D0385914

MARC SORENSON, Ed.D.

For Vicki,

my companion in business and in life

CAUTION!

THE INFORMATION CONTAINED IN THIS BOOK IS NOT INTENDED TO REPLACE MEDICAL CONSULTATION. ONE WHO IS ILL SHOULD NOT ALTER MEDICATIONS NOR CHANGE DIETARY HABITS EXCEPT AS ADVISED BY HIS OR HER PHYSICIAN.

Table of Contents

Acknowledgements

Writing a book on health and fitness is a simple enough project if one simply communicates his views on the causes of various diseases and then suggests life-style changes which might prevent, mitigate, or reverse those diseases. Such a book, however, could be viewed as opinion and might not withstand, in the reader's mind, the onslaught of differing views existing in the world of health literature.

To avoid that dilemma, I determined to produce a treatise which would be perceived as more than another author's assumption about health. To accomplish this, I documented (from the best medical and nutrition journals and professional books) nearly all of the statements made in the text, especially those of a controversial nature. It was a monumental task, and had I looked at the scope of the undertaking in its entirety, the project might have appeared overwhelming. Inch by inch, however, the task was completed, due in no small part to the assistance of excellent people and excellent technology.

Kudos to my wife, Vicki, who directed our fitness resort in her usual precise and caring manner while I pounded the word processor. Her support in this project was critical, since the duties of running a successful business cannot be neglected. Not only did Vicki direct the business, but she also cared for our home, thereby creating an atmosphere which was conducive to thought and writing.

Mildred Sorenson, my mother, and her friend Marilyn Staker, deserve a great deal of thanks for months of searching the stacks at the University of Utah medical library to locate and copy the scientific literature necessary to document this work. My mother also proofread the manuscript and offered suggestions. I am grateful for her caring and her expertise. Her assistance and her expertise in English were invaluable.

Colleen Cummings, who along with Vicki created many of the recipes and prepared them for taste testing, is deserving (as you will see) of accolades for her culinary efforts. And to her husband, Todd, who enthusiastically supported this project, I also give my thanks.

I am particularly indebted to Ralph Ofcarcik, Ph.D., our resident food technologist who researched and wrote much of the last three chapters. Dr. Ofcarcik devoted months to this project—time which I'm sure he might rather have spent hiking and camping. He also meticulously reviewed the content of this text for accuracy and made many suggestions for improvement. His knack for graphic illustration has added a clarity to this work which would have otherwise been unattainable.

My 18-year-old daughter, Suzanne, deserves my gratitude for endless hours of filing as the spate of research arrived. Her intense interest in human physiology enabled me to share my excitement with her as I discovered new concepts in health and fitness. To my other children, Marc, Katie and Samantha, I give my love for their unwavering support.

It is in order to offer a special word of appreciation to my friend, Dr. Fred Bushnell, a physician who helped set up the *Grateful Med* software for my Northgate computer system. The program enabled my computer to communicate freely with its counterpart at the National Library of Medicine in Bethesda, Maryland, thereby keeping me abreast of the latest research into the subjects covered.

I am also grateful to Dr. Ethel Nelson and Dr. T. Colin Campbell, who so graciously gave of their time in granting interviews regarding their landmark works in the fields of nutrition and health. And to Dave Beck, a friend and fellow bicycling fanatic, I give thanks for the training sessions which helped me to maintain a high level of physical fitness, and for the words of positivism which helped me stay motivated.

Gratitude is expressed to Dr. John McDougall, a California physician whose painstaking work in his medical/nutritional practices in Hawaii and California have inspired me for years. His philosophy has indelibly influenced the program of nutrition which we use at National Institute of Fitness, and his books have become our nutritional bibles. A statement made by Dr. McDougall as we did a talk show has become the health slogan for our institute: "If people wish to be healthy and slim, tell them to stuff themselves with starch and take a walk."

Finally, thanks to the thousands of "Niffers" who have attended our resort, spread the word to their friends, and made both our livelihoods and this book a reality.

Preface

by
NEAL D. BARNARD, M.D.

When I was in medical school, I was taught that heart disease is largely irreversible, that cancer is mainly due to factors beyond our control, and that diabetes was to be treated with drugs and little else. Well, we were wrong. As Dr. Sorenson has meticulously documented in this unique volume, the power of dietary choices to affect our health is surprising and often dramatic.

Heart disease can often be reversed. Cancer is usually due to identifiable factors that are within our control. Diabetes is very strongly linked to specific nutrient factors. The research world has turned a corner in these and many other areas. The next step is to take the findings to the general public. Medicine has largely failed in this mission. I will never forget the faces of women who died of breast cancer which should have been prevented by dietary changes, of men who were paralyzed by strokes that never had to occur, of children whose cholesterol levels were already rising to dangerous levels because their parents had been sold short in knowledge that should have come from physicians but sadly was never conveyed at all.

The book you hold in your hands will change that. It is readable and informal. It will give you a working knowledge of vital information that is currently known to relatively few people. I hope you will not only read the book but share it with those you love. The information it holds will give them the power to improve their health and vitality and even to add years to their lives.

I wish I had written this book.

Neal D. Barnard, M.D.
President, Physician's Committee for Responsible Medicine
Author of *The Power of Your Plate*

Foreword

by

JOHN McDOUGALL, M.D.

The truth that proper diet and lifestyle are the essential foundations for good health cannot be spoken too often. Dr. Sorenson has helped thousands of people at his live-in program, National Institute of Fitness, follow principles of eating and living that bring about excellent health. He now offers you his well-researched viewpoint in his book, *Megahealth*.

Many people understand (and find non-threatening) the importance of exercise, clean air and water, adequate rest, and psychological comfort for good health. Even though scientific research established beyond a doubt more than 40 years ago that a diet based on starches with the addition of vegetables and fruits as the best diet for people, dissemination of this information among the sickly American public is still in its infancy.

Greed and gluttony are the two primary reasons for the slow spread of life-saving nutritional information to Americans. Greed: Meats, dairy products, eggs and processed foods are the high-profit food items in the food industry. Also, the medical business is undeniably paid for sickness and therefore has no compelling reason to insist on an immediate change in the American diet. Gluttony: As Americans, we feel it is our birthright to eat the richest foods money can buy; historically, the foods of kings and queens. Of course, the expected consequence of all this feasting has to be health problems that were notorious for the royalty of past ages—obesity and gout, at the very least.

The usual consequence of a lifetime of rich foods, sedentary activity, and poor health habits are obesity, heart disease, strokes, cancer, adult-onset diabetes, arthritis, and an overabundance of bowel problems. Knowing the cause of illness allows you to take preventive action, and the result will be a better life for you and your family. If you're already in trouble, a change in diet and lifestyle means the progress of the disease can be slowed or stopped, and in most cases the healing capacity of the body finally catches up, and "cure" is a common outcome.

Even though the benefits of a healthier diet and lifestyle are established (beyond doubt) for health and healing, few people seem to change even after they have the information. The reason is that change is difficult, and it is a process that takes time and learning experiences. Negative, unpleasant experiences come in the forms of sickness, medications, surgery and hospitalization. The preferable way to help you along the path of better eating and living is through positive, pleasant experiences of feeling good, enjoying new foods, and learning about good health. People, individually and as a nation, are making changes, even if the pace seems slow. Hopefully you will learn soon enough to incorporate these principles before a real tragedy, such as a heart attack or breast cancer, happens to you.

One of the best ways for you to speed your transition from a typical sickly, overweight American to a person enjoying excellent health is to take advantage of learning experiences, such as a stay at National Institute of Fitness, and reading this book. *MEGAHEALTH* is a comprehensive discussion of scientific research and principles that will someday be the standard by which the health industry advises people to live. You have no reason to wait for the rest of the world to accept these time-honored ideas. Take advantage of Dr. Sorenson's efforts to help you understand what you can do to avoid illness and regain lost health through these simple, cost-free, self-help practices you can start today.

John McDougall, M.D.
Medical Director of the McDougall Live-in Program
at St. Helena Hospital and Health Center.
Author of *The McDougall Plan, McDougall's Medicine—A Challenging Second Opinion, The McDougall Program—Twelve Days to Dynamic Health*

A Word About
National Institute of Fitness

National Institute of Fitness (NIF), founded by Marc Sorenson, Ed.D., and managed by him and his wife, Vicki, is one of the best-known health resorts in the world and is consistently ranked as one of the top ten "spas" in the United States. The Sorensons do not really consider their resort to be a "spa," but rather a retreat where guests can learn life-style changes while participating in a low-fat nutrition program and a variety of physical activities. These activities include hiking and walking, tennis, racquetball, aerobic dance, water exercise, swimming and weight training, as well as cardiovascular conditioning on a variety of treadmills, stair climbers and cross-training machines. Although some pampering activities such as massage, facials, manicures and hairstyling are made available, they are definitely *not* the focus at NIF.

Rooms and meals are provided by the Institute, along with maid service. Food is plentiful and always available in keeping with the "eat more" philosophy of NIF. Weight loss, because of the low-fat, high fiber foods and the aerobic exercise, averages about a pound per day for men and about one-half pound per day for women. Other changes experienced by guests often include dramatic drops in blood pressure, blood sugar, and serum cholesterol levels.

Lectures on a variety of health subjects are given by Dr. Sorenson and Dr. Ralph Ofcarcik. Occasionally, presentations are made by other experts who have been invited by the Sorensons to address the guests.

Lectures in positive thought and action are also given regularly. Tapes by Earl Nightingale, Zig Ziglar, Dennis Waitley and others are made available to help change thought patterns that may be destructive to happiness.

Many walking awards are given to guests. These awards are given based on the total number of miles walked during a stay. These awards, however, are tied to a requirement for listening to the positive action tapes.

The average stay at NIF is about 4½ weeks, but rewards of health and fitness accrue even after a one-week stay. Some guests have checked in for a year, during which time they have completely transformed themselves in terms of weight, health, and attitude. This is made possible by a price that has been described as the "best bargain in the industry." In 1991 dollars, the average stay costs about $550 per week, but some programs cost as little as $425. Other "spas" which offer less charge as much as $3750 per week.

Vicki Sorenson, the Director of Operations, sees that the facilities are maintained in a top condition and that the program structure meets the needs of the guests.

NIF is located at the base of the geologically spectacular Snow Canyon State Park, near St. George, Utah. The area features year-around hiking in a desert climate. (Snow Canyon was named for an early pioneer in the area, not for the white stuff.) Located within a few hours drive are several national parks, including Great Basin National Park (the newest national park in the U.S. at the time of this writing), Grand Canyon, Zion, Bryce, Canyonlands, and Arches. Lake Powell National Recreation Area and Lake Mead are also located nearby.

Those who attend are known affectionately to their peers and to the team at NIF as "Niffers." There are usually more than 100 Niffers in attendance at any given time, and 70-80% of them are repeaters or have been referred by friends, which speaks well for the reputation of the Institute.

If you or someone you know would like to receive information on National Institute of Fitness, call 801-673-4905 or write:

NIF
202 North Snow Canyon Road, Box 938
Ivins, Utah 84738.

Introduction

During the past 17 years as the owner and operator of the health resort known as National Institute of Fitness (NIF) I was privileged to witness many of our guests recover from serious or life-threatening diseases. During those years, myriad tons of weight were lost, scores of people lowered cholesterol to healthful levels, and hundreds saw their diabetes disappear, never to return. Others recovered from various ailments too numerous to mention.

Many of the recipients of these health benefits described their changes as "miraculous." No miracle, however, was involved. They were simply educated as to the cause of their maladies. They then made the changes required to produce good health and consequently became well.

Not everyone, however, can come to NIF for a healthful vacation and education experience. I therefore determined to produce a manual for the correct care of the human body—a manual which would allow a vastly larger number of people to access the concepts taught at NIF. The book you hold is the end product that determination. It is a book of rules. If you will abide by the precepts herein, you will have the best possible chance to live a long and disease-free life.

The attainment of vibrant health, like all other aspects of success, is indeed dependent on adherence to a set of rules or laws. Just as there are rules for aviation which, if followed, will enable a pilot to fly his aircraft safely without serious incident, there are also rules for protecting and achieving health and well-being.

Some rules are obvious. One shouldn't step in front of speeding trucks, because to do so would certainly influence health in a less than positive manner. Nor is it a good idea to jump from an airplane without a parachute. In either case, the results of breaking the rules are quick and lethal. Non-adherence to other rules of good health may not produce such quick, dramatic and obvious results, but the consequences of the rule-breaking are equally predictable.

The good news is that adopting a lifestyle based on correct principles can add "life to years and years to life." This is a book of rules that offers the reader the knowledge necessary to take control of health.

It may come as a surprise to many people that *health is a matter of law and not luck.* They assume, incorrectly, that poor health (especially in terms of degenerative disease) is an inescapable part of living—a natural process of aging. When they observe someone who has lived a long life, free of debilitating disease, they describe him or her as "lucky," or they chalk it up to "good genes."

Many feel that the best they can hope for is a drug that might slow the disease process or palliate pain. Pain, however, is not meant to be the inevitable, chronic companion of humans as they age; rather, it is a *warning signal* which alerts us that something is wrong—something that needs to be corrected. To mitigate the pain through the use of drugs—without removing the cause of the malady—serves no purpose other than to make people more comfortable as they proceed toward debility and demise. Individuals who rely on such "treatment" may be likened to the man who was awakened in the middle of the night by the wailing of his smoke alarm. Irritated by the noise, he cut its wires and went back to bed while his house burned down. Just as surely, millions are allowing their health to smolder while they remove the annoyances of pain.

Poor health is not our heritage. A simple look at the systems of the body that protect it from accident, injury and disease should be sufficient to convince the most skeptical individual that the natural course of human existence is one of strength and wellness. We possess ears and eyes capable of warning us of imminent danger; immune systems which fight valiantly against encroaching microorganisms; cleansing systems which filter away toxins that find their way into the body through our food, water and air. When injured, our bodies perform the miracle of healing. We also possess brains and central nervous systems which allow us to learn from previous experiences, thereby enabling us to avoid repetitions of injurious situations. The human body possesses no systems that work for early death and illness; rather, it has systems that strive for optimal health and longevity. If one does not overwhelm those systems with a plethora of poisons, health will be the natural state.

Though there are many rules for good health, this book will concentrate on establishing rules in the areas in which there is the most controversy and where there currently exists the greatest potential for positive change: namely, in the areas of proper fuels and proper exercise.

The body must be given proper fuels. As the gasoline engine does not perform well on diesel fuel, neither does the human body function correctly while using fuel befitting a cat, calf, bear or rat. Such fuels are toxins to human beings, and when ingested in sufficient quantities, they damage the body at a rate that overwhelms its capacity to heal.

The body is also meant to move. Without regular, vigorous movement, the body deteriorates and becomes susceptible to a host of diseases. Many texts on health have focused on the influences of nutrition on disease, while excluding (or barely mentioning) the profound influence of proper exercise. Others have focused almost exclusively on exercise while treating nutrition as a mere bagatelle. The truth is that neither of these areas can be neglected if optimal health, or MEGAHEALTH, is to be achieved and sustained.

There are other rules, of course, which concern the breathing of clean air, drinking of good water, and avoidance of radon gas and other pollutants. These rules, however important, are not the focus of this text. Rather, it focuses on proper foods and proper exercise. It is an extensively documented treatise which leaves little room for doubt as to the path to health and fitness.

A massive, elucidating body of evidence indicates that habits of nutrition and exercise (or the lack thereof) can either extend life and produce optimal health or produce physical, mental and emotional misery while subtracting many years from the normal life span. The presentation of this evidence is my purpose. Then, the CHOICE is yours.

1.

PART 1:

Eat and Live; Diet and Die.

1. Part 1: Eat and Live; Diet and Die.

> *The belief that obese people overeat is so widespread that one wonders if this conviction will give way to the data on this question.*[1]
>
> —Dr. Sandra Wooley

Let's face facts: if diets worked, publications such as the *National Enquirer* and *Woman's Day Magazine* would have made the population thin long ago. After all, don't such magazines carry the "ultimate" diet nearly every month? Still, the desperate hordes await the next "miracle," with the hope that finally they will discover the method which produces a slim and attractive physique or figure. And, as long as the market exists, there will be a plethora of products ready to pander to it. It's the American way.

Obesity **is not** caused by overeating, nor is it caused by consuming too many calories. Obesity results from high-fat nutrition, failure to exercise, and intermittent starvation programs commonly called "diets." Research has established conclusively that fat people eat no more than, and in most instances considerably less than, thin people. FAT PEOPLE DIET AND THEREBY BECOME FATTER. A primary cause of obesity, then, is *undereating*.

Despite all that is said about heart disease, diabetes, cancer, and osteoporosis, there is no doubt more concern with overweight than with all other health problems. In fact, more mental anguish is endured and more time wasted fretting over extra pounds than in the combined anxiety over any other five burdens, including personal finances, AIDS, the national debt, the war on drugs or the threat of nuclear holocaust. Thinness is the national preoccupation—not because obesity is a grave threat to health, but because of its visibility. Occlude an artery and no one notices; develop a small cancerous lump and no one sees, but add ten pounds to the hips and mid-section and the whole world observes.

OUR NATIONAL OBSESSION

It is, perhaps, unfortunate that cosmetic preoccupations seem more important than health concerns, but such is often the case. People who refuse to give up dietary fat to decrease the risk of cancer will eat cat manure while standing on their heads if they believe it will help them lose a few pounds.

Ah, if we could only develop such commitment in the heart disease patient who needs to curtail his consumption of high-fat food to survive! What a contrast between the half-hearted attempts to improve health and the obsessive-compulsive behavior of the dieters who assiduously pursue the latest weird diet fad in order to weigh just a bit less, including: living on a single food for long periods of time, wiring the jaws shut to prevent eating, having the stomach stapled to decrease the amount of food that can be consumed, inducing vomiting, starving until death, and engaging in other health-destroying practices such as purging with emetics or dehydrating with diuretics.

Although overweight people are accused of having little willpower, nothing could be further from the truth. Witness the fact that liquid-protein diets have caused the deaths of more than 60 people.[2][3] More than 60 people have had the willpower to diet themselves to death! The good news: they were probably the *only* 60 people who managed to diet and then keep their weight off! We certainly cannot fault their willpower. If the truth were known, the number of deaths attributable either directly or indirectly to dieting is astronomical. The obsession to be thin, and the use of aberrant dieting methods to attain that thinness, are two of the great tragedies of our modern world. *DIETING (RESTRICTING CALORIES AND/OR FOOD) DOES NOT WORK. IN FACT, IT CAUSES OBESITY.*

Methods such as liquid-protein diets, as dangerous as they are, require unbelievable commitment and willpower because they are painful, enervating and psychologically devastating—especially when they produce only ephemeral success. In addition to liquid protein, we have endured the grapefruit and egg diet, the drinking man's diet, the junk-food diet, the vinegar and vitamin B-6 diet, the Beverly Hills diet, and so on, *ad dietary infinitum.* Dieting has been, and continues to be, a futile and debilitating waste of time. Nevertheless, both the diet industry and the American waistline continue to expand.

We want what we lack.

Why the obsession with girth control? Because that which is rare is nearly always in great demand. Achieving "sveltness" is so difficult that it has become synonymous with glamor, power, wealth and even goodness. The opposite of leanness, of course, has become an object of loathing. In our business, we often hear the statement, "I hate my thighs!" Or, if not the thighs, the target of animosity is usually the stomach or some other guiltless part of the anatomy.

WEIGHT AND PREJUDICE

Prejudicial treatment of overweight people, both by themselves and others, is rampant. The prototypical fat person is limned as lazy, gluttonous and lacking in character—a portrayal which is groundless and false. Some of the most dynamic and hard-working people in the world possess a few more pounds than is currently considered fashionable. The traits of laziness and gluttony may exist in a few fat people but certainly not to a greater extent than among thin people. Even those who are heavy often see themselves or other overweight individuals as having some basic flaw. Such statements as, "You can never be too thing nor too rich" evince the undue and exaggerated importance that society places on the size of the body. Society condemns obese persons as being not quite as good as thin persons. After all, if they (the overweight individuals) were good people, wouldn't they take care of themselves? This attitude is prejudice in its most ignorant form.

Neither thinness nor fatness determines a person's goodness or his character. The basic difference between fat people and thin people is that fat people are fatter. Yet, as stated in jest by E.B. Astwood, *"Obesity in America is regarded along with narcotic addiction as something wicked, and I shall not be surprised if soon we have a prohibition against it in the name of national security."* Though humorous, this statement comes entirely too close to the truth. It is time to stop condemning obesity and to start understanding it; time to realize that to the extent that overweight is a problem, it is a problem of physiology and environment, not character or psychology.

We are so concerned with overweight in this country that we spend billions of dollars on products and services that actually contribute to the problem. Twenty-six percent of all soda pops consumed are diet sodas, amounting to 47 gallons per year for every man, woman and child in America. Thirty thousand people per year have their jaws wired shut, and another 100,000 go through liposuction. Thirty—three billion dollars are spent yearly on weight loss schemes, including $5.5 billion on programs sponsored by doctors and hospitals.[4]

The population, however, is still becoming fatter.[5] Between 1963 and 1980, there was a 54% increase in the rate of obesity among children six to eleven years old, and nearly a doubling of superobesity (defined as 100% or more above ideal weight).[6] It may come as a surprise that these children are consuming no more calories, and perhaps slightly fewer calories, than they were in 1963. What *is* making them fatter? Certainly not the consumption of excessive food energy.

DO FAT PEOPLE EAT MORE?

The strange behavior in which dieters engage might make sense if fat people ate more than thin people, but they do not. Dieting, which we will define as restricting calories and/or food consumption, is not part of the solution to weight control; *it is part of the problem.* Dieters succeed in losing weight initially, but the lost weight is regained—usually with a few extra pounds for good measure. As Dr. Kelly Brownell of the University of Pennsylvania stated in regard to curing obesity by reducing weight to its ideal level and maintaining it for five years: "A person is more likely to recover from most forms of cancer."[7] Dr. William Bennett perhaps described the dieter's dilemma most succinctly when he stated that, "Dieting as a therapy for obesity is about as effective as the 19th century practice of treating pneumonia by bloodletting."[8]

Both of these gentlemen are correct. Five years after losing weight on a diet, the rate of recidivism is about 99%.[9] [10] Most dieters, as we will learn, also gain back considerably more weight than they lost during their diets.

OBESITY: A PROBLEM OF PSYCHOLOGY OR PHYSIOLOGY?

Psychologists have had a field day analyzing the reasons that corpulent people (presumably) consume too many calories. Behavior-modification techniques ranging from food-aversion therapy to electric shock to hypnosis have been used to help people eat less. The perpetrators of this foolishness need to realize that those who are overweight already eat far less per pound of weight than do lean people![11] No amount of scientific inquiry will bring any worthwhile answers to the researcher who is working on a problem that *does not exist!*

While psychoanalysis probes the reasons for eating disorders, the population continues to fatten. Eating disorders have been produced, quite clearly, by dieting. Dieting is a method of eating that initially makes one leaner, yet ultimately makes one larger. Wouldn't that produce strange behavior in anyone? *Weight control, in the beginning, is strictly a physiological problem, not a psychological problem.* It becomes psychological only after a person has driven himself over the edge by dieting, thereby developing strange relationships with food.

Indeed, the result of the preoccupation with dieting is that bodies are becoming larger, not smaller.[5] [12] This is in spite of the millions of pieces of advice in the forms of books, articles, and media programs that have shown people how to eat fewer calories. That advice, by the way, has been quite effective. People eat less now than in the past when there was less obesity.[5] The diet craze has exerted its influence in assisting a nation of maniacal dieters to eat less both in terms of food bulk and food energy. *What it hasn't done is help them to become thinner.*

How prevalent is the dieting mania? Among adolescents in the 1960s, 30% of girls and 6% of boys were dieting on the day they were questioned.[13] Twenty years later, this figure had increased to 63% for girls and 16.2% for boys![14] Considering that people are dieting more, eating less and becoming heavier, can it be that dieting is making them fat?

PRESENTING THE UNDIET

Yes, dieting causes obesity. Those who eat less will ultimately have a higher percentage of body fat than those who eat more. Dieting is, in fact, the very best method of causing obesity, especially when combined with such other factors as high-fat nutrition and sedentary living. This chapter will expose the health problems associated with dieting (the calorie-restriction method of weight control) and present a solution that involves a change in exercise and nutrition. Rather than present another starvation plan which would be doomed to failure, it will present a method that results in the consumption of more food and, ultimately, more calories. It will be a method for becoming leaner while eating more and moving more. We will label this method the "Undiet."

OBESITY, DIETING AND HEALTH

Now . . . before you accuse me of having scrambled brains, please read on. After all, if you have tried to maintain weight loss through dieting, you know as well as I that it simply does not work. Perhaps it is time to look for a different method.

Make no mistake—although the current obsession with weight has led to greater obesity, there is no doubt that obesity and overweight are health problems of astronomical proportions; not because of the obesity itself, but because of the way in which obesity is produced. The health problems associated with obesity cost the American public nearly $40 billion per year.[14.1]

Approximately 40% of the female population of the U.S. is overweight.[15] When ideal weights for health are considered, however, it has been shown that the least risk for heart disease is possessed by those who are 6% underweight as assessed by the height-weight charts established by insurance companies.[16] If this low weight is really the "ideal" weight, then it is likely that 90% of women and 70% of men are overweight.

A KILLER OF MAJOR PROPORTIONS— OR IS IT?

Obesity is often defined as being at least 20% over the "ideal weight" established by the Metropolitan Life Insurance Company. This level of weight has been established as a health hazard by experts from the National Institutes of Health. The higher the weight beyond the 20% figure, the greater the hazard becomes.[17]

For instance, the prevalence of hypertension is 2.9 times as high for the obese as the nonobese (5.6 times as high for people 20-44 years of age). Hypercholesterolemia (blood cholesterol levels over 150) is 2.1 times higher in obese people; diabetes is 2.9 times higher; cancer of the colon, rectum, prostate, gallbladder, breast, uterus and ovaries are all considerably more prevalent in the obese compared to the nonobese. In the case of uterine cancer, the rate for women who are severely obese is 5.4 times that of nonobese women.

Extreme obesity is also associated with up to a 1200% increase in death from all causes.[17] As men and women become older, the death-dealing influence of obesity becomes more pronounced. Figure 1 illustrates the relationship of obesity to mortality in the age group 15 to 39 for men;[17] Figure 2 shows the increasing chance of death from heart disease for women as weight increases.[16] We should also note at this point that it is not a good idea to be more than 25% *underweight.* At this weight, the death rate also begins to climb, though not so dramatically as with overweight.

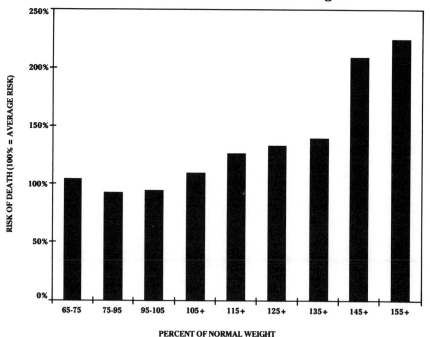

FIGURE 1:
Death Risk for Men 15-39
Relative To Percent of Normal Weight

FIGURE 2:
**Heart Attack Risk for Women
(5'4½") with Increasing Weight**

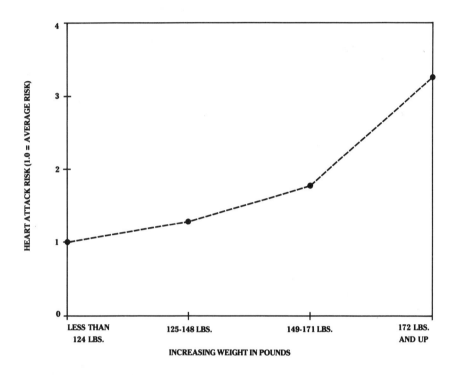

HEALTH AND THE DEADLY DIET:
IS IT REALLY LOW-CALORIE DIETS
THAT DESTROY HEALTH?

Having observed many dieters who look fatigued and unhealthy, I often felt that calorie-restricted dieting was a far greater threat to health than obesity itself. On reading an excellent article in the *Journal of Psychology*, written by Dr. Esther Rothblum,[18] I became even more convinced. I am indebted to Dr. Rothblum for acquainting me with several of the research studies cited in the first three sections of this chapter.

When animals are put through a series of low-calorie diets, they begin to exhibit a greater preference for fatty foods than animals who don't diet.[19] Obese people also show a proclivity for fatty foods.[20] [21] [22] (We will discuss in subsequent chapters the health havoc wrought by excessive dietary fats.) Increased fat intake after dieting may be much more important in causing disease than obesity itself. Dieters, whether obese or not, have higher levels of triglycerides than non-dieters[23] and show an increased risk of hypertension, heart failure, and diabetes, as well as neuromuscular, digestive and kidney problems.[24] [25] [26]

A recent article in the *New England Journal of Medicine*[26. 5] points out how important dieting may be as a cause of heart disease. Researchers who analyzed over 3000 health records of the famous Framingham Heart Study found that those with fluctuating weight had a 75% greater risk of dying from heart disease than those whose weights remained stable. Yo yo dieting seemed particularly dangerous to men, who had a 93% greater risk of death from heart disease with fluctuating rather than stable weight, compared to a 38% greater risk in women.

During low-calorie diets, many patients experience excessively low blood pressure, elevated cholesterol levels, weakness, elevated uric acid levels, abnormal heart beats, diarrhea, anemia, gallstones, nausea and severe headaches.[27]

There is no doubt that a low-calorie diet will initially lower blood pressure and reduce cholesterol levels,[28] as well as improve blood sugar levels.[29] However, when the weight is regained, the negative influence of dieting on these factors becomes increasingly apparent and exceeds the positive influences experienced during the diet.[30] How unfortunate that doctors recommend low-calorie diets to their patients with high blood pressure and high cholesterol. Such a program ensures that their patients will ultimately be fatter and less healthy.

It may come as a surprise to learn that body fat per se, when not associated with dieting, has little influence on the length of life.[31] In view of that fact, we can state unequivocally that *dieting is far more dangerous than the obesity which it is designed to overcome.*

More dangerous still are drastic surgical procedures. Stomach stapling (which limits the capacity of the stomach to hold food) has been linked to ventral hernia, urinary tract infection, anemia, osteoporosis, vomiting, stomach cancer, constipation, diarrhea, malnutrition and death.[18] Intestinal bypass (which greatly restricts the amount of food which can be absorbed) has been linked to intestinal obstruction and subsequent death.[18]

Those who survive such procedures also find that their bodies adjust to the decreased calorie consumption, with the lost weight returning even though the bypass or stapling is still in place. At National Institute of Fitness, we have worked with people with stomach staples (still in place) who had regained their weight even after initial losses of up to 150 pounds. These procedures aren't just bad, they are potentially fatal! They are based on the premise that fat people eat more than thin people—*a premise which is wholly and unequivocally false.*

CALORIES AND OBESITY: A CRITICAL ERROR IN THINKING

In order for a weight-control program to work and in order for pertinent research to be of value, that program and research must be based on correct premises. Nearly all of the plans which purport to fight obesity are based on the premise that fat people eat more than thin people. And, until lately, most research studies have searched for the reasons *why* fat people eat too much. As previously stated, *one cannot find the answers to a problem that does not exist!* It is no wonder that obesity has frustrated the best efforts of the diet and medical industries. These organizations have been belaboring a false premise!

Therefore, the mistake repeatedly made in attempting to treat the epidemic of obesity has been the advice to restrict consumption of calories. The method works initially, but the results are fleeting. The weight gained after a low-calorie diet ranges from about 108%-120% of the weight which was lost![32 33 122]

It requires, on average, about twice as long to gain back the weight, plus the extra, as it did to lose it (although, as we will see, this process can be greatly accelerated through multiple diets). Before anyone can attain lasting success in controlling weight at healthful levels, he or she must become convinced that OBESITY IS NOT CAUSED BY EATING TOO MUCH! If it were true that excessive eating caused overweight, then we would expect that people who consume more calories would be the people with the largest weights. This is not the case.

An extensive study by Dr. Leonard Braitman and his colleagues measured calorie intake versus body weight.[11] It revealed that thin people ate considerably more actual calories and far, far more calories per pound of weight than their obese counterparts. *The less people ate, the more they weighed,* until their body weights were 149% above ideal weight. At weights above 149% over ideal, calorie consumption began to increase. This increase was possibly due to the fact that larger bodies burn more calories in transporting themselves. Nevertheless, even these "morbidly" obese subjects ate fewer calories than the thin subjects until their weights were considerably beyond the 149% figure. At that point, these very obese subjects began to consume a greater number of calories than thin people but still far *fewer calories per pound of body weight.* The authors of this study concluded that "Neither the caloric intake nor the caloric intake adjusted for physical activity level was higher in the obese subjects . . . factors other than overeating should be given increased consideration in the etiology [cause] of obesity."

Figure 3 illustrates the relationship between calories consumed and weight.[11] It is obviously an inverse relationship. The heavier people become, the fewer calories they consume. Considering the fact that thin people consume more calories than fat people, does it not make perfect sense that RESTRICTING CALORIES MAKES A FAT PERSON MORE LIKE A FAT PERSON THAN EVER?

How to fatten a hog

There are those in the livestock industry who have understood and used the fattening capabilities of dieting for decades. An acquaintance from a small farming community described to me his method for fattening hogs: "We restrict the amount of food the hogs receive for several days, until they are so hungry and uncomfortable that we can hear their squealing at the ranch

FIGURE 3:
Caloric Intake At Varying
Percentages of Optimum Weight — Female

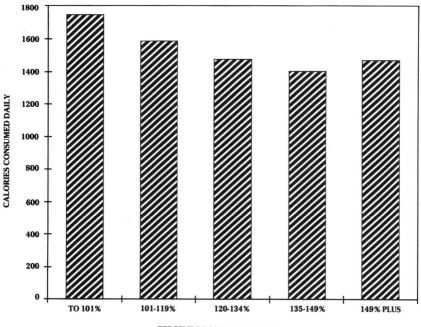

PERCENT OF OPTIMUM WEIGHT

house. At that point we feed the hogs freely for a few days and then repeat the process. We have found that the animals will become fatter and go to market at a heavier weight than can be produced by any other method." COULD IT BE THAT THE PREFERRED METHOD FOR WEIGHT LOSS (I.E., CALORIE RESTRICTION) IS ACTUALLY THE MOST EFFECTIVE METHOD FOR PRODUCING OBESITY THAT HAS EVER BEEN CONCEIVED?

The study by Dr. Braitman is hardly the only research to refute the commonly held theory that overweight people eat excessively. There is an abundance of research indicating either no relationship between calories consumed and the degree of overweight or a slight inverse relationship.[34][35][36][37][38][39][40][41][42][43][44][45][46][47][48][49][50][51][52][53] Studies conducted with young people, however, have indicated a *very strong* inverse relationship between calories consumed and obesity. One of these studies showed that the most obese secondary school girls consumed 740 *fewer* calories *per day* than the thinnest girls.[54] Another study conducted with boys in a camp situation showed that thin boys consumed about 1200 calories per day *more* than obese boys.[55] The thinnest boys actually consumed a whopping 4628 calories per day, on the average, yet remained thin!

Other research which compared eating habits of families and individuals who were obese to those who were non-obese found eating habits to be nearly identical in all subjects.[56 57 58 59 60]

The February 1991 issue of the *American Journal of Clinical Nutrition*[60.1] published the results of research which should forever put to rest the misconception that excessive eating causes obesity. In this research women volunteered to take part in an experiment which measured their daily calorie intakes, their body weights, and their percentages of body fat. Forty women who ingested the least number of calories per day (approximately 1500) were classified as "small eaters." Another 40 who consumed approximately 2400 calories per day were termed "large eaters." On assessing the weight of the two groups, it was found that those who were *large eaters weighed approximately nine pounds less than those who were small eaters. Assessment of body composition revealed that the large eaters were 22% fat. Small eaters were 33% fat!*

The excess calorie theory simply does not hold up under scrutiny. It is assumption only. When societies with little or no obesity (such as the Chinese) are compared to societies with epidemic obesity (such as the U.S.), it is found that people in the "thin" societies consume considerably more calories per pound of body weight than people in the "fat" societies.[61] Chinese consume about 2700 calories per person per day compared to 2400 calories per day for Americans. Nevertheless, Chinese are about 25% thinner than Americans.

It is also interesting to note that animals that are pregnant and obese eat far fewer calories than those that are pregnant and lean.[62] Nevertheless, those that are initially obese put on far more weight during the pregnancy than those that are initially lean, in spite of the fact that the lean animals continue to consume far more food during the pregnancy.

If dieting produces fat bodies, what is it that makes a person feel the need to diet in the first place? In other words, what causes the initial overweight condition which is worsened by restricting calories?

COULD IT BE DIETARY FAT?

A major difference between the Chinese people in the study just mentioned and Americans is the contrast in consumption of dietary fat. The Chinese consume a diet very low in fat, averaging about 14.5% of total calories but as low as 5.9% in some segments of that society. Most of the calories come from rice—the typical citizen ingesting 19 oz. (dry weight) of rice per day.[61] This compares with the typical American's consumption of approximately 37% of calories from fat. Could it be that fat, calorie per calorie, is much more fattening than starchy foods such as rice? It is well established that people who are obese eat a higher percentage of their food as fat and a lesser percentage as carbohydrate.[63] Does fat beget fat?

That question has been aptly answered in a study on rats.[64] One group of rats was given a low-fat diet and another group was given a diet which derived 42% of its calories from fat. All of the rats were allowed to eat as much food as they wanted. After 60 weeks of the experiment, the percentage of fat weight on the rats' bodies was determined. The rats eating the low-fat diet had 30% of body weight in fat; the rats on the high-fat diet had 51% of body weight in fat. The most interesting aspect of this research was the fact that *the rats in each group ate nearly the same number of calories.* Actually, the low-fat rats ate slightly more. The fat-eating rats were also *28% heavier than their low-fat counterparts.* It is quite obvious that fat, not calories, was the factor that triggered the gain in body fat and weight. Other animal studies corroborate that high-fat diets can produce obesity without increasing the number of calories consumed.[65][66][67][68][69]

The same applies to humans. Although obese people do not consume more calories than thin people, they definitely consume a greater percentage of their calories as fat.[20][21][22] The Chinese, as mentioned, consume almost 300 more calories per day and *20% more calories per pound of body weight* than Americans, yet they are 20% thinner than their American counterparts. Seventy-seven percent of their calories come from starch, not fat.[61] Obviously, a person with a weight problem simply cannot afford to eat fatty foods.

This is hardly news. It has been known since the 1950s that high-fat diets create severe obesity;[70][71] yet, as weight-control methods have been introduced, there has been a preoccupation with calories rather than fat.

Literally dozens of studies have established the obesity-producing effects of high-fat nutrition. Rats fed standard laboratory chow, which is about 6% fat, generally have only about 10 to 20% of their body weights as fat.[72] When the percentage of dietary fat is increased to 30-60%, rats rapidly gain weight and dramatically increase their percentage of body fat.[73] Some strains of rats fed a high-fat diet will gain weight until they weigh more than twice as much as littermates fed a low-fat grain diet.[73]

Perhaps it should be stated that the animals in the study just mentioned were bred to be genetically obese. *Yet, obesity was produced only by feeding a high-fat diet.* Let us state unequivocally that when there is a hereditary tendency toward obesity, proper nutrition and exercise can prevent the tendency from manifesting itself. Therefore, lifestyle choices are always far more important than our genetic makeups. We cannot excuse ourselves for overweight conditions by chalking them up to fate.

COULD IT BE LACK OF STARCH?

It should be obvious from the studies mentioned that *all calories are not created equal.* Eat starchy foods such as those which the Chinese eat—even when consuming large numbers of calories—and fat bodies will not result. Eat fatty foods such as Americans consume, and obesity will prevail in much of the society.

A study which focused on the effects of high-and-low-protein diets and their influences on cancer development in rats, found that when animal proteins were replaced with carbohydrates to produce a low-animal-protein diet, the animals consumed more calories but gained less weight than other animals that received fewer carbohydrates and consumed fewer calories.[74] One likely explanation of the "slimming" effect of starch is the fact that diets higher in starch give off more heat during their processing. Twenty percent more calories are used to process carbohydrates than are used to process fats. Fats, however, are converted to fatty tissue very efficiently, with little use of calories in the process.[75] [76] [77] [78] [79]

Thus we see that a high-starch, low-fat eating plan is as essential to the prevention and treatment of obesity as it is to the prevention and treatment of diabetes, osteoporosis, cancer, heart disease, kidney disease, gallbladder disease and others which we will discuss. Remember that it is not the number of calories nor the amount of food consumed which is important; it is the *type* of food that is a prime factor in causing obesity.

Starch resists conversion to fat

There is another advantage to the high-starch diet. Starches don't "like" to be converted to fat. In humans it is very difficult to convert carbohydrates of any kind to fat.[80] [81] [82] [83] In experiments where radioactive material was combined with carbohydrate, only 3% of the radioactive material could later be found in the fat stores of the body.[80] [81] Diets high in carbohydrates also cause an increase in the quantity of fat which is metabolized (burned) in the body.[82]

One researcher, in reviewing the merits of high-starch, low-fat nutrition for treating obesity, stated that due to the inability of humans to convert carbohydrate to fat and due to the increased fat-burning capacity of a high-carbohydrate diet, it should be easy to produce a negative fat balance in obese people by use of the low-fat program.[84]

COULD IT BE SUGAR?

Animals given sugar in addition to their regular meals (or whose diets are changed to include more sugar) usually gain more weight and increase their percentage of body fat compared to animals that do not receive sugar.[85] [86] [87] [88] [89]

Sugar, like fat, is a strong promoter of obesity in animals. Animals that are fed a high-table-sugar (sucrose) diet often eat less food than those fed a high-starch diet, yet gain more weight than the starch-fed animals.[88] A diet high in fructose (fruit sugar) produces similar effects but not to the same extent as sucrose.[88] Other studies with rats suggest that sugar alone may be as effective as fat alone in producing obesity.[90]

Interestingly, rats offered sugar in solution (sugar mixed with water) in addition to their regular rat chow, consume far more calories and gain much more weight than littermates who are fed only rat chow.[89] The actual weight of the food consumed is less for the sugar-fed rats, though the calories consumed are greater. When two groups of rats are limited to a specific number of calories, however, those which have access to sugar gain more weight and add more fat to the body than those eating a low-sugar diet.[91]

When sugar and fat are increased, they cause the "set point" for body weight to increase, which produces a temporary increase in the number of calories ingested. After the weight has been gained, however, the more obese subjects will eat less than their thinner counterparts. "Set point" can be defined as that weight which the body insists on maintaining. It is regulated by the hypothalmus, which is a control center in the central nervous system located at the base of the brain. The hypothalamus is influenced by factors such as exercise and composition of the diet. As we discuss set point later on, this phenomenon will become clearer.

Although sugar may cause obesity in rats, it is less likely to do so in humans, because as mentioned in the previous section on starches, it is very difficult for humans to convert carbohydrates to fat. It also appears that in humans, carbohydrates may increase metabolic rates, thereby helping to burn fat.[82] Sugar cannot be recommended in any case, since it may have adverse influences on dental health, diabetes and other diseases.

COULD IT BE THE COMBINATION OF SUGAR AND FAT?

The fattening effects of sugar may also be linked to the tendency to consume it with large quantities of fat,[92] such as in pastries, chocolate candies, ice cream, etc. Sugar may simply make the fat palatable and thereby cause a person to ingest more fat than he would otherwise consume. For instance, could anyone eat a round, white-flour sponge soaked in grease unless it was sweetened with sugar? Yet, that is exactly what a doughnut is. Cutting down on sugar is apt to substantially decrease the consumption of fat.

Several research results have shown that a "supermarket" diet consisting of such delicacies as chocolate-chip cookies, salami, cheese, marshmallows and condensed milk, has a very fattening effect on rats.[72] [93] [94] [95] The blend of sugar and fat may have a synergistic effect on producing obesity—in other words, an effect greater than that produced by either fat or sugar alone. The mixture has proven to cause spectacular weight gains when a high-fat diet by itself produced only modest gains in weight. When "supermarket" fed rats were compared to littermates fed normal rat chow (containing about 10% of calories as fat and free of sugar), the supermarket rats gained 2.7 times as much weight in the same period of time.[72] These foods, of course, are exactly the kinds of foods consumed regularly by most Americans. Is it any wonder that obesity is epidemic in this country?

Sugar ⟶ *Insulin* ⟶ *LPL* ⟶ *Fat storage* ⟶ *Obesity*

The fattening effect of the sugar-fat mixture just described is accomplished to a great extent by the insulin-stimulating influence of sugar. As we will learn later, insulin is necessary to move fat into the fat cells. It accomplishes this by stimulating both the action and quantity of a potent, fat-storing enzyme known as adipose tissue lipoprotein lipase (LPL). As would be expected, therefore, the consumption of sugar increases the quantity of insulin which is produced, thereby increasing the body's LPL activity and its ability to store fat. With the excess of fat available in the American diet, insulin, and consequently LPL, have a ready supply to move into storage. Sugar, then, is a triggering mechanism which can start a fat-storage process.

COULD IT BE LACK OF EXERCISE?

There is no doubt that lack of exercise is a cause of obesity. As people become less active, they tend to put on weight. Researchers at the New England Medical Center in Boston discovered that for each hour per day that a teenager watches T.V., his obesity increases by 2%[96] Considering that the average American watches 6 hours and 55 minutes per day,[97] it is no wonder that lack of exercise helps to create a problem of obesity in youngsters and adults alike. Many people feel that they "just don't have time for exercise." An apparent (and seemingly responsible) suggestion would be to reduce TV viewing to 6 hours per day and use 55 minutes to exercise. Such a change could hardly be called a sacrifice! As discussed in the chapter on fitness and health, it is also possible to exercise while watching the tube, thus missing none of the precious television time.

Just how important is television viewing as a predictor of obesity? Figure 4 illustrates the relationship between obesity and hours per week spent watching T.V. The more we watch, the fatter we become! There is the possibility, of course, that as people get fatter, they tend to watch more T.V. Personally, I believe that the sedentary living associated with the tube is a cause of obesity and not a result.

FIGURE 4:
Relationship of Time Spent
Viewing TV To Rate of Obesity

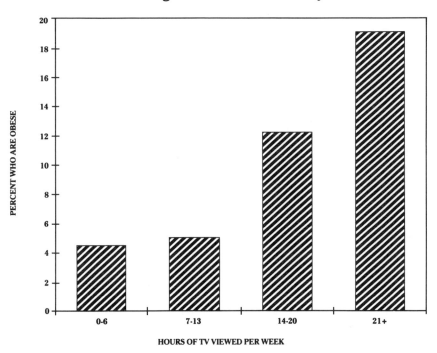

HOURS OF TV VIEWED PER WEEK

THE MECHANISMS BY WHICH
DIETING MAKES US FAT

We can be sure of one fact: Only fat people diet. Thin people, as we have pointed out, eat more and stay thinner, and livestock raisers actually use "dieting" as a method of fattening their animals. Eating fat and sugar, coupled with a sedentary life style, may initiate the overweight condition, but intermittent starvation programs (dieting) really put the icing on the cake.

There are several mechanisms by which dieting causes physiological changes that enhance fat storing capabilities of the body. These changes nearly always result in a recovery of the weight lost and a gain of *extra* pounds in excess of the starting weight. As one group of researchers reported, *prior weight loss is the strongest predictor of weight gain.*[98]

Changes in metabolic rate

One of the mechanisms by which dieting causes the body to store more fat is through lowering the rate of metabolism. Metabolism is the process of using energy for the myriad functions of the body, such as the unconscious functions of breathing, heart beat and glandular secretion, as well as physical activities which are under conscious or unconscious control. Those who diet dramatically decrease the number of calories which they metabolize, not only during exercise but throughout the day.[99 100 101 102 103 104 105 106 107 108 109 110 111] The decrease does not take long to accomplish. Within one to two days metabolic rate can decrease from 15-30%[111.1] This would indicate that the body senses a state of starvation during the diet and resolves to slow down the metabolic rate as a means of conserving energy, thereby (from the body's point of view) preserving life for the longest period of time.

In the scientific literature, people who have lost weight are called "reduced-obese." These people might better be termed "temporarily thinner."

Some of the reduction in *resting* metabolic rate is due to the decrease in the size of the body which is being maintained. According to one research study, if the dieter is able to maintain reduced body weight, the drop in metabolic rate may be solely attributed to the decrease in body size.[112] Other studies, however, do not agree that metabolic rates decrease only to the extent that body weight is reduced. Most research shows that the resting metabolic rate is still far lower in reduced-obese subjects after correcting for reduced body size.[101 113 114]

The largest difference in decreased calorie use by the formerly-obese person is not in *resting* metabolic rate but in *non-resting* metabolic rate—the number of calories expended during non-resting periods.

In a landmark study by Dr. David Weigle and his colleagues at the University of Washington,[104] some amazing facts regarding non-resting energy expenditure were discovered.

When dieters who had lost substantial amounts of weight were compared with people of the same weights who had not dieted, it was shown that the dieters burned 824 fewer calories per day than *the non-dieters.* In this study all of the reduced ability to burn calories occurred as a result of non-resting energy expenditure.

Women who are restrained eaters (dieters) eat an average of 410 fewer calories per day than non-dieters, but they burn 620 fewer calories per day than those who are not dieting.[115] *These women are also significantly heavier than the non-dieters.*

The decrease in non-resting energy expenditure could make it doubly tough on dieters, who often do not feel like exercising. Indeed, it has been demonstrated that there is a considerable reduction in spontaneous physical activity during a diet.[116]

When "temporarily thinner" persons are not sleeping or resting, they do not burn nearly as many calories as non-dieters of exactly the same weight. This means that if the reduced-obese person begins to consume the same number of calories as the non-dieter, the 824 calories per day not used in energy expenditure will be stored in the fat cells, adding an extra 8 pounds of fat every 35 days! It is no wonder that dieters become frustrated. They can truly "eat like birds" and gain weight on the same number or even fewer calories than are required simply to maintain the non-dieter's weight.

Dieters lose both muscle tissue and body fat during their diets. When weight is regained, however, nearly all of it comes back as fat, and the metabolic rate remains depressed during the refeeding period.[117]

Further proof of decreasing energy expenditure are studies on animals. After rats are forced to diet and lose weight, they quickly return to the weight of their non-dieting littermates, even when they are allowed to consume only the same number of calories (or even fewer calories) than their free-feeding friends.[118] The weight gain occurs even though the calories denied during the diet phase are never replaced in the refeeding phase. This can only be true if metabolic rate is lowered. The calories not burned (due to that lowered metabolic rate) are obviously deposited in the fat cells.

Ah, the plight of the dieter! He is forced to eat fewer calories than his non-dieting counterpart just to maintain his lowered weight. If he eats the same number of calories, he will become obese again very rapidly. In one amazing piece of research, rats were starved to 80% of normal weight. *When allowed to eat freely, they ate slightly less than their free-feeding littermates. Yet, they gained weight 18 times as fast as those littermates!* [119]

If one diet is a problem, then a series of diets is a disaster.

Repeated dieting and bingeing is known as "weight cycling" among scientists and "yo-yo dieting" by the general public. We previously mentioned that weight loss and regain had a detrimental influence on health, raising cholesterol levels and exacerbating diabetes. It has an even more profound affect on metabolism. Each diet lowers the metabolic rate more than the previous diet, and it takes longer each time for the metabolic rate to recover.[120] Weight is gained more rapidly after each diet, and the same low-calorie diet becomes less and less effective at removing weight from the dieter's body with each successive try.

Perhaps the study most descriptive of the metabolic adaptation to dieting was one in which rats were given a low-calorie diet. They lost a great deal of weight in 21 days. When allowed to eat normally, the rats regained the weight in an average of 46 days. The rats were then placed on another diet which contained exactly the same number of calories as the first diet. *This time, rather than lose the weight in 21 days, it took 46 days.* When allowed to eat freely, however, the rats gained back their weight in only 15 days—*three times as fast as after the first diet!* When compared to animals which were kept obese on a high-fat diet, these "cycled" rats were found to store fat four times more efficiently than their littermates.[121]

Accelerated weight gain and more difficult weight loss have also been produced by weight-cycling in humans, with the added problem that those who lost weight during the first diet cycle gained 120% of the weight lost between cycles![122] *Diets are deadly; multiple diets are more deadly.*

Medically-supervised fasting: the worst of the lot

Medically supervised fasting perhaps provides the most dramatic evidence for the existence of a set point for body weight. These programs are so futile that it is amazing that the hospitals and doctors who administer these horrors can justify them. Granted, fasting can be successful in the short term, but it is also the surest way to become excessively obese. At National Institute of Fitness, we have worked with several individuals who have been subjected to these medically-supervised programs.

The stories of these people are appalling. All of them have been very successful in losing weight to begin with, shedding up to 110 pounds. *In fact, one fasting victim lost 110 pounds twice on one of the best-known programs only to regain 130 pounds back each time.* Another lost 90 pounds and regained 110 pounds. These programs are probably more fattening than anything yet conceived.

A commentary in the *Journal of the American Medical Association* (JAMA)[123] in January 1990 discussed the "responsible" and "irresponsible" use of very-low-calorie diets. "Responsible" was defined as a program which included regular consultation and behavior modification techniques and supervision by a physician to prevent complications and fatalities. (Is this a bit frightening?) The authors indicated that these programs were "associated with only minor complications when administered to carefully selected patients by physicians trained in their use." They then recommended: "The diets should be limited to persons who are a minimum of 30% overweight, have received a recent medical examination and electrocardiogram with satisfactory results, and are free of contraindicating conditions, including a recent myocardial infarction; a cardiac conduction disorder; a history of cerebro-vascular, renal or hepatic disease; cancer; type 1 diabetes; or significant psychiatric disturbance." Sounds like a *great* program, right? A program that may kill the patient if he is not a very healthy and strong individual.

In a letter to the editor concerning the commentary, Dr. Thomas Flynn[124] noted that with the best in behavioral therapy treatment for the "fasting" patients (as recommended by the commentary authors), between 74 and 85% of the lost weight had been regained in three years.[125] It appears that at best, starvation programs combined with behavior therapy may prolong the agony a bit. Dr. Flynn concluded his letter with the following: "As the commentary states, there are many risks associated with irresponsible use, *but is there such a thing as responsible use?* [my emphasis] I am discouraged by the profit motive, the use of personality testimonials, the half-truths, the research results, and my own personal experience—and I run one of these 'responsible' programs." Dr. Flynn is medical director of the OPTIFAST program at the Humana Hospital in Orange Park, Florida. You are correct, Dr. Flynn. There is no "responsible" use of a low-calorie diet nor of a medically supervised fast.

The most widely publicized case of diet futility is the case of Oprah Winfrey, whose OPTIFAST program enabled her to fit into a pair of size 10 Calvin Klein jeans. But, alas, two years later, much of the lost weight had returned, and Oprah declared to a nationwide audience on her television program of November 5, 1990: . . . . "I'll never diet again. I will certainly never fast again."[126] In describing the rapidity with which the weight can come back, Oprah gave one of the best portrayals ever: ". . . if you set a five-pound limit [for regained weight], five pounds is only a meal away from seven. Seven is just a weekend away from ten. Ten is a day from twelve, and twelve is just really three days away from fifteen."

On hearing of Oprah's disavowal of her fasting program, the executive director of OPTIFAST stated, "We don't think that her show was devastating at all to OPTIFAST. It reinforced our philosophy that this [obesity] should be treated as a long-term disease."[127] One more starvation program shows its true colors; one more person realizes the futility of a weight-loss method which uses caloric restriction. One more diet pusher is stuck for a decent answer to explain the egregious failure of his methods to keep the weight off.

In one study of patients who had lost up to 91 pounds through a medically supervised fast, a two-year follow-up showed that only 3% managed to keep the weight off.[128] Given a few more years, nearly everyone fails to keep the weight off.

Other studies of weight loss through calorie restriction indicate similar results. Weight returns inexorably to its former level,[129] despite numerous attempts to halt that return through dieting.

The results of these severely restrictive programs suggest the existence of a *set-point mechanism* that forces the body to regain the weight it has lost (more on this later). They have about as much chance of working for sustained weight loss as does the aforementioned program used by my hog-raising acquaintance to fatten his hogs. Isn't it interesting that a hog farmer would be wiser than the people who sell these starvation programs and the physicians who administer them?

Exercise during dieting reduces the metabolism-lowering effects of dieting to an extent but not enough to overcome them.[130] [131] The more severe the diet, the less exercise helps to overcome the effects of lowered metabolism. Adolescent wrestlers often starve themselves in order to compete in a lower weight category. Then they regain the weight. This process may take place many times in a wrestler's career. When young men who have been through these weight cycling periods are compared to wrestlers who have not cycled, they show a resting energy expenditure 14% lower than the non-cycled wrestlers.[132]

Carbohydrate and metabolism

There is another factor that changes the influence that dieting has on metabolic rate. That factor is starch. One research study used an 800-calorie-per-day diet that was very high in starch. The diet allowed weight to be lost without lowering the metabolic rate.[133] However, in spite of its high starch content, the program produced fatigue, hunger and anxiety, along with a loss of muscle tissue. (For this reason, I question the validity of the statement that metabolic rate was not lowered, since muscle tissue is related closely to the ability to burn calories.) Seventeen percent of the weight lost (28 pounds in 16 weeks) was muscle. Another group that ate unlimited starches was able to lose a substantial amount of weight (14 pounds in 16 weeks) without any of the adverse symptoms experienced on the 800-calorie diet. Nearly all of the weight lost was fat.

Perhaps it is starch restriction rather than calorie restriction per se that has a most profound effect on lowering of the resting metabolic rate. Nonetheless, I believe that dieting by caloric restriction is dangerous to metabolic rates, regardless of food choice, especially in the non-resting phase of energy expenditure. The fatigue experienced on the low-calorie diet in the study just described, in my opinion, is a manifestation of reduced non-resting energy expenditure. At any rate, why would anyone go through the miseries of dieting when substantial weight can be lost very comfortably by simply changing from nutrition that is high in fat to nutrition that is low in fat and high in starch?

Dieting, thyroid, and metabolism

A final note about metabolism: When men are put on a program of underfeeding (a euphemism for diet), the production of thyroid hormone decreases by 28.3% in a period of only six weeks.[134] Similar reductions are observed in animals who are starved.[135 136 137]

Thyroid hormone is a metabolic stimulant that physicians often prescribe in pill form for their overweight patients. This is usually done because the patients' blood tests indicate an underproduction of that hormone. In most cases, the low levels are probably due to dieting and not to any inherent physiological problem. TSH, the hormone which stimulates the production of thyroid hormone, is also depressed when calories are restricted.[138 139 140]

Although I know of no research indicating that a program of low-fat nutrition and exercise increases the production of thyroid hormone, it is logical that such a program—which would remove the cause of lowered thyroid hormone (low-calorie dieting)—would return those hormone levels to normal.

Often, people who are overweight—and are having difficulty losing weight by dieting—are diagnosed through blood testing as having low thyroid output. Many are subsequently prescribed thyroid pills by their physicians. But low thyroid is not the *cause* of their problems—it is a *result* of their dieting. The pills, although they may help a person to lose weight initially, will probably have the effect of reducing the person's thyroid output even further. I personally observed the blood tests of one inveterate dieter who, due to other complications involving the drug, stopped taking thyroid medication after 17 years. This person's thyroid output at that time was almost nil. However, after a few months away from the pills and using a low-fat, vegetarian nutrition plan, the thyroid output recovered completely to normal. It is best to eat as human beings are intended to eat, exercise as they are intended to exercise, and then let nature take its course. Any attempt to improve on the system is ill-advised.

Enzymes and fat storage

A fascinating enzyme called adipose tissue lipoprotein lipase (LPL) has a great deal to do with the body's ability to become fat. In fact, transporting fats from the blood to the fat cells depends on it.[141] When found in the capillaries of fat tissue, this enzyme causes circulating fat to be taken from the blood and stored as body fat.[142] It may also signal the central nervous system to initiate processes which increase the consumption of food following a diet.[143] In obese subjects who restrict calories to lose weight, the activity and quantity of LPL is greatly increased.[144]

What does this mean to the person who is restricting calories? It means that the action of dieting greatly increases the quantity and activity of a potent, fat-storing enzyme which will subsequently cause that person to eat sufficient food to make up for the restriction, thereby regaining all of his lost weight, plus a few extra pounds.

Are all fats created equal?

All calories are not created equal. Even the calories in different types of fat have varying abilities to fatten. For example, animals fed animal fats become much heavier than those fed vegetable fats, even though the numbers of calories ingested are identical.[145] [146] Animal fats fatten by increasing the activity of LPL in the fat cells.[146] Vegetable fats increase LPL activity to a much lesser extent. This is not meant as an endorsement of vegetable fats—far from it. But in terms of the ability to fatten, they are the lesser of two evils. All fats, however, are very fattening.

Insulin drives LPL.

In the chapter on diabetes, we will discuss the fattening effects of insulin. We will point out that both dietary fat and body fat cause resistance to insulin, resulting in a greater secretion of that hormone.[147] Insulin also stimulates the quantity and activity of LPL, which may be the prime method by which it fattens. (See the chapter on diabetes.) Insulin is so important to the storage of fat that type 1 diabetics (those diabetics who do not produce insulin) become emaciated and die when denied an external source of insulin. Type 2 diabetics often produce far more than the normal amount of insulin, a prime contributor to the extreme obesity of those afflicted.

Insulin is also adept at slowing metabolic rates. One study pointed out that when heavy insulin injections were used to keep tight control of blood sugar in diabetics, daily consumption of calories *decreased* by 500 calories per day per person during one year on the program.[148] *Yet, the average gain in weight was 11 pounds.* This is one more example of the fact that obesity is not caused by eating too much but rather by metabolic disorders resulting from improper nutrition, low calorie dieting, and lack of exercise.

In addition to changes in LPL, diets may induce changes in the quantity and action of an enzyme known as sodium-potassium ATP-ase. This enzyme is a fat-burning enzyme which is significantly lower in obese individuals.[149] Dieting may therefore increase fat-storing enzymes while lowering fat-burning enzymes; not exactly what the dieter is seeking!

DIETING DESTROYS ENERGY.

As anyone knows who has tried to starve for a time, lethargy is something to be expected. As the diet period is extended, it becomes very difficult to perform heavy labor. Thus, calories are conserved which would otherwise have been burned in activity. Obese people become very efficient at conserving calories by accomplishing identical tasks with much less motion than their thinner counterparts. Even when sitting, obese people use less energy per pound than thin people who are also sitting. It is as if the obese body wants to conserve all of the fat that it can and tenaciously protects its fat stores. This results in the reduction in non-resting energy expenditure described earlier.

IS THE FAT IN THE GENES?

Yes, heredity does make a difference, but it is far from being a vital factor in obesity. If we juxtapose two people of the same sex, age, activity level, history of dieting and current nutritional habits, we will undoubtedly find that one is fatter than the other. Certainly such a comparison would indicate a genetic difference between the two. This does not mean, however, that either is doomed to be fat or that neither would put on weight if environmental factors were conducive to weight gain.

Several studies on genetic obesity, which were reported in the *New England Journal of Medicine*,[150] [151] [152] have created quite a stir. Two of these found that twins reared apart tended to be quite similar in the amount of fat which they accumulated on their bodies. This might indicate that they were victims of their heredity.[150] [151]

The other study showed that among twins who were given a fattening diet, there was a much greater tendency of twins to either gain weight in similar amounts or to resist that weight gain. One set of twins might gain very rapidly, whereas another set might gain more slowly on the same fattening diet.[152]

Investigations of obesity and metabolic rate among the Pima Indians have also shown a genetic tendency toward a low metabolic rate among those who are obese.[153] Personally, I doubt that the Pimas are victims of their genetics. We have discussed the dramatic metabolism-lowering influence of insulin. The Pimas have learned to love the high-fat diet of their White neighbors. In fact, they seem to have an even greater liking for fatty, sugary foods. This may also be a genetic preference. The extreme high-fat, high-sugar diet of the Pimas likely increases insulin production, which in turn lowers their metabolic rates. (See the section on insulin.) This combination of fat and sugar has made the Pima the most obese people in the world. Unfortunately, other American Indians are not far behind.

These "genetic" studies have some value, especially in terms of educating the public to the grave error of stereotyping fat people as lacking in character, willpower or goodness, or perhaps suffering from some mental aberration which causes them to overeat. These beliefs are unkind and untrue—overeating has nothing to do with obesity, and neither does character. Given the same atrocious nutrition, one person may become fat and another may stay thin. Most of us have heard such unkind and cruel statements as, "How can he let himself be like that?" or "If I were fat, I'd have the guts to do something about it." Such statements are unfair, especially since fat people do not eat as much, on the average, as thin people. If research into the genetics of obesity helps to quell these unfounded biases, so much the better.

The downside of such studies is that many who read about them in the popular media may be imbued with a sense of hopeless resignation, believing that they are destined to be fat due to genes inherited from their progenitors.

One concerned physician, who wrote an editorial in response to the previously mentioned articles on genetic obesity, stated that the popular press may now declare that what goes on in the home makes no difference. That, he says, would be a mistake.[154]

His concerns were well founded. Shortly after the articles were published in the *Journal, Time Magazine* ran an article of their own entitled, "Chubby? Blame Those Genes."[155] To a person who is desperate to lose weight, such a headline might bring despair. She might start wishing that she had chosen her parents a bit more wisely. Fortunately, for those who read the entire article, the last paragraph stated the truth about heredity and overweight: "People may indeed inherit a propensity to obesity, but it need not be their destiny." Well stated indeed!

The *Time* article also pointed out that a low-fat diet and

exercise can be a great help in offsetting heredity. This would be consistent with previously discussed research that showed that as societies become richer (which is nearly always accompanied by an increase in the consumption of animal products and fat), there is a rise in degenerative diseases and obesity.[156]

Have genetics changed in American Indians?

When the food becomes richer and physical activity diminishes, obesity manifests itself. Anyone who has observed adult American Indians has probably observed that they are quite likely the most obese people on earth. Yet it was not so before the White man endowed them with dietary fat and sugar. Tribes who were formerly very lean are now obese,[157] and whereas these people had little or no diabetes, they now suffer the highest degree of diabetes in the world. Navajo children of today are 18.7% heavier (girls) and 28.8% heavier (boys) than were Navajo children of 35 years ago.[158]

Has the genetic makeup of the American Indian changed in the past 50 years? Not at all. How much has his nutritional environment changed? Immensely! (For a discussion of the changes in nutritional habits of the Indians, read the section on the Pima Indians in the chapter on diabetes.)

As with heart disease, familial tendencies become important in the production of obesity only when the toxins that cause the disease are already in place. At that point the propensity toward obesity becomes obvious. Without the toxins, we would never know who had a predisposition to obesity and who didn't. (See the chapter on heart disease for a more complete discussion of familial tendencies to disease.)

At this point we should mention another important fact: At the turn of the century, only about 5% of the U.S. population was overweight, compared with current estimates of up to 70% now. Can it be that our genetics have undergone such a dramatic change in the past 91 years? To make such a claim would certainly fly in the face of common sense. One of the big changes, other than moving from a society of relatively high physical activity to a society of low activity, is the change in the composition of the diet. Fat provided 31% more of our calorie intake in 1976 than in 1910, and yet in 1976 fewer calories were consumed on the average than 1910.[21]

One group of researchers, in discussing the interaction between environment and genetics, stated, "Our view is that some individuals are more susceptible to environmental forces that stimulate an imbalance of energy intake over expenditure. Because the genetic makeup of the population could not have changed substantially over past decades, changes in environmental forces and their impact on individual behaviors (both physical and diet) must be responsible for recent increases in obesity."[5]

Anyone who would blame a change in genetics for the increasing levels of obesity would also flunk a basic kindergarten course in reasoning. The fat may be in our *jeans*, but it is certainly not in our *genes*.

If it is neither heredity nor gluttony that causes overweight, and if it is true that calorie-restricted diets result ultimately in obesity, what is the explanation? The most simple, consistent, and logical explanation is known as the "set-point theory."

1.

PART 2:

Resetting the Set Point

1. *Part 2: Resetting the Set Point*

We have established that the number of calories consumed is of little importance in obesity, as long as the calories are derived from starches and other low-fat foods. We have also established that caloric intake is inversely proportional to body weight. If the number of calories are not responsible for obesity, then what regulates body weight? What is it that increases body weight when fat and sugar are eaten but does not do so when starch is eaten? What makes the dieter more lethargic than the non-dieter? What makes the dieting person expend significantly fewer calories during his or her non-resting hours? The fascinating theory of *set point* provides answers to these provocative questions.

A person's set point weight, according to the theory, is that weight which the body tenaciously defends. People who diet to lose weight gain back the weight, and people who are force fed to gain weight lose the weight when they are allowed to eat normally. Something demands that the body weigh a certain amount. That something is the hypothalamus, an important organ in the central nervous system which is located at the base of the brain. It is involved in many functions that have to do with growth and development, sexual maturity, body temperature and regulation of appetite.[159]

The hypothalamus regulates body mass by "setting" the weight of the body according to what it perceives as appropriate at a given time. (This action of the hypothalamus will be discussed later in this section.)

There are many systems of the body that operate on the "set point" principle. For instance, sugar levels in the blood are usually maintained within a certain safe range except in cases where something occurs to temporarily raise or lower those levels. When that happens, the body makes certain quick adjustments to bring the sugar levels back into the normal range. When sugar floods into the blood as a result of a meal filled with sweets, the pancreas is activated to produce insulin, which transports the excessive sugar out of the blood, thus ensuring that the sugar level does not become dangerously high. If the level of sugar becomes too low due to excessive insulin, the person begins to crave food. When the food is eaten, sugar is absorbed into the blood, thereby raising blood-sugar levels to a safe range.

However, as discussed in the chapter on diabetes, something may happen to "reset" the set point to a higher level. In the case of diabetes, that factor is usually a high intake of dietary fat. When this happens, the person becomes hyperglycemic (excessive sugar in the blood). If the cause of the high set point is not removed, the person will have chronically high blood sugar levels and will be diagnosed as an adult-onset diabetic. Remove the cause of the high set point, however, and the sugar levels will quickly normalize. The *set point* for blood sugar, thus, will drop.

The example of blood sugar levels is one of perhaps millions of set point mechanisms which work in the human body. Some of these, such as blood-sugar levels and body weight, can become out of balance and be set to very high levels, whereas others, such as PH balance of the blood and body temperature, are maintained within very close limits. If they were not closely regulated, death would come quickly as the body became too acidic or too alkaline; too hot or too cold. Nevertheless, even the set point for body temperature can be raised when a person has a fever and may remain elevated until the cause of the fever (fighting a foreign organism) has been removed. The theory follows that set point for body weight is regulated in the same manner. This set point is often very high due to environmental causes. When those causes are removed, the set point will be reset to a lower level.

If the set point theory for weight is correct, then like other set points (such as the blood-sugar set point previously described), we should expect that it exerts its influence in both directions. We should expect also that those who have gained weight purposely by force feeding would have a very difficult time keeping the extra weight on—perhaps as difficult a time as the dieter has in keeping weight off.

What is the evidence that a set point for weight exists?

When people are living life styles that are constant—in other words, not doing anything that would influence weight in the short term (such as dieting or force feeding)—their weights remain very constant.[160] [161] [162] Variations in body weights are usually only about ½%, either up or down. When something disturbs that constancy (such as dieting or force feeding), the body may make substantial, albeit temporary, changes in weight. Weight returns to its previous level after the alteration in energy intake is stopped.

When a subject who gains weight through a force-feeding program is allowed to eat normally, he unconsciously decreases his caloric intake to a level far below his baseline intake (the number of calories ingested prior to the force feeding). His weight also returns to its baseline level. Those who have been starved, when allowed to eat normally, dramatically increase caloric consumption and quickly return to baseline weights. This indicates that weight is regulated around a particular level and that the body is quite capable of manipulating food and energy intake to maintain that level. This weight which the body insists on maintaining is called the set point level.

Numerous studies substantiate the set point theory. When people are force fed and gain weight, the weight returns quickly to normal when the force feeding program ends.[163] In some experiments, subjects have a very hard time gaining any weight at all, even when overfeeding themselves thousands of extra calories per day.[164] To maintain the gained weight after a force-feeding program, it is necessary to continue to eat large numbers of calories. Otherwise, the weight is lost rapidly. The force feeder, therefore, must work very hard to keep his gained weight. If he lessens his calorie intake, he loses weight rapidly, even if the number of calories he is eating greatly exceed the number he ate prior to his force-feeding program. *It is necessary to consume 50% more than the usual number of calories to maintain a weight gain of about 20%.*[165]

Further evidence of the difficulty of retaining weight which has been gained by overfeeding comes from experiments on animals. If animals are starved (put on a diet), they will lose a considerable amount of weight and fat. When they are allowed to eat normally, they will automatically increase the amount of food they consume until they return to their former weights.[166] If animals are force fed, however, they will gain weight to the point of obesity. When allowed to eat freely, they will lower their food consumption markedly until they return to their previous weights.[167]

The dieter, on the other hand, cannot keep off the weight he has lost, even when restricted to fewer calories than he ate prior to beginning his diet. It is quite obvious that the body regulates weight around a set point. Overfeed, and all of the gained weight will be lost when the program ends. Diet, and all of the lost weight will be regained when the program ends.

Let's use an example of another set point which controls oxygen levels in the body and then relate it to the set point for weight. This will increase the understanding of the battle the dieter faces in trying to overcome his body's natural physiology.

The oxygen set point

All cells require oxygen to sustain life. Therefore, if the oxygen in the body is decreased, the body will respond dramatically to bring it back to its previous level. When we jog or walk, for example, the muscle cells begin to burn large quantities of oxygen to support the activity. This lowers the oxygen content of the muscles below the level which the body feels is appropriate, or in other words, below the *set point* for oxygen.

Lowering the oxygen level produces what is known as an oxygen debt. As the level of oxygen moves below the set point, there exists a "gap" between that level and the level which the body would like to maintain. That gap must be filled for the body to survive and be comfortable. The debt must be paid.

As the body senses a lowering of the oxygen level, the respiratory rate is immediately increased, which brings a larger quantity of oxygen into contact with the blood in the lungs. This increases the quantity of oxygen which is absorbed into the blood, thereby increasing the amount available for transport to the "oxygen-deprived" muscles. Heart rate is also increased, and the volume of blood that the heart pumps out with each beat, known as stroke volume, is also increased. These physiological changes increase the quantity of oxygen delivered to the cells, thus preventing oxygen levels from becoming dangerously low.

If the body were not able to increase oxygen delivery in response to exercise, death would be the quick and unavoidable outcome. The body, however, is very adept at self-preservation and will not allow the oxygen level to drop very far. Anyone who has tried sprinting up a hill for a few seconds while holding his breath (not recommended) knows just how intensely the body works to pay the oxygen debt or fill the gap. Someone performing such an experiment would quickly focus his thoughts on only one thing—breathing. He would frantically await the end of the sprint in anticipation of ending his discomfort by breathing, which would pay the oxygen debt incurred.

Let us suppose, now, that the sprint has ended and that the sprinter sits down on the side of the road. Does his rate of breathing or his heart rate return immediately to normal? Of course not. He will breathe very hard and deeply until the debt has been paid. He will "BINGE" on oxygen until the debt has been paid or until the gap has been filled. Only then will the sprinter's heart and respiratory rates return to normal.

Now let's relate the dieting experience to the experience of the "breath-holding sprinter" described above. When a person diets, he becomes like the sprinter running up the hill. The body weight does come down (just as the level of oxygen comes down in the sprinter). The set point for weight, however, remains at the same level or even increases. This creates a gap between the weight which the body considers to be appropriate and actual weight, which is now below set point. This is not an oxygen debt but a fat debt which must be repaid. Diets, like sprints, are very uncomfortable, and it is well known that people who diet generally think of little else but eating—a similar phenomenon experienced by the oxygen-depleted sprinter. He can think of little else but breathing. The "food-obsessed" mentality observed in the dieter, therefore, indicates no inherent psychological flaw. It exists for purposes of survival.

When a diet finally ends, as it must, the dieter will binge for a period of time until the weight is regained and eating patterns return to normal. This is similar to what happens when the sprinter is recovering from his oxygen deprivation. He continues to deliver oxygen at a high rate until his debt is repaid and the oxygen gap is filled. He can then breathe normally without the need to "binge" on oxygen. Binge eating is not a psychological problem but a self-preserving reality. Nothing is more natural than breathing heavily after a period of oxygen deprivation. Likewise, nothing could be more natural than eating heavily after a period of food deprivation. This explains the "overeating" which is frequently observed among obese people. Contrary to popular opinion, it is not the result of a willpower deficit or some intrinsic flaw in the grey matter. People whose weights are below set point weights will eat as if there were no tomorrow in an attempt to fill the "fat gap." These people *are not gluttonous, they are hungry.* It is dieting, not obesity, that accounts for this behavior.[168] [169] [170]

People do not really overeat. A person who has held his breath for a period of time will then breathe long and hard until he has paid his oxygen debt, but we do not accuse him of "over breathing." A person who has gone without water will likewise drink copious quantities of water until his thirst is sated. We do not accuse him of "over drinking." A person who has restricted food intake for a period of time. . . . You get the point.

We established earlier that over a long period, the obese person eats no more, and probably less, than the thin or "normal-weight" individual. In view of this fact, "overeating" is a myth. The pattern of eating is simply changed from one of regular, unrestrained eating to one of bingeing and starving, resulting in a similar or lesser caloric intake among obese people. If anything, obese people *"undereat."*

The Minnesota Experiment

One of the first dramatic examples of body weight regulation by the set point mechanism was a study known as the Minnesota Starvation Experiment.[32] In this study, men were given a low-calorie diet for a period of 24 weeks. During that time they lost about 20% of their original weight. Toward the end of the 24-week period, weights had stabilized, although the number of calories they were receiving were constant throughout the program. Metabolic rates had decreased by 29%. When they were allowed to eat freely after the diet (which was referred to as a starvation program), they regained weight very rapidly, until, at the end of 33 weeks of unrestricted eating, they had become about 10% heavier than they had been prior to the diet. In other words, the set point had actually been set *higher* by the diet. The amount of fat on their bodies, moreover, had increased by 40%! This indicated a substantial loss of muscle mass—mass that was replaced by fat. This makes perfect sense, since muscle is the only tissue that can burn fat for energy. Decreasing the muscle mass would be a great solution to cutting back on the number of calories burned, thereby preserving life during a "famine."

More than a year after the 24-week starvation period, the weights of the men had nearly returned to pre-starvation levels, meaning that the set point had lowered. The body-fat percent had also dropped, indicating that some of the lost muscle tissue had returned. "Undieting" proved to be an effective method to lose the weight which they had gained through dieting.

Suppose, however, that the men in this study had been typical dieters, i.e., not taking part in an experiment but rather attempting to lose weight for cosmetic purposes. On finding themselves heavier after their diet experience, they would probably have panicked and begun another diet. This would have prevented the weight from stabilizing at lower levels and would have initiated another cycle of dieting, characterized by initial weight loss and eventual weight gain.

When people give up dieting in frustration, they will usually lose weight, just as the men in the Minnesota experiment did. We have worked with two people who became so disgusted with their diet experiences that they swore never to diet again. Within a year of beginning their "undiets," they each lost about 50 pounds. For the obese person, it appears that the *undiet* is far more successful for sustained weight loss than the diet. "Not dieting" is one method by which the set point may be set to lower levels.

Your hypothalamus determines your weight.

Other experiments have been performed in which lesions (injuries) were surgically induced in the hypothalami of rats. This operation caused the rats to lose considerable weight and then defend that new, lowered weight tenaciously.[171] One of these "lesioned" rats was force fed to increase its body weight to the level of normal rats. Then it was allowed to eat as it wished. Its weight quickly returned to the new lowered level produced by the surgery.[172] Obviously, the surgery had lowered the set point. These experiments indicate that the hypothalamus controls body weight. The hypothalamus is the "set point control center."

When rats with surgically-induced, lowered set points were placed on a calorie-restricted diet, they were able to further lower their weights by about 20%. When allowed to eat normally, however, their weights immediately returned to the higher level. This level, of course, was still far below their original weight prior to the hypothalamic lesion.[172]

Hypothalamic surgery, then, might be one method of losing weight which would ensure that the weight stayed off. But, before we start searching for a surgeon who can perform such surgery, we should be reminded that there are natural ways to influence the hypothalamus to lower the set point. Those methods will be discussed later in the chapter.

Why does the set point work?

To the dieter it may seem contradictory that dieting initiates fat-conservation mechanisms and that force feeding programs do exactly the opposite. It may appear that God, or nature, made a mistake in creating the human body, since efforts to become thin (through dieting) result in an increased body weight and an increased body-fat percentage.

With closer scrutiny it becomes clear that God, or nature, made no mistake. The system is perfect and operates exactly as intended. Let's take a look at this paradox and some explanations that elucidate the operation of the set point and reasons for its existence.

Fundamental premise: The body operates on the "survival principle." There are perhaps millions of functions which are intended to sustain life, and many of them operate on the set point principle. The body knows nothing about size 8 dresses and 30-inch waists. It knows nothing about looking "svelte" for the high school reunion. What the body understands is survival.

When something threatens that survival, the body responds as appropriately as possible, making adjustments which will mitigate the dangerous circumstances.

The aforementioned example of the sprinter shows how dramatically the body responds. Without oxygen, he would soon die, but his physiology prevents that from happening. No matter how great his willpower, it will be overridden by his desire to breathe. Some people believe that they can totally control their physiological responses if they have the willpower to do so, but they cannot. Try sometime to lower your body temperature 20 degrees using willpower. Your body will simply not let you do it because to do so would threaten your survival.

The body assumes that a long-term period of calorie restriction is a famine. It thus relies on stored fat when food supplies are short. When the diet begins, the body has no way of knowing how long this particular "famine" will last and consequently initiates survival responses—slowing itself down to conserve as many calories as possible to postpone the day of death by starvation. By so doing it can survive for the longest period of time, using only the least amount of energy to maintain vital processes.

We have established that during dieting, fat-storing enzymes increase while fat-burning enzymes decrease. Muscle tissue is also decreased, and the person who is starving (dieting) becomes lethargic. All of these changes conserve energy, allowing for a type of "hibernation" until food supplies are restored.

But the body is very smart. It learns from its painful experience. If it can just survive this famine, it will make sure that it has a greater quantity of energy stored for the next famine. With each succeeding diet, the body gets smarter, adding a few more pounds of fat to its "savings account" to guard against the next disaster. Thus the set point rises with each diet, and more fat is stored. When famines stop for a year or two, however, the body begins to "forget" about them. It becomes more complacent, willing to give up some of the stored energy that it has heretofore considered essential to survival. Hence, those who give up dieting tend to lose considerable weight over a period of time.

How would you respond to a real famine?

If it is hard for you to visualize this problem from the body's point of view, then perhaps another analogy is in order. Let's create a little scenario to illustrate your response if you were put in a situation in which very little food was available. Suppose that the truckers who transport food go on strike. Suddenly there is no food in the supermarkets. A newscast informs you that this situation will last for at least three weeks, but on checking your refrigerator and pantry, you find only a one-week supply of food. Since there is no other food available except that small amount, you, as an astute individual, ration the week's supply to make it last three weeks. You also become lethargic in order to conserve the food normally needed to provide energy for exercise.

You will, of course, learn from the experience. You might say to yourself, "I am not about to let this happen again! When the famine is over, I will store more food to protect myself against another famine."

Finally, the "famine" ends, and you scurry to the grocery store, which is once again well-stocked. As expected, everyone at the store is buying massive quantities of food to hedge against the next famine. You buy a three-week supply of food, feeling confident and well-prepared for any future interruption in the food supply.

Alas, a few months later, another disruption of the food supply occurs, which is predicted to last for at least six weeks. You, however, have only a three-week supply of food. Again, you are forced to repeat the rationing process, but this time you *really* get smart. This time you put away a nine-week supply! You become smarter with each succeeding famine, storing a bit more food each time to ensure your survival.

The body responds in exactly the same manner, storing more food after each famine (as in the example of the man who had lost 110 pounds twice on the medically-supervised fast and gained back 130 pounds each time). The body's storage pantries are the fat cells, and after each cycle of starving and bingeing, they collect a bit more fat to prepare for the next period of deprivation. This makes sense and is a perfect system. No, God did not err when He programmed the body for survival.

How to put weight on a thin person

People who are naturally thin may have a difficult time gaining weight by the usually prescribed method of eating more food. Although they may gain a pound or two, the weight is lost rapidly following the "overeating" period. I have been told of an organization, however, which specializes in helping chronically underweight people gain body mass.

You can probably guess the method. They place the person on a low-calorie diet until several pounds have been removed from the already-too-thin frame. Afterward, the person is allowed unrestricted eating. He gains back all of the lost weight plus a few extra pounds. The process is repeated, and as we would expect, he is finally able to fatten his body. Remember that THE DIET IS PROBABLY THE MOST EFFECTIVE METHOD OF FATTENING EVER DEVELOPED. I do not endorse this method, even for underweight people, due to the many deleterious influences of diet cycling heretofore discussed.

There is an amusing, ironic and perhaps tragic aspect of this method. It is exactly the same program that overweight people have used for decades in a futile attempt to become slim! DIETING GIVES THE BODY A PERFECT REASON TO BECOME FATTER: TO PROTECT ITSELF AGAINST FUTURE DIETS.

LOWERING THE SET POINT

From the preceding discussion it becomes clear that the set point mechanism is not intimidated by attempts to manipulate body weight through calorie restriction or caloric glut. It resists such attempts strongly, creating binges when starvation ceases, thereby filling the "fat gap." One group of authors likens the set point to a thermostat.[173] This is an excellent analogy which serves to illustrate the futility of "fighting" the set point. The following is my version of the "fat thermostat" and its relationship to the set point.

The Fat Thermostat analogy

Suppose that there is a room with a thermostat set at 70 degrees. This thermostat is a control center for both a heater and a cooler. We determine that we want to increase the heat in the room to 90 degrees. Not being very smart, we bring in wheelbarrows full of hot coals and set them in the room in order to produce the desired increase in room temperature. As expected, the temperature rises to 90 degrees, but as the room warms, the cooler is activated. It works tirelessly until the coals have burned themselves out. The temperature is then brought back to 70 degrees (which is where the thermostat is set).

Still a bit obtuse, we determine to cool the room to 50 degrees. We bring in blocks of ice and place them around the room, and as expected, the room temperature is soon cooled to 50 degrees. During the cooling period, however, the furnace is activated. It works arduously until the ice is melted and the temperature is once again at 70 degrees.

Suddenly we see the light. We decide that if we want to maintain the room at a temperature other than its presently "set" temperature of 70 degrees, perhaps we should walk over to the thermostat and reset it to a lower temperature. How intelligent we have become!

We should use the same method with the thermostat (set point) for weight. If we can't fight it, we had better reset it to a lower setting.

The questions now arise: *How does one lower the fat thermostat to produce a lower weight setting?* How do we influence the hypothalamus to turn down the setting a few pounds? Do we try hypothalamic surgery?

We have already presented various ways in which the set point can be raised. High-fat diets, high-sugar diets, and sedentary living raise the set point. Dieting also raises the set point, perhaps more dramatically than any other method. We might suspect, then, that ceasing to diet, ceasing the high-fat nutrition, and engaging in a good exercise program would lower the set point. Information regarding dieting and high-fat nutrition has been amply discussed; now let's assess the influence of exercise in becoming lean.

The critical importance of exercise

Just as the calorie-restricted diet gives the body a perfect reason to become fatter, exercise gives it a perfect reason to become leaner and lighter.

Suppose that a person has dieted for years and in the process has become very obese. Finally, she gives up dieting and commences an exercise program consisting of a long, slow walk up a nearby hill. As she begins her walk, she also begins to experience, perhaps for the first time, some sustained physical discomfort. She is not accustomed to exercising. Within a short time, every fiber in her body is saying, "If you were a whole lot smaller, this would be a whole lot easier."

Aerobic exercise gives the body a reason to be smaller. Slimmer, lighter bodies carry themselves up hills—or anywhere else for that matter—more effortlessly and more easily than do heavy bodies. Thus, her body suddenly has a reason to be smaller and lighter. The hypothalamus, sensing this change, lowers the set point to a level more conducive to comfort in the new lifestyle. Combined with low-fat, high-fiber nutrition, exercise will lower the set point at a steady and reasonable rate until the excess weight is removed.

The above example is not meant to suggest that exercise should be a torturous experience to be effective; yet, it cannot be totally comfortable, or the body will have no reason to make the change to a lighter weight. If the exercise makes one hurt severely, however, the program has as much chance of surviving as a snowball in the Sahara. People do not continue in programs that make them miserable.

Many people ruin their chances for success by attempting to exercise far beyond their capabilities. They hurt themselves so badly that they give up in despair. If instead they begin slowly, building strength and endurance gradually, exercise becomes a successful and rewarding habit. It improves not only physical health but also self-image. Weight is lost at a realistic rate, and as the weight comes off, the exercise becomes easier.

This is the rule for exercising to lower the set point: Exercise must be sufficiently uncomfortable to convince the body to lower the set point but not so uncomfortable that it becomes a misery. The *aerobic zone* (discussed in the chapter on fitness) defines that magic area of intensity where one experiences neither comfort nor misery. Something as non-threatening as a brisk morning walk for 30 minutes or more can produce astounding, positive changes, particularly when combined with a high intake of complex carbohydrates (starches).

The formula for successful weight control, then, is to fill oneself to satiety with carbohydrates and to move the body regularly and vigorously. CONSULT YOUR PHYSICIAN PRIOR TO STARTING YOUR EXERCISE PROGRAM.

Exercise as a weight-loss method

A near-universal, yet totally erroneous belief is that large amounts of exercise create a bigger appetite. Whereas this is certainly true *after* the weight is lost, it is most assuredly not true *during* the weight-loss program; provided, of course, that low-fat nutrition is also used.

Exercise is somewhat effective in reducing weight even when it is not combined with a good nutrition program. A study that used an aerobic exercise program to rehabilitate cardiac patients produced an average fat loss of about 15 pounds over nine months.[174] This was accomplished without placing any restrictions on nutrition. Undoubtedly, if a low-fat nutrition program had been used, a much greater weight loss would have occurred.

Recently the results of a study which compared *exercise alone* to *diet alone* or *diet plus exercise*, showed that dieting alone virtually guaranteed a "yo-yo" cycle of losing weight and regaining it.[175] The human subjects were placed in one of three weight-loss programs. Fifty dieted, 50 dieted and exercised, and 50 exercised without dieting. All of those who dieted regained all of their weight back in two years or less. Those who dieted and exercised gained most of it back, and those who just exercised kept all of the weight off and continued to lose after two years. Another advantage of exercise is the fact that when weight is lost by exercise alone, there is no reduction whatsoever in metabolic rate, despite reductions in body size.[176]

Exercised rats, when fed a high-fat diet, gain much less weight than their littermates who are fed the same diet but not exercised.[93] However, the exercised rats on the high-fat diet still gain more than twice as much weight as littermates on a low-fat diet who also exercise.

One study indicates that aerobic exercise elevates the metabolic rate for a period of 24 hours after the exercise session.[177] Still other research affirms that the weight-reducing effects of exercise are much greater than those that could be expected from the body fat burned during the exercise period.[178] [179]

Though exercise is effective, we cannot overemphasize the importance of keeping dietary fat to an absolute minimum. Although exercise may partially (but effectively) lower a fat person's set point, it cannot fully work its magic without proper nutrition habits. Animals confined to cages—which severely limits their activity—never become severely obese if they consume a very-low-fat diet.[180] [181] Faulty nutrition is always the initial cause of obesity. Sedentary living, and also dieting, simply accelerate the process.

Watching the set point come down

In working with thousands of overweight guests at our fitness resort during the past 17 years, we have observed what might appear to the uninitiated to be a strange phenomenon. Our guests are seldom hungry while they lose weight. Of course, if they do become hungry, we require them to eat as much brown rice or potatoes as it takes to assuage that hunger. Many guests find it hard to eat all of the food they are given at meals, and yet men lose an average of one pound per day whereas women lose approximately one-half pound per day. Our program is based on unlimited complex carbohydrate (starch) nutrition along with large quantities of exercise.

During the National Institute of Fitness program, many of our guests walk from 2 to 20 miles per day, and a few average more than 20 miles per day. Yet, many of them find it impossible to consume all of the high-carbohydrate, high-bulk food that is offered. We constantly hear the comment, "I love the food, but I'm just not hungry." One of the young men on our program recently lost 92 pounds in 84 days without suffering hunger and only occasionally needed extra potatoes or brown rice. His energy level was superb throughout his program. Eventually, he became fit and lean enough to became a walking instructor for our institute. As an instructor, he lost another nine pounds. No hunger, no restriction of calories, and terrific energy. Now that he is lean, of course, he needs to consume far more food than he ever did when he was fat. There is a great lesson to be learned here. *The leaner you become with this method, the more you will need to eat.* One of the young women in our program recently lost 40 pounds in her first 28 days. She also, like most others, had a very high energy level throughout that time and needed little food beyond the basic meals. The thinner she becomes, however, the greater will be the amount of food she needs.

Granted, these are exceptional results, although they are by no means unusual. As mentioned before, the average weight loss is about a pound per day for men and a half-pound for women. As might also be expected, the larger the person, the greater the weight loss.

The lack of hunger, accompanied by good levels of energy, is easy to explain in terms of the set point mechanism. We have established that exercise lowers the set point for body weight. Starchy nutrition also lowers the set point. A study previously cited indicated that those people who were fed an unlimited starchy diet automatically cut back on their calories without hunger and lost a considerable amount of weight.[15] We find that this is also true with our program but to a much greater degree.

As previously mentioned, when animals and people who have been force fed are allowed to eat normally, they instinctively and unconsciously reduce their caloric intake, quickly returning to their previous weights. In view of these facts, let's take a look at the reason for the decreased appetite and high energy of those guests who attend National Institute of Fitness. We will use the example of a woman who has a set point weight and current body weight of 200 pounds. On the scale on the following page, this is represented by a point along a continuum between 120 and 210 pounds.

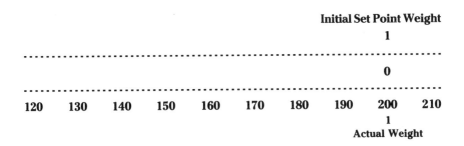

As she begins to exercise and eat the set-point-lowering foods, her set point drops to 190 pounds. Her actual weight, however, is still at 200 pounds. The distance between the actual weight and set point weight is the "fat surplus" which her body now recognizes. Her body "thinks" that she is ten pounds too heavy.

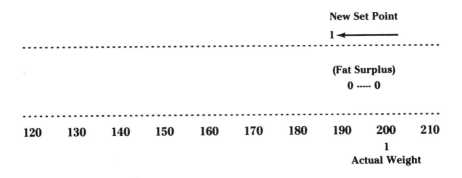

In order for her body to have energy to work, there are two sources it can turn to. She can either eat food to furnish that energy or she can use the energy which is stored in her body (primarily in fat cells). Since her body now considers itself to be ten pounds overweight, it chooses to derive much of its energy from the fat stores, thereby reducing her weight until it comes in line with her new, lowered set point. This depresses the appetite, since only modest amounts of food will be needed to furnish essential nutrients. Her level of energy is good, because her body willingly relinquishes its fat stores in order to lower weight.

As she continues to exercise and eat proper foods, her set point weight and her actual weight continue to drop. As long as she keeps her set point weight below her actual weight, her fat surplus continues to be a primary energy source. This heightened fat metabolism makes it unnecessary to eat large quantities of food for energy. Thus, her appetite remains depressed until her actual weight is lowered to the level of the set point weight.

What happens, however, when her body becomes as lean and as light as it desires to be? In other words, when she has become as small as she should be to maintain good health? Suppose that this occurs at a weight of 130 pounds. The set point weight and actual weight are now one and the same, and the set point will no longer drop, since further reduction is potentially dangerous.

On the day that set point and actual weight stabilize at the same low level, let's assume that she takes a ten-mile walk. Since her body will not lower the set point any further, the loss of calories during the hike moves her weight slightly under the set point. The body now senses a slight *fat debt*, and she becomes very hungry. When she finds food, she eats voraciously until she has re-supplied her body with sufficient calories to replace those used on the hike.

From this time on, she eats large quantities of food whenever she exercises vigorously, since she no longer has a fat surplus to work from. She stays thin and is able to enjoy all the food (the right kind, of course) that her heart desires. As we have established, thin, active people eat far more food than heavy, sedentary people.

In contrast, a calorie-restricted diet does nothing to lower the set point and, in fact, raises it, causing the body to experience the "fat debt." In that case, the body does not wish to let go of its fat stores, believing that it should weigh more, not less. Hunger is constant rather than depressed. If only people could learn that simple principle. Only fat people diet. Thin people can eat copious quantities of food—especially when it is the correct food.

With our set point scale, we can also explain the loss of weight which occurs *after* a program of force feeding. Suppose that we start with an individual who has a set point weight and an actual weight of 150 pounds.

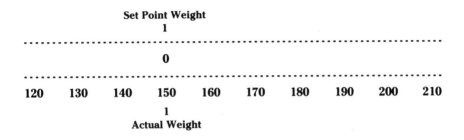

Now force feed this person to increase his weight to 160 pounds. His weight increases, but his set point remains at 150. This creates a fat surplus of ten pounds.

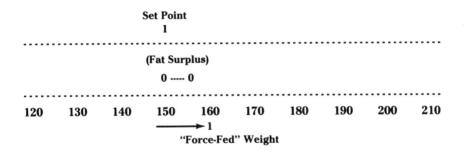

With a fat surplus of ten pounds, this individual experiences a depressed appetite in the same manner as the person who lowers the set point through proper nutrition and exercise. When allowed to terminate the force feeding program, he will eat very little until he returns to his base-line weight, at which time his appetite will be re-established. During the weight loss period, most of his energy requirements are supplied from his fat surplus.

In each of our examples, the set point is below the actual weight. In each case, appetite remains depressed until set point and weight are once again equal. This explains why force fed animals and humans return rapidly to previous weights when the excessive consumption of food ceases.

Finally, let's illustrate what occurs when a person with a set point of 190 pounds undertakes a severely restricted diet (such as a medically supervised fast) and loses 50 pounds.

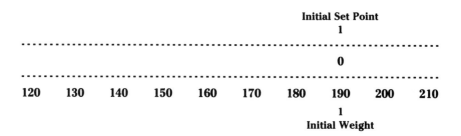

Now, through the fasting program, the actual weight is reduced by 50 pounds. The set point weight, however, is raised ten pounds as the body prepares to increase its fat supply when the "famine" is over. This creates a huge fat debt of 60 pounds.

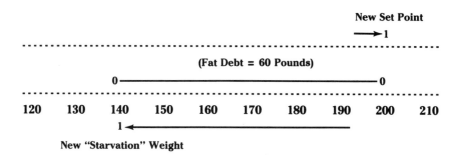

With this large fat debt, the "faster" experiences fatigue, hunger and lethargy in an effort to conserve fat. Ultimately, of course, the fat debt is paid, and the body weight stabilizes at the new set point of 200 pounds. During the rapid climb in weight to 200 pounds, the person will likely eat everything that doesn't crawl away. Even if she were restricted to the number of calories she ate prior to the starvation program (diet), her weight would move inexorably, though at a slower rate, to the 200-pound level. She is now prepared, with another ten pounds of fat in her savings account, to withstand the next "famine."

Imagine the dilemma of the person who has lost 50 pounds through starvation and who looks at a height-weight chart to determine "ideal" weight. Though she weighs 140 pounds, the chart tells her that she should weigh 120 pounds, according to her frame size and age. Statistically, she is 20 pounds overweight. Her body, however, "believes" that she is 60 pounds underweight! You can be assured that her body is not impressed by the chart on the wall of her physician's office. She will inevitably regain the 60 pounds unless she undertakes measures to lower her set point through a program of sound nutrition, exercise and "undieting."

A program of low-fat, high-starch nutrition and exercise is essential for successful weight control. We are not talking about a moderate decrease in fat content of the diet but really LOW-fat nutrition! The fat content of the diet should not exceed 10% of total calories. We discussed earlier the fact that the Chinese eat far more calories than Americans and yet have virtually no obesity and little degenerative disease. Many Chinese eat foods that average fewer than 10% of calories in fat. The lower the fat content the less is their chance of obesity and degenerative disease.[182] Those who believe that they will stay slim on any other nutrition program are dreaming the impossible dream.

When hunger becomes unbearable, the end of the diet is near. The famished, soon-to-be-fat-again dieter is forced to ask, "What now?" The answer, of course, is that he binges and regains the weight. Another diet rears its ugly head. This unfortunate person lives a life that revolves as much around food denial as it does around family, friends and career. This is no way to live!

A program of low-fat, healthful nutrition may require giving up such delicacies as steaks, pastries, butter, margarine, mayonnaise, and alcoholic beverages; but think of the freedoms that result. Food becomes the ally rather than the enemy. No more starvation; no more worrying about whether or not there is a psychological problem; no more weirdness such as grapefruit and egg diets. No more food aversion therapy.

EAT MORE, NOT LESS, FOR GOOD HEALTH.

It is believed by some that the way to a long and healthy life is to live on a low-calorie diet forever. The theory stems from studies that indicated that rats which were forced to live in a state of semi-starvation lived longer than littermates who were allowed to eat freely.

This has no practical value, since most humans cannot live in a state of semi-starvation unless, like the rats, they are confined to cages. Secondly, if one were able to extend the life span by living in hunger, would he do it? I personally like to eat (lots), and a program of lifetime hunger does not sound like fun to me. If I must live in such a manner to extend my life, I believe that I will opt for a shorter life.

The good news is that we can learn to eat *more* of the good food and expect to live *longer* lives. If there are still those who believe in starving themselves into "svelteness," perhaps we should examine a few facts about calorie intake and health in humans.

A study that compared nutrient intake with the rate of high blood pressure (hypertension) showed that those with normal blood pressure consumed nearly 16% more calories, amounting to 300 calories more per day, than those with high blood pressure.[183] The data presented in this study also showed that among all subjects, hypertensive or not, *those who were leaner ate the greatest number of calories.*

Another study showed that men who consumed the fewest calories had 2½ times the death rate from heart disease as those who consumed the greatest number of calories.[184] Other research confirms the fact that those who eat less die more readily of heart disease[185] [186] [187] and also stroke.[188] It is quite obvious from these studies and others that restricting calories is not good for the health!

Eating is also good therapy for the diabetic. People who eat more food—and more calories—have substantially lower blood sugar levels than those who eat less.[189] As previously mentioned, diabetics who were given insulin injections to closely control their blood sugar levels decreased their calorie consumption by more than 500 calories per day over a one-year period. At the same time, they gained an average of 11 pounds! It is quite apparent that calorie restriction is not what it is cracked up to be. It is dangerous, frustrating, enervating and fattening! The real need is for dietary fat restriction along with an ultimate increase in total calories; those calories being consumed in the form of starchy foods and vegetables.

In the chapter on exercise and health, it is noted that those who are the most physically fit live longer, and with fewer diseases, than those who are unfit. Is there any doubt that those who exercise and stay lean must eat far more calories than those who are inactive? *If you wish to be as healthy and as lean as possible, you must eat plenty of good food!*

Regular exercise, coupled with a high-starch, low-fat nutrition program, disposes of any calories the body might view as excessive. The studies that indicated a shorter life span among rats who ate a greater number of calories might be explained by the fact that rats in a cage become sedentary when they are allowed all that they want to eat. Also, unlike humans, rats tend to become more active when their calories are restricted.[190]

Humans, on the other hand, tend to hibernate, becoming lethargic as they try to conserve the fat on their bodies. The rat may therefore live longer on a diet, provided he is caged. Among human beings, there is no doubt that those who consume more calories live longer, healthier and slimmer lives. For those who like to eat, that is good news. Remember, however, that the calories we consume need to be high in complex carbohydrates and very low in fat and sugar.

Eating too little food may cause breast cancer.

In a study that investigated the influence of dietary fat and breast cancer, it was found that women who consumed more than 2355 calories per day had only 58% of the number of breast cancer cases as women who consumed less than 1792 calories per day.[191] Or, stated another way, for every 100 breast cancer cases among those women who ate *less* than 1792 calories per day, there were only 58 cases among those who consumed more than 2355 calories. The same research also showed a strong *inverse* correlation between total carbohydrate intake and breast cancer. Are we surprised? Obviously, those who ate more were consuming most of the extra calories in the form of carbohydrate, not fat.

HOW DIFFICULT CAN IT BE?

Some say that they could never give up their toxins in order to be slim. These same people sometimes eat nothing but grapefruit and eggs for months on end in an abortive attempt to achieve a goal weight. Surely a program of unlimited starches is easier than that! Coupled with a beautiful, brisk daily walk of 30 to 90 minutes, such an eating program can produce the slim, healthy body that seems to be at such a premium.

Pay no attention to the hucksters who insist on pushing you into the latest method of starvation. Look them squarely in the eyes and tell them "fat chance!"

OTHER CONSIDERATIONS

Diet pills

Diet pills have long been used to help dieters suppress appetite and thereby eat less. Ultimately this diet method, like others discussed, makes a person fatter rather than thinner, because it is one more way to starve. This fattening effect, however, might not be the most dangerous aspect of these pills. It has been documented more than 100 times that diet pills containing the drug phenylpropanolamine (contained in more than 70 over-the-counter preparations) have been associated with psychiatric, neurological and cardiovascular disorders.[192][193][194] Yet, diet pills cost consumers $400 million per year.[193]

WHAT HAVE WE LEARNED?

1. Dieting by calorie restriction is the most effective method of fattening ever developed.

2. Those who consume fewer calories weigh more than those who consume more calories. Diets produce fat bodies.

3. Dieting is deadly and is related to a host of physical and psychological problems. It has, in some cases, caused death. It is quite probable that most of the health risks associated with obesity are really deleterious effects of dieting.

4. Weight is regulated by a set point mechanism controlled by the hypothalamus. The number of calories consumed is not a critical factor in weight control.

5. Exercise is absolutely essential in a program to reduce and control weight.

6. Those who consume fewer calories suffer poorer health than those who consume more.

7. To become lean and fit, one must eat more starches, less fat, and less sugar. This enables a person to lose weight or maintain weight with no hunger and with a high energy level.

REFERENCES

[1] Wooley, S. Theoretical, practical, and social issues in behavioral treatments of obesity. J Appl Behav Anal. 1979; 12:3-25.

[2] Liquid protein and sudden death. FDA drug bulletin. 1978:8:18-19.

[3] Centers for Disease Control. Liquid-Protein diets. Atlanta: U.S. Public Health Service 1979. Publication # EPI-78-11-2.

[4] New Way to Lose Weight: Let's Get Tall. Washington Post, Oct. 1990.

[5] Gortmaker, S. Inactivity, diet, and the fattening of America. J Am Diet Assoc 1990; 90:1247-1252, 1255.

[6] Gortmaker, L. Increasing pediatric obesity in the United States. Am J Dis Child 1987; 141:535-540.

[7]Brownell, K. Quoted in the Washington Post, Oct. 1990.

[8]Bennet, W. Quoted in the Washington Post, Oct. 1990.

[9]Allon, N. The stigma of overweight in everyday life. In Wolman, B. Psychological Aspects of Obesity. Van Nostrand Reinhold, publishers, New York, 1982.

[10]Foryet, J. Limitations of behavioral treatment of obesity: Review and analysis. J Behav Med 1981; 4:159-173.

[11]Braitman, L. Obesity and caloric intake: The National Health and Nutrition Examination Survey of 1971-1975. J Chron Dis 1985; 38:727-732.

[12]Harlan, W. Secular trends in body mass in the United States, 1960-1980. Am J Epidemiol 1988; 128:1065-1074.

[13]Dwyer, J. The social psychology of dieting. J Health Soc Behav 1970; 11:269-287.

[14]Rosen, J. Prevalence of weight reducing and weight gaining in adolescent girls and boys. Health Psychology 1987; 6:131-147.

[14.1]Obesity Update, July/August 1991, p. 1.

[15]Hammer, R. Calorie-restricted low-fat diet and exercise in obese women. Am J Clin Nutr 1989; 49:77-85.

[16]Manson, J. A prospective study of obesity and risk of coronary heart disease in women. N Engl J Med 1990; 322:882-889.

[17]Health Implications of Obesity. National Institutes of Health consensus development conference statement 1990; 5(9):7.

[18]Rothblum, E. Women and weight: Fad and fiction. J Psychol 1990; 124:5-24.

[19]Brownell, K. Yo-yo dieting. Psychology Today, January 1988:20-23.

[20]Romieu, I. Energy intake and other determinants of relative weights. Am J Clin Nutr 1988; 47:406-412.

[21]Dreon, D. Dietary fat: Carbohydrate ratio and obesity in middle-aged men. Am J Clin Nutr 1988; 47:995-1000.

[22]Miller, W. Diet composition, energy intake, and exercise in relation to body fat in men and women. Am J Clin Nutr 1990; 52:426-430.

[23]Hibscher, J. Obesity, dieting and the expression of "obese" characteristics. J Compar Psychol 1977; 2:374-380.

[24]Bray, G. Obesity: A serious symptom. Ann Intern Med 1972; 77:779-805.

[25]Stunkard, A. Dieting and depression reexamined. Ann Intern Med 1974; 81:526-533.

[26]Ernsberger, P. The death of dieting. American Health 1985; 4:29-33.

[26.5]Lissner, L. Variability of body weight and health outcomes in the Framingham population. N Engl J Med 1991; 324:1839-1844.

[27] Polivy, J. Breaking the Diet Habit. Basic Books, publishers, 1983.

[28] Simopolous, A. Body weight, health, and longevity. Ann Intern Med 1984; 100:285-295.

[29] Bray, G. Obesity: Part 1—pathogenesis. West J Med 1988; 149:429-441.

[30] Ashley, F. Relation of weight change to changes in atherogenic traits: The Framingham study. J Chron Dis 1974; 27:103-114.

[31] Andres, R. Effect of obesity on total mortality. Int J Obesity 1980; 4:381-386.

[32] Keys, A. The Biology of Human Starvation. University of Minnesota Press, 1950:819-918.

[33] Higa, B. Staying—or Getting—Well. This People Magazine, Fall 1989, p. 18.

[34] Leslie, P. Effect of optimal glycaemic control with continuous subcutaneous insulin infusion on energy expenditure in type I diabetes mellitus. Br Med J 1986; 293:1121-1126.

[35] DCCT Research Group. Weight gain associated with intensive therapy in the diabetes control and complications trial. Diabetes care 1988; 11:567-573.

[36] Ohlsen, M. Longitudinal studies of food intake and weight of women from ages 18 to 56 years. J Am Diet Assoc 1976; 69:626-631.

[37] Keys, A. Coronary heart disease in seven countries. Am Heart Assoc monograph no. 29. Am Heart Association, Inc., 1970.

[38] Keen, H. Nutrient intake, adiposity and diabetes. Br Med J 1979; 1:655-658.

[39] Wooley, S. Theoretical, practical and social issues in behavioral treatments of obesity. J Appl Behav Analy 1979; 12:3-25.

[40] Birbeck, J. Obesity, socioeconomic variables and eating habits in New Zealand. J Biosoc Sci 1981; 13:299-307.

[41] Baecke, J. Food consumption, habitual physical activity, and body fatness in young Dutch adults. Am J Clin Nutr 1983; 37:278-286.

[42] Kroumhout, D. Energy and macronutrient intake in lean and obese middle-aged men. (The Zutphen study.) Am J Clin Nutr 1983; 37:295-299.

[43] Endholm, O. The energy expenditure and food intake of individual men. Br J Nutr 1955; 9:286-300.

[44] Olson, R. Obesity as a nutritional disorder. Fed Proc Fed Am Soc Biol 1959; 18:58-67.

[45] McCarthy, M. Dietary and activity patterns of obese women in Trinidad. J Am Diet Assoc 1966; 48:33-37.

[46] Maxfield, E. Patterns of food intake and physical activity in obesity. J Am Diet Assoc 1966; 49:406-408.

[47] Cahn, A. Growth and caloric intake of heavy and tall children. J Am Diet Assoc 1968; 53:476-480.

[48]Lincoln, J. Caloric intake, obesity and physical activity. Am J Clin Nutr 1962; 25:390-394.

[49]Wilkinson, P. Energy intake and physical activity in obese children. Br Med J 1977; 1:756.

[50]Niederpreum, M. Contribution of dietary fat to body fatness in lean and obese adults. Med Sci Sports Exerc 1990; 22:S129.

[51]Romieu, I. Energy intake and other determinants of relative weights. Am J Clin Nutr 1988; 47:406-412.

[52]Dreon, D. Dietary fat: Carbohydrate ratio and obesity in middle-aged men. Am J Clin Nutr 1988; 47:995-1000.

[53]Rolland-Cachera, M. No correlation between adiposity and food intake: Why are working-class children fatter? Am J Clin Nutr 1986; 44:779-787.

[54]Johnson, M. Relative importance of inactivity and overeating in the energy balance of obese high school girls. Am J Clin Nutr 1956; 4:37-44.

[55]Stefanik, P. Caloric intake in relation to energy output of obese and nonobese adolescent boys. Am J Clin Nutr 1959; 7:55-62.

[56]Rosenthall, B. Differences in eating patterns of successful and unsuccessful dieters, untreated overweight and normal weight individuals. Addictive Behaviors 1978; 3:129-134.

[57]Adams, N. The eating behavior of obese and non-obese women. Behav Res and Therapy 1978; 16:225-232.

[58]Coates, T. The relationship between person's relative body weights and the quality and quantity of food stored in their homes. Addictive Behaviors 1978; 3:179-184.

[59]Wing, R. Differential restaurant patronage of obese and non-obese people. Addictive Behaviors 1978; 3:135-138.

[60]Coll, M. Obesity and food choices in public places. Arch Gen Psychiatry 1979; 36:795-797.

[60.1]George, V. Further evidence for the presence of "small eaters" and "large eaters" among women. Am J Clin Nutr 1991; 53:425-429.

[61]Campbell, T. A study on diet, nutrition and disease in the People's Republic of China. Division of Nutritional Sciences, Cornell University, Ithaca, New York 1989:1-9.

[62]Heng, J. Effects of maternal obesity on fasting metabolism in newborn rats. Int J Obesity 1990; 14:505-513.

[63]Miller, W. Diet composition, energy intake and exercise in relation to body fat in men and women. Am J Clin Nutr 1990; 52:426-430.

[64]Oscai, L. Effect of dietary fat on food intake, growth and body composition in rats. Growth 1984; 48:415-424.

[65]Schemmel, R. Dietary obesity in rats: Body weight and body fat accretion in seven strains of rats. J Nutr 1970; 199:1041-1048.

[66]Lemmonier, D. Effect of age, sex, and site on the cellularity of the adipose tissue in mice and rats rendered obese by a high-fat diet. J Clin Invest 1972; 51:2907-2915.

[67]Herberg, L. Dietary-induced hypertropic-hyperplastic obesity in mice. J Lipid Res 1974; 15:580-585.

[68]Jen, J. Sex differences in the effects of high-fat feeding on behavior and carcass composition. Physiol Behav 1981; 27:161-166.

[69]Wade, G. Obesity without overeating in golden hamsters. Physiol Behav 1982; 29:701-707.

[70]Fenton, P. The nutrition of the mouse: Responses of four strains to diets differing in fat content. J Nutr 1951; 45:225-234.

[71]Mickelsen, O. Experimental obesity: Production of obesity in rats by feeding high-fat diets. J Nutr 1955; 57:541-554.

[72]Sclafani, A. Dietary obesity. In Stunkard, A., Obesity. W. B. Saunders Co., publishers, 1980, pp. 166-181.

[73]Schemmel, T. Skeletal size in obese and normal-weight littermate rats. Clin Orthop 1969; 65:89-96.

[74]Schulsinger, D. Effect of dietary protein quality on development of Aflatoxin B-1 induced hepatic prenoplastic lesions. JNCI 1989; 81:1241-1245.

[75]Miller, D. Weight maintenance and food intake. J Nutr 1962; 78:255-262.

[76]Rubner, M. Quoted in Oscai, L. Effect of dietary fat on food intake, growth and body composition in rats. Growth 1984; 48:415-424.

[77]Black, A. Further experiments in the relation of fat to economy of food utilization. V fluctuations in curve of daily heat production. J Nutr 1949; 37:289-301.

[78]Ball, E. Some energy relationships in adipose tissue. Ann NY Academy of Sciences 1965; 131:225-234.

[79]Baldwin, R. Metabolic functions affecting the contribution of adipose tissue to total energy expenditure. Fed Proc 1970; 29:1277-1283.

[80]Bjorntorp, P. The glucose uptake of human adipose tissue in obesity. Europ J Clin Invest 1971; 1:480-485.

[81]Bjorntorp, P. Carbohydrate storage in man: Speculations and some quantitative considerations. Metabolism 1978; 27 (suppl 2):1853-1865.

[82]Acheson, K. Nutritional influences on lipogenesis and thermogenesis after a carbohydrate meal. Am J Physiol 1984; 246:E62-E70.

[83]Acheson, K. Glycogen synthesis versus lipogenesis after a 500 gram carbohydrate meal in man. Metabolism 1982; 31:1234-1240.

[84]McCarty, M. The unique merits of a low-fat diet for weight control. Med Hypothesis 1986; 20:183-197.

[85]Faust, I. Diet-induced adipocyte number increase in adult rats: a new model for obesity. Am J Physiol 1978; 235:E-279-E286.

[86]Hirsch, E. Overeating, dietary section patterns, and sucrose intake in growing rats. Physiol Behav 1982:8.

[87]Castonguay, T. Palatability of sugar solutions and dietary selection. Physiol Behav 1981; 27:7-12.

[88]Allen, R. Some effects of dietary dextrose, fructose, liquid glucose and sucrose in the adult male rat. Br J Nutr 1966; 20:349-357.

[89]Kanarek, R. Dietary-induced overeating in experimental animals. Fed Proc 1977; 36:154-158.

[90]Oscai, L. Dietary-induced severe obesity: Exercise implications. Med Sci Sports Exerc 1985; 18:6-9.

[91]Sclafani, A. Scurose and polysaccharide-induced obesity in the rat. Physiol Behav 1984; 32:169-174.

[92]Lucas, F. Hyperphagia in rats produced by a mixture of fat and sugar. Physiol Behav 1990; 47:51-55.

[93]Sclafani, A. Dietary induced obesity in adult rats: Similarities to hypothalmic and human obesity syndromes. Physiol Behav 1976; 17:461-471.

[94]Sclafani, A. Effects of atropine and vagotomy on appetite in hypothalmic hyperphagic rats. Society for Neuroscience Abstracts 1979; 5:223.

[95]Sclafani, A. Effects of age, sex, and prior body weight in the development of dietary obesity in adult rats. Physiol Behav 1977; 18:1021-1026.

[96]Aviation Medical Bulletin. Bell Curve Association, Atlanta, GA, July 1990.

[97]A. C. Nielsen Co. Quoted in Hope Health Letter, September 1989.

[98]Colditz, G. Patterns of weight change and their relation to diet in a cohort of healthy women. Am J Clin Nutr 1990; 51:1100-1105.

[99]Grande, F. Changes of basal metabolic rate in man in semistarvation and refeeding. J Appl Physiol 1958; 12:230-238.

[100]Bray, G. Effect of caloric restriction on energy expenditure in obese patients. Lancet 1969; 2:397-398.

[101]Leibel, R. Diminished energy requirements in reduced-obese patients. Metabolism 1984; 33:164-170.

[102]Ravussin, E. Energy expenditure before and during energy restriction in obese patients. Am J Clin Nutr 1985; 41:753-759.

[103]de Boer, J. Adaptation of energy metabolism of overweight women to low-energy intake, studied with whole-body calorimeters. Am J Clin Nutr 1986; 44:585-595.

[104]Weigle, D. Weight loss leads to a marked decrease in non-resting energy expenditure in ambulatory human subjects. Metabolism 1988; 37:930-936.

[105]Apfelbaum, M. Effect of caloric restriction and excessive caloric intake on energy expenditure. Am J Clin Nutr 1971; 24:1405-1409.

[106] Drenick, E. Energy expenditure in fasting men. J Lab Clin Med 1973; 81:421-430.

[107] Krotkiewske, M. Effects of long-term training on adipose-tissue cellularity and body composition in hypertropic and hyperplastic obesity. Int J Obesity 1977; 2:395-398.

[108] Ballor, D. Exercise training attenuates diet-induced reduction in metabolic rate. J Appl Physiol 1990; 68:2612-2617.

[109] Steen, S. Metabolic effects of repeated weight loss and regain in adolescent wrestlers. JAMA 1988; 260:47-50.

[110] Jequier, E. Energy metabolism in human obesity. Soz Praventivmed 1989; 34:58-62.

[111] Foster, G. Controlled trial of the metabolic effects of a very-low-calorie diet: Short- and long-term effects. Am J Clin Nutr 1990; 51:167-172.

[111.1] Brownell, K. Weight regulation practices in athletes: Analysis of metabolic and health effects. Med Sci Sports Exerc 1987; 19:546-556.

[112] Wadden, T. Long-term effects of dieting on resting metabolic rate in obese outpatients. JAMA 1990; 264:707-711.

[113] Heshka, S. Weight loss and change in resting metabolic rate. Am J Clin Nutr 1990; 52:981-986.

[114] Elliot, D. Sustained depression of the resting metabolic rate after massive weight loss. Am J Clin Nutr 1989; 49:93-96.

[115] Tuschl, R. Energy expenditure and everyday eating behavior in healthy young women. Am J Clin Nutr 1990; 52:81-86.

[116] deGroot, L. Adaptation of energy metabolism of overweight women to alternating and continuous low energy intake. Am J Clin Nutr 1989; 50:1314-1323.

[117] Dulloo, A. Adaptive changes in energy expenditure during refeeding following low-calorie intake: Evidence for a specific metabolis component favoring fat storage. Am J Clin Nutr 1990; 52:415-420.

[118] Levitsky, D. The ingestion of food and the recovery of body weight following fasting in the naive rat. Physiol Behav 1976; 17:575-580.

[119] Boyle, P. Increased efficiency of food utilization following weight loss. Physiol Behav 1978; 21:261-264.

[120] Brownell, L. Physical activity in the development and control of obesity. In Stunkard, A. Obesity. W.B. Saunders, publishers, p. 305.

[121] Brownell, K. The effects of repeated cycles of weight loss and regain in rats. Physiol Behav 1986; 38:459-464.

[122] Blackburn, G. Weight cycling: The experience of human dieters. Am J Clin Nutr 1989; 49:1105-1109.

[123] Wadden, T. Responsible and irresponsible use of very-low-calorie diets in the treatment of obesity. JAMA 1990; 263:83-85.

[124]Flynn, T. Letter. JAMA 1990; 263:2885.

[125]Wadden, T. Three-year follow-up of the treatment of obesity by very-low-calorie diet, behavior therapy, and their combination. J Consult Clin Psychol 1988; 56:925-928.

[126]Winfrey, O. Regaining Weight. Transcript of the Oprah Winfrey Show, #1081, November 5, 1990, p. 3.

[127]Trebe, A. Oprah doesn't shy away from weighty subject. USA Today, Nov. 6, 1990, p. 1.

[128]Stunkard, A. Behavior modification in the treatment of obesity: The problem of maintaining weight loss. Arch Gen Psychiatry 1979; 36:801-806.

[129]Johnson, D. Therapeutic fasting in morbid obesity. Long-term follow-up. Arch Intern Med 1977; 137:1381-1382.

[130]Ballor, D. Exercise training attenuates diet-induced reduction in metabolic rate. J Appl Physiol 1990; 68:2612-2617.

[131]Van Dale, D. Repetitive weight loss and weight regain: Effects on weight reduction, resting metabolic rate, and lipolytic activity before and after exercise and/or diet treatment. Am J Clin Nutr 1989; 49:409-416.

[132]Steen, S. Metabolic effects of repeated weight loss and regain in adolescent wrestlers. JAMA 1988; 260:47-50.

[133]Hammer, R. Calorie-restricted low-fat diet and exercise in obese women. Am J Clin Nutr 1989; 49:77-85.

[134]Katzeff, H. Calorie restriction and iopanoic acid effects on thyroid hormone metabolism. Am J Clin Nutr 1990; 52:263-266.

[135]Young, R. Hepatic conversion of thyroxine to triiodothyroine in obese and lean Zucker rats. Life Sci 1984; 34:1783-1790.

[136]Goldberg, J. Altered triiodothyroine metabolism in obese Zucker fatty rats. Endocrinology 1988; 122:689-693.

[137]Katzeff, H. Decreased thyroxine secretion and decreased type Ideiodinase activity each contribute to the decrease in triiodothyroine production in Zucker fatty rats. Clin Res 1989; 37:254A.

[138]Vinick, A. Fasting blunts the TSH response to synthetic thyrotropin-releasing hormone. J Clin Endocrinol Metab 1975; 40:509-511.

[139]Kleinmann, R. The effects of iopanoic acid on the regular of thyrotropin secretion in euthyroid subjects. J Clin Endocrinol Metab 1980; 51:399-404.

[140]Burman, K. Iopdate restores the fasting-induced decrement in thyrotropin secretion. J Clin Endocrinol Metab 1983; 57:597-602.

[141]Cryer, A. Tissue lipoprotein lipase activity and its action in lipoprotein metabolism. Int J Biochem 1981; 13:525-541.

[142]Eckel, R. Lipoprotein lipase. A multifunctional enzyme relevant to common metabolic diseases. N Engl J Med 1989; 320:1060-1068.

[143]Kern, P. The effects of weight loss on the activity and expression of adipose-tissue lipoprotein lipase in very obese humans. N Engl J Med 1990; 322:1053-1059.

[144]Schwartz, R. Increase of adipose-tissue lipoprotein lipase activity with weight loss. J Clin Invest 1981; 67:1425-1430.

[145]Mercer, S. Effect of high-fat diets on energy balance and thermogenesis on brown adipose tissue of lean and genetically obese ob/ob mice. J Nutr 1987; 117:2147-1253.

[146]Shimomura, Y. Less body-fat accumulation in rats red a safflower oil diet than in rats fed a beef tallow diet. J Nutr 1990; 120:1291-1296.

[147]Fried, S. Nutrition-induced variations in responsiveness to insulin effects on lipoprotein lipase activity in isolated rat fat cells. J Nutr 1990; 120:1087-1095.

[148]DCCT Research Group. Weight gain associated with intensive therapy in the diabetes control and complications trial. Diabetes Care 1988; 11:567-573.

[149]Remington, D. How To Lower Your Fat Thermostat. Vitality House International, publishers, p. 90.

[150]Stunkard, A. The body-mass index of twins who have been reared apart. N Engl J Med 1990; 322:1483-1487.

[151]MacDonald, A. Body-mass indexes of British separated twins. N Engl J Med 1990; 322:1477-1482.

[152]Bouchard, C. The response to long-term overfeeding in identical twins. N Engl J Med 1990; 322:1477-1482.

[153]Ravussin, E. Energy expenditure in the obese: Is there a thrifty gene? Infusionstherapie 1990; 17:108-112.

[154]Sims, E. Destiny rides again as twins overeat. N Engl J Med 1990; 322:1522-1523.

[155]Chubby? Blame those genes. Time Magazine, June 4, 1990, p. 80.

[156]Zimmet, P. Epidemiology of diabetes and its macrovascular manifestations in Pacific populations: The medical effects of social programs. Diabetes Care 1979; 2:144-153.

[157]West, K. Diabetes in Americans and other native populations of the new world. Diabetes 1974; 23:841-855.

[158]Sugarman, J. Evidence for a secular change in obesity, height, and weight among Navajo Indian school children. Am J Clin Nutr 1990; 52:960-966.

[159]The Human Body. Marshall Editions Limited. Arch Cape Press, publishers, New York, 1989.

[160]Durnin, J. Appetite and the relationships between expenditure and intake of calories in man. J Physiol, London 1961; 156:294-306.

[161]Robinson, M. Day to day variations in body weight of young women. Br J Nutr 1965; 19:225-235.

[162]Khosha, T. Measurement of changes in body weight. Br J Nutr 1964; 18:227-239.

[163]Sims, E. Endocrine and metabolic adaptation to obesity and starvation. Am J Clin Nutr 1968; 21:1455-1470.

[164]Sims, E. Studies in human hyperphagia. In Bray, G. Treatment and Management of Obesity. Harper and Row, publishers, New York, p. 29.

[165]Sims, E. Endocrine and metabolic effects of experimental obesity in man. Recent Prog Horm Res 1973; 29:457-487.

[166]Brooks, C. A study of the effect of limitation of food intake and the method of feeding on the rate of weight gain during hypothalamic obesity in the albino rat. Am J Physiol 1946; 147:695-707.

[167]Cohn, C. Influence of body weight and body fat on appetite of "normal" lean and obese rats. Yale J Biol Med 1962; 34:598-607.

[168]Herman, C. Anxiety, restraint, and eating behavior. J Abnorm Psychol 1975; 84:666-672.

[169]O'Neil, P. Restraint and age at onset of obesity. Add Behav 1981; 6:135-138.

[170]Ruderman, A. Restraint theory and its applicability to overweight individuals. J Abnorm Psychol 1983; 92:210-215.

[171]Powley, T. Relationship of body weight to the lateral hypothalamic feeding syndrome. J Comp Physiol Psychol 1970; 70:25-36.

[172]Keesey, R. A set-point analysis of the regulation of body weight. In Stunkard, A. Obesity. W. B. Saunders, publishers, 1980, pp. 149-150.

[173]Remington, D. How To Lower Your Fat Thermostat. Vitality House International, publishers, 1983.

[174]Bjorntorp, P. Effects of physical training on glucose tolerance, plasma insulin and lipids and on body composition. Acta Med Scand 1972; 192:439-443.

[175]Hellmich, N. Exercise is the way to weight loss that lasts. USA Today, Oct. 17, 1990.

[176]Frey-Hewitt, B. The effect of weight loss by dieting or exercise on resting metabolic rate in overweight men. Int J Obesity 1990; 14:327-334.

[177]Allen, D. The role of physical activity in the control of obesity. Med J Aust 1977; 2:434-435.

[178]Mayer, J. Regulation of food intake and obesity. Science 1967; 156:328-337.

[179]Oscai, L. Effects of weight changes produced by exercise, food restriction, or overeating on body composition. J Clin Invest 1969; 48:2124-2128.

[180]Oscai, L. Dietary-induced severe obesity: A rat model. Am J Physiol 1982; 242:R212-R215.

[181] Oscai, L. Effect of dietary fat on food intake, growth and body composition in rats. Growth 1984; 48:415-424.

[182] Campbell, T. Cornell Nutrition Department, Ithaca, N.Y. Telephone interview with author, May 1990.

[183] McCarron, D. Blood pressure and nutrient intake in the United States. Science 1984; 224:1392-1398.

[184] Morris, J. Diet and heart: A postscript. Br Med J 1977; 2:1307-1314.

[185] Kushi, L. Diet and 20-year mortality from coronary heart disease. N Engl J Med 1985; 312:811-818.

[186] Yano, K. Dietary intake and the risk of coronary heart disease in Japanese men living in Hawaii. Am J Clin Nutr 1878; 31:1270-1279.

[187] Garcia-Palmeri, M. Relationship of dietary intake to subsequent coronary heart disease incidence: The Puerto Rico Heart Health Program. Am J Clin Nutr 1980; 33:1818-1827.

[188] Khaw, K. Dietary potassium and stroke-associated mortality: A 12-year prospective study. N Engl J Med 1987; 316:235-240.

[189] Keen, H. Nutrient intake, adiposity, and diabetes. Br Med J 1979; 1:655-658.

[190] Remington, D. Personal communication.

[191] Knekt, P. Dietary fat and risk of breast cancer. Am J Clin Nutr 1990; 52:903-908.

[192] Weintraub, M. Letter. JAMA 1990; 263:2886.

[193] Dilsaver, S. Complications of phenylpropanolomine. Am Fam Physician 1989; 39:201-206.

[194] Mueller, S. Neurologic complications of phenylpropanolomine use. Neurology 1983; 33:650-652.

2.

Diabetics, Fat, and Fat Diabetics

2. *Diabetics, Fat and Fat Diabetics.*

> *"With an excess of fat, diabetes begins and from an excess of fat diabetics die, formerly of coma and recently of atherosclerosis."*[1]
>
> —Dr. E.P. Joslin, 1927
>
> *"A potential diabetic can be transformed into a completely diabetic individual by administration of the time-honored carbohydrate-free meal of meat and fat."*[2]
>
> —Dr. I.M. Rabinowich, 1930
>
> *"In the curves of subjects fed on carbohydrate there is an insignificant rise in the blood sugar. . .Those in the carbohydrate group are all strikingly within normal limits. . .Those who were placed on the fat diet and those who were starved manifested a definite decrease in sugar tolerance."*[3]
>
> —Dr. J.S. Sweeney, 1927

Adult-onset diabetes is *not* a sugar disease. It is a *fat* disease—a result of excessive dietary fat or excessive body fat. Provided that the disease has not progressed to the point of severe pancreatic damage, it can usually be reversed and cured through proper nutrition and exercise.

The above quotes come from medical professionals who published their findings six decades ago in the best medical journals of the day. At least two of the men understood that fat, not sugar, was the primary cause of adult-onset diabetes. Yet, 60 years later, most physicians fail to recommend diets sufficiently low in fat to rid their patients of the disease. In the interim, millions have died needlessly of this most easily cured of all degenerative diseases. Diabetes claims at least 34,000 lives and contributes to another 95,000 deaths per year, at a cost of $13.8 billion annually.[4]

At National Institute of Fitness, we use a low-fat, high-carbohydrate nutrition plan to assist guests in shedding excess pounds without hunger and to fuel their muscles for the walking, hiking and other exercise. Since diabetics are usually overweight, a large number of them enroll in our weight-control program—not necessarily to mitigate their diabetes but to lose weight.

We were surprised to find that many of our diabetic guests were cured of their diabetes in very short periods. In many cases, people who had been injecting more that 70 units of insulin per day became free of the needle in as little as four days. Others who did not decrease insulin dosages were experiencing low blood sugar.

I had read some material on diabetes written by Nathan Pritikin which addressed the association between diabetes and the high-fat diet. Nonetheless, I was amazed at the dramatic reduction in blood-sugar levels occurring on our low-fat nutrition program. We began warning our diabetic guests to stay in contact with their physicians and to watch blood-sugar levels closely if they were taking either insulin injections or "diabetic pills" (hypoglycemic drugs). If this was not done, they were in danger of becoming severely hypoglycemic or going into insulin shock, since they no longer needed injected insulin or hypoglycemic drugs to process the carbohydrates they were consuming.

A near disaster

One of our guests did not heed this advice. He had been injecting 50 units of insulin each day for more than five years and had participated in two diabetic clinics in Mexico and one in the U.S. He carried with him a device known as a glucometer, which measures blood-sugar levels almost instantly when a drop of blood is applied.

The low-fat, high-fiber nutrition program produced such a rapid drop in sugar levels that he was able to stop injecting insulin after five days. The morning following his cessation of insulin shots, he felt poorly and decided that he had been premature in his actions. Without consulting the glucometer, he injected 25 units of insulin and went into insulin shock but remained conscious. Had he consulted his glucometer prior to injecting insulin, he would have found that his blood sugar was low, not high. The injected insulin further lowered his sugar to dangerous levels. Fortunately, his condition was brought to the attention of our nurse, who gave him fruit juice to raise his levels to normal. This incident occurred nine years ago, and as of the time of this writing, he has never since needed to inject insulin. He has also lost 50 pounds and usually walks several miles daily to keep fit.

This man's story is by no means unique. More than 100 others attending National Institute of Fitness have dropped insulin injections and hypoglycemic drugs in the past few years. One lady was confined to a wheelchair and was in danger of amputation of the left foot due to diabetes-related circulation problems. She was able to rid herself of the wheelchair, her diabetes, and the fear of amputation in a two-week period. Her program was quite simple: An instructor would assist her to walk a few steps without the wheelchair and then let her rest until she could walk a few more steps. On arriving at the swimming pool, she would do a few light water exercises. This, combined with the low-fat nutrition, enabled her to walk two blocks nonstop after a two-week program. Her need for insulin dropped from 65 units per day to 0. She attended our program three times and on the third visit walked three miles nonstop.

Other stories could be told of the many guests who have made spectacular progress in ridding themselves of diabetes, but those stories could easily fill an entire book.

WHAT IS THE CAUSE OF ADULT-ONSET DIABETES—INSULIN DEFICIENCY OR INSULIN RESISTANCE?

Insulin is a hormone produced in specialized areas of the

pancreas gland known as the Islands of Langerhans. It removes excessive sugar from the blood and stores it in the cells, thereby regulating sugar levels. When insulin is not present in sufficient quantities or cannot do its job properly, blood-sugar levels become excessive, causing the body to spill sugar into the urine as a method of eliminating part of the excess. This causes the urine to become sweet. To flush the load of sugar from the body, urination is profoundly increased, causing a constant thirst due to the loss of water used in the process.

Chronic high-blood sugar causes many problems in the body, not the least of which is impaired circulation. In severe cases, the lack of circulation may lead to gangrene and amputation. Heart disease is also affected adversely by diabetes. Diabetics have 2½ times the rate of death from heart disease as non-diabetics. Kidney damage is widespread among diabetics, and blindness due to cataracts and retinal impairment is common.[5]

It is mistakenly assumed by many that adult-onset diabetics do not produce sufficient insulin to process the carbohydrates they eat. The fact is that these diabetics in general produce ample insulin and often have higher blood-insulin levels than non-diabetics.[6] [7] [8] [9] Surprisingly, obese diabetics as well as obese non-diabetics respond to sugar ingestion with two to four times as much insulin production as normal-weight persons![10]

DOES FAT CAUSE DIABETES?

If adult-onset diabetes is not caused by a lack of insulin, then we must look elsewhere for an explanation of the disease. It has long been known that high blood fats interfere with the action of insulin.[10] [11] [12] [13] [14] [15] [16] This interference renders insulin less effective in transporting excessive sugar from the blood. In one study, a researcher injected insulin and sugar (glucose) into both normal subjects and subjects who had high blood fats. In subjects with high blood fats, sugar levels stayed much higher than in normal subjects. This was true even though the amount of insulin injected was identical in each group.[10] Those with a high degree of fat in the blood, then, are *insulin insensitive* and may not be able to efficiently remove sugar from the blood despite the availability of copious quantities of insulin.

One group of researchers investigated the relationship of blood fats to insulin effectiveness. They concluded that "within a group of subjects similar to the kinds of patients seen by the average physician, on a diet which attempts to approximate that of the average American, we have shown that insulin resistance leads to hyperinsulinemia [high blood insulin] and subsequent hypertrigliceridemia (high blood fats)."[16]

The opposite is also true. It might be further stated that the typical American diet leads to high blood fats (as we will establish in the chapter on heart disease) which are responsible for resistance to insulin, which leads to adult-onset diabetes.

Is fat the major cause of adult-onset diabetes? It might be interesting to look at studies that have placed diabetic patients on low-fat diets. We could then determine whether such changes have been beneficial in reducing blood sugar levels.

THE LOW-FAT DIET AS THERAPY: A CURE FOR MOST TYPE 2 DIABETICS

Such a study was done in 1955. It confirmed that proper nutrition was effective therapy for adult-onset diabetics. Eighty diabetic patients were put on very low-fat diets. In six weeks, 60% of those patients no longer required injections. After a few more weeks, 70% were insulin free, and those still needing insulin needed far less than their original dosages.[17]

Another more recent study was reported in the journal *Diabetes Care* in which diabetic patients were put on an exercise program and a very low-fat diet that was high in starch.[18] Twenty-three patients were taking diabetic pills, known as oral hypoglycemic agents, and 17 more were taking insulin shots. In a 26-day program, 21 of the 23 who were on oral medication were able to discontinue their medication. Of the 17 taking insulin injections, all but four were able to discontinue their injections. Of the four, two had cut their insulin dosage to 50%.

The group also averaged a nine-pound weight loss during the program.

Numerous other studies have confirmed that a low-fat, high-starch nutrition program quickly lowers both blood sugar and insulin dependency in diabetics.[19 20 21 22 23 24 25 26] This enables them in most cases to discontinue use of insulin injections and oral hypoglycemic agents. A high-fiber, high-carbohydrate eating plan increases sensitivity to insulin even among those who are not diabetic.[27 28 29]

THIS IS NOT NEW INFORMATION.

In 1933 and again in 1949, Professor H.P. Himsworth warned of the diabetes-causing properties of high-fat diets[30 31] and pointed out that in times of war, when fatty foods were scarce, diabetes also became scarce. In 1949 he stated, "The progressive rise in diabetic mortality in western countries in the last 50 years coincides with a gradual change towards higher-fat and lower-carbohydrate diets; the protein and calorie values have altered little. The diabetic mortality rate is high in countries whose diets tend to be high in fat and poor in carbohydrate and low where the opposite tendency prevails. . . . Race is not a predominant factor in determining diabetic mortality. Immigrant races manifest the mortality rate of their new country in proportion as they acquire its dietary habits. . . . There thus seems to be a universal relation between diet and diabetic mortality. The dietetic factor most closely related is fat consumption."[31]

Dr. Himsworth noted that people living in rural areas had lower fat-consuming habits and a concomitantly lower incidence of diabetes than those living in urban areas.

Has anyone been listening?

It makes one wonder, with the diabetic pills and insulin injections prescribed by physicians, if anyone read the research by Dr. Himsworth or Drs. Joslin, Rabinowich and Sweeney, who were quoted at the beginning of this chapter. We have cited only a few of the articles on the subject which have been written more recently. Are we so indoctrinated to drugs that we neglect to inform the diabetic patient that his disease can probably be completely controlled or cured by a low-fat, high-carbohydrate diet?

Many diabetics who come to our resort tell us that they have never heard of the therapeutic effects of a very low-fat diet for diabetes. The abundance of research in and since Himsworth's time makes it clear that most diabetics are simply suffering from a "fat disease."

CHANGING NUTRITIONAL STYLES AND RATE OF DIABETES

Further evidence indicting the high-fat diet comes from epidemiological studies which show that as the quantity of fat consumption increases in a population, there is a subsequent and predictable increase in diabetes.

Africa

In Africa, as the diet becomes more "Westernized," those Africans who have moved from a rural society with a low-fat diet to an urban society with a high-fat diet show a marked increase in the incidence of diabetes.[32] [33] [34]

Japan

Japanese who have migrated to Hawaii have a greater rate of diabetes than those who remained in Japan. They also have a greater rate of diabetes than Caucasians living in Hawaii. In the 1950s, Japanese immigrants to Hawaii had only half the rate of diabetes as Caucasians living there. By the 1970s, as the diet of these immigrants had changed to mimic that of the Caucasian population, the rate of diabetes had increased to 1.6 times that of the Caucasians![35] Among Hawaiian Japanese, the number of calories consumed was nearly identical to the number consumed by Japanese in Japan, but the Hawaiian Japanese consumed a far greater portion of those calories as fat and much less in starch.

The Japanese in Japan who suffered from diabetes also had a decreased death rate from the disease compared to the Japanese living in Hawaii. This may indicate that the high-fat diet continues its death-dealing blows long after the diabetes has developed. *Diabetes is a well-known risk factor for heart disease; yet, it has been pointed out that there is a greater risk for heart attack among non-diabetic Japanese Americans than among diabetic Japanese living in Japan.*[35]

It is obvious that the high-fat, low-fiber diet is the prime factor in causing both heart disease and diabetes. It is also obvious that diabetes is a risk factor for heart disease only when blood-cholesterol levels are above 150 (as we discuss in the chapter on heart disease). It is unlikely that the cholesterol levels of the Japanese living in Japan were very high, since they consume fewer saturated fats and cholesterol. They were therefore far less susceptible to the deleterious influence of diabetes on heart disease. It is not surprising that the death rate from heart disease was less in diabetic Japanese in Japan than in non-diabetic Japanese Hawaiians.

Studies of Japanese men living in King County, Washington show them to have four times the rate of diabetes as men in Japan and twice the rate of the Caucasian population of the same area.[36] The diabetics, it is found, consume a higher percentage of fat and animal proteins than the non-diabetics.

The high diabetic rate among Japanese-Americans (compared to Caucasian Americans) is likely due to a genetic component, since the two groups are similar in their eating habits. Yet, the Japanese in Japan have much less diabetes than the Caucasian Americans. They also eat far less fat and far more starch. Let us emphasize that a genetic predisposition to a disease will manifest itself only when the toxins which cause the disease are present. Otherwise, those people with the genetic predisposition will never know. (For a discussion of genetic factors and disease, see the chapter on heart disease.)

Nauru

Another spectacular example of the high-fat diet and its diabetes-causing properties is the tragedy of the people of the island of Nauru, an island in Micronesia.[37] For most of their history, these people lived primitively and consumed a low-fat, high-carbohydrate diet. After World War II, they became wealthy through selling one of the island's natural resources (phosphorous) which was in great demand in industrialized countries. With some of the riches produced by selling this resource, Nauruans began to import rich foods from Australia, resulting in a "Westernized" eating style. Daily meals included the consumption of several kinds of meat and fish. Whereas diabetes was a rare occurrence before their new-found wealth, it has increased to the point that more than 34% of the adult population now have the disease. What a dear price to pay for their new, wealthy lifestyles!

Pima Indians of Arizona

Still, the Nauruans take second place to the Pima Indians in terms of the prevalence of diabetes.[38] The Pimas now have one of the highest per-capita fat consumptions in the world, but this was not always true. This style of eating among the Pimas developed only in the past few generations.

The Pimas also have the highest prevalence of diabetes in the world—more than 50% of all adults over 35 years of age are diabetics—and diabetes has increased more than 40% just since 1970. For hundreds of years the Pimas lived on healthful native foods such as prickly pears, tempary beans, mesquite pods and corn. They were then reported to be exceptionally healthy people, with diabetes being a rare occurrence.

The White man's "poison"

As the Pimas began to take jobs outside the reservation and serve in the military, they developed a taste for the high-fat foods eaten by Caucasians. They then became obese and diabetic. The prevalence of both obesity and diabetes among the members of the tribe is a testimony to the dangers of the high-fat diet. In Arizona alone, there are more than a quarter million Indian diabetics; and it is estimated that it will cost the Grand Canyon State $2 billion per year to treat its Indian diabetics by the year 2000.[39]

The high degree of fat in the diet and obesity among the Pimas undoubtedly contributes to insulin resistance and exacerbates the problems of high-blood sugar. Insulin is known to be very fattening itself. It is likely that a return to the native, low-fat diet would quickly cure not only the diabetes but the high prevalence of obesity.

Return to traditional foods— a cure for the Pima's diabetes?

The Pima's traditional low-fat foods were recently analyzed to determine their effects on the blood sugar levels of healthy non-diabetics.[40] It was found that these foods slowed the digestion of carbohydrates and dramatically lowered blood-sugar levels as well as insulin production.

The *Phoenix Gazette* carried an interesting article about an Arizona Indian who returned to eating his native-American diet:[41]

Earl Ray, a Pima, once weighed 239 pounds. He lived on a fast food diet consisting of pizza, burgers and alcohol.[41] On the advice of Gary Nabhan, who studies native American foods and their relationship to diseases, Earl gave up his high-fat fare and booze in 1983 and switched to the foods eaten by his forefathers. He now weighs less than 150 pounds, and hardly anyone believes that he is a Pima Indian. He reversed his diabetes and overcame arthritis, hair loss, and stomach problems.

There is a very simple answer to the epidemic problems of diabetes and obesity among the Indians in Arizona, and it won't require the expenditure of $2 billion per year.

The Pimas are not the only group of American Indians who suffer from diabetes. Dr. Kelly West points out that prior to 1940, the Indians in Oklahoma there were lean. By 1974 they were obese.[46] *There were no cases of diabetes and no death by the disease before 1939. By 1974, the rate of death from diabetes among the Indians there was 2.3 times that of the White population!* The difference may indeed be due to a genetic component which makes the Indians less capable of handling the high-fat diet of their Caucasian counterparts. But, without eating the White man's diet, the Indians would never have known of their susceptibility to diabetes.

Did the entire Indian nation suddenly change its genetic make-up to become susceptible to this disease? Or, are the White man's diet and activity pattern responsible? Anyone who suggests that the Indians have a genetic problem, as opposed to an environmental problem, is blind to reality. Remove the fat and sugar from their diets, and the Indians will not suffer from diabetes to any greater extent than their forefathers.

Conventional drug therapy for adult-onset diabetes is insane. People get well when they stop eating fat and sugar and start eating complex carbohydrates. How simple can it be? Yet we still see articles such as a recent one in *Time Magazine* which indicates that scientists are still looking for the cause and cure for this disease.[42] Has the world gone mad, or is it simply blind?

The examples given above are only a few which illustrate the cause and effect relationship between the higher-fat diets and the rate of diabetes. Numerous other research studies have confirmed that as people move from "primitive" to "developed" environments, the rate of diabetes increases dramatically.[43] [44] [45] [46]

DIABETES IS A RISK FACTOR FOR HEART DISEASE

Diabetes is one of the strongest risk factors for heart disease.[47] [48] [49] [50] [51] [52] It causes up to a 340% increase in mortality.[48] When stroke and heart disease are combined, the death risk increases to 410%.

Even a small decrease in the ability to metabolize sugar may increase the risk of dying from heart disease.[53] Those with blood-sugar levels above 96 two hours after a glucose-tolerance test are at approximately double the risk of death from heart disease as those who are below those levels. This is an interesting finding, because levels under 115 are not usually considered to be diabetic. Even a tendency toward diabetes may predict an increased chance of death from heart disease.

As might be expected, a low-fat diet can prevent both heart disease and diabetes in nearly every case. Other methods may control sugar levels but can increase the risk of death from heart disease. Oral hypoglycemic drugs, which lower blood sugar, have been shown, in some cases, to increase the rate of death from heart attacks by 250%. The drug Tolinase carries a warning label stating the increased risk of death.[54]

A prominent California physician considers these drugs to be so dangerous that he always removes diabetics from these medications immediately and then treats them with a low-fat, high-starch nutrition program.[55] He has stated that, "Because nowadays the primary purpose of diabetes treatment is to reduce the complications of the disease, prescribing a drug which doubles the risk of heart disease makes no sense."[54] It is hard to argue with that logic.

INSULIN IS FATTENING!

When animals are given injections of insulin, they become fatter than other animals that consume the same number of calories but do not receive the insulin.[56] When calories are not restricted, the animals receiving insulin usually increase the amount of food they eat and become fat even faster.[57] Insulin may raise the "set point" and thereby create a "fat gap," which must be filled. (See the set point discussion in the chapter on obesity.) In humans, however, this is not necessarily true. Rather than increase consumption of food, insulin may cause a considerable *decrease* in consumption of both food and calories. This ultimately results in a greatly *increased* body weight in spite of the decreased calorie consumption.[58] [59]

Insulin increases fat storage by activating a potent fat-storing enzyme called *adipose tissue lipoprotein lipase* or LPL.[60] [61] (See the chapter on obesity.) LPL pulls fat into the fat cell. Its source for this fat is that which is contained in capillaries feeding fat tissue.[62] High-fiber diets reduce the quantity of insulin produced in response to food[63] [64] [65] [66] and would therefore be expected to lessen the amount of LPL produced. With a lessened LPL level, we would expect less fat to accumulate in the fat cells. This is exactly the case.[67]

A study reported in the journal *Diabetes Care* established that after a year of intensive insulin therapy, subjects' average daily calorie consumption *decreased* by more than 500 calories per day. Body weight, however, *increased* by an average of more than 11 pounds![59]

In the chapter on obesity, it was mentioned that obese people eat no more, and in many cases less, than people who are thin. Could it be that the extra insulin produced by obese people lowers metabolic rates sufficiently to produce this paradoxical effect? One study showed that intensive insulin therapy produced a drop in metabolic rate of 90 calories per day.[58] Of further interest is the fact that among subjects who eat more food, sugar levels are much lower than in those who eat less.[68] Dr. Harry Keen and his colleagues reported in the *British Medical Journal* that the increasing blood-sugar levels associated with decreased food intake "is largely accounted for by highly-significant *inverse* [my emphasis] correlations between food-energy intake and adiposity."[68]

If fat causes insulin resistance and if diabetics often respond to sugar with excessively high insulin production, then it is not hard to understand why so many diabetics are obese. They produce excessive insulin—which is then rendered ineffective by the presence of fat. The excessive insulin causes them to become fatter, which makes them even more resistant to insulin. Pastries such as doughnuts and eclairs, which contain a load of sugar, stimulate insulin production. They also contain a load of fat, which causes insulin resistance. Hence, they are the quintessential killers in terms of diabetes.

When insulin injections are prescribed as therapy, the prescription is for more body fat. Fuel is added to the fire, and the resultant obesity produces the need for still more insulin as the body becomes more resistant to its effects. This vicious cycle can be broken by changing to a low-fat, high-starch nutrition program, coupled with a sensible exercise plan.

EXERCISE AS THERAPY

A low-fat, high-fiber nutrition program is essential for the treatment of diabetes, but exercise is also good therapy. Trained athletes usually have normal blood-sugar levels and decreased blood-insulin levels.[69] [70] This is an indication that their bodies are more sensitive to the smaller amount of insulin that is produced and may be partially responsible for the leanness which is usually observed in the well-trained athlete. A lower level of insulin would let an athlete escape the fattening effects of that hormone.

Obese and non-obese people who exercise require far less insulin in response to a large load of sugar,[71] [72] indicating an increased sensitivity to that drug through exercise. The increased sensitivity to insulin occurs even when there is no weight loss. This shows that exercise exerts its influence independent of its usual effects of reducing body weight.[73] Exercise is so effective in increasing insulin sensitivity that it has been found to correlate directly with increasing physical fitness levels as diabetics train and become more fit.[61]

INCREASING DIETARY FIBER: GOOD THERAPY FOR DIABETES

Plant fiber is effective in treating diabetes. A study by Dr. James Anderson shows what occurs when diabetics are placed on a diet rich in fiber.[23] Twenty diabetic men were given conventional, low-fiber, high-fat foods for seven days and then switched to a diet very high in fiber. The diet was designed to prevent loss of weight; easily accomplished since the men were relatively lean. In 16 days, 11 of the men were able to discontinue insulin injections completely, and most of the others greatly reduced their dosages.

A serendipitous side benefit of this treatment was a spectacular drop in cholesterol from an average of 208 to 147. That is a drop of more than 28% in a period of 16 days! This is not surprising in view of the cholesterol-lowering capabilities demonstrated in numerous studies reviewed in the chapter on heart disease. Remember that for every 1% drop in cholesterol, there is a 2% drop in the chance of death from heart disease. Thus the diabetics had reduced their risk by 56% in a period of 16 days! They further reduced their risk of mortality by lowering their blood sugar levels significantly.

The study by Dr. Anderson indicated that a high-fiber diet is effective in treating diabetics, even when the subjects do not experience weight loss. Before we run out to buy oat bran to add to our high-fat diets, however, it should be stated that only 9% of the calories in Dr. Anderson's program came from fat. This was without doubt one of the prime reasons for the decrease in insulin need. Other research *has* indicated a moderate lowering of blood sugar by adding fiber to a conventional diet.[74] [75] High-fiber diets, however, are usually low in fat, which gives the diabetic the best of both treatments.

WILL THE MEGAHEALTH PROGRAM HELP THE TYPE 1 DIABETIC?

Type 1 diabetics will always need insulin treatments, since they cannot produce sufficient insulin to take care of the carbohydrates which they consume. We have found that type 1 diabetics who use our methods of nutrition usually cut their need for insulin injections by 50% in a few days.

Dr. John McDougall suggests that the type 1 diabetic cut the insulin dosage immediately by 30% after starting a low-fat, high starch program.[55] All such dietary changes should, of course, be carefully monitored by a physician in the case of both type 1 and type 2 diabetes.

In type 1 diabetes, there is damage to the pancreas which prevents it from producing sufficient insulin. The cause of this damage is not known; however, the disease occurs much more frequently in areas of high fat consumption[76] and has recently been shown to correlate closely to the consumption of cow's milk.[77]

WHAT HAVE WE LEARNED?

1. Adult-onset diabetes is an unnecessary disease. It can be prevented, and in most cases reversed, by a low-fat, high-carbohydrate nutrition program combined with proper exercise.

2. Type 2 (adult-onset) diabetics usually produce plenty of insulin—more than non-diabetics.

3. Dietary fat and body fat both inhibit the action of insulin, forcing the pancreas to secrete more than normal to compensate for the decreased ability of insulin to do its job.

4. Obesity increases insulin insensitivity, which increases the severity of the diabetes.

5. Diabetic drugs (hypoglycemic agents) help to control blood-sugar levels but increase the chance of death by heart disease by as much as 250%.

6. Sensible nutrition, combined with the recommended exercise, can usually alleviate all diabetic symptoms within a matter of a few days to a few weeks. Best results will be obtained when the diet contains at least 70% of its calories in complex carbohydrates.

7. For the type 1 diabetic, or juvenile-onset type, the same program will greatly decrease the need for insulin and certainly enhance the quality of life.

There should be no argument. If we fail to use methods known to prevent or cure diabetes, then the carnage will proceed, along with blindness, heart disease, kidney failure and other manifestations of this unnecessary infirmity. A pharmaceutical cure is not forthcoming. If you or someone you know is a diabetic, share this chapter with your physician and then get started on this life-saving program.

REFERENCES

[1] Joslin, E. Atherosclerosis and diabetes. Ann Clin Med 1927; 5:1061-1080.

[2] Rabinowich, I. Experiences with a high-carbohydrate, low-calorie diet for the treatment of diabetes mellitus. Can Med Assn J 1930; 23:489.

[3] Sweeney, J. Dietary factors that influence the dextrose-tolerance test: A preliminary study. Arch Intern Med 1927; 40:818-830.

[4] National Diabetes Data Group: Diabetes in America. NIH publication #1468, 1985.

[5] The Human Body. Arch Cape Press, publishers, 1989.

[6] Seltzer, H. Insulin secretion in response to glycemic stimulus: Relation of delayed initial release to carbohydrate intolerance in mild diabetes mellitus. J Clin Invest 1967; 46:323-335.

[7] Perley, M. Plasma-insulin responses to glucose and tolbutamide of normal-weight and obese diabetic and non-diabetic subjects. Diabetes 1966; 15:867-874.

[8] Bagdade, J. The significance of basal insulin levels in evaluation of the insulin response to glucose in diabetic and non-diabetic subjects. J Clin Invest 1967; 46:1549-1557.

[9] Kipnis, D. Insulin secretion in normal and diabetic individuals. Adv Intern Med 1970; 16:103-135.

[10] Kane, J. Studies of carbohydrate metabolism in idiopathic hypertriglyceridemia. Metabolism 1965; 14:471-486.

[11] Farquar, J. Glucose, insulin, and triglyceride responses to high and low-carbohydrate diets in man. J Clin Invest 1966; 45:1648-1656.

[12] Davidson, P. Insulin resistance in hyperglyceridemia. Metabolism 1965; 14:1059-1070.

[13] Ford, S. Interactions of obesity and glucose and insulin levels in hypertriglyceridemia. Am J Clin Nutr 1968; 21:904-910.

[14] Abrams, M. Oral glucose tolerance and related factors in a normal population sample. II Interrelationship between glycerides, cholesterol, and other factors with the glucose and insulin response. Br Med J 1969; 1:599-602.

[15] Tzagourinis, M. The role of endogenous insulin in different hyperlipidemic states. Diabetologia 1972; 8:215-220.

[16] Olefsky, J. Reappraisal of the role of insulin in hypertriglyceridemia. Am J Med 1974; 57:551-560.

[17] Singh, I. Low-fat diet and therapeutic doses of insulin in diabetes mellitus. Lancet 1955; 1:422-425.

[18] Barnard, J. Response of non-insulin-dependent diabetic patients to an intensive program of diet and exercise. Diabetes Care 1982; 5:370-374.

[19]Bruznell, J. Improved glucose tolerance with high-carbohydrate feeding in mild diabetes. N Engl J Med 1971; 284:521-524.

[20]Bruznell, J. Effect of a fat-free, high-carbohydrate diet on diabetic subjects with fasting hyperglycemia. Diabetes 1974; 23:138-142.

[21]Simpson, H. A high-carbohydrate-leguminous-fibre diet improves all aspects of diabetic control. Lancet 1981; 1:1-5.

[22]Anderson, J. Hypolipidemic effects of high-carbohydrate, high-fiber diets. Metabolism 1980; 29:551-558.

[23]Anderson, J. High-carbohydrate, high-fiber diets for insulin-treated men with diabetes mellitus. Am J Clin Nutr 1979; 32:2312-2321.

[24]Kiehm, T. Beneficial effects of a high-carbohydrate, high-fiber diet on hyperglycemic diabetic men. Am J Clin Nutr 1976; 29:895-899.

[25]Ney, D. Decreased insulin requirement and improved control of diabetes in pregnant women given a high-carbohydrate, high-fiber, low-fat diet. Diabetes Care 1982; 5:529-533.

[26]Van Eck, W. The effect of low-fat diet on the serum lipids in diabetes and its significance in diabetic retinopathy. Am J Med 1959; 27:196-211.

[27]Anderson, J. Plant fiber: Carbohydrate and lipid metabolism. Am J Clin Nutr 1979; 32:346-363.

[28]Villaume, C. Long-term evolution of the effect of bran ingestion on meal-induced glucose and insulin responses in healthy men. Am J Clin Nutr 1984; 40:1023-1026.

[29]Fukagawa, N. High-carbohydrate, high-fiber diets increase peripheral insulin sensitivity in healthy young and old adults. Am J Clin Nutr 1990; 52:524-528.

[30]Himsworth, H. The physiological activation of insulin. Clin Sci 1933; 1:1.

[31]Himsworth, H. Diet in the etiology of human diabetes. Proc Roy Soc Med 1949; 42:323-326.

[32]Wicks, A. Insulinopenic diabetes in Africa. Br Med J 1973; 1:773-776.

[33]Trowell, H. Dietary-fiber hypothesis of the etiology of diabetes mellitus. Diabetes 1975; 24:762-765.

[34]Trowell, H. Definition of dietary fiber and hypotheses that it is a protective factor in certain diseases. Am J Clin Nutr 1976; 29:417-427.

[35]Kawate, R. Diabetes mellitus and its vascular complications in Japanese migrants on the island of Hawaii. Diabetes Care 1979; 2:161-170.

[36]Tsunehara, C. Diet of second-generation Japanese-American men with and without non-insulin-dependent diabetes. Am J Clin Nutr 1880; 52:731-738.

[37]Ringrose, H. Nutrient intakes in an urbanized Micronesian population with a high diabetes prevalence. Am J Clin Nutr 1979; 32:1334-1341.

[38]Nabhan, G. Native Seeds Search Information Packet, Tucson, Arizona, 1990.

[39]Nabhan, G. Food, health and Native-American agriculture. J Gastronomy, 1990; 68-81.

[40]Brand, J. Plasma glucose and insulin responses to traditional Pima Indian meals. Am J Clin Nutr 1990; 51:416-420.

[41]Coates, B. Traditional diet helps Pima Indian. Phoenix Gazette, Wednesday, June 27, 1990.

[42]Nash, M. A Slow, Savage Killer. Time, November 26, 1980, pp. 52-59.

[43]Sloan, N. Ethnic distribution of diabetes mellitus in Hawaii. JAMA 1963; 183:419-424.

[44]Campbell, G. Diabetes in Asians and Africans in and around Durban. S Afr Med J 1063; 37:1195-1208.

[45]Bennett, P. Diabetes mellitus in American (Pima) Indians. Lancet 1971; 2:125-128.

[46]West, K. Diabetes in American Indians and other native populations of the new world. Diabetes 1974; 23:841-855.

[47]Kannel, W. Diabetes and cardiovascular disease: The Framingham study. JAMA 1979; 241:2035-2038.

[48]Jarrett, R. The Bedford survey: Ten-year mortality rates in newly-diagnosed diabetics, borderline diabetics and normoglycemic controls and risk indices for coronary heart disease in borderline diabetics. Diabetologia 1982; 22:79-84.

[49]Yano, K. Glucose intolerance and nine-year mortality in Japanese men in Hawaii. Am J Med 1982; 72:71-80.

[50]Pan, W. Relationship of clinical diabetes and asymptomatic hyperglycemia to risk of coronary heart disease mortality in men and women. Am J Epidemiol 1986; 123:504-516.

[51]Kleinman, J. Mortality among diabetics in a national sample. Am J Epidemiol 1988; 128:389-401.

[52]Rosengren, A. Impact of cardiovascular risk factors on coronary heart disease and mortality among middle-aged diabetic men: A general population study. Br Med J 1989; 200:1127-1131.

[53]Fuller, J. Coronary heart disease risk and impaired glucose tolerance: The Whitehall study. Lancet 1980; 1:1373-1376.

[54]McDougall, J. McDougall's Medicine: A Challenging Second Opinion. New Century, publishers, 1985, pp. 210-211.

[55]McDougall, J. The McDougall Program: Twelve Days to Dynamic Health. Nal Books, publishers, 1990, pp. 337-338.

[56]Remington, D. The Bitter Truth About Artificial Sweeteners. Vitality House International, publishers, 1987, p. 9.

[57]MacKay, E. Hyperalimentation in normal animals produced by protamine insulin. J Nutr 1940; 20:59-66.

[58]Leslie, P. Effect of optimal glycemic control with continuous subcutaneous insulin infusion on energy expenditure in type 1 diabetes mellitus. Br Med J 1986; 293:1121-1126.

[59]The DCCT Research Group. Weight gain associated with intensive therapy in the diabetes control and complications trial. Diabetes Care 1988; 11:567-573.

[60]Ashby, P. Effects of insulin, gluco-corticoids and adrenalin on the activity of rat adipose tissue lipoprotein lipase. Biochem J 1980; 188:185-192.

[61]Parkin, M. Effects of glucose and insulin on the activation of lipoprotein lipase and protein synthesis in rat adipose tissue. Biochem J 1980; 188:193-199.

[62]Eckel, R. Lipoprotein lipase: A multifunctional enzyme relevant to common metabolic diseases. N Engl J Med 1989; 320:1060-1068.

[63]Jenkins, D. Dietary fibres, fibre analogues and glucose tolerance: Importance of viscosity. Br J Med 1978; 1:1392-1394.

[64]Albrink, M. Effect of high and low-fiber diets on plasma lipids and insulin. Am J Clin Nutr 1979; 32:1486-1491.

[65]Vachon, C. A rat model to study postprandial glucose and insulin responses to dietary fibers. Nutr Rep Int 1988; 37:1339-1348.

[66]Blackburn, N. The mechanism of action of guar gum in improving glucose tolerance in man. Clin Sci 1984; 66:329-336.

[67]Deshaies, Y. Attenuation of the meal-induced increase in plasma lipids and adipose tissue lipoprotein lipase by guar gum in rats. J Nutr 1990; 120:64-70.

[68]Keen, H. Nutrient intake, adiposity, and diabetes. Br Med J 1979; 1:655-658.

[69]Lohman, D. Diminished insulin response in highly trained athletes. Metabolism 1978; 27:521-524.

[70]Le Blanc, J. Effects of physical training and adiposity on glucose metabolism and I-insulin binding. J Appl Physiol 1979; 46:235-239.

[71]Bjorntorp, P. The effect of physical training on insulin production in obesity. Metabolism 1970; 19:631-638.

[72]Bjorntorp, P. Effects of physical training on glucose tolerance, plasma-insulin and lipids and on body composition in men after myocardial infarction. Acta Med Scand 1972; 192:439-443.

[73]Soman, V. Increased insulin sensitivity and insulin binding to monocytes after physical training. N Engl J Med 1979; 301:1200-1204.

[74]Jenkins, D. Unabsorbable carbohydrates and diabetes: Decreased postprandial hyperglycemia. Lancet 1976; 2:172.

[75]Miranda, P. High-fiber diets in the treatment of diabetes mellitus. Ann Intern Med 1978; 88:482-486.

[76]McDougall, J. The McDougall Program. Nal Books, publishers, New York, 1990, p. 336.

[77]Scott, F. Cow milk and insulin-dependent diabetes mellitus: Is there a relationship? Am J Clin Nutr 1990; 51:489-491.

3.

Matters of the Heart: The Prevention and Reversal of Heart Disease

3. Matters of the Heart: The Prevention and Reversal of Heart Disease.

"When you see the Golden Arches, you're probably on the road to the pearly gates."[1]

—William Castelli, M.D.

Heart disease kills thousands of people each day and costs over $100 billion dollars per year in the U.S in terms of treatment, lost wages and lost productivity. The deaths and the dollars spent are equally unnecessary and ludicrous. This disease has a specific cause—without the cause, the disease will never develop. Remove the cause in a person suffering the disease, and the disease will go away.

Approximately once every half minute, an American experiences an excruciating pain and clutches his chest, feeling as if he has been crushed by a semi truck. Sweating, nausea and shortness of breath follow as he strives to sustain life—caught in the grasp of the number one killer. It will require a lot of luck and some excellent medical care if he is to survive.

With good medical care, his chance of surviving will be slightly better than the chance of dying, but in 44% of the cases, his first symptom of serious disease will also be his last.[2]

We are, of course, talking about a heart attack or myocardial infarct, which is often the first and last manifestation of the silent killer, heart disease.

WHAT IS THE CAUSE?

Heart disease is the scourge of the "developed Western world." It is an insidious and unnecessary malady which is CAUSED EXPLICITLY BY THE CONSUMPTION OF ANIMAL PRODUCTS AND SATURATED FATS and is exacerbated by smoking, sedentary living, diabetes and various drugs. It is predictable, preventable, reversible and wholly unnecessary; yet, heart disease and other vascular diseases costs the American public $101 billion per year in lost wages, hospital care, and lost productivity.[3] Heart disease also exacts an incalculable toll in suffering and debility. Approximately 3000 Americans per day die of this disease, making it by far the largest epidemic in the country.[3]

Nearly 1,000,000 people die from heart disease and other vascular diseases each year in the U.S., accounting for 45.3% of all deaths. By comparison, cancer kills about 500,000 people yearly and AIDS about 16,000.[3] Though both AIDS and cancer are serious diseases, we seem less concerned about the million deaths from vascular diseases.

The underlying cause of vascular diseases is a buildup in the arteries of fat and a waxy substance known as cholesterol. As this buildup occurs, the arteries become progressively occluded—a condition known as atherosclerosis or hardening of the arteries. Muscle cells in the arteries also proliferate and become swollen with fat. Blood flow is reduced by the progressive occlusion, and clots may form in the narrowed arteries, leading to the interruption of the oxygen flow to dependent tissues. Such a blockage ultimately causes death to the tissues involved, since cells cannot survive without oxygen. The illustration on the following page depicts this process.

When atherosclerosis affects the coronary arteries which carry blood into the muscle of the heart, it restricts blood flow into that muscle. This is known as coronary artery disease (CAD). Should a complete blockage occur in one of these narrowed arteries, the event which results is the heart attack or myocardial infarct, previously described. Usually the blockage occurs in an area of the artery narrowed by atherosclerosis. This narrowing, in turn, has been caused by a high level of cholesterol in the blood.

PROGRESSION OF ATHEROSCLEROSIS

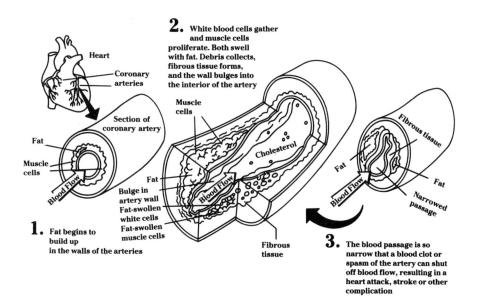

1. Fat begins to build up in the walls of the arteries

2. White blood cells gather and muscle cells proliferate. Both swell with fat. Debris collects, fibrous tissue forms, and the wall bulges into the interior of the artery

3. The blood passage is so narrow that a blood clot or spasm of the artery can shut off blood flow, resulting in a heart attack, stroke or other complication

THE FIRST SIGNS OF
HEART DISEASE

The first manifestations of this disease are seen as fatty streaks in the arteries, especially in the aorta,[4] the large artery which carries blood away from the heart to other structures of the body. The aorta branches like a tree after leaving the heart. The branches form other smaller branches until the arteries become microscopic. These tiny blood vessels are called capillaries. Capillaries deliver oxygen and nutrients from the blood to all living cells of the body. At the base of the aorta, near its attachment to the heart, small branches called coronary arteries travel back to the heart muscle to supply this tremendous pump with the oxygen it needs. These are the arteries where heart disease or CAD occurs.

However, the process of atherosclerosis takes place in all arteries of the body, not just in the heart. If it occurs in the brain, it is known as cerebrovascular disease, and its end result is often a stroke. A stroke occurs when part of the brain is deprived of oxygen due to an occluded or ruptured vessel. With few exceptions, the cause of stroke is the same as heart attack. Thus, our discussion of heart disease covers cerebrovascular disease as well.

DO CHILDREN HAVE HEART DISEASE?

The aorta, being the trunk of the spectacular branching circulatory system, is large enough to be easily studied for signs of atherosclerosis. In our society, which has one of the highest rates of heart disease in the world, atherosclerosis has been observed in the aortas of three-year-olds![5] It is also common in the arteries of teen-age children.[6] Autopsies performed on young men killed in the Korean and Vietnam Wars showed advanced atherosclerosis in the coronary arteries.[7] [8]

Early atherosclerosis is seen as a fatty streak in the inner lining of the artery and later as an irregular fatty mass known as a plaque. Plaques grow from the inner lining of the artery into the bloodstream. The disease is usually progressive, and the locations of fatty streaks in young arteries are the same locations at which full-blown plaques develop in later ages.[9] [10]

This should not be construed to mean that age, in itself, is a risk factor for heart disease, although it is assumed to be such by many. THE REASON THAT OLDER PEOPLE USUALLY HAVE A MORE ADVANCED FORM OF THE DISEASE IS OBVIOUS. THEY SIMPLY HAVE HAD MORE TIME TO SELF-DESTRUCT. The disease is progressive, but only when factors responsible for the disease remain in the system. It makes sense, then, that a person who is older would have a greater cholesterol plugging of the coronary arteries. As will be discussed later in this chapter, the disease will regress and reverse when the toxins have been removed.

PRIMARY CAUSE: CHOLESTEROL

What is cholesterol? Despite all of its bad press, it is not all bad; in fact, we could not live without it. Cholesterol is a necessary chemical produced in the liver and is an essential structural component in all cell membranes. It serves as a raw material for the production of such hormones as estrogen, testosterone and other steroid hormones, as well as for bile salts which are necessary for digestion. In the skin, it forms a barrier against harmful substances which would otherwise be absorbed into the body. The barrier also prevents the evaporation of excessive water.[11] Cholesterol becomes harmful only when it becomes excessive, in which case, it becomes one of the most insidious toxins known to man.

How much cholesterol is needed?

Cholesterol is available from two sources: (1) that which we produce in the body and (2) that which we consume as part of our nutrition. Our bodies manufacture all of the cholesterol necessary to perform the functions delineated above. Rarely does the body produce more than a safe amount. Therefore, the plaque that builds up in our arteries is due to consuming too much (a) dietary cholesterol or (b) *saturated fat*, which can independently increase the quantity of cholesterol in the blood[12]—a quantity known as *serum cholesterol level*.

Dietary cholesterol is found only in animal products and exists in both the fat and lean portions of those products.

Saturated fats are those fats which are solid at room temperature and are also derived primarily from animal products. Some vegetable fats, such as coconut oil, are also saturated, and when taken in large quantities, can be devastating in their promotion of atherosclerosis.[13] These fats are as adept as dietary cholesterol at raising serum cholesterol levels.[14] Moreover, they are doubly dangerous in that they increase blood viscosity and promote thrombosis (clotting), increasing the likelihood that a clot will form in an area narrowed by atherosclerosis.[15] [16] [17]

Plants do not contain cholesterol. Dietary cholesterol is ingested only by consuming animal products. Cholesterol in the arteries becomes excessive due to the consumption of animal foods and/or large quantities of the aforementioned saturated vegetable fats.

Cholesterol begins to accumulate in the arteries only when it reaches a certain level in the blood. The serum cholesterol level is the primary predictor of atherosclerosis and subsequent heart disease.[18] [19] [20] [21] [22] [23] [24] [25] [26]

Extensive studies of cholesterol levels and heart disease, performed over the past several decades, conclude that as cholesterol levels rise, deaths from heart disease rise concomitantly.

Framingham and MRFIT

The longest ongoing study of the relationship between cholesterol and death rate from heart disease (and other causes) is known as the Framingham study. The researchers in this study, under the direction of Dr. William Castelli, have followed the blood-cholesterol levels and death rates of over 5,000 men for a period of more than 40 years. One of the interesting findings of this study was that heart disease did not develop unless serum cholesterol was above 150. This was true even when the subjects with low cholesterol smoked, had high blood pressure, or led inactive lives.[27] THEREFORE, IT IS ESTABLISHED THAT A HIGH-SERUM-CHOLESTEROL LEVEL IS THE ONE CRITICAL FACTOR IN HEART DISEASE. When elevated cholesterol *is* present, however, other factors accelerate the growth of plaque in the arteries or increase the chance of blockage. A raised level (above 150) is the most important risk factor for heart disease, with an increasing rate of death as levels increase beyond that threshold mark.[28]

Another large study is known as the Multiple Risk Factor Intervention Trial, or by its acronym, MRFIT. This research measured cholesterol levels of approximately 360,000 men, ranging in age from 35 to 57, and then followed them over the next six years to determine the risk of death from heart disease. The men were divided into ten groups according to their cholesterol levels, with the first group being comprised of those who had cholesterol levels below 167, the second group from 168-181, the third group from 182-192, and so on up to the tenth group, with levels above 264.

Dr. Jeremiah Stamler, who coordinated the project, said that the total cholesterol level was the primary predictor of a heart attack. As cholesterol level went up, so did death from heart attacks in every group. Dr. Stamler stated that, "In every one of these groups, this relationship held consistently, systematically and without contradiction, and in every one of them it was continuous, strong and graded from the second per cent of serum cholesterol (182-202) on up."[29]

In almost every instance, the greater the cholesterol level, the greater the rate of heart disease at any age.[29] Figure 1 illustrates the increasing incidence of heart disease that occurs with increasing serum-cholesterol levels.[29] The graph contains all ten categories of cholesterol levels and subsequent death rather than starting at the 182 level as mentioned in Dr. Stamler's statement. This is done to illustrate the continuing decline in death as cholesterol levels drop below 182. I suspect that the data for a category below 150 was not evaluated because the analysis was based on death rate per thousand. The researchers probably could not find a significantly large population sample among the 356,222 total who had cholesterol levels that low! Or, perhaps they could find no deaths from heart disease among people with cholesterol levels below 150.

Serum cholesterol is expressed in milligrams percent, meaning the number of milligrams of cholesterol per 100 milliliters of blood. Although levels of 165 and over are considered atherogenic (capable of developing atherosclerosis),[30] there is little chance of having a heart attack for those people who have maintained levels of 180 or less for a lifetime.[31] [32] This is likely due to a slow progression of

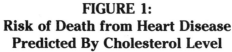

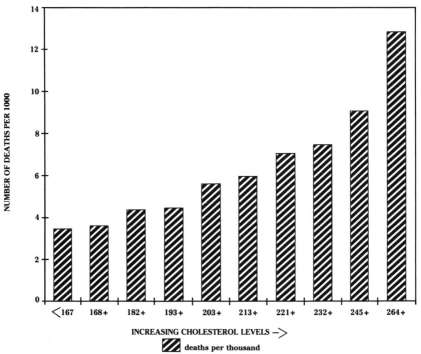

FIGURE 1:
Risk of Death from Heart Disease
Predicted By Cholesterol Level

atherosclerosis whereby heart disease does not develop to life-threatening levels. Plaque would be present but minimal. However, for those who have previously had high cholesterol levels, 180 is not an adequate goal; rather, they should try to achieve a level well below 150.

If it is true that there are almost no deaths from heart disease when cholesterol levels drop below 150, we might alter the above graph to indicate a progression starting at zero deaths per 1000 and becoming progressively higher as serum cholesterol levels rise. Figure 2 shows that progression in line graph form.

It has been proven that atherosclerosis can be reversed,[33] and it appears that at levels of 150 and below, this reversal can take place. Heart disease is virtually unknown in societies that have levels under 150. In China, for instance, where there is a

FIGURE 2:
Risk of Death from Heart Disease
Predicted By Cholesterol Level

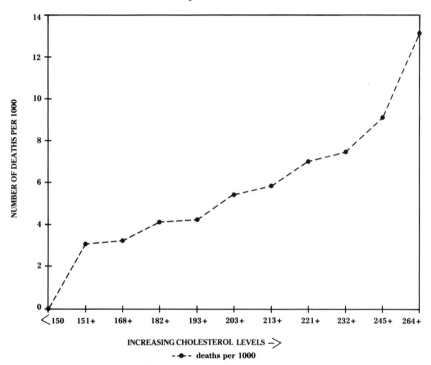

INCREASING CHOLESTEROL LEVELS –>
- –•– deaths per 1000

great variance in nutritional habits among people living in the 65 different counties, cholesterol levels range from 110 to 200, with an average of 127. This compares with an average of 212 for Americans.[34] The heart disease rate is very low in China and declines to .03% as animal-product consumption decreases.[35] On the other end of the spectrum are cholesterol levels near 300. That level predicts a 90% chance of having a heart attack![36]

There are, then, no absolute cut-off points for cholesterol safety, although heart attacks among those with levels below 150 are nearly unknown. "Low risk" or "normal" levels for heart disease are generally considered to be at or below 200,[37] in spite of the obviously elevated risk with levels above 150. American Heart Association recommendations are for cholesterol levels to be at or below 180. This level is obviously too high—heart disease still exists at 180.

The probable explanation for these "low" levels being excessively high is the erroneous assumption that a certain number of people will die from heart disease as they age, and when cholesterol levels are around 200, the chance of death is greatly reduced (compared to levels of 260 and above). The assumption continues that "this is the best that we can do." A cholesterol level below 200 is considered quite low in a society where the average cholesterol level for men is about 212 and where many have levels well above 300. *We need to realize that the person who has average cholesterol is in grave danger of death from heart disease!*

It is amazing, yet understandable in light of our atrocious eating habits and extremely high cholesterol levels, that CAD is considered to be a normal and predestined process of aging. Many feel that at best we can reduce, but not eliminate, CAD. This opinion assumes, of course, that people are destined to be sick rather than well, which is simply not true. Heart disease has a cause. Remove the cause, and the disease will regress until, in some cases, it no longer exists.[38] Remove the cause from a person who does not yet suffer the disease, and the disease will never develop.

It should also be noted that as people in "developed societies" age, their cholesterol levels tend to increase; but this is not true of societies who consume low-fat, low-cholesterol diets.[39] Let's reiterate: Aging per se is not a cause of heart disease! Older people who reside in a fat and cholesterol-consuming society simply have had more time than young people to experience the cumulative effects of the dietary toxins. Obviously, then, blockages in older arteries would be larger.

As previously stated, the rate of death from heart disease at cholesterol levels of 200 is only one-fifth of that occurring at 260.[29] This should not, however, deter someone from lowering levels until the risk reaches zero. When a person aspires to attain Megahealth, he or she is not interested in decreasing a high risk of death from heart disease by 80%. *Zero risk* is the only sensible goal. In my opinion, it is entirely possible to reduce the risk of death from heart disease to zero in individuals who are willing to make substantial changes in nutrition and activity.

An article entitled "What's Your Risk? A Layman's Guide to

Cardiovascular Disease" appeared in the journal *Physician and Sports Medicine.*[40] In it, the following information was presented:

Total Cholesterol	Incidence of CAD Per 1000 Men
Under 200	69.8
200-219	93.8
220-239	171.6
240-250	195.9
Over 250	335.4

Such information serves to corroborate the abundance of research confirming the relationship between increasing cholesterol levels and increased incidence of heart disease. It may even convince someone with cholesterol levels over 200 to make an effort to decrease it. A disservice is done, however, to those who have levels between 150 and 200. Such information could be interpreted as meaning that once a person brings his level under 200, there is little use in doing anything further. Without a category for those under 150, it is likely to be assumed that anyone under 200 would have the same risk, regardless of whether the level was at 199 or 125. Nothing could be further from the truth. If the chart were to accurately reflect the chance of developing heart disease, it would contain one more category which would look like this:

Under 150   Zero

It is an error to think that a risk of zero per 1000 is not infinitely better than a risk of 69.8 per 1000! We must convince the public to stop believing that a certain number of people will die of heart disease irrespective of eating habits or cholesterol levels.

Knowing that it is possible to prevent and reverse heart disease, the committed individual has a real goal on which to focus. It is a reachable goal. Many who attend National Institute of Fitness lower their cholesterol levels from high risk to low risk in as little as two weeks, and many achieve levels below 150 during their stays.

Others share this view about the protective effects of very

low cholesterol. Dr. John McDougall, a physician from Santa Rosa, California, is so convinced of the parallel relationship between cholesterol levels and death that he sets a goal of 150 or less for his patients.[41] This contrasts with many other physicians who give their patients a clean bill of health if their levels are at 200 or below.

When cholesterol levels exceed the threshold mark of 150, other factors become catalysts in the development of the disease. The most important of these factors are family history of heart disease, cigarette smoking, sedentary living, type and amount of fat in the diet, blood sugar levels, blood pressure levels, and the type of cholesterol in the blood. Let's consider each of these factors separately.

FAMILY HISTORY OF HEART DISEASE. IS IT REALLY A FACTOR?

There is little doubt that heart disease runs in families and that genetics play a key role in its development.[42 43 44 45 46 47] Those who have not chosen their parents wisely are certainly at a greater risk but only if they are consuming the dietary toxins which produce the disease. In societies which consume few or no animal products, heart disease rates approach zero, and there is no observable familial tendency to the disease.

Such a society is the Tarahumara Indian tribe who live in central Mexico. These people thrive on a diet of corn, beans and fruit, with animal products being eaten only sparingly. Cholesterol consumption is only about 70 milligrams daily.[48] They are capable of unbelievable feats of strength and endurance, including running continuously for 175 miles while playing kickball for 48 hours, running 500 miles in five days, and carrying a 100 pound pack for 110 miles in 70 hours.[49] They are completely free of heart disease, hypertension, diabetes and obesity.[47 48]

One might ask, "Why is there no familial tendency to heart disease among these people and, in fact, *no trace* of heart disease?" The answer is quite clear. Their blood cholesterols are in the 120-130 range,[47] which is well below the level required to produce the disease. The small amount of meat which the Tarahumaras consume is sometimes obtained by running after a deer until the animal collapses from exhaustion.[50] It is no wonder that the Tarahumaras eat little meat!

We will recognize familial tendencies only when we have ingested sufficient dietary "toxins" to create the disease! Then and only then will we observe that certain families are more or less capable of handling the toxins than others.

Primitive Mexican societies other than the Tarahumaras have in the past subsisted primarily on corn tortillas, beans and chili peppers. Dr. R.K. Anderson, in 1948, stated that such a diet was nutritionally sound and that nutritional deficiencies were uncommon.[51] He also stated: "To try to impose the food pattern recommended for a United-States population on a country like Mexico, with its present resources and economic and social conditions, might lower rather than improve the nutritional status of the people." His ideas were prophetic. By 1975, a terrible increase in the incidence of heart disease among the urban Mexicans had been reported as they adopted a more "Americanized" diet.[52]

At our resort, many Mexican guests attend who have become accustomed to typical American fare. They suffer from heart disease, diabetes, and obesity. Indubitably, there are now families of Mexicans who have tendencies toward more heart disease than other families, but no one could ever have known this without the change in nutrition that produced the disease in the first place.

Let's play out an interesting scenario: Suppose that we were to perform an experiment in which we daily administered a small amount of poison to everyone living in a particular country and that we continued to poison that populace for a period of years. It is predictable that we would be able to observe some families who were more resistant to the poison. Some would die quickly; others would take more time. To the poor souls whose parents died early of poisoning, someone might suggest that they "cut back a bit on their poison consumption!"

There is a dose-response, cause-effect relationship between heart disease and consumption of animal products and saturated fats. Should we eliminate the toxins or just "cut back"? We cannot blame our illnesses on our heredity, and as Dr. McDougall says, "We cannot do a thing about our heredity, so we had better concentrate on those factors which we can change."[53]

Some say that it is important to know our familial tendencies in order to identify those individuals who should make changes in nutrition. That is tantamount to suggesting that we need to find out who should be poisoned and who should not!

There is little doubt that the Tarahumaras would suffer heart disease if they ate heavy quantities of animal products. Is it not also certain that familial tendencies toward the disease would then develop? One thing is certain: We will not know the answers to that question as long as the Tarahumaras continue to eat as they do.

This much we do know: When the Tarahumaras are switched from a low-cholesterol diet to a totally cholesterol-free diet, their serum-cholesterol levels drop from an average of 120 to 113. When they are subsequently fed a high-cholesterol diet for three weeks, their levels increase by 30%, to an average of 147.[54]

The Chinese and heart disease: Is it in the genes?

Let's look at another example: Dr. T. Colin Campbell and his colleagues are conducting a massive study of the eating habits and disease rates among Chinese people in 130 different locations in China.[55] In a recent interview with Dr. Campbell, I asked if there was a dose-response relationship between consumption of animal products and the rate of heart disease.

Dr. Campbell replied that in the populations of Chinese counties that consume the smallest quantity of animal products, and thereby the smallest quantity of saturated fats and cholesterol, the rate of heart disease decreases to almost zero. In fact, in the counties that have the lowest consumption of animal products, the rate of heart disease is about .03%. Dr. Campbell was adamant that "animal products" included fish, pork, and fowl and not just red meat.[56]

Contrast that .03% to the approximately 50% of Chinese

who die of the disease in "developed" societies.[58] We are finding three people in 10,000 (in the counties with least animal consumption) who show signs of this disease compared to about 5,000 people in 10,000 who will die from it in the U.S. This means that the rate of atherosclerotic disease among the population of the U.S.A. is approximately 1,666 times higher than in the counties of China whose people consume the fewest animal products. Expressed in percentage, that is about 166,000% higher!

The rate of heart disease in China is very low compared with the U.S., even in the counties where the residents tend to consume more animal products. The average serum cholesterol level is 127, with a range of 88 to 165, meaning that their high levels nearly match U.S. lows. The levels in the U.S. usually range from 155 to 274.[57] It might be deduced, therefore, that the entire Chinese population enjoys genetic protection from high cholesterol levels and subsequent death from heart disease.

The above idea has been put to rest by Dr. Ethel Nelson, who along with her surgeon husband, moved to Thailand in 1951 to practice medicine in the Bangkok Mission Hospital. In doing post-mortem examinations on persons who died of various causes, Dr. Nelson observed a complete absence of coronary heart disease and myocardial infarcts (heart attacks). She found no significant coronary cholesterol deposits in the autopsied hearts of two of the three ethnic groups found in Bangkok: The Thai and Chinese. Indians, another ethnic group, did not permit post-mortem exams at that time.[58]

Ten years later, in 1961, at the invitation of the Nelsons, pathologist Dr. Albert Hirst came to Bangkok for the sole purpose of determining why the indigenous population in Thailand had so few heart attacks. While in Bangkok, Hirst examined 108 hearts of routinely autopsied patients. He found only three hearts showing any scarring indicative of past heart attacks. This was one-eighth the rate of Americans dying in Los Angeles, California during the same period.[59]

By 1978, the rate of heart attacks as a cause of hospital deaths in the Bangkok Mission Hospital had risen to about 15%. Dr. Nelson became intrigued with the increasing number of heart attacks among the three ethnic groups which had been free of the malady in 1951. She began a retrospective examination to determine when and why this startling increase in heart disease had begun. Unfortunately, there were no medical records saved in the hospital prior to 1958. Nonetheless, she knew that heart disease had been non-existent in 1951. She found supporting evidence for Hirst's study that the rate of heart attack in 1958-1961 was still extremely low—only 0.3 per 1,000 hospital admissions in both the Thai and Chinese patients. However, by this time there were already 6.2 deaths per 1,000 among Indians. This was compared by Dr. Nelson to a rate of 11.2 per 1,000 admissions in an American Hospital in New England. Indians living in Bangkok at that time, then, already had more than half the rate of death from heart attacks as Americans.

Heart attacks among Chinese and Indians began to increase steadily from 1962-1965 until they reached a peak in 1978-1981. The Chinese rate increased from 0.3 per 1,000 to 11.8 per 1,000 during that period, which exceeded the rate of death from heart attack in America. In the Indians, the rate peaked at 30.2 per 1,000 admissions or more than 2½ times the American rate! The native Thai rate increased to 23% of the U.S. rate, about an 8-fold increase from 1958—still much lower than either the Chinese or Indians.

Dr. Nelson explains that in the 1960s, due to the involvement of Americans in nearby Vietnam, there was a deluge of Americans into Bangkok. These Americans wanted to eat and live as they had in the U.S., and the people of Bangkok were willing to oblige, constructing luxury hotels, residences and restaurants in the Western style. As a result, the indigenous population became prosperous, consequently enriching their native cuisine as well as adopting Western ways of eating.

As part of the investigation, Dr. Nelson noted the differences in eating habits of the three ethnic groups, correlating this information with death from heart attack. The Thai, although they began eating richer foods, still made rice their staple, eating this grain with coconut gravy and spiced curries that contained small amounts of meat or chicken. Their usual dessert was fresh tropical fruit. Some Chinese, who have historically liked to feast on special occasions, became wealthy enough to feast daily on many quick-fried meat dishes, sometimes including fish, shellfish, pork, chicken and duck in a single meal. Their desserts were invariably sweetened lotus seeds or canned lichees, a tropical fruit.

The Chinese food was obviously much richer in fat and higher in animal products than that of the Thai. Consequently, the rate of heart disease increased to more than four times that of the Thai, even though the heart attack rate for the Thai had already increased dramatically since the sweeping changes in their nutrition had occurred.

Dr. Nelson described the Indian cuisine as far richer than even that of the Chinese. Whereas the Chinese and Thai used eggs sparingly and used no milk, the Indian population used huge quantities of clarified butter (ghee) in preparation of nearly all their foods, including vegetables. The use of butter is an especially important factor, since a recent study has shown that the consumption of butter relates more closely to the rate of heart attacks among women than any other food—even higher than ham, salami, red meat, total fats and coffee.[60]

Characteristically, the Indians served their meat with gravy containing a visible layer of fat. Desserts such as custards were made with milk, eggs, butter and sugar. Other desserts included deep fried pastries and cakes covered with syrups. More than 50% of the calories in the Indian diet came from fat! This compared to about 37% of the calories from fat in the typical American diet. On this cholesterol-laden, high-fat diet, 48% of the Indian heart attack patients had serum-cholesterol levels above 250. Is it any wonder that the Indians had a rate of death from heart attack 2½ times that of Americans?

Recently Dr. Nelson and her colleagues instituted an 8-point program called NEWSTART, which emphasizes exercise and a strict vegetarian diet, low in refined sugar and fat and high in complex carbohydrate (starch). Substantial improvements in health are already occurring as these people return to the types of food that humans are intended to eat.[61]

In summarizing her research, Dr. Nelson states, "Bangkok is no different from the United States. An enriched diet, no exercise, stress, and general neglect of basic health principles lead to degenerative diseases. These diseases *are not familial,* not racial, not infectious—but are preventable and reversible."[58]

Yes, familial tendencies to heart disease and other degenerative diseases may occur but only when the toxins that cause the diseases are consumed. It is time we stop pussyfooting with the American public and call a spade a spade: ANIMAL PRODUCTS ARE TOXIC TO HUMAN BEINGS. THEY CAUSE HEART DISEASE!

When comparing the Chinese of Dr. Campbell's study with that of the Chinese in Bangkok as described by Dr. Nelson, it becomes obvious that the Chinese have no natural immunity toward heart disease. The low rate observed by Dr. Campbell and his colleagues in the Chinese study is due to the fact that the Chinese in China consume a diet much lower in animal products than the Chinese population in Bangkok. Neither familial tendencies nor ethnic tendencies are involved.

CIGARETTE SMOKING— A DEADLY HABIT FOR THE HEART

The health-destroying effects of smoking are so well known that they deserve little attention here. When cholesterol levels are above the threshold level for heart disease, smoking greatly increases the chance of death. Smoking also causes an increase in the severity of other risk factors.

On the other hand, a decrease in smoking reduces the severity of risk factors.[62] [63] [64] [65] [66] [67] [68] [69] Smoking is so devastating that in one study it was found to reduce the average life span by almost 18 years![70] This may be due in part to a considerable increase in cholesterol levels among those who smoke. Each cigarette smoked per day raises cholesterol levels by one-half point.[71] One who smokes two packs per day raises cholesterol levels by about 20 points. When smoking ceases, cholesterol levels return to their original levels. Those who wish to live long and healthfully cannot afford to smoke. Enough said!

SEDENTARY LIVING CAN DESTROY YOUR HEART

In the chapter on fitness we establish that exercise dramatically reduces the chance of death from heart disease. It appears that exercise, or the lack thereof, lessens or increases the developmental rate of the disease indirectly. Exercise does this by influencing risk factors such as blood sugar levels, hypertension, type of fat in the blood, and obesity. Yet, exercise is also capable of exerting its own positive influence independent of those risk factors. (See the chapter on fitness for the in-depth research and discussion.)

There is one aspect of exercise that cannot be overemphasized: It is capable of reducing the death rate from all causes. Drug therapy for high cholesterol levels has proven to reduce the number of deaths from heart disease per se, but it has not proven to reduce the rate of death from all causes, especially during the treatment period. In other words, although heart attacks have lessened, death from violence, accidents and suicides have actually increased with drug therapy. (More on this disturbing finding later.)[72] Therefore, exercise is far superior to drug therapy for those who refuse to change their habits of nutrition.

The terrible tube

Cholesterol levels in children relate closely to the amount of time spent watching television.[73] Dr. Kurt Gold of The University of California indicates that children who watch two to four hours of T.V. per day have a 50% greater risk of high cholesterol than those who watch less than two hours.[74] Those who watch more than four hours have four times the risk.

ARE THERE GOOD FATS
AND BAD FATS?

Saturated fats—The worst of the lot

It is generally accepted that the type of fat in the diet is very important. Saturated fats—those which are solid at room temperature—cause an elevation of blood cholesterol levels[11] and, as previously mentioned, increase the coagulability of the blood, leading to an increase in the likelihood of clotting in narrowed areas of arteries. These fats are usually of animal origin but may also come from a few vegetable sources.[75]

Although the rate of heart disease is increased by the use of saturated vegetable fats, most societies that eat little or no animal products have very low rates (or no rate) of heart disease. For instance, the Thai population of Bangkok, which was discussed earlier, uses coconut oils in curries and gravies and some of their desserts. But, until they started eating more animal products, heart disease was unknown among them. An exception is the population of Sri Lanka, which ingests a very, very heavy amount of concentrated coconut oils and has a relatively high rate of heart disease.[71] A low-fat diet is important, whether the fats are from vegetable or animal sources.

Polyunsaturate: A two-edged sword

Conversely, increasing the quantity of polyunsaturated fats (fats which are liquid at room temperature), while at the same time reducing saturated fats by a like amount, decreases serum cholesterol levels.[76 77 78]

The reduction in total cholesterol is accomplished mainly by reducing LDL or "bad" cholesterol.[79 80 81 82]

These reductions of cholesterol levels are not very large when compared to the dramatic drops produced with a cholesterol-free, low-fat diet. It should be remembered that polyunsaturated fats are strong promoters of cancerous tumor growth[83] and that all fats are fattening. Therefore, adding polyunsaturates to the diet cannot be recommended. It has also been demonstrated that when total fat concentration is high, atherosclerosis can progress even when cholesterol is limited to less than 100 mg per day. This is true even when most of the fat is of the polyunsaturated variety.[84]

A process called hydrogenation is often used to change the texture and increase the shelf life of polyunsaturates. This process is accomplished by forcing hydrogen ions into the fats, which in effect causes them to become saturated. Hydrogenated fats are particularly dangerous in that they are more capable than other saturated fats of decreasing "good" HDL cholesterol and increasing the ratio of total cholesterol to HDL.[85]

Something's fishy

A type of polyunsaturated fat known as omega 3, contained in fish fats, reduces the risk of death from heart attack.[86] [87] [88] Omega 3 has the capability of decreasing blood platelet activity,[89] [90] [91] thereby preventing the blood from clotting in the arteries. All else being equal, then, one would be expect a reduced number of heart attacks with the use of fish fat. However, those who eliminate saturated fats and animal foods from the diet would not receive any benefit from fish fats. And, like other drugs, fish fats treat symptoms, not causes. If there were no plaque in the arteries to begin with, then there would be no need to decrease clotting potential.

These fats are far from being panaceas. There are three distinct problems with the use of fish fats: (1) They raise the level of "bad" LDL cholesterol,[92] [93] [94] thereby favoring increased atherogenesis. (See the discussion on HDL and LDL which follows later in this chapter.) (2) Fish and all other cholesterol-containing animal products raise cholesterol levels when those levels are initially low.[95] [96] [97] [98] (3) Both fish and poultry consumption have also been shown to raise triglycerides in women to a greater degree than red meat consumption.[97] [98] Fish-fat therapy also adversely affects diabetes, dramatically increasing blood-sugar levels and increasing the need for insulin.[98.1]

Fish fats do lower cholesterol levels when taken in high doses, provided that the level of triglycerides in the subjects is also very high.[92] When triglycerides are not elevated, however, even large doses of fish oil are not capable of lowering cholesterol levels and, in fact, raise the total cholesterol level by 4.8% and LDL levels by 9.1%. Some of the earlier studies, which indicated a lowering of cholesterol, substituted fish fats for saturated fat. The decrease in saturated fat was likely the real reason for the drop in cholesterol levels.

The results of many studies indicate that the protective effect of fish fat is in preventing a heart attack and not in preventing heart disease. Heart disease may actually increase with fish oil use. Thus a person who consumes fish fats may delay the inevitable for a time—perhaps until he dies of something else such as a stroke.

Dr. Neal Barnard, a physician who heads the Physician's Committee for Responsible Medicine, points out that "Eskimos, who eat a great deal of fish, are much more likely to die of brain hemorrhages than those who eat less fish, perhaps because of their disrupted blood-clotting system."[99] He further describes fish as "a mixture of protein and fat, seasoned with toxic chemicals."

All cholesterol and fat-containing animal products, including fish, cause atherosclerosis and heart disease. Fish eaters do show a decreased incidence of heart attack compared to those who eat red meat, eggs, etc.[88] This does not mean that the underlying cause has been removed. It simply means that fish fats delay the tragic event. If we insist on poisoning ourselves with animal products, then fish may indeed be the best of the "poisons."

Eat fish fats and bleed to death?

Fish fats are not only effective in preventing clotting in the arteries. They are effective in preventing clotting, period. A physician who works with the Eskimos, and who is a patron at our health institute, told me that a major medical problem among the Eskimos is excessive bleeding. It is almost impossible, he said, to stop the flow of blood from any injury—even something as seemingly innocuous as a nosebleed. Research backs him up. There is a considerable increase in bleeding time among heavy consumers of fish or those treated with fish fats.[89] [100] [101]

The physician also brought to my attention the high degree

of osteoporosis among Eskimos. We must not forget that osteoporosis is caused primarily by consumption of animal proteins and that as the consumption of these proteins increases, there is a concomitant rise in the quantity of calcium lost in the urine. Increasing fish consumption as a method of decreasing the chance of heart disease may carry with it a large price in terms of weaker bones. (See the chapter on osteoporosis.)

Fish fats are fattening!

The third reason to steer clear of fish fats is that all fats are fattening. Guests at our institute have often complained of gaining several pounds after starting a prescription of fish oil capsules. Thus, when the problem of osteoporosis from the fish proteins is eliminated (by separating the fat from the fish and processing that fat in the form of fish oil supplements), we increase the already epidemic rate of obesity.

MONOUNSATURATES: THE BEST OF THE WORST

Another fat, known as a monounsaturate, has recently received attention. The most widely known monounsaturates are olive oil, canola oil and avocado oil. In areas where large quantities of monounsaturates are consumed, the rate of heart disease is lower than in areas where more saturated fats and polyunsaturates are consumed.[102] Olive oil is used widely in the Mediterranean regions, and the rate of heart disease there is considerably lower than in areas where more saturated fats are consumed. This is not surprising. Caution is in order here, however. Fats are still fattening, and increasing consumption of total fat relates closely to death rate from cancers of the breast, prostate and colon.[103] People who live in the Mediterranean area have a higher rate of cancer than those who consume a lower-fat diet. (See the charts in the chapter on cancer.)

If a person insists on using fats, then monounsaturates may indeed be the best of a very poor lot. They are not medicine, however, and they will not produce any miracle cures. The people of the Mediterranean do have heart disease. It makes little sense to add monounsaturates to the diet in order to be more like a society which has *fewer* heart problems. Rather, we should mimic the diets of those who have virtually no heart disease. A low-fat, cholesterol-free nutrition program is the only "miracle cure." Expecting miracles from fish fats or monounsaturates is a pipe dream that ultimately leads to health problems, because we are led away from the real solutions.

Total fat

Although saturated fats have received the bulk of the bad press in terms of heart disease, the importance of total fat content of the diet cannot be overemphasized. Viscosity of the blood, along with coagulant (clotting) activity is related very closely to total fat intake.[104] And, a low-fat diet, even when the proportion of saturated fat is relatively high, reduces the potential of clotting in the arteries.[105] This could be partially due to an increase in antioxidant vitamins and minerals such as beta carotene, vitamin E and selenium, which are usually higher in a diet which is high in vegetables and grains. These nutrients have been shown to decrease clotting potential in the blood.[106] Beta carotene supplements per se have been shown to decrease stroke, heart attack and death from heart disease by 49% among those who suffer from angina.[106.1]

HIGH BLOOD-SUGAR LEVELS MAY CAUSE HEART ATTACKS.

Diabetics have a significantly higher rate of death from heart attacks.[107] [108] [109] Even non-diabetics with elevated sugar levels have a greater risk of heart disease.[110] High blood glucose levels impair circulation, thus compounding the problem of impaired circulation in the arteries of the heart. It has been suggested that the inability to remove sugar causes an inability to handle fats in the blood.[111] As blood sugar levels rise, there is a tendency for cholesterol levels to rise also.[107]

Both diseases have the same underlying cause: NAMELY, THE CONSUMPTION OF TOO MUCH FAT. The relationship between fat and adult-onset diabetes is incontrovertible, as established by research cited in the chapter on diabetes. It is also a disease that can usually be "cured" in a short time.

At National Institute of Fitness, well over 100 adult-onset diabetics have been able to stop insulin injections and hypoglycemic drugs. Usually this takes place in less than two weeks but has taken as long as five months and as little as four days. The physicians who work with these people are often amazed at the rapid return to health of their patients. (A full explanation of the mechanisms that result in high blood-sugar levels is given in the chapter on diabetes.)

Another point: Diabetic drugs which control blood-sugar levels have been known to increase the rate of sudden death from heart attack by as much as 250%.[112] How does one gain by lowering his sugar levels with a drug that drastically increases his chance of sudden death?

The usual treatment for adult-onset diabetes is injecting insulin. However, it is known that adult-onset diabetics already produce plenty of insulin[113] and that insulin is very fattening. (See the chapters on diabetes and obesity.) Since obesity is associated with an increased risk of heart disease,[114] it is likely that part of the increased risk of heart disease among diabetics is due to the fattening influence of excessive insulin.

For almost all adult-onset diabetics, insulin injections become unnecessary when they (the diabetics) follow a low-fat nutrition program. With insulin, as with most other drugs, the "cure" is often worse than the disease. The use of this drug is one more abortive attempt to improve on the perfect, God-given drugstore contained in each human being. Eating correctly will dramatically decrease or eliminate insulin need in the type 2 diabetic and thereby decrease obesity and its adverse effects on heart disease.

HIGH BLOOD PRESSURE IS A SYMPTOM OF VASCULAR DISEASE.

Hypertension, or high blood pressure, is strongly associated with death from both heart disease and stroke.[115] Both high-systolic (upper number) and high-diastolic (lower number) blood pressure are potent risk factors.[116] As blood pressure increases, the risk of death from heart disease increases in a stair-step fashion, beginning at low levels. Atherosclerosis weakens the artery walls over a period of time to the point that even slightly elevated pressure may cause the wall to rupture.[117]

Hypertension is not a disease.

High blood pressure itself is not a disease. The relationship of heart disease to hypertension is often one of a disease and its symptom. When blood vessels are partially closed due to atherosclerosis, the pressure in the circulatory system increases, since more pressure is required to move the blood through a narrower pipe.[108]

Blood also becomes viscous and sticky when laden with saturated fats and cholesterol, creating the need for greater pressure to move it through the arterial system.[118] [119] This is similar to pushing honey through a pipe—a task which would require a good deal of pressure. If the honey were diluted with water, however, the pressure required to push it would decrease, because the substance would be thinner and less viscous.

A low-fat diet thins the blood. Blood cells under the influence of a high-fat diet, however, tend to stick together in clumps and can block or severely retard circulation as well as cause blood vessels to constrict.[120] [121] [122] These factors cause blood pressure to rise.

Another well-known element which raises blood pressure in susceptible individuals is the accumulation of excessive fluid in the arteries. Salt and other sodium-containing chemicals are the usual cause.[123] (See the chapter on salt.)

The vegetarian diet as therapy for hypertension

We can quickly thin the blood and reduce clumping by reducing the amount of fat and cholesterol in the diet. We would expect this to lower the blood pressure. Vegetarians have far lower blood viscosity than those who eat mixed diets,[124] and we might expect that switching from a mixed diet to a vegetarian diet would lower blood viscosity and subsequently lower blood pressure.

Three studies show that when people switch to a vegetarian diet, the blood pressure drops, whether the blood pressure is in "normal" ranges or elevated.[125] [126] [127] One study used a vegan diet (no meat, fish, fowl, milk or any other animal product) to treat 26 subjects who were medicated for long-term high blood pressure.[128] After one year on the program, 22 were free from all adverse symptoms, and the other four showed fewer symptoms. Twenty of 26 subjects stopped all medications. Even without the medications, pressures dropped about 8 points systolic and 5-10 points diastolic. This occurred in spite of the fact that most of the subjects had brought their pressures into the "normal" range *with* medication prior to the study.

As a therapy for hypertension, the low-fat, cholesterol-free nutrition program is far superior to antihypertensive drugs. We might add that it is also a lot less expensive.

Antihypertensive drugs:
Are they more harmful than hypertension?

Hypertensive patients are often advised to use a low-sodium diet to help high blood pressure and are often given drugs. Diuretics are frequently prescribed to reduce the amount of fluid in the system. Another group of drugs called beta blockers are used to decrease the strength and frequency of heart contractions. Since the heart is the pump which drives blood through the system, it stands to reason that decreasing the strength of that pump would decrease blood pressure.

There are distinct problems arising from the use of these medications. Diuretics raise cholesterol levels by as much as 8% and cause significant increases in "bad" LDL cholesterol and in triglycerides.[129] [130] [131] [132] Beta blockers also promote increases in triglycerides and notable drops in "good" HDL cholesterol.[133] [134] [135] [136] One gains little by reducing blood pressure when he increases factors which accelerate the atherosclerotic process. Some antihypertensive drugs also interfere with the ability to exercise,[137] which, as we will establish in the chapter on fitness, is a prime method for prevention of death by heart disease.

Withdrawal may be dangerous.

Withdrawal from beta blockers is dangerous when the person taking them suddenly stops. Within the first two weeks of sudden cessation of beta blockers, a person has four times the chance of having a heart attack.[138]

Those who decide to stop taking a drug should do so only under the supervision of a physician who can help them to withdraw slowly. It is noteworthy that treatment with antihypertensive drugs has been shown to decrease the number of deaths from atherosclerosis but has not decreased the overall death rate.[139] This must mean that the drugs in this study increased the number of deaths from causes other than vascular diseases. Nor is the death rate from heart disease always decreased. One study showed that people with severe atherosclerosis, undergoing hypertensive drug treatment, had a 500% *increase* in the number of heart attacks.[140]

Hypertension is a symptom of trouble, and as such, is related to death from heart disease. It does not, however, cause the disease. Hypertension is not caused by a lack of beta blockers or a deficiency of diuretics, nor is it caused by aging. Whereas blood pressure tends to rise with age in our fat-and-cholesterol-consuming society,[141] no such rise is seen in societies which consume a low-fat, low-cholesterol diet.[142] [143] It is well known that American Blacks have epidemic rates of hypertension.[144] Yet, in primitive African societies where low-fat nutrition is typical, blood pressures remain very low for a lifetime.[145] [146]

Among our guests at National Institute of Fitness we often see blood pressures drop precipitously within a few days of beginning the program. Physicians who work with these people generally remove them from antihypertensive medication within two weeks. Participants in Dr. John McDougall's 12-day program at the St. Helena Hospital in California are usually free of medication within a few days![147] His program consists of vegan nutrition, walking and education. How simple can it get?

CAN CHOLESTEROL BE GOOD OR BAD?

There are different types of cholesterol in the blood, each named for the protein which carries it. Cholesterol is carried by protein "packages" of different densities. When these proteins combine with cholesterol, they are called high-density lipoprotein (HDL), low-density lipoprotein (LDL), and very-low-density lipoprotein (VLDL). VLDL is of little importance in heart disease. Therefore the two types of cholesterol with which we are most concerned are HDL and LDL.

HDL is important in that it protects against atherosclerosis in those who have elevated cholesterol levels.[148] [148.1] It is known as "good" cholesterol because it transports cholesterol from the tissues back to the liver where it can be broken down and disposed of. LDL is known as "bad" cholesterol and is plaque forming; exactly the opposite of HDL. It is highly predictive of death from heart disease.[149] LDL lodges itself in the arterial walls, thus blocking circulation by contributing to the atherosclerotic process.

HDL/LDL RELATIONSHIPS

When total cholesterol is high, an accompanying high level of HDL furnishes some protection against heart disease.[148] If HDL is low, then a high cholesterol level is much more dangerous. HDL and LDL are the two primary components of cholesterol. Therefore, when HDL is high, LDL tends to be low and vice versa.

When cholesterol is lowered, both HDL and LDL are usually lowered. When cholesterol levels rise, both usually rise. *High levels of HDL are not protective in themselves because they may reflect nothing more than a very high level of total cholesterol.* To be protective, they must be accompanied by low levels of LDL.

CHANGING THE HDL/LDL RATIO

It is important, then, for those with high total-cholesterol levels (above 150) to increase the HDL portion while decreasing the LDL portion of total cholesterol. This can be accomplished in several ways:

Exercise increases HDL.

Sustained aerobic exercise, as described in the chapter on fitness, alters HDL/LDL relationships by increasing HDL and decreasing LDL.[150] [151] [152] [153] Thus, regular exercise may be protective to the person who consumes animal products and has a high total-cholesterol level.

This blood-fat altering effect of exercise may be partly responsible for the life-saving influences of exercise and fitness established by Dr. Steven Blair and his colleagues at the Institute for Aerobic Research. (See the chapter on fitness.) They found that those subjects who were very fit with high cholesterol levels had only half the rate of death from heart disease as those who were unfit with "low" cholesterol levels. We must remember that "low" in this study meant under 200, which is really quite high.

Had the authors of this study defined low levels as below 150, then they would have found little or no protective effect of exercise, since people with those levels are usually free of heart disease.[27] Fitness provides protection against heart disease primarily in people who insist on consuming foods which cause the disease. (This statement is not meant to disparage exercise. Nevertheless, we must not lose sight of the primary preventive factor for heart disease, which is an animal-free nutrition program.) We should note that the subjects in Blair's study who were very fit, yet exhibited high cholesterol levels, experienced twice the rate of death from heart disease as highly-fit individuals with low levels. "Fit" persons in the Blair study were those who were capable of staying on a treadmill for the longest periods of time. Those in the top one-fifth of those tested (in terms of their treadmill performances) were considered "highly fit."

In the primitive Tarahumara Indian society discussed earlier, the HDL levels were surprisingly low in spite of an extremely high level of exercise. Yet, they had no heart disease.[55] This indicates that low HDL, like other risk factors for heart disease, becomes a problem only when total-cholesterol levels exceed the threshold mark of 150. It also indicates that high LDL levels (in relation to HDL) are damaging only when the total cholesterol levels are sufficiently high to cause the disease.

Some research has indicated that for exercise to be of value in increasing HDL levels, the heart must beat at 75% of its maximum rate for a sustained period.[154] For a person who suffers from heart disease, this should be attempted only on the advice of a physician, who will likely prescribe training at a lower pulse rate for a period of time.

Niacin therapy influences HDL/LDL ratios.

Niacin, when given in megadoses, has the ability to lower total cholesterol by decreasing the harmful LDL fraction and increasing the helpful HDL fraction.[155] [156] In such high doses, however, this vitamin must be considered a drug, and like other drugs has some very unpleasant side effects, including flushing and tingling, dry skin, intestinal disorders, and liver problems.[157] If a drug must be used, then niacin may be the best of the lot but certainly not without the advice of a physician.

HDL, LDL and polyunsaturates

Increasing polyunsaturated fats in the diet lowers total cholesterol by lowering LDL,[158] [159] [160] [161] [162] [163] and some studies also indicate an increase in HDL,[164] [165] a decrease in HDL[166] [167] or no change.[168] [169] As previously mentioned, these fats cannot be recommended as a therapy because they are fattening and because total fat consumption relates to a variety of cancers.[170] [171] Polyunsaturates by themselves are also known to be strong promoters of cancerous growths in laboratory animals.[172] [173]

OTHER FACTORS ADVERSELY AFFECTING HDL/LDL RELATIONSHIPS

Factors which adversely influence HDL/LDL ratios include milk, coffee, fish fats, lack of exercise, and the consumption of other animal products which contain cholesterol.

Milk consumption can plug your arteries.

A study at the Harvard Medical School compared vegans (those who consume no animal products) with lactovegetarians (those who eat no animal products except dairy products).[174] The effects of milk consumption on total cholesterol, HDL and LDL fractions were measured. The research indicated that the consumption of milk increased total cholesterol profoundly and that the increase was accomplished by raising the harmful LDL fraction three times faster than the "good" HDL fraction. Milk, then, is doubly harmful, since it raises cholesterol to dangerously high levels and causes an adverse balance between HDL and LDL.

Fish fats

Fish fats, one of the latest fads for heart disease, have been shown to increase LDL levels without a proportionate increase in HDL. See the preceding discussion on fish fats.

Coffee influences blood fats.

Although coffee has recently been downplayed as a risk factor for heart disease,[175] it can do no one any good. Coffee has been shown in some studies to greatly increase total cholesterol levels,[176] [177] [178] primarily by increasing LDL.[178]

Although the research is not consistent, coffee has been strongly implicated in heart disease per se. In one piece of research which compared heart-attack rate among women to various products which were consumed as either food or drink, heavy coffee consumption was related to an increased heart-attack rate of about 80%.[88] In fact, the relationship between coffee consumption and heart attack rate was greater than the association between heart attacks and meat! Butter was the only product that related more closely to heart attack than coffee. Figure 3 illustrates the association of heavy consumption of various foods to the rate of heart attacks in women.

There is the possibility that some other important heart disease risk factors (such as stress or the tendency of smokers to drink coffee) leads to a higher consumption of coffee. At the very least, coffee does no one any good.

Another study showed that men who drank nine or more cups of coffee per day had 2.2 times the rate of heart attack as those who drank less than one cup per day.[179] Women who consumed nine cups had 5.5 times the rate of heart attack as those who drank less than one cup. Coffee appeared to increase the rate of heart attack over and above its effect on raising cholesterol.

Coffee is a drug, and as such can easily be abused. Such abuse has very undesirable consequences for the heart health of the user.

Sedentary living—move it or lose it!

The positive association between exercise and higher levels of HDL was already discussed. Conversely, lack of exercise correlates with high levels of LDL and decreased levels of HDL. This may be another reason for the significantly increased risk of death in people who are not physically fit.[180]

FIGURE 3:
Heart Attack Risk in Women
with High Consumption of Various Foods

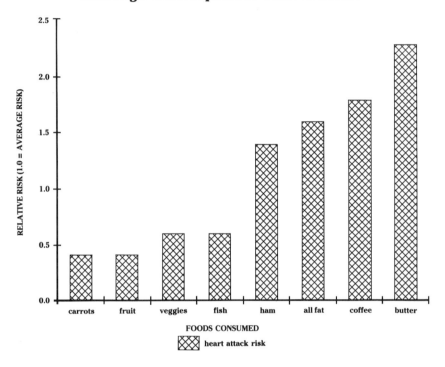

Animal-product consumption

A switch to a pure vegetarian diet will lower LDL about twice as fast as HDL,[181] producing a much healthier ratio. As consumption of dietary cholesterol increases, the accompanying increase in total cholesterol is accomplished by raising LDL about five times as fast as HDL.

One study indicated that feeding cholesterol in the form of eggs increased total serum cholesterol by 31% in a period of only three weeks.[181] Nearly all of that increase was due to an elevation of LDL cholesterol.

IS ALCOHOL GOOD FOR THE HEART?

Another factor which influences HDL and LDL is alcohol consumption. Surprisingly, alcohol has been shown to raise the HDL levels and to relate to a lower rate of death from heart disease.[182] It is misguided, however, to prescribe alcohol as a method of preventing heart disease since any advantage in that realm will be negated by increases in blood pressure.[183] [184]

The devastation caused by alcohol outside the realm of heart disease should also be taken into consideration. More than 105,000 deaths are attributed annually to alcohol, accounting for the loss of 2.7 million years of life. The use of alcohol has been linked closely to various cancers, mental disorders, digestive diseases, and of course, death due to injuries, both intentional and unintentional.[185] (See the section on alcohol.)

THE TOTAL CHOLESTEROL/HDL RATIO: DETERMINING THE RISK

To determine the risk of heart disease based on lipoprotein levels, it is common to use the ratio of total cholesterol to HDL. As an example, if total cholesterol is 250 and HDL is 50, then the ratio is 5.0. This ratio represents the average risk for heart attack in our country. As Dr. Julian Whitaker points out in his book, *Reversing Health Risks,* "Since about 50% of American men die from heart disease, it is quite dangerous to walk around with average risk."[186] It should again be noted that these ratios are important only in people who have elevated cholesterol levels. The Tarahumara Indians, whose cholesterol levels average about 130, have no heart disease in spite of very low HDL levels. They also have total cholesterol to HDL ratios of about 4.2, which, in a society with high cholesterol levels, predicts a high rate of heart attack. As with other risk factors, *the total cholesterol/HDL ratios lose their ability to predict death from heart disease when cholesterol levels are below 150.*

We should remember Dr. Stamler's statement that the

relationship between serum cholesterol and heart disease is "continuous and graded." There should be no false sense of security due to a "desirable" ratio.

A prime example of this is mentioned by Dr. Kenneth Cooper in his book, *Running Without Fear.*[187] He points out that Jim Fixx, a famous runner and author, had a "good" cholesterol/HDL ratio of 3.48. Jim died of a heart attack which occurred while he was running—this in spite of his high level of HDL. His cholesterol level was 254, and he suffered severe atherosclerosis in several coronary arteries, one of which was 99% occluded.

Dr. Cooper notes that Jim had a poor familial history of heart disease, since his father had died of a heart attack at the age of 43. Perhaps Jim's running helped him to outlive his father, but what might have happened had he not eaten the cholesterol-raising foods? My opinion is that he would still be running and writing today.

Exercise is wonderful, but it is no panacea. Coronary heart disease develops as a result of improper eating. It is lunacy to consider it "normal" for a certain percentage of our population to die of heart disease and other vascular diseases. Efforts to reduce the rate of this killer make little sense until we are willing to remove the cause of the disease.

DO PROTEINS PLAY A PART IN HEART DISEASE?

Cholesterol and saturated fats may be assisted in their atherogenesis (building of plaque) by the action of animal proteins.[188] When subjects were placed on a diet consisting of 20% of calories in either soy protein or casein (milk protein), those consuming the casein had LDL levels 16% higher than those consuming the soy proteins. The dangerous effects of milk and other animal products are obviously not limited to those effects produced due to saturated fat and cholesterol. The adding of low-fat, cholesterol-free animal products such as skim milk may help to lower cholesterol somewhat but not to the extent to which it could be lowered without animal proteins.

Not only are animal proteins able to raise cholesterol and LDL levels, but there is ample indication that vegetable proteins can reduce those levels.[188.1] [188.2] [188.3] In one study, a low-fat diet with soy proteins reduced cholesterol levels in a few weeks. The same degree of cholesterol reduction, using a conventional low-fat diet, took several months.[189] When subjects who had been on a soy-protein, low-fat diet were switched to a low-fat diet containing animal proteins, cholesterol levels and LDL levels climbed sharply. When cholesterol was added to the diet of subjects on a high-soy-protein diet, the soy proteins were protective against an increasing cholesterol level.[190]

Soy proteins were used in the above study, but it is likely that any vegetable protein has the same effect. This may be the reason that the Seventh-day Adventists, who are lacto-ovo vegetarians, have significantly lower levels of cholesterol than meat eaters. These people consume far more vegetable proteins than the rest of the population; thus they are at least somewhat protected from the ravages of the milk and eggs by the vegetables they eat.[189] Animal studies have confirmed the hypocholesterolemic (cholesterol-lowering) and LDL-lowering effects of vegetable proteins, including those derived from soy, wheat, rice[190] or cottonseed.[191] In fact, one of the studies showed wheat protein to be slightly superior to soy or rice in lowering cholesterol levels.[190]

DIETARY CHOLESTEROL VS. SATURATED FAT— WHICH IS WORSE?

It is quite clear that cholesterol consumption raises blood cholesterol levels. Yet, there are those who believe that only saturated fat causes elevated levels and that cholesterol consumption is inconsequential. They therefore consume products lower in saturated fat but nonetheless very high in cholesterol. Such products include chicken, turkey, fish, shellfish and lean cuts of red meat.

Whereas saturated fats are indeed strong promoters of atherosclerosis, the harm from dietary cholesterol cannot be overemphasized. Up to a point, dietary cholesterol is a strong elevator of cholesterol levels—even in the absence or near absence of saturated fats. This cholesterol-raising effect is seen even when people are exercising regularly and vigorously.[181] [182]

Low-fat meat is lower in calories than high-fat meat but contains approximately the same quantity of cholesterol, ounce for ounce. Therefore, if one eats 1000 calories of lean meat, it will require a larger consumption of that meat than if he ate fat meat.

To illustrate, let's suppose that each ounce of meat, lean or fat, contains *30* milligrams of cholesterol. *Fat meat contains 200 calories per ounce. Lean meat, due to its lower fat content, contains 100 calories per ounce.* Now let's suppose that a person decides to eat 1000 calories of either lean or fat meat.

He will be required to consume *five ounces of fat meat to obtain his 1000 calories.* This amount of fat meat will contain *150 milligrams of cholesterol.*

He will be required to consume *ten ounces of lean meat to obtain 1000 calories.* This amount will contain *300 milligrams of dietary cholesterol.*

In this illustration, 1000 calories of fat meat contains 150 milligrams of cholesterol. One thousand calories of lean meat contains 300 milligrams of cholesterol. Lean meat, therefore, would contain *twice as much cholesterol per calorie* as fat meat.

This means that there is more cholesterol per calorie in lean meat than in fat meat. Consuming lean meat in the same number of calories as fat meat, then, would dramatically increase dietary cholesterol intake. It would also produce an increase in the quantity of animal protein consumed.

Knowing that these proteins raise cholesterol levels and that low-fat meats contain as much cholesterol per calorie as high-fat meats, we cannot recommend low-fat meat products. At best they may be the lesser of two evils. At best they may be the lesser of two evils. In addition to raising cholesterol, these animal proteins (which would increase on a diet of low-fat meat products) are the prime cause of osteoporosis. (See the chapter on bone strength.) Low-fat diets should always be no-cholesterol *and* no-animal-protein diets.

Dietary cholesterol is capable of causing death from heart disease even when increased consumption of this toxin does not raise cholesterol levels. This is true at any given blood-cholesterol level.[193] In other words, if someone has a cholesterol level of 200 and consumes a high cholesterol diet, he has a 58% greater chance of death from heart disease than the person who has a 200 level but who consumes much less cholesterol. Thus, consuming dietary cholesterol increases the chance of death from heart disease even when cholesterol levels are "low." The same holds true for people with higher cholesterol levels. Those who consume a greater amount of dietary cholesterol have a far greater chance of death than people with identical cholesterol levels who consume far less toxin.[193]

Further illustrating the important influence of dietary cholesterol are studies that indicate a dramatic increase in death by heart attack in countries that consume large quantities of cholesterol. Figure 4 illustrates the increasing chance of death from heart disease with increasing consumption of dietary cholesterol in various countries.[194]

A recent editorial in the *New England Journal of Medicine* sounded as if it might have been written for a vegetarian journal.[195] In it, physicians Walter Willet and Frank Sacks state that, "The optimal intake of cholesterol is probably zero, meaning the avoidance of animal products; people will need to balance their desire to minimize the risk of coronary heart disease against their taste for meat and dairy foods."

We must not be lulled into a false sense of security by using low-fat animal products in the belief that saturated fats are the real culprits and that dietary cholesterol is of little consequence. Many low-fat animal products are loaded with cholesterol.

This is not to say that dietary cholesterol is more dangerous than saturated fat in causing heart disease. Both are very important. The authors of the *Journal* article quoted above also state, "Most recommendations suggest that total saturated fats be reduced to about ten percent of energy intake, but the optimal level may be much lower." The fact that such statements were published in the medical profession's most prestigious journal is indication that the medical community is awakening to the truth

FIGURE 4:
Relationship of Dietary Cholesterol Consumption
To Death from Heart Disease

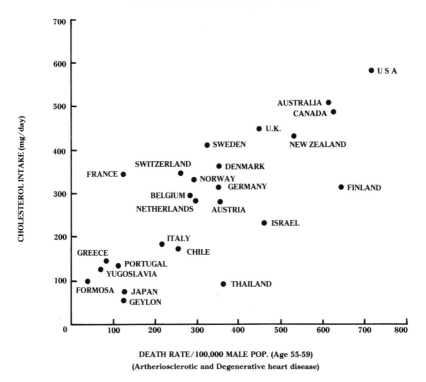

DEATH RATE/100,000 MALE POP. (Age 55-59)
(Artheriosclerotic and Degenerative heart disease)

about the real causes of degenerative diseases. This is good news indeed!

THE INCREDIBLE KILLER EGG

It would not be appropriate to conclude a discussion on dietary cholesterol without mentioning the egg. Controversy as to the cholesterol-raising influence of eggs has raged for some time, but that controversy is really unnecessary. Eggs cause dramatic and rapid rises in cholesterol levels in people who have initially low levels. When researchers want a source of cholesterol which will raise levels spectacularly, they choose the egg.[181] [196] [197] Eggs are actually a more potent blood-cholesterol raiser than pure cholesterol dissolved in oil![198]

The researchers who conducted the previously discussed study of the Tarahumaras used *eggs* to raise the levels of cholesterol by 31% in three weeks—most of the increase coming as LDL.

The egg contains about 213 to 250 milligrams of cholesterol and derives 70% of its calories from saturated fat! Nathan Pritikin stated that the human body could stand no more than 100 mg per day of dietary cholesterol. He who understands that fact, yet still chooses to eat a three-egg omelette, must have a death wish!

The controversy over eggs has arisen from several studies that have shown that increasing egg consumption doesn't significantly raise blood-cholesterol levels.[199] [200] [201] [202] [203] These studies, with one exception, were sponsored by the egg industry and used subjects who were already ingesting large quantities of cholesterol. It is a well known fact that beyond a certain point of cholesterol consumption, eating more cholesterol will not raise cholesterol levels.[32] [39]

It appears that the threshold at which dietary cholesterol ceases to raise levels in the blood is about 300 to 475 mg per day.[39] Cholesterol consumptions of 400 to 4800 mg per day have approximately the same effect on cholesterol levels.[204] [205] [206] No differences, then, could be expected in blood cholesterol levels when comparing people who consume cholesterol in amounts above the threshold.

The cholesterol-raising effects of dietary cholesterol have been known since at least 1960.[207] It was probably not by accident that the researchers who performed the "harmless egg" studies used subjects who were already consuming large quantities of cholesterol. The use of such subjects would ensure no correlation between egg intake and cholesterol levels.

When eggs are eaten by subjects who normally consume little cholesterol, a quick and dramatic increase in blood-cholesterol levels occurs.[208] [209] [210] [211] Don't be misled—eggs are replete with cholesterol and saturated fat. There is no magic in the egg that will prevent its toxic influence on the arteries. If 100 milligrams is the maximum daily cholesterol most human beings can ingest without causing atherosclerosis, then eating a product that contains up to 250 milligrams per helping is a form of slow suicide.

From the above discussion, one might conclude that if he or she is already consuming a large quantity of cholesterol, eating more will not hurt, since it is unlikely to raise cholesterol levels. In other words, once past the threshold, one might as well eat cholesterol levels to his heart's content, since all possible harm has been done. This is wishful thinking. The consumption of dietary cholesterol increases the chance of death from heart disease at any cholesterol level.[193] A final note on the egg: Salmonella-contaminated eggs were responsible for more than 2000 reported cases of food poisoning in 1990.[212] With all of their death-dealing properties, is it worth the risk to eat them?

CAN LIFESTYLE CHANGES REDUCE THE CHANCE FOR HEART DISEASE DEATHS?

That question may seem a bit silly in view of what has been discussed. Any thinking person would suspect that if he changed the habits that led to the disease, his chance of dying from it would decrease. There are those, however, who profess to believe that dietary changes or drug therapy do little to either lower cholesterol levels or decrease the chance of death from heart disease. Yet, as the American public increased its consumption of fat from 34% of total calories to 42% of total calories in the 1960s, there was a concomitant rise in death due to heart disease. Fat consumption decreased again to approximately 36% of total calories by 1984, and a decline in death from heart disease accompanied that decrease.[213] Dietary changes obviously exert their influence on the death rate for heart disease.

An article in the *Atlantic Monthly* entitled "The Cholesterol Myth"[214] caused a considerable stir among physicians and lay people alike. One of the precepts of this article was that lowering cholesterol was futile in terms of any life-saving effect. I can imagine a few million people breathing a collective sigh of relief as they realized that they had finally found the pied piper who would tell them what they wanted to hear.

One of the main contentions of the article was that changing the diet was not effective in lessening the degree of deaths from heart disease and that there was really only a small drop in total serum cholesterol which could be expected from such changes. These ideas seemed to spring from analyzing the data from the Multiple Risk Factor Intervention Trial (MRFIT) study referred to earlier, which showed very little decrease in deaths from changing to a diet slightly lower in fat and by using cholesterol-lowering drugs.

The *Atlantic* article conveniently passed up all the evidence that eating too much cholesterol and saturated fat can plug the arteries.[215] It also failed to mention other studies that prove conclusively that lower cholesterol levels, achieved through diet and drug therapy, do indeed lessen the risk of death from coronary heart disease. For instance, a study conducted in Oslo, Norway showed a 47% decrease in death from heart disease when the subjects changed to a low-fat diet.[215] Another study which used a cholesterol-lowering drug for seven years, produced a 19% decrease in death from heart disease.[216]

Follow-up on the MRFIT research also indicates that the criticism of this study might have been a bit premature. Those Those subjects who made changes that lowered cholesterol levels are now experiencing a 24% reduction from heart attacks and an all-cause death rate 8% lower than those who were not treated.[217] Those who were hypertensive (suffering from high blood pressure) are experiencing a 50% drop in death from all causes after ten years of follow-up.[218]

As Dr. Glen Griffin states in an editorial in the journal *Postgraduate Medicine*,[215] "The Cholesterol Myth Club is on a par with the Flat Earth Society." He also states that "in the very serious cholesterol matter, Mr. Moore [the author of the *Atlantic* article] is joined by a few doctors who have their heads in the sand when it comes to understanding that eating less cholesterol and saturated fat can decrease the risk of having a heart attack."

Nonetheless, two of the points in the "Cholesterol Myth"

article are well taken. The author admits that there is a slightly reduced risk of death from heart disease in the studies that have used cholesterol-lowering drugs along with a cholesterol-lowering diet. He contends, however, that there is only a small reduction in the number of actual deaths due to heart disease. This assessment is correct—at least during the time of drug treatment. As just mentioned, follow-up studies are more positive.

To illustrate how interpretation may mislead, let's analyze the lipid study just mentioned, which divided 3806 men into a treatment group and a comparison group that received no treatment. The treatment group, after follow-up for 7.4 years, had 155 deaths or non-fatal heart attacks, whereas the non-treatment group had 185 such events. This represents a 19% decrease in events when comparing the groups to each other. However, when comparing the actual number of events in each group to the number of people in each group, there were about 9.8% of the people in the non-treatment group who had a fatal or non-fatal event as compared to 8.1% of the people in the treatment group. This means that only 1.7% more of the people in the non-treatment group died or had a non-fatal event. Viewed in this light, there is hardly a significant difference.

Nevertheless, preventing 30 fatal or non-fatal events through drugs and dietary changes might be worthwhile if it were not for the fact that those who were on the treatment program experienced nearly a 300% increase in death by accidents and violence! These deaths actually exceeded the lives saved through the treatment. We will elaborate on these findings a little later on.

The use of drugs is often a huge disappointment, and it is certainly not the answer to heart disease. One statement in the *Atlantic* article, however, is ludicrous. To quote, "Diet has hardly any effect on your cholesterol levels." This is poppycock. What a person eats makes quick and profound changes in cholesterol levels, as we have already established. Obviously, the author of this article, and many health professionals, are blind to the influence of nutrition on cholesterol levels. They look only at research that makes small and hardly noticeable changes in nutrition and then complain when prodigious results are not forthcoming.

Typical of this attitude is a recent article written in the *Journal of the American Medical Association*, entitled "What If Americans Ate Less Fat?"[218.1] In it the authors point out that lowering dietary fat intake to 30% of total calories (as recommended by the AHA) will probably extend life span in the United States by about 3-4 months. A diet which is 30% calories in fat, of course, is a high-fat diet and could not be expected to substantially reduce mortality. As we will repeat throughout this text, the definition of a low-fat diet is one which contains 10% or less of total calories in fat.

It is unfortunate that much of the medical community is ignorant of the profound influence of "real" dietary changes on cholesterol levels and subsequent death from heart disease. As I spoke to a church group some time ago, one of the men in the group told me that his son was being taught in medical school that dietary changes could lower cholesterol levels by a maximum of about 15%. It is astounding that a medical school could be teaching such a flagrant falsehood! At our resort, we have seen people drop serum cholesterol levels from 25% to 50% in a period of four weeks!

Two years ago, my mother-in-law, Colleen, expressed concern that her cholesterol level was 360, and no type of cholesterol medication seemed to budge it. Her husband, Todd, also had an elevated cholesterol level of 226. At the time, he was taking blood-pressure medication, yet his pressure remained elevated. I convinced them to try a low-fat, low-cholesterol program similar to that which Nathan Pritikin advocated, since they were not willing to try the pure vegetarian program that I recommended as being the best plan.

The program worked beautifully for Todd. His cholesterol level dropped from 226 to 156 in 28 days (a 31% reduction), and his blood pressure normalized without medication. Colleen, however, did not have any change. Her cholesterol remained at 360. I convinced her to switch to a pure vegetarian (vegan) program for the next four weeks, and her level dropped from 360 to 204 (43%)!

The professional journals are replete with examples of dramatic lowering of cholesterol levels by dietary means. At

National Institute of Fitness, we consistently see drops of 100 points or more in four to six weeks when levels are in the 300 range. In the Heart-disease-reversing research of Dr. Dean Ornish, cholesterol levels dropped an average of 24.3%, and LDL levels dropped by 37.4% in the subjects who participated in his vegetarian, low-fat diet for one year.[219] This occurred even though his patients had reduced their fat consumption (and probably cholesterol levels) prior to the beginning of the experimental period. Fifteen percent indeed!

One really does have his head in the sand if he believes that high cholesterol levels cannot be dropped more than 15% by dietary means. However, as in the case of Colleen, some cannot reduce levels on a diet which contains "just a little toxin." These people need to eschew all animal products.

Before we come down too hard on those who espouse the "cholesterol myth" theory, let me say that I understand where such nonsense gets started. So many of the studies require only small changes in dietary habits. They usually advocate the recommendations of the American Heart Association[220] (AHA), which suggests a reduction of total fat consumption from 37% of total calories (the American average) to 30% of total calories.

The AHA also recommends a reduction in cholesterol intake from the American range of about 450 to 700 milligrams of cholesterol per day to 250 to 300 milligrams per day. This is tantamount to suggesting that someone poison himself at a slower rate. This advice, if heeded, will lower cholesterol levels somewhat, and it will slightly decrease the risk of heart attack. The AHA diet, however, is still harmful. As Nathan Pritikin once remarked, "The American Heart Association diet does not prevent heart disease, it causes it."[221]

It is understandable that poorly informed individuals perceive dietary changes as producing little in the way of positive effects. They are comparing severely harmful programs with programs only slightly less harmful. The results are predestined to be disappointing. If we wish to ascertain the benefits of a low-fat diet, we cannot eat a diet that has 30% of total calories in fat. That is a high-fat diet! Nor can we expect dramatic improvements in heart health with a cholesterol intake of 250 milligrams per day. That is a high-cholesterol diet! This is not to say that lowering fat content to 30% is futile. Such a change will help. The person who makes such a change will at least deteriorate at a slower rate.

Societies that have little or no heart disease, such as the Tarahumaras and the Chinese discussed earlier, consume diets ranging between 6% and 15% fat. What happens when people with severe heart disease are put on a diet with a very-low-fat content and no cholesterol? Has anyone made such a seemingly obvious study?

HEART DISEASE IS REVERSIBLE.

The answer to that question has been aptly answered by Dr. Dean Ornish of the University of California, San Francisco Medical School.[219] Dr. Ornish studied 41 heart disease patients who had advanced coronary heart disease. Half of the patients were placed on a diet that contained 8% of its calories in fat and was purely vegetarian except for some skim milk and egg whites. The diet contained less than 5 milligrams of cholesterol per day.

In a period of one year, 82% of the subjects on the vegetarian diet had experienced a partial regression of the plaque in their arteries; the closer the adherence to the diet, the greater the regression. One subject, who adhered strictly to the program, reduced the plugging of his arteries by 23%. The average regression was 5%.

Perhaps if all of the subjects had adhered strictly to the diet, the average regression would have been in the 20% range. This is pure speculation but feasible. We have discussed the fact that animal proteins themselves exert an upward influence on cholesterol levels. What might have happened if no protein from eggs and milk had been allowed?

The American Heart Association Diet:
Does it simply poison us slower?

The other half of the patients in the study were given diets based on the changes recommended by the American Heart Association (AHA). At the end of the year, 53% of them had more atherosclerosis than at the beginning of the program. The average increase in plugging of the arteries was 8%, compared to a 5% regression or "unplugging" with the low-fat diet used by Dr. Ornish. This means that there was a 13% swing toward better heart health by using the low-fat, low-cholesterol program as opposed to the AHA program. Although other studies have demonstrated a reversal of heart disease in some patients, Dr. Ornish's research is the first (with which I am acquainted) to conclusively prove reversal without the use of any drugs whatsoever.

One of Dr. Ornish's patients followed the American Heart Association diet, along with an exercise program, for one year after learning that one of his coronary arteries was 37% blocked. At the end of the year, the artery was 77% blocked! On Dr. Ornish's low-fat, low-cholesterol program, the blockage decreased to 59% in the next year.[222]

One 75-year-old patient's angina (heart pain) was so severe that he could hardly cross the street. One year later, after participating in Dr. Ornish's program, he was able to hike for six hours in the Grand Teton Mountains at an altitude of 8,000 feet!

One publication described Dr. Ornish's program as a "radical vegetarian diet."[223] It is interesting that a program which reverses heart disease, and on which humans thrive, could be termed "radical." It is, however, radically different than the toxic diet most Americans consume.

To me, Dr. Ornish's work substantiates Pritikin's statement about the American Heart Association diet. The AHA diet increases atherosclerosis in more than half of the people who have the disease. This is hardly a recommendation for such a diet, which at best will probably allow the person who is susceptible to heart disease to kill himself more slowly.

How much dietary cholesterol is too much?

Another comparison might be made between the results of Dr. Ornish's work and a study in which subjects with severe heart disease were placed on a two-year diet containing less than 100 milligrams of cholesterol per day. Saturated fats were also decreased in the diet while increasing the quantity of unsaturated fats.[224] After the experimental period of two years, more than half of the subjects experienced *progression* of the disease; their arteries were more plugged than when the experiment began.

From such a study we might learn two things: (1) 100 milligrams of cholesterol per day might be too much for individuals who are susceptible to heart disease. (2) A very low-fat nutrition program is required to be of value in reversing the disease. Manipulating the type of fat is far less effective than just ridding the diet of its excessively high fat content.

Other examples of reversal

To most people, it comes as quite a shock to learn that heart disease is not only avoidable but reversible. Yet, there have been many other studies that indicate that the disease can indeed be reversed. Vegetarian animals (herbivores) develop atherosclerosis and heart disease when they are fed cholesterol along with their regular foods. When they are allowed to return to their natural diets, regression of the disease occurs.[225]

Human subjects who undergo surgery or a combination of drug and dietary therapy have also shown regression,[226] [227] [228] [229] although not to the extent of Dr. Ornish's subjects. One recent study showed a regression of atherosclerosis in some patients who received intensive drug therapy, but many of the subjects in this study also had progression of the disease.[230]

A great example of reversal was Nathan Pritikin himself, who had severe heart disease before he developed the "Pritikin Diet," which is very low in fat and animal products. When Mr. Pritikin died after many years on his diet, his autopsy revealed that he had experienced nearly complete reversal of the disease and had the heart of a healthy young boy.[231] We should note that he also had two forms of cancer, which were diagnosed 27 years prior to his death. He was given 30 days to live. His ability to survive these cancers for such an extended time is remarkable and probably due to his very-low-fat diet.

When Mr. Pritikin was originally diagnosed as having heart

disease in 1955, his cholesterol level was 280. By September of 1958 he had decreased it to 122; by June 1960 it was 120, and in November of 1984 it was an astounding 94! Dr. Jeffrey Hubbard, reporting in the *New England Journal of Medicine*, stated that, "in a man 69 years old, the near absence of atherosclerosis and the complete absence of its effects are remarkable."[208] Mr. Pritikin, in his death, proved what he said in his life—that he had the answers to heart disease. His own complete reversal of the disease proved that he knew how to cure it.

Some might suggest that Pritikin's low cholesterol levels may have contributed to his cancer. Not so. At one time during the year that he was diagnosed as having cancer, his cholesterol level was still elevated at 210. Cancer takes a considerable time to develop, meaning that Pritikin's cancer began and progressed during the time in which his cholesterol level was extremely high. It is far more likely that the *high* levels of cholesterol *caused* the cancer (since in societies which eat the way that Pritikin recommended, the higher the cholesterol level, the higher the cancer rate).[232]

Not only has heart disease proven to be reversible, but a recent study demonstrated that even a more moderate reduction in fat intake can stop the progression of plaque formation in some individuals.[233]

No, cholesterol is not a myth, and yes, dramatic reductions in cholesterol levels and plaque can be produced by intelligent, positive changes in dietary habits. These changes can result in reversal of heart disease. Isn't it time we stop deceiving the American public and tell them the real truth about this unnecessary, preventable, and reversible condition?

According to Dr. Michael Klaper, in a lifetime the typical American eats 15 cows, 211 hogs, 900 chickens, and 12 sheep.[234] Add to this multi-thousands of eggs, tankers of milk, untold gallons of ice cream, buckets of frozen yogurt, thousands of pounds of cheese, massive quantities of fish, and tons of saturated fats in the form of butter, margarine and lard. It is not hard to see why heart disease is the most devastating epidemic ever known.

Can low-cholesterol levels be dangerous?

The discussion of heart disease would be conspicuously lacking without putting to rest two concerns about blood cholesterol and its contribution to other causes of death. The first concern, as previously mentioned, is cancer; particularly colon cancer. The second is death from all causes.

Although the death rate from heart disease decreases as a result of using cholesterol-lowering drugs and increasing polyunsaturated fats, the risk of death from all causes (during treatment) declines very little or not at all.[235] In some studies, an increased death rate from cancer appears to result from these treatments to lower cholesterol.[236] [237] This is interesting in view of the fact that patients with colon cancer often exhibit lower cholesterol levels than those without cancer.[238]

Of even more interest, one report shows that the decrease in heart disease mortality accomplished by using the drug Cholestyramine was negated by a four-fold increase in deaths from violence and accidents.[239] Other drugs and conventional dietary programs have fared no better in terms of all-cause mortality.

Dr. Matthew F. Muldoon recently made a report which assessed the combined results of several major studies on cholesterol lowering and its influence on the rate of death from heart disease and death from all causes.[72] The combined total subjects numbered 24,847. After following these patients for an average of 4.6 years, it was found that those who were being treated to lower cholesterol showed 28 fewer deaths per 100,000 from heart disease, *but 29 more deaths from suicides, homicides and accidents!*

However, as noted previously, years after the treatments with drugs, those who lower their cholesterol and blood pressure do show a considerable decrease in deaths from all causes. To me, this indicates that if a person can survive the initial treatment with the drugs, he will live longer because he lowered his cholesterol.

How long he has to survive to reap the benefits is another question. In a recent report in the *Journal of the American Medical Association,*[239.1] it was shown that Finnish heart patients did not fare well with a program of drugs and dietary therapy.

Although they experienced a decrease of 46% in heart disease death during five years of treatment (compared to those who had no therapy), the treatment could hardly be termed successful. A five-year follow-up showed that those who had used the drug and dietary programs had two and one-half times the death rate from heart disease as those who did not. There were 13 times as many deaths due to violence among those who had the drug and diet therapy!

It is my opinion that God, or nature, if you prefer, has given the human being a perfect drugstore and that efforts to manipulate that drugstore are usually ill-advised and dangerous. *When a drug lessens the chance of heart disease only to increase the risk for another cause of death, the only entity to benefit from the use of the drug is the pharmaceutical company!* The primary change to the individual is a change in the mode of death and a change in the weight of the pocketbook. And, those changes are not positive. Even though long-term follow-up on drug treatment indicates that those who survive the therapy may suffer less from heart disease, resorting to drug therapy seems a ridiculous idea when effective, *no-risk* methods are available.

The answer lies neither in drug therapy nor conventional dietary wisdom as espoused by the American Heart Association. Rather, we need to eat as human beings are intended to eat and keep our bodies physically fit.

DO LOW CHOLESTEROL LEVELS CAUSE CANCER?

Some research, other than that discussed previously, indicates that lower blood-cholesterol levels correlate with an increased incidence of cancer, especially colon cancer.[240] [241] [242] [243] [244] [245] Such studies are welcomed with alacrity by those who are praying for an excuse to pursue their self-destructive habits. "Why should I try to lower my cholesterol if it increases my chance of death from cancer?"

It is far more likely that colon cancer somehow lowers blood cholesterol, causing a mistaken interpretation of the correlation.[246] In other words, cancer lowers cholesterol; low cholesterol does not cause cancer.

It should have been obvious that something strange was happening to produce a positive correlation between low-cholesterol levels and colon cancer. Many studies on both humans and animals have shown strong associations between increasing intake of fat and cholesterol and increasing colon cancer.[247] [248] [249] [250] The intake of cholesterol and fat usually causes spectacular increases in cholesterol levels. Colon cancer also relates closely to the intake of fat and cholesterol. How, then, could a low-cholesterol level possibly relate to an increased rate of colon cancer? It could only happen if colon cancer, once developed, lowered the cholesterol levels. Nothing else makes sense.

Recent research confirms that colon cancer is not caused by low cholesterol levels. Dr. Sven Tornberg and his colleagues studied the rates of colon cancer in 92,000 Swedish subjects who had their cholesterol measured and then were followed up to determine the rates of cancer which developed over the years.[251] Men who had high cholesterol levels in the beginning year of the study had a colon cancer rate 62% higher and a rectal cancer rate 70% higher than those with lower cholesterol levels. The follow-up period in this research averaged nine years from the assessment of cholesterol levels to the diagnosis of cancer.

Obviously, high cholesterol levels are associated with the development of cancer of the colon, *after which* the cancer lowers blood cholesterol levels.

Some studies which showed lowered cholesterol related to increased colon cancer probably used subjects who had undiagnosed colon cancer, which could have been in the process of reducing the cholesterol levels. Later, when diagnosed as having the cancer, they would manifest an even lower cholesterol level.[252] When people with similar cholesterol levels are compared, those who are later diagnosed with colon cancer experience a drop of 13% in cholesterol levels, whereas those who do not contract the cancer raise their cholesterol by about 2% in the same period.[253]

Another way of putting to rest the low-cholesterol, high-colon-cancer idea is to determine whether the pre-cancerous structures called adenomas are more common in people with high or low cholesterol levels. These structures are small tumors which occur in the colon and thereafter may become cancerous.[254] [255] The size and number of these adenomas correlate in a dose-response fashion to subsequent colon cancer.[252] If there is a cause and effect relationship between low cholesterol levels and colon cancer, then there should be a similar relationship between low cholesterol and the pre-cancerous condition. If there is an opposite relationship, then it can be assumed that once the adenomas become cancerous, the cancer lowers the cholesterol levels.

There is no doubt that a direct relationship exists between the incidence of these pre-cancerous adenomas and high cholesterol levels.[253] Therefore, if there is a dose-response relationship between adenomas and colon cancer, there is also a dose response relationship between cholesterol levels and subsequent colon cancer. THE HIGHER THE INITIAL LEVEL OF CHOLESTEROL, THE GREATER WILL BE THE CHANCE OF DEATH FROM COLON CANCER.

Finally, we observe societies that consume little cholesterol and saturated fat and therefore have low cholesterol levels. In such a society, if the low-cholesterol, high-colon-cancer theory were correct, we should expect to see massive numbers of people suffering from colon cancer. In fact, we should observe far greater numbers of cancer patients than in countries such as the U.S., which have high-cholesterol levels. This is not the case. In China, for instance, where the rate of colon cancer is much lower than in the U.S., the cholesterol levels are also far lower.[232]

In an interview with Dr. Ethel Nelson (who conducted the Bangkok study referred to earlier), I asked if colon cancer had increased in Bangkok as the consumption of fat and cholesterol had increased. She replied that colon cancer had considerably increased.[58] She also mentioned that fiber intake had decreased, which also has a definite bearing on colon cancer. (See the chapter on cancer.)

POLYUNSATURATES, HEART DISEASE AND CANCER

What of the increased incidence of cancer among those who have lowered their cholesterol levels with a high intake of polyunsaturated fat? Polyunsaturates produce cancer growth in laboratory animals.[256] [257] A low-fat nutrition program is necessary for optimal health, and switching to a different type of fat may do nothing more than change the instrument of death.

THE ASPIRIN FAD

One of the latest in a series of treatments for heart disease is aspirin. Aspirin, like fish oil, has the ability to decrease blood-platelet activity[258] and thereby decrease the chance of a blood clot which might occlude an artery. There is no doubt that taking several aspirin per week can decrease the risk of a heart attack. This does not mean, however, that heart disease has been abated. And, as with other drug therapies, there is a price to be paid.

One piece of research[259] showed that regular aspirin use is associated with a "non-significant" increase in the rate of stroke of 20 to 30%, a significant increase in kidney cancer in men, a significant increase in colon cancer in both sexes, and a significant increase in heart disease in both sexes! Aspirin also causes considerable damage to the lining of the digestive tract, producing erosions and bleeding of the mucosal linings.[260] [261] [262]

Aspirin is a drug, and like other drugs is laden with problems. It masks symptoms which could warn us of impending disaster and, as in the case of fish fats, may actually increase the severity of the disease. The blood can be thinned and the risk of clotting substantially reduced in a day or two on a nutrition program free of animal products and saturated fats. Since this program will also reverse heart disease, it makes much more sense than to artificially thin blood with aspirin. Heart disease is not due to an aspirin deficiency.

The use of aspirin, fish oil, and polyunsaturates may seem

like the answers to the prayers of those who say," Please, Lord, let me find the cure for my problems in a pill. Don't make me change my eating habits, and for goodness sake don't make me exercise!"

The danger in such foolishness does not lie in the fact that people are using these products to lessen their chances of death from heart disease. The danger is not that such methods may cause more harm than they prevent. The real crime is that a proven method of prevention and reversal is readily available. The method will not be used, however, if the "dreamer" believes his answer lies in polyunsaturates or chemicals. To deny himself the remedy while pursuing his imaginary "will'o the wisp" is to deny himself the opportunity of ridding himself of the disease.

OTHER CONSIDERATIONS

Oat bran

Eating oat bran lowers serum cholesterol levels.[263] [264] [265] However, whether this effect is due to oat bran itself or to some other factor is debatable. Other grain fibers are also adept at lowering cholesterol levels.[266] *Perhaps adding oat bran calories to one's diet causes him to consume fewer calories from animal products and saturated fats.*[267] [268] [269]

However, it does appear that oat bran has a cholesterol-lowering influence superior to that from the fiber from other grains. Recent research has indicated that oat bran lowers cholesterol levels much better than either wheat bran or rice bran.[270] Oat bran also is superior to corn bran in lowering cholesterol levels.[271] Various fibers, other than those found in oat bran, are known to be beneficial, and it is likely that all of them would have some influence in decreasing heart disease. Fiber does bind some cholesterol in the intestine, thereby ensuring that it is transported out of the body rather than being absorbed or re-absorbed. The water-soluble fiber found in oat bran seems to do this best.

Whatever the cause of the lowered cholesterol levels, this much we know: A nutrition program that features little or no animal products, along with large quantities of grains, fruits, vegetables and legumes, will be very high in fiber and very low in fat and cholesterol. Fiber is no panacea, though it is a necessary nutrient. However, the person who believes that he will prevent heart disease by doing nothing more than spooning a bit of oat bran into his cereal is dreaming, especially if that cereal is covered with milk or cream and followed by a fried egg.

Obesity

Obesity relates very closely to heart disease.[272] Women who are 6% or more lower than "ideal" weight have the fewest heart attacks. ("Ideal" weights are those listed on height/weight charts developed by the Metropolitan Life Insurance Company.) For those 5% below ideal weight to 14% above, the rate of heart attacks is increased by 30%. From 15% to 29% above ideal, the rate of heart attacks is 80% greater, and for those who are more than 30% overweight, the rate is 230% greater. This is logical, since both heart disease and obesity have many of the same underlying causes. Figure 5 displays the influence of increasing weights on the rate of heart attacks in women.

We know that people who are lean consume more calories and considerably more calories per pound of body weight than those who are obese[273] (See the chapter on obesity.) Therefore, we can state unequivocally that there are two basic factors that make people obese: (1) What they are eating—not how much and (2) Lack of exercise. Both of these factors also relate closely to the incidence of heart disease.

Surgery

Bypass surgery, in which a vein from the leg or chest cavity is removed and used to bypass an occluded artery in the heart, is an operation which has little value in saving lives. It also causes a great deal of debility and possible brain damage.[274] The bypass is aptly named. It bypasses the problem rather than eliminating it. The operation is done primarily in response to a severe heart pain called angina. Angina is a response to plugging of the coronary arteries which reduces oxygen flow to the heart

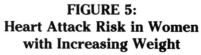

FIGURE 5:
Heart Attack Risk in Women
with Increasing Weight

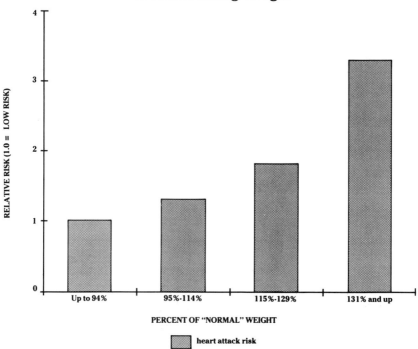

PERCENT OF "NORMAL" WEIGHT

heart attack risk

muscle. It is one of the few warning signals of heart disease, but unfortunately it does not occur until the disease is advanced.

Dr. John McDougall of St. Helena Hospital in California manages a marvelous 12-day program in which his patients follow a pure vegetarian nutrition program and walk regularly. Angina usually disappears shortly on this program.[275] At National Institute of Fitness, we observe the same results. Most of our participants who enter the program with angina are free from the pain in less than three weeks.

The person who suffers angina and switches to a program of pure-vegetarian nutrition can expect to save about $40,000 on a bypass operation and at least another $100 per month on the food bill, since inexpensive starchy foods such as wheat, rice and potatoes will be the staples of his new, healthful way of eating.

We must not forget the previously mentioned work of Dr. Dean Ornish that proves that heart disease is reversible through dietary therapy and other worthwhile lifestyle changes. It certainly seems that a person should try to achieve that reversal through dietary means before submitting oneself to such drastic surgery.

Other techniques such as laser surgery, balloon angioplasty and a "roto rooter" treatment with a mechanical device, are available. These techniques also "bypass" the problem. They are temporary measures at best and will usually require another operation in a few months to a few years.

At the very least, the first therapy should be the program outlined in this book. It should be monitored by the patient's physician, who can make recommendations for safe and effective exercise. The program can do no harm and may save the patient untold agony as well as a great deal of money.

Triglyceride

Triglyceride fat is the type of fat found in the fat cells—an important source of stored energy. When broken down to products known as free fatty acids, it becomes a readily available energy source for the muscles and all other tissue except brain cells.[276]

This fat is also found in the blood, and when excessive, is suspected of contributing to the atherosclerotic process.[277] [278] Triglycerides may, in fact, be the most important risk factors for heart disease and stroke in women.[277] Carbohydrates can raise triglycerides,[278] but I believe that high triglycerides are primarily due to the combined excessive consumption of sugar and fats.

We continually see triglycerides drop on our program of high-starch, low-fat nutrition (provided those levels are high to begin with). Levels above 150 are usually lowered on this regimen, since 70% or more of the calories in our program come from starch. One of our guests, using our very-high-complex carbohydrate program, lowered his triglyceride level from 1300 to 85!

A triglyceride level below 100 is considered ideal, although many people have excellent health with higher levels. The

Tarahumara society referred to earlier has triglycerides higher than 100, but due to their low-fat, low-animal consumption, they have no heart disease. If triglycerides are above 150, it is certainly a good idea to cut back on sugar intake and to eliminate all animal fats and concentrated vegetable fats.

Stress

There are those who make a strong case for stress as a primary contributor to heart disease.[279] I am not convinced, because in World War II the rate of heart disease in Europe was greatly reduced. Granted, the stress must have been overwhelming. But since the people in Europe were cut off from their supplies of animal products, sugar and fat (during the periods of rationing), rates of heart disease fell. As one researcher stated, "Before the late war, mortality from diseases of the circulatory system was rising each year in Norway. This rise ceased during the war, and from 1941 to 1945 there was a well-marked fall in mortality from these diseases. Since the war, there has been a rapid rise in mortality towards the pre-war level."[280] He also mentioned that there were severe dietary restrictions, especially of foods containing fat and cholesterol.

Perhaps excessive stress, like other risk factors for heart disease, contributes to the atherosclerotic process when blood-cholesterol levels rise above 150. Certainly, high levels of stress cannot be good for the health; but then, neither can levels of stress that are too low. Good social relationships, good marriages, and good businesses involve a certain amount of stress, and these stresses strengthen the system if not carried to excess.

Exercise itself is a stress, but without exercise, the system weakens and deteriorates. With the correct amount of exercise, we become much healthier and less apt to die of heart disease and cancer. Exercise carried to the extreme, however, can result in fractures, illness and fatigue.

The personality of the stressed individual appears to be of great importance. Recent research indicates that the busy, harried, overworked person does not necessarily have more heart attacks than anyone else, whereas a person with a hostile, angry personality has a great deal more risk.[281] The person who becomes enraged at slow drivers or who snaps at people who don't respond quickly enough to his or her requests may be in trouble.[281] Lawyers who had high hostility scores on a personality test experienced four times the rate of death from heart disease as those whose personalities were classified as "easygoing."

Anger is obviously a matter of choice, just as surely as eating "killer" foods is a choice. Both choices develop into habits that have the potential to devastate a person's mental and physical health. If one cannot make the choice to be more loving, accepting and forgiving, then it is of paramount importance that he remove animal products from his diet!

WHAT HAVE WE LEARNED?

1.   Heart disease is endemic only to those societies whose citizens are consumers of saturated fats and animal products. It is caused by the consumption of those products.

2.   Heart disease is virtually unknown among people whose blood cholesterol levels are consistently below 150.

3.   When cholesterol levels are below 150, risk factors for heart disease such as hypertension, smoking, sedentary living and high blood sugar cease to be risk factors.

4.   Familial (genetic) tendencies toward heart disease are of consequence only to those people who are consuming the products which can cause the disease. Unless these toxins are consumed, no one will ever know who has a tendency toward heart disease and who does not.

5.   HDL and LDL levels are important when total cholesterol is above 150. Positive changes in these levels can be produced through reducing or eliminating animal products and saturated fats and through regular aerobic exercise.

6.   Fish oil and aspirin as therapy for heart disease may be of some value in preventing heart attacks but not heart

disease and may actually promote atherosclerosis.

7.   The use of drugs to lower cholesterol levels has been proven to reduce death from heart disease but may increase death from cancer, accidents, suicides and other violence.

8.   For the person who has heart disease or has high blood cholesterol, physical fitness attained through regular exercise is the second best of all therapies to prevent death from the disease. As good as it is, however, it does not come close to a pure vegetarian diet in terms of its life-saving potential.

9.   Eggs raise cholesterol levels as fast or faster than any other food. Don't be fooled by the hype from the egg industry.

10.   Heart disease is a reversible condition. It can be reversed with a low-fat, cholesterol-free nutrition program.

11.   Hostility, and not stress per se, is a possible risk factor for heart disease, provided that the cholesterol level is above the threshold level of 150. Learning to rid oneself of anger and hostility is good therapy for not only heart disease but many of life's other dilemmas.

A parting shot—Impotence

If one is willing to take his chances with heart disease and stroke in order to enjoy a fat-laden diet, perhaps he should consider one more factor: Heart disease and cerebrovascular diseases are not the only vascular disorders. Male impotence is another. The risk factors for heart disease are also risk factors for impotence.[282]

The arteries that supply the erectile tissue of the penis can become plugged in the same manner as other arteries, making erection virtually impossible. Hypertensive drugs can also exacerbate the problem of impotence[283] and are in fact the most commonly reported problem with the use of these drugs among men. Diabetes, which injures the nerves, also contributes. All of these factors are engendered by improper eating habits. Certainly potential impotence is another very good reason to prevent or reverse the plugging of arteries through proper nutrition.

REFERENCES

[1]Castelli, W. Quoted in Barnard, N. *The Power of Your Plate*. Book Publishing Company, publishers, Summertown, TN, 1990, p. 20.

[2]Whitaker, J. *Reversing Health Risks*. G.P. Putnams's Sons, publishers, New York, 1988, p. 137.

[3]American Heart Association. 1991 Heart and Stroke Facts, p. 13.

[4]Newman, W. Relation to serum lipoprotein levels and systolic blood pressure to early atherosclerosis. The Bogalusa heart study. N Engl J Med 1986; 314:138-144.

[5]Holman, R. The natural history of atherosclerosis: The early aortic lesions as seen in New Orleans in the middle of the 20th century. Am J Pathol 1958; 34:209-235.

[6]Strong, J. The natural history of atherosclerosis. Am J Pathol 1962; 40:37-49.

[7]Enos, W. Coronary disease among United States soldiers killed in action in Korea; preliminary report. JAMA 1953; 152:1090-1093.

[8]McNamara, J. Coronary artery disease in combat casualties in Vietnam. JAMA 1971; 216:1185-1187.

[9]Montenegro, M. Topography of atherosclerosis in the coronary arteries and aorta. Lab Invest 1968; 18:586-593.

[10]Idem. Fatty streaks in the coronary arteries and aorta. Lab Invest 1968; 18:560-564.

[11]Guyton, A. *Textbook of Medical Physiology*, sixth edition. W.B. Saunders, publisher, Philadelphia, 1981, pp. 857-858.

[12]Anderson, J. The independence of the effects of cholesterol and degree of saturation of the fat in the diet on serum cholesterol in man. Am J Clin Nutr 1976; 29:1184-1189.

[13]Mendis, S. The effects of replacing coconut oil with corn oil on human serum lipid profiles and platelet derived factors active in atherogenesis. Nutrition Reports International 1989; 40:773-782.

[14]Keys, A. Serum cholesterol response to change in dietary lipids. Am J Clin Nutr 1966; 19:175-181.

[15]Hornstra, G. Influence of dietary fat on platelet function in men. Lancet 1973; 1:1155-1157.

[16]O'Brien, J. Acute platelet changes after large meals of saturated fats. Lancet 1976; 1:878-880.

[17]Simpson, H. Hypertriglyceridemia and hypercoagulability. Lancet 1983; 1:786-789.

[18]Welch, C. Cineocoronary arteriography in young men. Circulation 1970; 42:647-652.

[19]Page, I. Prediction of coronary heart disease based on clinical suspicion, age, total cholesterol and triglycerides. Circulation 1970; 42:625-645.

[20]Zampogna, A. Relationship between lipids and occlusive coronary artery disease. Arch Intern Med 1980; 140:1067-1069.

[21]Cohn, P. Serum lipid levels in angiographically defined coronary artery disease. Ann Intern Med 1976; 84:241-245.

[22]Jenkins, P. Severity of coronary atherosclerosis related to lipoprotein concentration. Br Med J 1978; 2:388-391.

[23]Pocock, S. Concentrations of high-density lipoprotein cholesterol, triglycerides, and total cholesterol in ischaemic heart disease. Br Med J 1989; 298:998-1002.

[24]Rosengren, A. Impact of cardiovascular risk factors on coronary heart disease and mortality among middle-aged diabetic men: A general population study. Br Med J 1989; 299:1127-1131.

[25]Pekkanen, J. Risk factors and 25-year risk of coronary heart disease: The Finnish cohorts of the seven countries study. Br Med J 1989; 299:81-85.

[26]Benfante, R. Is elevated serum-cholesterol level a risk factor for coronary heart disease in the elderly? JAMA 1990; 263:393-396.

[27]Castelli, W. Epidemiology of coronary heart disease: The Framingham Study. Am J Med 1984; 76:4-12.

[28]Kannel, W. Cholesterol in the prediction of atherosclerotic disease: New perspectives based on the Framingham Study. Ann Intern Med 1979; 90:85-91.

[29]Stamler, J. Is the relationship between serum cholesterol and risk of premature death from coronary heart disease continuous and graded? JAMA 1986; 256:2823-2828.

[30]Pritikin, N. *The Pritikin Program for Diet and Exercise.* Grosset and Dunlap, publishers, 1979, p. 16.

[31]McDougall, J. *McDougall's Medicine, A Challenging Second Opinion.* New Century, publishers, 1985, p. 105.

[32]Connor, W. The key role of nutritional factors in the prevention of coronary heart disease. Prev Med 1972; 1:49-83.

[33]Ornish, D. Can lifestyle changes reverse coronary artery disease? Lancet 1990; 336:129-133.

[34]Campbell, T. Quoted in USA Today. In Healthful Living, East Beats West, June 6, 1990, p. 1D-2D.

[35]Campbell, T. Personal communication, May, 1990.

[36]Castelli, W. Quoted in the Aviation Medical Bulletin, May, 1990, p. 1.

[37]Cooper, K. *Controlling Cholesterol.* Bantam Books, publishers, New York, 1988, p. 42.

[38]Hubbard, J. Nathan Pritikin's heart. N Engl J Med 1985; 313:52.

[39]Connor, W. The plasma lipids, lipoproteins and diet of the Tarahumara Indians of Mexico. Am J Clin Nutr 1978; 31:1131-1142.

[40]What's your risk? A layman's guide to cardiovascular disease. Physician Sports Med 1990.

[41]McDougall, J. Healthy by choice. Vegetarian Times, June, 1990, p. 16.

[42]Moll, P. Total cholesterol and lipoproteins in school children: prediction of coronary heart disease in adult relatives. Circulation 1983; 67:127-134.

[43]Cuthbert, J. Detection of familial hypercholesterolemia by assaying functional low-density-lipoprotein receptors on lymphocytes. N Engl J Med 1986; 314:879-883.

[44]Williams, R. Evidence that men with a familial hypercholesterolemia can avoid early coronary death. JAMA 1986; 255:219-224.

[45]Reed, T. Young-adult cholesterol as a predictor of familial ischemic heart disease. Prev Med 1986; 14:292-303.

[46]Van Dipthout, W. Distributions and determinants of total and high-density-lipoprotein cholesterol in Dutch children and young adults. Prev Med 1985; 14:169-180.

[47]Seed, M. Relation of serum lipoproteins(a) concentration and apolipoprotein phenotype to coronary heart disease in patients with familial hypercholesterolemia. N Engl J Med 1990; 322:1494-1499.

[48]Connor, W. The plasma lipids, lipoproteins, and diet of the Tarahumara Indians of Mexico. Am J Clin Nutr 1978; 31:1131-1142.

[49]Pritikin, N. *The Pritikin Program for Diet and Exercise.* Grosset and Dunlap, publishers, New York, 1979, p. 25.

[50]Groom, D. Cardiovascular observations on Tarahumara Indians—the modern Spartans. Am Heart J 1971; 81:304-314.

[51]Anderson, R. Nutritional appraisals in Mexico. Am J Pub Health 1948; 38:1126-1135.

[52]Cerqueira, M. The food and nutrient intakes of the Tarahumara Indians of Mexico. Am J Clin Nutr 1979; 32:905-915.

[53]McDougall, J. The McDougall Tapes. Audiocassette program, 1989, P.O. Box 14039, Santa Rosa, California 95402.

[54]McMurry, M. Dietary cholesterol and the plasma lipids and lipoproteins in the Tarahumara Indians: A people habituated to a low-cholesterol diet after weaning. Am J Clin Nutr 1982; 35:741-744.

[55]Campbell, T. A study on diet, nutrition and disease in the People's Republic of China. Part 1. Division of Nutritional Sciences, Cornell University, Ithica, New York, pp. 1-8.

[56]Campbell, T. Personal communication. May 9, 1990.

[57]Campbell, T. Quoted in the New York Times, May 8, 1990, p. C-4.

[58]Nelson, E. Personal communication. November 15, 1990.

[59]Hirst, A. A comparison of atherosclerosis of the aorta and coronary arteries in Bangkok and Los Angeles. Am J Clin Pathol 1962; 38:162-170.

[60]Gramenzi, A. Association between certain foods and myocardial infarct in women. Br Med J 1990; 300:771-773.

[61]Nelson, E. Perils of prosperity. Saturday Evening Post, May/June 1990, pp. 14, 16, 106-110.

[62]Wilhelmsen, L. Nine year's follow-up of a maximal exercise test in a random population of middle-aged men. Cardiology 1981; 68: supplement 2:1-8.

[63]Sobloski, J. Protection against ischemic heart disease in the Belgian Physical Fitness Study: Physical fitness rather than physical activity? Am J Epidemiol 1987; 125:601-610.

[64]Pekkanen, J. Risk factors and 25-year risk of coronary heart disease in a male population with a high incidence of the disease: The Finnish cohorts of the seven-countries study. Br Med J 1989; 299:81-84.

[65]Stamler, J. Lifestyles, major risk factors, proof and public policy. Circulation 1978; 58:3-19.

[66]Rosengren, A. Impact of cardiovascular risk factors on coronary heart disease and mortality among middle-aged men: A general population study. Br Med J 1989; 299:1127-1131.

[67]Freestone, S. Effect of coffee and cigarette smoking on the blood pressure of untreated and diuretic-treated hypertensive patients. Am J Med 1982; 73:348-353.

[68]Goldman, L. The decline in ischemic heart disease mortality rates. An analysis of the comparative effects of medical interventions and changes in lifestyle. An Intern Med 1984; 101:825-836.

[69]Paffenbarger, R. Physical activity, all-cause mortality and longevity of college alumni. N Engl J Med 1986; 314:605-613.

[70]Meyers, Robert J., former chief actuary of the Social Security Administration. Quoted in the Salt Lake Tribune, Friday, May 11, 1990.

[71]Cholesterol and cigarettes per day. Aviation Medical Bulletin, May, 1990.

[72]Muldoon, M. Lowering cholesterol concentrations and mortality: A quantitative review of primary prevention trials. Br Med J 1990; 301:309-314.

[73]Friend, T. T.V. hours and kids' cholesterol. USA Today, November 14, 1990.

[74]Gold, K. Quoted in Friend, T. T.V. hours and kids' cholesterol. USA Today, November 14, 1990.

[75]Mendis, S. The effects of replacing coconut oil with corn oil on human serum lipid profiles and platelet derived factors active in atherogenesis. Nutr Reports International 1989; 40:773-782.

[76]Jackson, T. Influence of polyunsaturated and saturated fats on plasma lipids and lipoproteins in man. Am J Clin Nutr 1984; 39:589-597.

[77]Paul, R. On the mechanism of hypocholesterolemic effects of polyunsaturated lipids. Adv Lip Res 1979; 17:155-171.

[78]Goodnight, S. Polyunsaturated fatty acids, hyperlipedemia and thrombosis. Arteriosclerosis 1982; 2:87-113.

[79]Shepherd, J. Effects of saturated and polyunsaturated fat diets on the chemical composition and metabolism of low-density lipoproteins in man. J Lipid Res 1980; 21:91-99.

[80]Turner, J. Effect of changing dietary fat saturation on low-density lipoprotein metabolism in man. Am J Physiol 1981; 241:E57-E63.

[81]Lewis, B. Towards an improved lipid-lowering diet: Additive effects of changes in nutrient intake. Lancet 1981; 2:1310-1313.

[82]Vega, G. Influence of polyunsaturated fats on composition of plasma lipoprotein and apolipoprotein. J Lipid Res 1982; 23:811-822.

[83]Reddy, B. Effect of a diet with high levels of protein and fat on colon carcinogenesis in f344 rats treated with 1,2 dimethylhydrazine. JNCI 1976; 57:567-569.

[84]Artzenius, A. Diet, lipoproteins and the progression of coronary atherosclerosis. The Leiden Intervention Trial. N Engl J Med 1985; 312:805-811.

[85]Mensink, R. Effect of dietary *trans* fatty acids on high-density and low-density lipoprotein cholesterol levels in healthy subjects. N Engl J Med 1990; 323:439-445.

[86]Kromhout, D. The inverse relation between fish consumption and 20-year mortality from coronary heart disease. N Engl J Med 1985; 312:1205-1209.

[87]Bjerregaard, P. Mortality from ischemic heart disease and cerebrovascular disease in Greenland. Int J Epidemiol 1988; 17:514-519.

[88]Gramenzi, A. Association between certain foods and risk of acute myocardial infarction in women. Br Med J 1990; 300:771-773.

[89]Dyerberg, J. Hemostatic function and platelet polyunsaturated fatty acids in Eskimos. Lancet 1979; 2:433-435.

[90]Sanders, T. The effect of dietary supplements of omega-3 polyunsaturated fatty acid on the composition of platelets and plasma choline phosphoglycerides. Br Med J 1981; 45:613-616.

[91]Knapp, H. In vivo indexes of platelet and vascular function during fish-oil administration in patients with atherosclerosis. N Engl J Med 1986; 314:937-942.

[92]Zucker, M. Effects of dietary fish oil on platelet function and plasma lipids in hyperlipoproteinemic and normal subjects. Atherosclerosis 1988; 73:13-22.

[93]Wilt, T. Fish oil supplementation does not lower plasma cholesterol in men with hypercholesterolemia. Results of a randomized, placebo-controlled crossover study. Ann Intern Med 1989; 111:900-905.

[94]Sztern, M. Short-term effects of fish oil on human lipid levels. J Nutr 1991; 2:255-259.

[95]O'Brien, B. Human plasma-lipid responses to red meat, poultry, fish and eggs. Am J Clin Nutr 1980; 33:2573-2580.

[96]Fehily, A. The effects of fatty fish on plasma lipid and lipoprotein concentrations. Am J Clin Nutr 1983; 38:349-351.

[97]Flynn, M. Serum lipids in humans fed diets containing beef, fish or poultry. Am J Clin Nutr 1981; 34:2734-2741.

[98]Flynn, M. Dietary "meats" and serum lipids. Am J Clin Nutr 1982; 35:935-942.

[98.1]Glauber, H. Adverse metabolic effect of omega-3 fatty acids in non-insulin-dependent diabetes mellitus. Ann Intern Med 1988; 108:663-668.

[99]Barnard, N. *The Power of Your Plate.* Book Publishing Co., publishers, Summertown, TN, 1990, p. 23.

[100]Sanders, T. Cod-liver oil, platelet fatty acids, and bleeding time. [Letter] Lancet 1980; 1:1189.

[101]Sanders, T. Effect on blood lipids and hemostases of a supplement of cod-liver oil, rich in eico-sapentaenoic and docosadhexaenoic acids, in healthy young men. Clin Sci 1981; 61:317-324.

[102]Grundy, S. Comparison of monounsaturated fatty acids and carbohydrates for lowering plasma cholesterol. N Engl J Med 1986; 314:745-748.

[103]Carroll, K. Experimental evidence of dietary factors and hormone-dependent cancers. Cancer Res 1975; 35:3374-3383.

[104]Miller, G. Fat consumption and factor VII coagulant activity in middle-aged men: An association between a dietary and thrombogenic coronary risk factor. Atherosclerosis 1989; 78:19-24.

[105]Marckmann, P. Effectsd of total fat content and fatty acid composition in diet on factor VII coagulant activity and blood lipids. Atherosclerosis 1990; 80:227-233.

[106]Salonen, J. Effects of antioxidant supplementation on platelet function: A randomized pair-matched, placebo-controlled, double-blind trial in men with low antioxidant status. Am J Clin Nutr 1991; 53:1222-1229.

[106.1]Gaziano, J. Beta Carotene therapy for chronic stable angina. Abstract presented to the American Heart Association 63rd scientific sessions, November 12-15, 1990.

[107]Pan, W. Relationship of clinical diabetes and asymptomatic hyperglycemia to risk of coronary-heart-disease mortality in men and women. Am J Epidemiol 1988; 128:389-401.

[108]Jarrett, R. Type 2 (non-insulin dependent) diabetes mellitus and cardio-vascular disease-putative association via common antecedents; further evidence from the Whitehall study. Diabetologia 1988; 31:737-740.

[109]Fuller, J. Mortality from coronary heart disease and stroke in relation to degree of glycemia. The Whitehall study. Br Med J 1983; 287:867-870.

[110]Urberg, M. A correlation between serum cholesterol and glycostylated hemoglobin in non-diabetic humans. J Fam Pract 1989; 28:269-274.

[111]Neighbor, W. Commentary. J Fam Pract 1989; 28:273-274.

[112]McDougall, J. *McDougall's Medicine: A Challenging Second Opinion.* New Century, publishers, Piscataway, NJ, 1985, p. 211.

[113]Kipnis, D. Insulin secretion in normal and diabetic individuals. Adv Intern Med 1970; 16:103-134.

[114]Health Implications of Obesity. National Institutes of Health Consensus Conference Statement. 1990; 5(9):4.

[115]Veteran's Administration Cooperative Study Group on Antihypertensive Agents. Effects of treatment on morbidity in hypertension: Results in patients with diastolic blood pressures averaging 115 through 129 mm hg.

[116]Rosenman, R. A study of comparative blood pressure measures in predicting risk of coronary heart disease. Circulation 1976; 54:51-58.

[117]McDougall, J. *McDougall's Medicine: A Challenging Second Opinion.* New Century, publishers, Piscataway, NJ, 1985, pp. 170-200.

[118]Freis, E. Hemodynamics of hypertension. Physiol Review 1960; 40:27-54.

[119]Frolich, E. Reexamination of the hemodynamics of hypertension. Am J Med Sci 1969; 257:9-23.

[120]Freidman, M. Effect of unsaturated fats upon lipemia and conjunctival circulation. JAMA 1965; 193:110-114.

[121]Williams, A. Increases blood-cell agglutination following ingestion of fat; a factor contributing to cardiac ischemia, coronary insufficiency and anginal pain. Angiology 1957; 8:29-40.

[122]Cullen, C. Intravascular aggregation and adhesiveness of the blood elements associated with alimentary lipemia and injections of large molecular substances. Circulation 1954; 9:335.

[123]Dahl, L. Salt intake and salt need. N Engl J Med 1958; 258:1152.

[124]Ernst, E. Blood rheology in vegetarians. Br J Nutr 1986; 56:555-560.

[125]Rouse, I. Blood-pressure-lowering effect of a vegetarian diet: Controlled trial in normotensive subjects. Lancet 1983; 1:5-10.

[126]Margetts, B. Vegetarian diet in mild hypertension: A randomized controlled trial. Br Med J 1986; 293:1468-1471.

[127]Beilin, L. Vegetarian diet and blood pressure levels: Incidental or causal association. Am J Clin Nutr 1988; 48:806-810.

[128]Lindahl, O. A vegan regimen with reduced medication in the treatment of hypertension. Br Med J 1984; 52:11-20.

[129]Ames, R. Elevation of serum lipid levels during diuretic therapy of hypertension. A Veteran's Administration-National Heart, Lung and Blood Institute cooperative study on antihypertensive therapy: Mild hypertension. Am J Med 1976; 61:748-757.

[130]Goldman, A. Serum lipoprotein levels during chlorothalidone therapy. JAMA 1980; 244:1691-1695.

[131]Grimm, R. Effects of thiazide diuretics on plasma lipids and lipoproteins in mildly hypertensive patients. Ann Intern Med 1981; 94:7-11.

[132]Weidmann, P. Effects of antihypertensive therapy on serum lipoproteins. Hypertension 1983; 5:120-131.

[133]Shaw, J. Beta blockers and plasma triglycerides [letter]. Br Med J 1978; 1:986.

[134]Day, J. Metabolic consequences of atenolol and propranolol in treatment of essential hypertension. Br Med J 1979; 1:77-80.

[135]England, J. The effect of metoprolol and atenolol on plasma high-density lipoprotein levels in man. Clin Exper Pharmacol Physiol 1980; 7:329-333.

[136]Leon, A. Blood lipid effects of antihypertensive therapy: A soluble blind comparison of the effects of methyldopa and propranolol. J Clin Pharmacol 1984; 24:209-217.

[137]Chick, T. The effect of antihypertensive medication on exercise performance: A review. Med and Sci of Sports and Exerc 1987; 20:447-454.

[138]Psalty, M. The relative risk of incident coronary heart disease associated with recently stopping the use of B-blockers. JAMA 1990; 263:1653-1657.

[139]Medical Research Council Working Party. MRC trial of mild hypertension: Principal results. Br Med J 1985; 291:97-104.

[140]Stewart, I. Relation of reduction in pressure to first myocardial infarction in patients receiving treatment for severe hypertension: Principal results. Lancet 1979; 1:861-865.

[141]Why does blood pressure rise with age? [Editorial] Lancet 1981; 2:289.

[142]Freis, E. Salt, volume and the prevention of hypertension. Circulation 1976; 53:589-595.

[143]Connor, W. The plasma lipids, lipoproteins and diet of the Tarahumara Indians of Mexico. Am J Clin Nutr 1978; 31:1131-1142.

[144]Roberts, J. Blood pressure levels of persons 6-74 years. United States, 1971-1974. DHEW publication #78-1648 203, 1977, pp. 1-31.

[145]Shaper, A. Cardiovascular disease in the tropics III. Blood pressure and hypertension. Br Med J 1972; 3:805-808.

[146]Kaminer, B. Blood pressure in Bushmen of the Kalahari Desert. Circulation 1960; 22:289-292.

[147]McDougall, J. Personal communication, September 1988, St. Helena, California.

[148]Castelli, W. Incidence of coronary heart disease and lipoprotein levels. The Framingham study. JAMA 1986; 256:2835-2838.

[148.1]Stampfer, M. A prospective study of cholesterol, apolipoproteins, and the risk of myocardial infarction. N Engl J Med 1991; 325:373-381.

[149]Gordon, T. High density lipoprotein as a protective factor against coronary heart disease. Am J Med 1977; 62:707-714.

[150]Enger, S. High-density lipoprotein (HDL) and physical activity: The influence of physical exercise, age and smoking on HDL-cholesterol and the HDL-total cholesterol ratio. Scand J Clin Lab Invest 1977; 37:251-255.

[151]Adner, M. Elevated high-density lipoprotein levels in marathon runners. JAMA 1980; 243:534-536.

[152]Hartung, G. Relationship of diet to HDL in middle-aged marathon runners, joggers and inactive men. N Engl J Med 1980; 302:357-361.

[153]Danner, S. Effect of physical exercise on blood lipids and adipose tissue composition in young, healthy men. Atherosclerosis 1984:53:83-90.

[154]Stein, R. Effects of different training intensities on lipoprotein cholesterol fractions in healthy middle-aged men. Am Heart J 1990; 119:277-283.

[155]Council on Scientific Affairs. Dietary and pharmacologic therapy for the lipid risk factors. JAMA 1983; 250:1873-1879.

[156]Paoletti, R. Influence of Bezafibrate, Fenofibrate, and nicotinic acid and Etofibrate on plasma-high-density lipoprotein levels. Am J Cardiol 1983; 52:21B-27B.

[157]Cooper, K. *Controlling Cholesterol.* Bantam Books, publishers, New York, p. 247.

[158]Stein, E. Lowering of plasma cholesterol levels in free-living adolescent males; use of natural and synthetic polyunsaturated foods to provide balanced-fat diets. Am J Clin Nutr 1975; 28:1204-1216.

[159]Shepherd, J. Effects of saturated and polyunsaturated fat diets on the chemical composition and metabolism of low-density lipoproteins in man. J Lipid Res 1980; 21:91-99.

[160]Turner, J. Effect of changing dietary fat saturation on low-density lipoprotein metabolism in man. Am J Physiol 1981; 241:E57-E63.

[161]Lewis, B. Towards an improved lipid-lowering diet: additive effects of changes in nutrient intake. Lancet 1981; 2:1310-1313.

[162]Vega, G. Influence of polyunsaturated fats on composition of plasma lipoprotein and apolipoprotein. J Lipid Res 1982; 23:811-822.

[163]Jackson, R. Influence of polyunsaturated and saturated fats on plasma lipids and lipoproteins in man. Am J Clin Nutr 1984; 39:589-597.

[164]Hjermann, I. The effects of dietary changes in high-density-lipoprotein cholesterol. The Oslo study. Am J Med 1979; 66:195-209.

[165]Brussard, J. Effects of amount and type of dietary fat on serum lipids, lipoproteins and apoproteins in man. Atherosclerosis, 1980; 36:515-527.

[166]Ernst, N. Changes in plasma lipids and lipoproteins after a modified-fat diet. Lancet 1980; 2:111-113.

[167]Schaefer, E. The effects of low-cholesterol, high-polyunsaturated-fat and low-fat diets on plasma lipid and lipoprotein cholesterol levels in normal and hypercholesterolemic subjects. Am J Clin Nutr 1981; 34:1758.

[168]Harris, W. The comparative reduction of the plasma lipids and lipoproteins by dietary polyunsaturated fats: Salmon oil vs. vegetable oils. Metabolism 1983; 32:179-184.

[169]Becker, N. Effects of saturated, monounsaturated, and w-6 polyunsaturated fatty acids on plasma lipids, lipoproteins and apoproteins in humans. Am J Clin Nutr 1983; 37:355-360.

[170]Weisburger, J. Nutrition and cancer. On the mechanisms bearing on causes of cancer of the colon, breast, prostate, and stomach. Bulletin of the New York Academy of Medicine 1980; 56:673.

[171]Hill, P. Environmental factors and breast and prostatic cancer. Cancer Res 1981; 41:3817-3818.

[172]Hill, P. Diet and endocrine related cancer. Cancer 1977; 39:1820-1826.

[173]Nishizuka, Y. Biological influence of fat intake on mammary cancer and mammary tissue: Experimental correlates. Prev Med 1978; 7:218-224.

[174]Sacks, F. Plasma lipoprotein levels in vegetarians: The effect of ingestion of fats from diary products. JAMA 1985; 254:1337-1341.

[175]Grobbe, D. Coffee, caffeine, and cardiovascular disease in men. N Engl J Med 1990; 323:1026-1032.

[176]Bonaa, K. Coffee and cholesterol: Is it all in the brewing? Br Med J 1988; 297:1103-1104.

[177]Thelle, D. Coffee and cholesterol in epidemiological and experimental studies. Atherosclerosis 1987; 67:97-103.

[178]Williams, P. Coffee intake and elevated cholesterol and apolipoprotein B levels in men. JAMA 1985; 253:1407-1411.

[179]Tverdal, A. Coffee consumption and death from coronary heart disease in middle-aged men and women. Br Med J 1990; 300:566-569.

[180]Blair, S. Physical fitness and all-cause mortality. A prospective study of healthy men and women. JAMA 1989; 262:2395-2401.

[181]McMurry, M. The absorption of cholesterol and the sterol balance in the Tarahumara Indians of Mexico fed cholesterol-free and high-cholesterol diets. Am J Clin Nutr 1985; 41:1289-1298.

[182]Handa, K. Alcohol consumption, serum lipids and severity of angiographically determined coronary artery disease. Am J Cardiol 1990; 65:287-289.

[183]Intersalt Cooperative Research Group. Intersalt: An international study of electrolyte excretion and blood pressure. Results for 24-hour urinary sodium and potassium excretion. Br Med J 1988; 297:319-328.

[184]Kaelber, C. Symposium on alcohol and cardiovascular diseases. Circulation 1981; 64, suppl III:1-84.

[185]Shultz, J. National Centers for Disease Control. Quoted in the Flagstaff Sun, Sunday, March 25, 1990, p. 4.

[186]Whitaker, J. *Reversing Health Risks*. G.P. Putnam's Sons, publishers, 1988, p. 44.

[187]Cooper, K. *Running Without Fear.* M. Evans and Co., publishers, 1985, pp. 33, 43.

[188]Meinertz, H. Soy protein and casein in cholesterol-enriched diets: Effects on plasma lipoproteins in normolipidemic subjects. Am J Clin Nutr 1989; 50:786-793.

[188.1]Meinertz, H. Soy protein and casein in cholesterol enriched diets: Effects on plasma lipoproteins in normolipidemic subjects. Am J Clin Nutr 1989; 50:786-793.

[188.2]Pesciatini. Treatment of dyslipedaemia with a simple low-fat diet and with a combination of a low-fat diet and a formulation containing soybean protein. Int J Clin Pharm Res 1985; 5:199-204.

[188.3]Jenkins, D. Hypocholesterolemic effect of vegetable protein in a hypocaloric diet. Atherosclerosis 1989; 78:99-107.

[189]Sirtori, C. Soybean-protein diet in the treatment of type-II hyperlipoproteinaemia. Lancet 1977; 1:275-277.

[190]Alladi, S. Lipids, lipoproteins and lipolytic activity in plasma with dietary protein changes. Nutrition Reports International 1988; 40:653-661.

[191]Radcliffe, J. A comparison of the effects of dietary casein and cottonseed isolate in serum and hepatic lipids in the rat. Nutrition Reports International 1989; 40:821-826.

[192]Johnson, C. Effects of exercise, dietary cholesterol, and dietary fat on blood lipids. Arch Intern Med 1990; 150:137-141.

[193]Shekelle, R. Dietary cholesterol and ischemic heart disease. Lancet, 1989; 1:1177-1178.

[194]Connor, W. The key role of nutritional factors in the prevention of coronary heart disease. Prev Med 1972; 1:48-83.

[195]Willet, W. Chewing the fat. How much and what kind. N Engl J Med 1991; 324:121-123.

[196]Connor, W. The key role of nutritional factors in the prevention of coronary heart disease. Prev Med 1972; 1:48-83.

[197]Wells, V. Egg yolk and serum cholesterol levels: The importance of dietary cholesterol intake. Br Med J 1963; 1:577-581.

[198]Connor, W. The interrelated effects of dietary cholesterol and fat upon human serum lipid levels. J Clin Invest 1964; 43:1691-1696.

[199]Slater, G. Plasma cholesterol and triglycerides in men with added eggs in the diet. Nutr Rep Int 1976; 14:249-252.

[200]Porter, M. Effect of dietary egg on serum cholesterol and triglyceride of human males. Am J Clin Nutr 1977; 39:490-495.

[201]Flynn, M. Effect of dietary egg on human serum cholesterol and triglycerides. Am J Clin Nutr 1979; 32:1051-1057.

[202]Flaim, E. Plasma lipid and lipoprotein cholesterol concentrations in adult males consuming normal and high-cholesterol diets under controlled conditions. Am J Clin Nutr 1981; 34:1103-1108.

[203]Dawber, T. Eggs, serum cholesterol, and coronary heart disease. Am J Clin Nutr 1982; 36:617-625.

[204]Connor, W. Dietary cholesterol and the pathogenesis of atherosclerosis. Geriatrics 1961: 16:407-415.

[205]Connor W. The serum lipids in men receiving high-cholesterol and cholesterol-free diets. J Clin Invest 1961; 40:894-901.

[206]Connor, W. Effect of dietary cholesterol upon serum lipids in man. J Lab Clin Med 1961; 57:331-342.

[207]Beveridge, J. The response of man to dietary cholesterol. J Nutr 1960; 71:61-65.

[208]Mattson, F. Effect of dietary cholesterol on serum cholesterol in man. Am J Clin Nutr 1972; 25:589-594.

[209]O'Brien, B. Human plasma-lipid responses to red meat, poultry, fish, and eggs. Am J Clin Nutr 1980; 33:2573-2580.

[210]Roberts, S. Does egg feeding (i.e., dietary cholesterol) affect plasma cholesterol in humans? The results of a double-blind study. Am J Clin Nutr 1981; 34:2092-2099.

[211]Sacks, F. Ingestion of egg raises plasma-low-density lipoproteins in free-living subjects. Lancet 1984; 1:647-649.

[212]Scrambled. Time Magazine, May 13, 1991, p. 50.

[213]Stephen, A. Trends in individual consumption of dietary fat in the United States, 1920-1984. Am J Clin Nutr 1990; 52:457-469.

[214]Moore, T. The cholesterol myth. Atlantic Monthly, September 1989, pp. 36-70.

[215]Griffin, G. Cholesterol Myth Club on a par with the Flat Earth Society. Postgrad Med 1990; 87:13, 16.

[216]The Lipid Research Coronary Primary Prevention Trial Results: 1. Reduction in incidence of coronary heart disease. JAMA 1984; 251:351-364.

[217]The Multiple Risk Factor Intervention Trial Research Group. Mortality rates after 10.5 years for participants in the Multiple Risk Factor Intervention Trial: Findings related to a priori hypothesis of the trial. JAMA 1990; 263:1795-1801.

[218]Multiple Risk Factor Interventions Trial Research Group. Mortality after 10½ years for hypertensive participants in the Multiple Risk Factor Intervention Trial. Circulation 1990; 82:1616-1628.

[218.1]Browner, W. What if Americans ate less fat? JAMA 1991; 265:3285-3291.

[219]Ornish, D. Can lifestyle changes reverse coronary heart disease? The lifestyle heart trial. Lancet 1990; 336:129-133.

[220]American Heart Association Bulletin.

[221]Remington, D. *The Bitter Truth about Artificial Sweeteners.* Vitality House International, publishers, 1987, p. 44.

[222]Shapiro, L. A new menu to heal the heart. Newsweek, July 30, 1980, pp. 58-59.

[223]Cholesterol reduction and the regression of coronary disease. Journal Watch 1991; 7:9.

[224]Artzenius, A. Diet, lipoproteins and the progression of coronary atherosclerosis. The Leiden Intervention Trial. N Engl J Med 1985; 312:1205-1209.

[225]Wissler, R. Studies of regression of advanced atherosclerosis in experimental animals and man. Annals of the New York Academy of Sciences 1976; 275:363-377.

[226]Buchwald, H. The partial ileal bypass operation in treatment of hyperlipidemias. Advan Exp Med Biol 1974; 63:221-230.

[227]Blankenhorn, D. Beneficial effects of combined colestipol-niacin therapy on coronary atherosclerosis and coronary venous bypass grafts. JAMA 1987; 257:3233-3240.

[228]Kane, J. Regression of coronary atherosclerosis during treatment of familial hypercholesterolemia with combined drug regimens. JAMA 1990; 264:3007-3012.

[229]Cashin-Hemphill, L. Beneficial effects of colestipol-niacin on coronary atherosclerosis: A 4-year follow-up. JAMA 1990; 264:3013-3017.

[230]Brown, G. Regression of coronary artery disease as a result of intensive lipid-lowering therapy in men with high levels of apolipoprotein B. N Engl J Med 1990; 323:1289-1298.

[231]Hubbard, J. Nathan Pritikin's Heart. N Engl J Med 1985; 313:52.

[232]Peto, R. Plasma cholesterol, coronary heart disease, and cancer. Br Med J 1989; 298:1249.

[233]Blankenhorn, D. The influence of diet on the appearance of new lesions in human coronary arteries. JAMA 1990; 263:1646-1652.

[234]Klaper, M. Vegan nutrition: Just what the doctor ordered. AHIMSA videotape #12. American Vegan Society, Malaga, NJ, 1989.

[235]Criqui, H. Epidemiology of atherosclerosis: An updated overview. Am J Cardiol 1986; 57:18c-223c.

[236]Pearce, M. Incidence of cancer in men on a diet high in polyunsaturated fat. Lancet, 1971; 1:464-467.

[237]Committee of Principal Investigators. A cooperative trial in the primary prevention of ischemic heart disease using clofibrate. Br Heart J 1978; 40:1069-1118.

[238]Feinleib, M. Summary of a workshop in cholesterol and non-cardiovascular-disease mortality. Prev Med 1982; 11:360-367.

[239]Reduction in the incidence of coronary heart disease: The Lipid Research Coronary Primary Prevention Trial Results, I. JAMA 1984; 251:365-374.

[239.1]Timo, E. Long-term mortality after 5-year multifactorial primary prevention of cardiovascular diseases in middle-aged men. JAMA 1991; 266:1225-1229.

[240]Rose, G. Colon cancer and blood cholesterol. Lancet 1974; i:181-183.

[241]Williams, R. Cancer incidence by levels of cholesterol. JAMA 1981; 245:247-252.

[242]Kark, J. The relationship of serum cholesterol to the incidence of cancer in Evans County, Georgia. J Chron Dis 1980; 33:311-322.

[243]Cambien, F. Total serum cholesterol and cancer mortality in a middle-aged population. Am J Epidemiol 1980; 112:388-394.

[244]Stemmerman, G. Serum cholesterol and colon cancer incidence in Hawaiian Japanese men. JNCI 1981; 67:1179-1182.

[245]Kagan, A. Serum cholesterol and mortality in a Japanese-American population: The Honolulu Heart Program. Am J Epidemiol 1981; 114:11-20.

[246]Rose, G. Plasma lipids and mortality: A source of error. Lancet 1980; 1:523-526.

[247]Colon cancer and diet, with special reference to intakes of fat and fiber. Am J Clin Nutr 1976; 29:1417-1426.

[248]Cruse, P. Dietary cholesterol is co-carcinogenic for human colon cancer. Lancet 1979; 1:752-755.

[249]Reddy, B. Effect of a diet with high levels of protein and fat on colon carcinogenesis in F344 rats treated with 1,2=dimethylhydrazine. JNCI 1976; 57:567-569.

[250]Broitman, S. Polyunsaturated fat, cholesterol and large-bowel carcinogenesis. Cancer 1977; 40:2455-2463.

[251]Tornberg, S. Risks of cancer of the colon and rectum in relation to serum cholesterol and beta-lipoprotein. N Engl J Med 1986; 315:1629-1633.

[252]Mannes, G. Relation between the frequency of colorectal adenoma and the serum cholesterol level. N Engl J Med 1986; 315:1634-1638.

[253]Winawer, D. Declining serum cholesterol levels prior to diagnosis of colon cancer. JAMA 1990; 263:2083-2085.

[254]Correa, P. The epidemiology of colorectal polyps. Prevalance in New Orleans and international comparisons. Cancer 1977; 39:2258-2264.

[255]Muto, T. The evolution of cancer of the colon and rectum. Cancer 1975; 36:2251-2270.

[256]Reddy, B. Effect of quality and quantity of dietary fat and dimethylhydrazine in colon carcinogenesis in rats. Proc Soc Exp Bio Med 1976; 151:237-239.

[257]Hopkins. G. Polyunsaturated fatty acids as promoters of mammary carcinogenesis induced in Sprague-Dawley rats by 7, 12-dimethlybenz[a]anthracene. JNCI 1981; 66:517-522.

[258]Rome, L. Aspirin as a quantitative acetylating reagent for the fatty acid oxygenase that forms prostaglandins. Prostaglandins 1976; 11:23-29.

[259]Paganinni-Hill, A. Aspirin use and chronic diseases: A cohort study of the elderly. Br Med J 1989; 299:1247-1250.

[260]Faust, T. Effects of aspirin on gastric mucosal prostaglandin E-2 and F-2 content and on gastric mucosal injury in humans receiving fish oil or aspirin. Gastroenterology 1990; 98:586-591.

[261]Cohen, N. Protection against aspirin-induced antral and duodenal damage with enprostil. A double blind endoscopic study. Gastroenterology 1985; 88:382-386.

[262]Hoftiezer, J. Effects of 24 hours of aspirin, Bufferin, paracetamol and placebo on normal gastroduodenal mucosa. Gut 1982; 23:693-697.

[263]Kirby, R. Oat-bran intake selectively lowers serum low-density lipoprotein cholesterol concentrations of hypocholesterolemic men. Am J Clin Nutr 1981; 34:824-829.

[264]Anderson, J. Hypocholesterolemic effects of oat bran or bean intake for hypercholesterolemic men. Am J Clin Nutr 1984; 40:1146-1155.

[265]Davidson, M. The hypocholesterolemic effects of B-glucan in oatmeal and oat bran: A dose-controlled study. JAMA 1991; 265:1833-1899.

[266]McIntosh, H. Barley and wheat foods: Influence on plasma cholesterol concentrations in hypercholesterolemic men. Am J Clin Nutr 1991; 53:1205-1209.

[267]Demark-Wahnefried, W. Reduced serum cholesterol with dietary change using fat-modified and oat-bran-supplemented diets. J Am Diet Assoc 1990; 90:223-229.

[268]Swain, J. Comparison of the effects of oat bran and low-fiber wheat on serum-lipoprotein levels and blood pressure. N Engl J Med 1990; 322:147-152.

[269]Connor, W. Dietary fiber—nostrum or critical nutrient? Editorial. N Engl J Med 1990; 322:193-195.

[270]Kestin, M. Comparative effects of three cereal brans on plasma lipids, blood pressure and glucose metabolism in mildly hypercholesterolemic men. Am J Clin Nutr 1990; 41:661-666.

[271]Anderson, J. Oat-bran cereal lowers serum total and LDL cholesterol in hypercholesterolemic men. Am J Clin Nutr 1990; 52:495-499.

[272]Manson, J. A prospective study of obesity and risk of coronary heart disease in women. N Engl J Med 1990; 322:882-889.

[273]Braitman, L. Obesity and caloric intake: The national health and nutrition examination survey of 1971-1975. (Hanes 1) J Chron Dis 1985; 38:727-732.

[274]McDougall, J. *McDougall's Medicine: A Challenging Second Opinion.* New Century, publishers, Piscataway, NJ, 1985, pp. 143-162.

[275]McDougall, J. *The McDougall Program: Twelve Days to Dynamic Health.* Penguin Books, publishers, New York, 1990.

[276]Guyton, A. *Textbook of Medical Physiology.* W.B. Saunders, publishers, Philadelphia PA, 1981, pp. 849-856.

[277]Lapidus, L. Triglycerides—Main lipid risk factor for cardiovascular disease in women? Acta Medica Scand 1985; 217:481-489.

[278]Cooper, K. *Controlling Cholesterol.* Bantam Books, publishers, 1988, p. 65.

[279]Ornish, D. *Stress, Diet and Your Heart.* Holt, Rinehart, and Winston, publishers, New York, 1982.

[280]Strom, A. Mortality from circulatory diseases in Norway 1940-1945. Lancet 1951; 1:126-128.

[281]Warning: Hostility can be dangerous to your health. University of Texas Lifetime Health Letter, October 1989, p. 1.

[282]Virag, R. Is impotence an arterial disorder? Lancet 1985; 1:181-184.

[283]Curb, J. Long-term surveillance for adverse effects of antihypertensive drugs. JAMA 1985; 253:3263-3268.

4.

Boning Up

4. *Boning Up*

> *"The first rule in formulating public health policy should be the assurance that the recommendations are not detrimental. It will be embarrassing enough if the current calcium hype is simply useless; it will be immeasurably worse if the recommendations are actually detrimental to health."*[1]
>
> —Dr. D.M. Hegsted

Osteoporosis is caused by multiple factors, the most important of which are the consumption of animal proteins and lack of vigorous exercise. The disease *is not* due to lack of dietary calcium, nor is it brought about by inadequate estrogen levels. Until we rid ourselves of both the estrogen and calcium manias, it is unlikely that the epidemic of brittle bones will abate.

Bone is among the strongest materials in nature. A cubic inch of healthy bone tissue can withstand loads of 19,000 pounds—about four times the strength of concrete and equal to the strength of aluminum.[2] Yet, bones become so brittle and weak in many people that the slightest impact or pressure can cause a fracture; even something as seemingly innocuous as stepping off a curb or being hugged by a well-meaning relative.

Osteoporosis, or thinning of the bones, afflicts more than 24 million Americans and is considered by many to be an inevitable product of aging. The end result of this disease, as just mentioned, is often a fracture of one of the bones, usually the hip, spine or wrist. If the fracture occurs at the hip, it is often fatal. The treatment of these fractures exacts a heavy economic toll in the United States, accounting for expenditures of $3.8 billion per year.[3] Total cost to treat osteoporosis has been estimated to be $6-8 billion per year.[4]

Since it is a well established fact that bones lose calcium during their progress to osteoporosis, the therapy most often recommended for the potential victim (usually a postmenopausal woman) is to saturate herself in calcium by means of capsule supplementation, calcium fortified foods or dairy products. Supposedly, calcium supplementation will slow bone loss.

Others believe that dietary calcium supplementation has no influence on bone. They believe that a very small quantity of calcium will suffice for good bone health.

Still others feel that calcium supplementation may help to build stronger bones only in the formative years, which would help prevent osteoporosis in later stages of life. Even those who advocate supplementation generally believe that at best such a method of treatment may retard the osteoporotic process but that it is not capable of halting or reversing the process of thinning bones.

As with cancer, heart disease and diabetes, many "experts" believe that a certain number of people will succumb to the disease and that the best any treatment can do is to retard the progression. They believe that osteoporosis is something that "just happens" as people get older. This is a most unfortunate and incorrect opinion, and it leads to the deaths of millions who could be saved through proper habits of nutrition and exercise.

CALCIUM SATURATION: AN EXERCISE IN FUTILITY?

The facts are these: (1) Osteoporosis is not an inevitable corollary of aging, and (2) calcium supplementation does only very little or nothing to retard bone loss and certainly does nothing to reverse the disease. Yet, a whole generation of women are basking in the false security that calcium supplements and dairy products are protecting them from this insidious and crippling malady. The calcium mania is one of the worst frauds perpetrated on the American public and does little good for anyone other than the hawkers of calcium pills and the dairy industry. Those entities, however, are doing quite well. In fact, $166 million was spent on calcium supplements in 1986, and it is estimated that the amount may rise to $1.7 billion in the future.[5] [6]

Do dairy products help?

As milk consumption increases, there is a concomitant increase in the amount of calcium lost in the urine. In one piece of research, women supplemented their diets with 1500 milligrams of calcium daily by consuming three glasses of skim milk. After one year, they were still in negative calcium balance, meaning that the amount of calcium leaving the body each day was more than the amount being ingested.[7] This indicates that bone was being lost in spite of the massive calcium dose. The more milk the women drank, the more calcium they lost each day.

Calcium supplements may indeed do something for osteoporosis—but, again, they may not—and dairy products may exacerbate the problem. The answers to osteoporosis are quite obvious. And, as will be seen in the remainder of this chapter, those answers do not include saturation in calcium. Still, calcium continues to be dumped into everything from soup to hay, and the dairy industry continues to sing the praises of its cholesterol-laden products.

These products, by the way, actually relate quite closely to the prevalence of osteoporosis worldwide.[1] It is noteworthy that countries such as the United States, whose populations consume large quantities of dairy products and calcium, have much higher rates of osteoporosis than countries which consume little or no dairy products and little calcium.[1] [8] [9] Figure 1, presented by Dr. Mark Hegsted in the *Journal of Nutrition*, shows the relationship of calcium consumption in various countries to the rate of hip fractures.[1]

If those people who consume more calcium have stronger bones, then we would expect to observe a general *downward* trend in the world-wide incidence of osteoporosis as calcium consumption increases. Yet, there is obviously a general *upward* trend in osteoporosis as calcium intake increases. It is not an exact relationship, because there are many other influences on osteoporosis which may come into play. Lack of exercise, dietary protein intake, caffeine consumption, smoking, obesity, corticosteroid use and antacid consumption all contribute to bone loss. However, if it is true that low-calcium intakes are a primary cause of osteoporosis, it would follow that those countries with the greatest per capita consumption of calcium

FIGURE 1:
The Relationship of Calcium Consumption To the Incidence of Hip Fractures in Various Countries

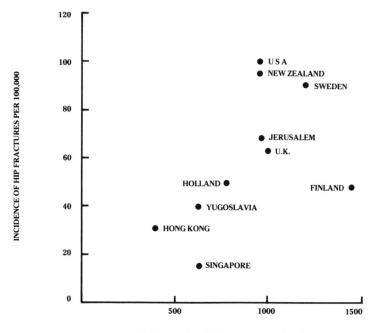

PER CAPITA CALCIUM CONSUMPTION (mg/day)

would generally suffer less, not more, osteoporosis.

The same relationship which is depicted in Figure 1 also exists (as we might expect) for skeletal size and calcium intake. It is a fact that populations that consume lower levels of calcium for a lifetime often have greater skeletal size than those who consume far more calcium.[10]

Among members of the Bantu tribe of Africa, calcium intake is very low (less than 300 milligrams per day per person), and the supposed drain on calcium stores very high.[11] [12] The typical Bantu woman bears six children and nurses each child for about ten months, which would be estimated to cause a loss of about half the body's calcium stores. Nonetheless, osteoporosis is nearly non-existent among those women. An estimated 10% of the Bantus are more than 60 years of age, indicating that osteoporosis would have manifested itself if it were going to be a problem.[1] Relatives of these same people in the United States have a high rate of osteoporosis.[14]

In general, however, rates of osteoporosis are lower among Black Americans than Caucasians.[15] Some would argue that Blacks have stronger bones and would consequently take many more years to develop osteoporosis. This argument states that we should not, therefore, compare the rates of osteoporosis of Blacks to Whites as a method of proving that calcium intake is not the prime factor in the disease.

While it is true that Blacks have stronger bones than Whites, it is also true that a large percentage of Blacks cannot tolerate milk due to an inability to digest lactose or milk sugar.[16] This would indicate a lower consumption of milk among both the African Bantu who do not use dairy products, and the American Blacks, who cannot tolerate milk very well.

The question then arises: How do Blacks initially develop the large, strong bones without a large quantity of calcium? The answer is simple: All people consume sufficient quantities of calcium if they are consuming adequate calories from a variety of foods.

Perhaps the most compelling study to refute the theory that osteoporosis is due to calcium deficiency is a massive study in China.[17] It compared dietary habits of thousands of Chinese living in different counties. Though the average consumption of calcium among the Chinese is less than half that of Americans, osteoporosis is rare. The Chinese live to an average age of over 70, suggesting that if the disease were going to be a problem, it would certainly have time to develop.

The reasoning behind the calcium glut sounds plausible enough at first. If calcium is being lost from the bones, then ingesting large quantities of calcium should reverse the process. As mentioned, however, the scientific research belies this error in thinking. Unless more calcium is retained than is lost, then the progress of this disease will be inexorable, regardless of the amount of calcium taken in.

Studies of calcium supplements confirm this fact. One piece of research showed that women consuming 1000 to 2000 milligrams of calcium per day, including 500 supplemental milligrams, lost bone just as rapidly as those who received no calcium except for the amount contained in their usual meals.[18]

More research on calcium supplements

Just how much good does calcium supplementation do in terms of preventing or retarding osteoporosis? A thorough review of the literature on calcium intake and osteoporosis was reported in the January 1989 issue of the *British Medical Journal.*[19] [20] It stated that the idea that increased dietary intake of calcium offsets losses in bones is "clearly misleading and not supported by experimental observation." As part of the review, the authors cited several pieces of research which came to the conclusion that bone is lost at equal rates regardless of the quantity of calcium ingested.

In a study of 103 postmenopausal women conducted in Denmark, calcium intakes of 1000 to 2000 milligrams per day, including 500 milligrams of supplemental calcium, were not effective in preventing bone loss in early menopause.[21] The woman in the study who consumed the most calcium (2350 milligrams per day) lost bone at the rate of 4-5% per year. Contrast this to the aforementioned Bantu women who have exceptionally strong bones with intakes of 250 to 400 milligrams per day.

It has been recommended that women ingest at least 1000 milligrams of calcium per day to prevent bone loss. That is ridiculous. Most women of the world consume far less than that amount and have little problem with osteoporosis. As Dr. Hegsted states, "The one thing we are certain about, however, is that if women generally needed a gram or more of calcium per day, the world should be falling apart with broken bones in the elderly. This is not happening."[22]

In an effort to test the claim that calcium supplements suppress bone loss, researchers supplemented a group of postmenopausal women for two years with 2000 milligrams of calcium per day and compared their rates of bone loss to another group who received a placebo containing no calcium.[23] Both groups of women in the study had profound and approximately equal losses in bone mineral during the two-year period of the study. Women who received estrogen treatments, however, retained their bone. Since estrogen treatments have been associated with several types of cancer, they cannot be recommended. (See the section on estrogen treatments.) Bone can be retained in a safe and natural way without resorting to either calcium pills or hormone treatments.

Dr. John Meulman, in an article in the journal, *Archives of Internal Medicine,*[6] indicates that no positive benefits of calcium supplementation have been proven. There are, according to Dr. Meulman, four potential problems with recommendations to arbitrarily supplement all postmenopausal women:

(1) Hypercalcemia (excessive calcium) in women with undiagnosed abnormalities in calcium metabolism

(2) Kidney-stone formation

(3) Decreased bone remodeling which leads to microfractures and eventual bone fragility

(4) A potential cost in the billions of dollars

Recently, another danger of calcium supplementation has emerged. Two articles in the *American Journal of Clinical Nutrition*[24] [25] have established that iron absorption is reduced substantially by calcium supplementation. The first showed that supplements would reduce iron absorption by 49-62% in a dosage of 300 to 600 milligrams per day when taken at meals. Calcium carbonate, one of three supplements used in the experiment, did not inhibit absorption of iron when taken between meals, whereas calcium citrate and calcium phosphate reduced iron absorption regardless of when they were taken.

The second study showed that a calcium supplement of only 165 milligrams per day taken as milk, cheese, or calcium chloride, reduced absorption of iron by 50-60%. It is no surprise that milk products relate to iron-deficiency anemia. (See the section on diseases.) The inhibiting influence of calcium on iron absorption has been known for some time, however. Many older studies show that iron absorption is severely inhibited by increasing calcium intake.[26] [27] [28] [29]

There are studies that do make a case for increased calcium

intake. One paper indicates that postmenopausal women need 1500 milligrams of calcium per day,[30] and another suggests that a sufficiently high calcium intake can reverse negative calcium balance (losing more calcium from the body than is taken in from foods).[31] Negative calcium balance results in a loss of bone. We will discuss calcium balance in the following pages.

Other studies that have tried to test the validity of these claims, however, have not been successful in halting bone loss through massive calcium supplementation, and in fact have seen little or no positive benefit of extra calcium for retardation of bone loss.[32] [33] [34] [35] [36] [37]

Are vegetarians at risk?

Research on vegetarians also belie the notion that those who consume more calcium have stronger bones. Vegetarians who have low levels of calcium intake have considerably stronger bones in old age than those who eat a mixed diet.[38] Studies on some vegetarian populations show that women in those populations do not develop postmenopausal osteoporosis—not even those with calcium intakes of only 400 milligrams per day. They also have greater bone density than Americans who consume more calcium along with a conventional diet.[39]

This is especially interesting in view of the fact that vegetarians have far lower blood estrogen levels than meat eaters.[40] [41] [42] Estrogen, as mentioned, protects against bone loss and is often prescribed in drug form for postmenopausal women. Many people believe that lack of estrogen is the prime risk factor for osteoporosis. Yet, as mentioned above, *those vegetarian women who have low calcium and low estrogen levels have better bone strength than meat-eating women who have high levels of calcium intake!* Obviously, lower calcium intake and lower estrogen levels are not causes of osteoporosis.

Past the age of 50, lacto-ovo vegetarians (those who eat no meat, fish or fowl but do eat eggs and milk) have significantly stronger bones than omnivorous women.[43] It might be thought that the greater bone mass among the vegetarians is due to an increased milk consumption, and thereby an increased calcium intake, but such is not the case. One study showed that vegetarians had milk intakes identical to omnivores, meaning that milk could not have been a factor in the increased bone strength of the vegetarians. Vegetarians eat much less animal protein than mixed-diet eaters since they ingest animal proteins only from milk and eggs, not from meat.

As we will establish, animal-product consumption is the prime factor in osteoporosis. For the meat eater, taking estrogen may be one of only two methods by which she can conserve her bones, the other method being a good exercise program. If she does take estrogen, however, she greatly increases her risk of various forms of cancer.

Is a pure vegetarian at risk for osteoporosis?

A vital point to be made to those who insist on calcium saturation is the fact that vegans (those who consume no animal products of any kind, including milk and eggs), generally have a much lower calcium intake than those who consume a typical diet. Yet, *there have been no reports of osteoporosis or any other type of calcium deficiency among vegans.*[44]

Vegan children who consume only about half or less than half of the recommended daily allowances of calcium, thrive on their vegan diets and show no signs of clinical deficiency of calcium.[45] [46] Contrast this with the Eskimos, who have one of the highest calcium intakes in the world at about 2000 milligrams of calcium daily. They also have one of the highest rates, if not the highest rate, of osteoporosis in the world.[47] Their consumption of animal products is also the highest in the world.

"Not even a trend"

In a study from the Mayo Clinic, no relationship was found between calcium consumption and osteoporosis. The study involved 106 women between the ages of 23 and 88 living in Rochester, Minnesota.[48] The researchers measured calcium intake and bone density. The women were followed for an average of 4.3 years and were found to have calcium intakes of 269 to 2000 milligrams per day, which were steady throughout the study period. After the data were gathered, Dr. Lawrence

Riggs, the lead researcher, reported that "We found no correlation between calcium intake and bone loss, not even a trend."[49] When Dr. Riggs compared the bone loss of women consuming more than 1400 milligrams per day to those consuming less than 500 milligrams per day, he found the rate of bone loss to be almost identical.

Considering the fact that high calcium intakes may cause kidney stones[50] and may also interfere with vitamin D, some researchers are telling their patients that calcium supplements should be used only as a last resort.[51]

Men also suffer from bone loss.

Whereas most people regard osteoporosis as an affliction of women, bone loss occurs in men at an equally alarming rate. Men, however, develop stronger bones during the formative years; therefore, it takes longer for the degenerative effects of osteoporosis to manifest themselves in the obvious symptoms of fractures and deformation. Since men live shorter lives on the average, the outward signs do not have as long to develop. Nonetheless, the calcium loss proceeds in men as well as women.

"Healthy" men lose an average of 2.3% of their vertebral bone mass per year in spite of calcium supplements of 1000 milligrams per day, along with large doses of vitamin D.[52] Since the average daily intake of calcium among these men is already over 1100 milligrams per day, they are losing bone on a whopping total calcium intake of 2159 milligrams per day!

There are better ways to
prevent and reverse osteoporosis.

Of more concern to the potential victims of this unnecessary disease is the fact that there are methods for retarding, preventing, and to an extent, reversing bone loss. None of these methods has anything to do with ingesting a plethora of calcium. Nevertheless, if people believe that calcium supplementation can do the job, then they are not apt to use the methods which can help them prevent or overcome the disease. Thus calcium supplementation, even if it were slightly effective in retarding bone loss, becomes more a bane than a boon by causing the potential victim to focus in an area which has at best only negligible positive effects and at worst may intensify the problem.

If osteoporosis is not caused by lack of calcium in the diet, just what is the reason for the epidemic of this disease? There are several important factors, but the basic cause of bone loss is losing more calcium from the body each day than is consumed in the daily diet.

EXCESSIVE CALCIUM EXCRETION IS THE CAUSE OF BONE LOSS.

To understand the mechanisms that cause osteoporosis, we must understand that it has little or nothing to do with the amount of calcium ingested so long as that amount meets the minimum requirements—which are very small—and so long as more calcium is retained in the body than is excreted. Calcium is consumed in the foods we eat, and any calcium not used by the body is excreted in the urine and feces. When a person excretes more calcium than is ingested, that person is in *negative calcium balance*, meaning that he or she is losing body stores of calcium.

Calcium is stored primarily in the bones; thus, the bones become brittle and weak with constant negative calcium balance. However, if more calcium is consumed than is lost, then one is said to be in *positive calcium balance.* In other words, if someone were to consume 1000 milligrams of calcium per day and excrete 1020 milligrams, she would be in a negative calcium balance of 20 milligrams per day, resulting in loss of bone. If excretion were only 990 milligrams, however, there would be a positive calcium balance of 10 milligrams, and no loss would occur. In fact, bone mass would probably increase.

However, it has been mentioned that some studies show calcium balance to be positively influenced by calcium supplementation. Nonetheless, bone mass does not seem to benefit, meaning that there is probably a flaw in measuring the excreted calcium. In other words, there is really a negative calcium balance, which is not showing up due to an inability to detect all of the calcium being lost.[53]

Studies on bone mass are also contradictory. There are a few that indicate a positive influence in slowing bone loss with greater calcium consumption.[54] [55] [56] Others show no benefit.[23] [53] [57] There is a possibility that what we are seeing in some studies (which show a benefit of calcium consumption) is a protective effect of obesity. Dairy products and other high-fat foods are quite fattening. People who are fatter have stronger bones, perhaps due to carrying the extra weight on the skeleton and perhaps due to the excess estrogen produced by obese people.

Another influencing factor in these studies is that people who have larger bones are generally larger and taller people who would consume more food than people of lesser stature, thereby showing an increased calcium consumption. A third factor may be that people who exercise regularly (or who have heavy-labor jobs) would also consume more food and more calcium. People who exercise regularly have far stronger bones than those who are sedentary. It is, therefore, likely that these studies are simply defining obese milk drinkers, large boned people with larger appetites, or people who consume more food and calcium due to heavy exercise.

Calcium and bone remodeling

Excessive calcium may also interfere with bone remodeling.[6] Bones retain their toughness and flexibility by continually eroding away old bone and replacing it with new bone. Cells called osteoclasts gather in concentrated masses in an area of the bone and eat away at the bone material until a small tunnel in the bone has developed. Thereafter, cells called osteoblasts begin depositing new bone, which is more flexible. This ensures that the bone does not become too brittle with age.[58] This process is absolutely necessary for bone strength, and it is a process which may be inhibited by excessive calcium.

Researchers who studied the effects of milk as a calcium supplement[7] stated that milk may have an advantage over calcium carbonate as a supplement because it "does not suppress bone remodeling as severely as calcium carbonate."

How can milk be recommended on the premise that it is less harmful than something else? Perhaps we should recommend smoking on the basis that it does not create heart disease as readily as eating meat! Their study also noted an increase in calcium lost in both the urine and feces with increasing milk consumption and a decrease in accretion (adding of new bone). Yet the authors concluded that "milk and milk products can be recommended as sources of calcium." So they can, but to what end? Bone mass was not increased one whit by supplementation with milk; calcium balance remained negative, and there was a decrease in bone accretion. How could anyone recommend using such a product? It might be noted that the study was sponsored by the National Dairy Council.

At least the researchers admitted that the poor performance in trying to achieve calcium balance could have been due to the increased dietary protein from the milk. The authors concluded that cutting back on protein from other sources (such as meat) might be the answer to achieving calcium balance. At least they were correct about the meat which, along with other animal proteins, is a prime cause of bone loss.

ANIMAL PROTEINS: THE PRIMARY FACTOR IN BONE LOSS

Consuming large quantities of animal protein causes an extreme loss of calcium, which ultimately results in thinning of the bones. The Eskimos referred to earlier not only have extremely high calcium intakes and extremely high rates of osteoporosis, but also have one of the highest animal-protein diets in the world.[47] People with excessive intakes of animal protein remain in negative calcium balance regardless of the quantity of calcium consumed.[59]

One researcher, making a computer search of the scientific literature, found 60 studies between the years of 1974 and 1988 that indicated a significant relationship between excess dietary protein and an increased calcium loss! One of the researchers, Dr. Angelo Licata, stated, "Increased dietary protein acutely causes a negative calcium balance in osteoporotic patients and may contribute to bone loss in this disease."[60]

As we will establish later, however, all dietary proteins are not equal in their abilities to weaken bones. Vegetable proteins may actually have a protective influence.

It is amazing that those who push dairy products, calcium, estrogen and drugs manage to gloss over animal-protein as a cause of bone loss. This concept is not exactly news. Dr. H.C. Sherman, in 1920, reported that meat consumption caused a net loss of calcium.[61] This finding has been corroborated consistently. Figure 2 portrays the relationship of dietary protein consumption to urinary calcium lost.[77]

Proteins cause acid blood.

The consumption of large quantities of animal proteins induces bone dissolution by acidifying the blood.[62 63 64 65 66 67] It also increases the filtration rate through the kidneys, which increases the quantity of calcium lost in the urine.[59 64 68 69 70 71 72 73]

Whereas excess carbohydrates and fats can be stored in the body, this is not the case with proteins. They are broken down to amino acids, which when excessive, saturate the blood and make it acidic. The blood, which must be maintained in a slightly alkaline state for good health, counteracts the acidity by dissolving bone, which can provide alkaline salts to neutralize the acid.

The liver ultimately breaks down the excessive amino acids and excretes the waste products of nitrogen and calcium through the kidneys. This causes the strong diuretic effect and a loss of calcium. Some of the calcium may be reabsorbed in the kidney, but because of a high sulfur content,[74] animal proteins interfere with the reabsorption process, forcing more calcium into the toilet. In severe cases of kidney disease, when the acid load cannot be successfully eliminated, the body pulls so much calcium from the bones to neutralize the acid load that 50% of the calcium stores of the skeleton can be lost in only three years![62]

Urinary calcium excretion on a high-protein diet is about 90-100 milligrams per day, which puts most women at risk for

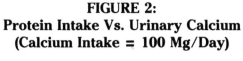

FIGURE 2:
Protein Intake Vs. Urinary Calcium
(Calcium Intake = 100 Mg/Day)

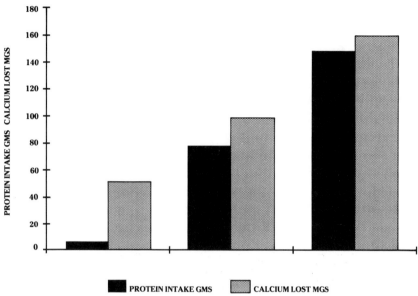

osteoporosis.[75] In an attempt to stem the tide of osteoporosis, the Food and Nutrition Board of the National Academy of Sciences has set the recommended daily allowances as follows:[76]

- 360-1200 milligrams per day for youth
- 800 milligrams per day for adults
- 1200 milligrams per day for pregnant or lactating women

These recommendations are excessively high, especially for a person who eats little protein. It has been shown that adults on a low-protein diet stay in positive calcium balance regardless of whether the calcium intake is 500, 800 or 1400 milligrams per day.[77] *Conversely, on a high protein diet, no amount of calcium will put the body in positive calcium balance!*[77] It is obvious that a plethora of protein causes a paucity of bone. Figure 3 depicts the relationship between protein consumption and hip fractures in several countries of the world.

FIGURE 3:
The Relationship of Protein Consumption To the Incidence of Hip Fractures in Various Countries

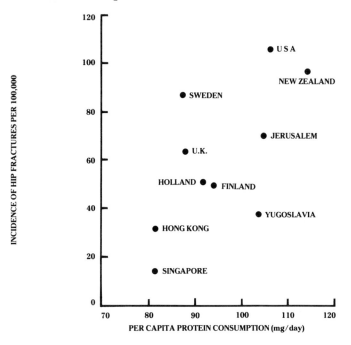

Compare Figure 3 with Figure 1. Both of these charts were presented by Dr. Hegsted in an article which appeared in the *Journal of Nutrition.*[1] In assessing the relationships of calcium intake, protein intake and osteoporosis, Dr. Hegsted made the following comment: "The hypothesis that high protein intakes may be involved is consistent with the epidemiology (occurrence and cause of the disease), whereas the calcium deficiency hypothesis is not."

There are, however, a few research papers which show no relationship between the consumption of meat and urinary calcium loss.[78] [79] [80] These studies were all conducted by the same researchers and were supported by the meat and dairy industries. The methodology of this research has been questioned,[81] and other researchers have stated that the studies are inconsistent with the preponderance of research indicating a direct relationship between protein consumption and calcium loss.[82]

The influence of phosphorous

Phosphorous, in some instances, has a somewhat protective influence against the loss of urinary calcium. Phosphorous exerts this influence by causing calcium to be reabsorbed in the kidneys rather than allowing it to wash out in the urine. Since phosphorous is contained in animal products, some people believe that it will negate the calcium-leaching influence of animal proteins. However, this is not the case. Although adding phosphorous to the diet does slow urinary calcium loss, it does not overcome the pernicious influence of the dietary proteins.[77] In fact, excessive consumption of phosphorous (usually by red meats and carbonated beverages) can decrease calcium absorption, reduce serum calcium, and may contribute to bone disease.[83]

Calcium absorption in the intestine

Absorption of calcium in the intestine is also an important consideration. If more dietary calcium is absorbed, then calcium balances might be improved. At higher protein and calcium intakes, more calcium is indeed absorbed, but the increased absorption cannot counterbalance the dramatically increased loss of calcium in the urine.[76] This is true even when there is a very large intake of calcium. Most of the large quantity of calcium which is ingested in the form of supplements simply passes out through the feces without being absorbed, and that which is absorbed is exceeded by the amount lost in the urine.

Vegetable proteins are safer.

Fortunately, when proteins come from vegetable sources, they do not cause a negative calcium balance, even when calcium intake is low.[84] [85] Vegetable proteins may actually have a protective effect against bone loss.[84]

DOES FIBER INHIBIT CALCIUM ABSORPTION?

There is some concern that the increased fiber and oxalic acid found in vegetarian diets may decrease the absorption of calcium from the intestines. Yet, if this were the case, then vegans would suffer from calcium deficiencies, which does not happen.

An interesting chemical, boron, may be part of the reason. Boron strongly reduces calcium excretion and is abundant in fruits and vegetables. These foods may therefore be very protective against osteoporosis.[86] [87] Could this be why the Chinese who were mentioned earlier have such low rates of osteoporosis in spite of low calcium intakes? Whatever the reason, it can be stated with certainty that fiber, at least as consumed naturally in whole foods, is not a threat to strong bones. The typical Chinese consumes three times as much dietary fiber as the typical American.

PROTEIN IS AMPLE ON A DIET FOR GOOD HEALTH.

We have established animal proteins as the prime factor in bone loss. But if we don't eat animal proteins, can we get enough protein for the maintenance of other parts of the body? The answer is an unequivocal yes. Research shows conclusively that human beings need very little protein.[88] All of the protein requirements for humans can be derived by eating any single starchy food such as rice or potatoes, provided the calorie consumption meets the daily need of the individual. All of the essential amino acids are in plentiful supply in any single starchy food or any combination of starches.[89]

Human breast milk contains only about 5% of its calories from protein,[90] and yet the infant is able to double its weight, including all of its protein structures, in a six-month period. It should be evident that the human will never again need as much as 5% of calories from protein since there will never again be a period of such rapid growth.

Research done on human subjects in 1955 indicates that a diet that furnishes only 2.5% of total calories as protein is adequate to maintain the protein stores of humans.[88] This is not the case with rats, which have a much higher protein need.[89] Unfortunately, our usual high-protein recommendations for human beings are based on studies performed on rats, and we are paying dearly for our rat-style nutrition based on that research. That price includes high rates of osteoporosis, cancer, heart disease, diabetes and numerous other infirmities. A mother rat's milk has ten times the protein concentration of human breast milk![89]

The ideal protein intake for man is probably about 20 to 40 grams per day.[88] Typically, Americans consume 2½ to 5 times that amount, which exceeds their abilities to handle the resultant acidity without decalcifying their bones.

Low-protein diets stop calcium loss.

Young adults easily stay in positive calcium balance when protein is restricted to 50 grams per day.[91] When protein intakes are increased to 95 or 142 grams per day, there is a corresponding increase in calcium lost in the urine, regardless of the intake of calcium. *Even at very high intakes of calcium, if protein intake is high, the calcium lost in the urine is greater than that absorbed in the intestine.*[77] This, of course, indicates a net loss of calcium from the bone.

Let us reiterate the importance of animal proteins in the cause of osteoporosis. *When protein content of the diet is low, calcium is retained in the bones, which do not demineralize, even when calcium intakes are very low. When protein content is high, calcium will be lost, and the bones will weaken regardless of an extremely high intake of calcium.*

Calcium saturation, then, is indeed an exercise in futility. A low animal-protein diet can stop the loss of calcium. If calcium supplementation helps at all, it simply helps to retard the progression of a disease which would not happen at all without excessive protein consumption.

One might ask why the researchers who originally determined protein requirements did not experiment on humans or apes rather than rats. Apes, at least, have a much closer physical resemblance to humans. The ape, on his mostly vegetarian diet, manages to build huge bones and muscles. He does this without the benefit of cow's milk or calcium supplements. Some of the calcium pushers might be quite surprised that apes don't crumble and fall apart on their "deficient" diets.

Calcium requirements for good health

Human beings need calcium; it is an essential mineral. But how much do we need for good health? When animal-protein consumption is low, we can easily supply our needs for calcium (about 200-400 milligrams per day) from vegetables, grains, legumes and fruits. It is being recommended by the "experts," nevertheless, that women consume 1000 to 1500 milligrams of calcium daily.[92] Few women in the world consume that much calcium. If the real calcium requirement is 200-400 milligrams per day, how easy is it to obtain that much from a pure vegetarian diet? Table 1 shows the amount of calcium in various foods. It is very simple to obtain sufficient calcium without supplements or dairy products. Now let's look at the calcium content of foods based on how much calcium is contained per 100 calories consumed. Table 2 shows that vegetables compare very well to dairy products as calcium sources.

It is apparent that vegetation is an abundant source of calcium. This should be obvious, since all calcium comes originally from the earth. The calcium is absorbed in vegetation, and animals then eat the plants which contain calcium. From this calcium, they build bones.

The calcium in cow's milk comes from vegetation, exactly the source from which humans should obtain theirs. We have

TABLE 1:
Calcium Content of Typical Portions of
Animal and Plant Foods

Animal Foods	Serving Size	Calcium Per Serving
Sardines, Canned in Oil.................	4 ounces	402 mg
Ham, Boneless, Roasted	4 ounces	trace
T-Bone Steak, Lean with Fat..............	4 ounces	7 mg
Leg of Lamb, Boneless, Roasted with Fat	4 ounces	11 mg
Milk, Whole	1 cup	272 mg
Turkey, Fryer, Roasted Meat and Skin	4 ounces	trace
Eggs, Jumbo Chicken, Poached	1 egg	34 mg

Plant Foods	Serving Size	Calcium Per Serving
Collard Greens, Boiled and Drained	1 cup	154 mg
Apple, 2¾" Diameter	1 apple	10 mg
Beans, Pinto, Dry, Cooked	1 cup	89 mg
Potato, Baked in Skin, 4¾"x2⅓" Diameter ...	1 potato	21 mg
Carrots, Sliced, Boiled and Drained	1 cup	75 mg
Orange, 2-7/8" Diameter	1 orange	51 mg
Rice, Brown, Cooked	1 cup	22 mg

TABLE 2:
Calcium Content of 100-Calorie Portions of Animal and Plant Foods

Animal Foods	Calcium Per 100 Calories
Sardines, Canned in Oil	114 mg
Ham, Boneless, Roasted	trace
T-Bone Steak, Lean with Fat	2 mg
Leg of Lamb, Boneless, Roasted with Fat	3 mg
Milk, Whole	181 mg
Turkey, Fryer Roasted, Meat and Skin	trace
Eggs, Jumbo Chicken, Poached	34 mg

Plant Foods	Calcium Per 100 Calories
Collard Greens, Boiled and Drained	570 mg
Apple	12 mg
Beans, Pinto, Dry, Cooked	39 mg
Potato, Baked in Skin	10 mg
Carrots, Sliced, Boiled, Drained	107 mg
Orange	78 mg
Rice, Brown, Cooked	10 mg

been told that we never outgrow our need for milk, and yet, adult cows do not drink cow's milk. They obtain calcium from vegetation. How could it possibly be important for adult human beings to drink cow's milk? Do we ever see cows with bad bones due to lack of cow's milk? *We need to think!*

Vegetables, grains, legumes and fruits are the foods consumed by the populations of the world who have the very best bone health, despite the protests of those who claim that calcium absorption is impaired on a vegan diet high in oxalates, phytates and fiber. It is obvious that those who consume these foods to the exclusion of all dairy products and supplements are quite efficient at retaining calcium. If it were not so, then vegans, who have "low" intakes of calcium and very high intakes of the factors that supposedly inhibit calcium absorption would have poor bone health, exactly opposite from the truth.

Animal proteins and kidney stones

Another result of increased calcium excretion through the urine is an increased risk of kidney stones.[93] [94] [95] [96] [97] This condition becomes excruciatingly painful when these stones try to pass through the urinary tract. Vegetarian populations show a decreased risk of kidney stone formation.[98] After World War II, when food supplies, especially animal products (which had been scarce during the war) became plentiful, there was an epidemic increase in kidney stones in many countries in Europe.[99] It is likely that the increased quantity of dietary protein was responsible.[100]

As discussed, when animal proteins are consumed, there is a profound increase in the quantity of calcium excreted in the urine. It is common sense that kidney stones, which are formed primarily from calcium, would increase on a diet high in animal proteins. While bone is being lost, stones form from calcium drawn from the victim's own bones!

MOVE IT OR LOSE IT!

A second major factor in bone loss is sedentary living. With little or no weight-bearing activity, bones lose part of their reason to exist and deteriorate rapidly. Bones are meant to move, bear weight, and work against resistance. When this doesn't happen, bone tissue is not sufficiently stimulated to stay strong. It is well known that when bones aren't used, they begin to lose their calcium stores, which results in a loss of bone.[101]

People who are bedridden lose bone rapidly. Healthy men who are restricted to bed rest lose calcium at the rate of 200-250 milligrams per day and will lose approximately 4% of their total calcium stores in a period of 30-36 weeks.[102] However, bone mass in the weight-bearing bones of the legs decreases as much as 25-45% in the same period! The good news is that when normal activity resumes, the process is reversible; bone is regained at about the same rate at which it was lost.

Some bones must have weight-bearing work.

Astronauts who experience long periods of weightlessness lose massive quantities of calcium from the bones of the legs; this in spite of the fact that they exercise vigorously in non-weight-bearing fashion.[103] [104] It appears that the bones which would normally bear weight must do exactly that to maintain their strength. This fact was first established in 1966 in a study that showed that the loss of urinary calcium was just as great in bed rest as in heavy exercise in bed on an exercise apparatus which involved no weight bearing.[105] The loss of calcium could be slowed but not eliminated by having the subjects stand quietly beside their beds, giving the weight-bearing bones the type of stimulation for which they were designed. Other research shows that bed rest is detrimental to bone mass, but that recovery of lost bone takes place when normal activity is restored.[106] One study involved 90 healthy young men who volunteered to subject themselves to bed rest from 5 to 36 weeks. All of them evinced extreme loss of calcium through the urine which could not be halted by exercise in bed, vitamin D supplementation, heavy calcium supplementation, or various other therapies.

Without the normal weight-bearing activity, bone-mineral content decreased at the rate of 5% per month![107]

It is a self-evident truth that neglected systems begin to atrophy. The bones are certainly no exception.

A most efficient method for producing osteoporosis, then, is to combine a high animal-protein diet with a lifestyle of no vigorous, weight-bearing activity. Unfortunately, this is exactly the *modus vivendi* of a large portion of the American public.

According to the *Morbidity and Mortality Weekly Report*, only about 8% of our population between the ages of 18 and 65 participate regularly in vigorous physical activity of sufficient duration to cause substantial positive changes in their health.[108] Much lip service is given to exercise, but few participate. It is no wonder that osteoporosis is epidemic in our society.

FITNESS: THE BEST THERAPY FOR THIN BONES

Now the positive side of the story. Fitness activities of the correct type work to slow, halt or even reverse the loss of bone. Both muscles and bones respond to the stress placed on them by becoming larger and stronger. It is well known that muscle mass increases in response to exercise, and it has been established that there is a positive correlation between muscle mass and bone mass.[109] [110] [111] Obviously, increasing strength through exercise increases the size and strength of bone.

This relationship between the load placed on bone and the resultant effect on bone mass was first noticed in 1683 by Galileo.[103] A little more than 200 years later, in 1892, a German anatomist named Julius Wolff stated that "every change in the function of a bone is followed by certain changes in internal architecture and external conformation in accordance with mathematical laws."[112] In plain English, this means that the size and shape of bones depends on the stresses placed on them. This is known as "Wolff's Law" and is a valid and self-evident truth. It behooves the victim or potential victim of osteoporosis to give up the easy chair and find a way to provide healthful, vigorous exercise for the skeletal system.

It can be easily observed that when stress is placed on the skin, such as by using the hands to hoe the garden or to lift barbells, calluses develop in response to that stress. When the work stops for a few weeks, and the skin is no longer placed in the stress situation, the calluses begin to disappear. They have lost their function, which is to protect the skin from the blistering and bleeding which would result if the skin were allowed to continue the work without toughening. Disuse of the eyes will cause blindness, and those who do not involve themselves in some form of intellectual stimulation are apt to lose their abilities to think and reason effectively. All parts of the body deteriorate with disuse.

Hippocrates stated that *"All parts of the body which have a function, if used in moderation and exercised in labors in which each is accustomed, become thereby healthy, well-developed and age more slowly, but if unused they become liable to disease, defective in growth, and age quickly."* This wisdom relates to all systems of the body, including the bones. The bones are not inert sticks but dynamic, living tissue which will grow with use and shrink with disuse. It is God's gift to mankind that bones tend to increase their mass until about the age of 35. After that time, it will require constant physical labor to maintain the bone mass at youthful levels.

ACHIEVING PEAK BONE MASS
WITH EXERCISE

During a lifetime, the greatest skeletal weight is usually attained prior to the age of 35, after which there tends to be a decline. If there were some method of increasing that skeletal weight prior to the period of decline, then the symptoms of bone loss and subsequent osteoporosis would take much longer to manifest themselves. Exercise is an effective method of increasing that peak bone mass.

Athletes such as baseball players, tennis players, bowlers and others who predominantly use one arm in their sports, develop the bones in that arm to a much greater extent than the arm that is not involved in the sport. In fact, the upper-arm bones of the playing arms of long-time tennis players are from 28 to 35% thicker than their non-playing arms.[113]

Athletes involved in vigorous training generally have bone densities (the concentration of bone minerals) about 11% greater than those who exercise regularly for fitness. Those who exercise regularly for fitness have bone densities which are 27% higher than non-exercisers.[114] When bone mass in athletes is measured, the very best athletes have 50% more bone than sedentary people of the same weight. This certainly illustrates the osteogenic (bone forming) capabilities of vigorous exercise during the first 35 years of life. There is an obvious positive influence of vigorous physical activity in achieving a greater bone mass during the important bone-forming years.[115] [116] [117]

Exercise is so effective in stimulating bone growth in the areas of hardest use that scientists can accurately assess a person's former level and type of activity by studying his or her skeleton. For instance, due to bone sizes and unusual bone formations, it can be determined whether a skeleton belonged to a baseball pitcher, a spear thrower, a clarinet player, or a golfer.[118] (A golfer develops a bone growth on the upper arm bone, and a baseball pitcher develops a bony ridge along the attachment points of the muscles of his throwing arm.) With a detailed examination of the skeleton, it would be possible to identify a clarinet-playing, kayak-paddling baseball pitcher![118]

Since peak bone mass enables an individual to carry stronger bones into old age, then exercise becomes a critically important factor in the prevention of osteoporosis.

Don't overdo a good thing.

At this point, a word of caution is in order for women who might be inclined to feel that if some exercise is good, more is better. There can certainly be too much of a good thing. Exercising to an extreme, especially when trying to restrict calories, may cause estrogen levels to drop far too low. This in turn may cause menstruation to cease and bone to erode. It has been established that amenorrheic (without menstruation) women runners have only about 89 to 91% of the lumbar (lower spine) bone mass of non-runners.[115] [116] Many female runners also restrict calories, which may be more significant in causing their bone loss than the reduction in estrogen production.

Female runners who menstruate normally, however, have 108 to 110% of normal bone mass. When compared to amenorrheic non-runners (anorexics—non-exercisers who have lost their menstrual cycles), amenorrheic runners still have 25% greater bone mass than their non-running counterparts.[119] Exercising to an extreme, obviously harmful to skeletal health, is still far superior to a program of sedentary starvation.

What happens when women change their habits of nutrition and excess running? They then return to normal menstrual periods and bone mass improves but remains lower than that of normal, menstruating non-runners.[120]

As to the carry-over effects of exercise for improved skeletal health in later years, there is considerable research which indicates stronger bones among exercisers. One of the most important studies was done by Dr. Nancy Lane and her associates and reported in the *Journal of the American Medical Association*.[121] The research showed that joggers between the ages of 50 and 70 had a 40% greater bone density of the spinal column than sedentary people of the same age categories. It was also noted that joint health, as measured by the width of the joints, favored the runners. Some fear that osteoarthritis may be caused by excessive joint use. Not so. Although the runners in this study used their joints and their bones to a greater extent than non-runners, their joint health was as good or better than those who were sedentary. The conclusion reached by Dr. Lane was that "running is associated with increased bone mineral, but not, in this cross-sectional study, with clinical osteoarthritis."

The increased bone strength in Dr. Lane's study could have been because the runners, through their active lives, built a greater peak bone mass in their younger years that carried over to their middle age. It could also have been due to the bone-retaining influence of exercise during their later years or perhaps even an increase in bone mass during those years as a result of vigorous activity. It was likely a combination of all three.

Other research indicates that the expected bone loss with aging does not occur in marathon runners.[122] As with many other diseases, we assume because older people suffer from osteoporosis, it is simply something to be expected as part of the aging process and that the best that can be hoped for is to retard its progress. This is simply not true. Older people succumb to these diseases because they have had more time for the deterioration caused by sedentary living and atrocious dietary habits. The "expected" loss of bone is a farce. It needn't happen if a person is willing to develop safe and sane modes of living.

Can we increase bone mass after 35?

The answer to this question is a definite yes. In one experiment, women walked for 45 minutes per day, four days per week while carrying weights around their waists. In one year, they were able to increase bone mass by 1.5% in their lower spines.[123] The impact of exercise on the bone health of these women is even more pronounced when it is considered that sedentary women lost 6.5% of their bone density during the same period. That amounts to a 7.5% swing in favor of increased bone health in one year.

Perhaps the most impressive study on the influence of exercise on bone mass was done by Dr. Raphael Chow and his colleagues at Queen Elizabeth Hospital in Toronto, Canada.[124] Dr. Chow placed healthy postmenopausal women on an exercise program which consisted aerobics plus strengthening exercise. In a year, the women increased bone mass about 8%. *This increase was accomplished with no calcium supplementation and no estrogen therapy!* The calcium intake of those who gained bone mass ranged from 500 milligrams to 1000 milligrams. This is important because many women are being prescribed as much as 1500 milligrams of supplemental calcium to retard bone loss.

Exercise is forever

In another study, a variety of physical activities such as stair climbing, walking and jogging were used.[125] Within nine months the participants increased their bone mass by an average of 5%! A word of caution is in order, however. When the women stopped the exercise program, the increased bone mass was quickly lost. This makes perfect sense, since a program of exercise is not meant to be a quick fix. Imagine the benefits to the osteoporotic woman who added 5% to her bone mass each nine-month period. Although a consistent addition of 5% each nine-month period is not likely to occur, certainly much bone mass could return with a program of progressive exercise.

An exercise program probably has its greatest value as a defense and a therapy for a disease that need never happen—a disease that would not exist among people who did not eat animal proteins and who performed hard physical labor.

Exercise gives the bones a reason to exist. Giving calcium supplements without exercise, and expecting them to build bones, is tantamount to stuffing protein down a person who does no exercise and expecting it to build muscle! Or as Dr. J.A. Kanis stated so beautifully in a review in the *British Medical Journal,* "It [calcium supplementation] has an intuitive appeal, but the logic is similar to that which might lead doctors to give ground up brains for dementia."[126] With or without supplementation, exercise is necessary for increasing bone strength.

Building bones in the elderly

Other research reports that bone mass increases in middle-aged or elderly women in response to exercise.[127] [128] [129] One of the most recent studies showed an increase in the mass of the forearm bones in elderly women after a program of ball squeezing.[129] The women squeezed a ball as hard as possible three times daily, which took less than 30 total seconds per day. The results were astounding. After six weeks, there was an increase in grip strength of 14.5% and a gain of bone mineral content which averaged 3.4%. What a magnificent return on an investment of 30 seconds of exercise per day!

The authors of the study concluded that grip strength in the forearm is a good indicator of bone-mineral content and that both strength and bone-mineral content are increased by brief periods of stressful exercise. They suggest that if exercise can be applied to the whole skeleton, it may provide a means of reversing osteoporosis.[129] This would indicate that a training program should include all muscles and bones of the body; not just those of the legs and back which are used in walking, jogging, cycling, etc.

It is, in fact, *imperative* that all of the bones be used if optimum bone health is to be realized. Women who exercised the legs to improve their cardiovascular fitness increased the bone-mineral content of the spine and legs but lost bone mineral in the arms at an accelerated rate—even faster than a control group which did no exercise.[130] When exercise programs were changed to include strengthening movements for the upper body, bone mineral also increased in the arm bones. The researchers hypothesized that bone mineral was transferred from the bones of the upper limbs to the lower limbs and spine during the time in which exercise was done only for the lower limbs.

A good total-body weight-training program which features at least three maximum contractions per each movement, three or four times per week, would serve to strengthen bones and muscles in the entire system. A maximum contraction can be defined as exerting as much force as possible into lifting the weight. The minuscule investment in time would produce prodigious results for increased bone health. *Such a program would take less than 20 minutes per week.*

Caution is in order

Maximum contractions against bones which have been severely weakened by loss of calcium might produce fractures, especially in the hip or vertebral column. Until one has sought the advice of a physical therapist or physician, it would be unwise to participate in maximal-contraction weight training or other maximal-contraction exercise. With a few months of sub-maximal training under a professional's care, however, it is likely that the increased bone strength would be adequate to handle the load of a maximal contraction.

It is an incontrovertible fact that exercise is good therapy to build and maintain bone strength. Outdoor activity may also be of importance. The skin produces vitamin D in response to sunlight. Vitamin D is also essential to good bone health. In a study reported in the *British Medical Journal*, elderly men and women who were in the lowest category of outdoor activity had 4.3 times the rate of hip fracture as those who were in the highest category.[131] *Those men and women who consumed the least calcium in this study had only 70% of the fractures as those who consumed the most.*

ESTROGEN THERAPY: BOON OR BANE?

Estrogen therapy is definitely effective for osteoporosis. It has been proven to slow bone loss in postmenopausal women, and at least one study indicated a non-significant increase in bone mass.[132] This study also showed that a large bone loss occurred when calcium supplements were used without estrogen treatments.

Whereas estrogen therapy is obviously effective in slowing bone loss, it cannot be recommended. The potential side effects of this drug can be devastating, and we have already established that there are better ways to retain bone.

Is estrogen therapy worth the risk?

Research indicates an increased risk of various cancers of the reproductive system and breast with estrogen therapy. In 1933, researchers—using animals as subjects—confirmed the cancer-causing effects of sex hormones.[133] Other early research confirmed these effects.[134] [135] Estrogen treatments are equally harmful in human beings.

Research reported in the *New England Journal of Medicine* in 1975 showed that the risk of endometrial cancer increased with the time a patient was treated with estrogen.[136] For one to five years of treatment, the risk was 5.6 times greater in the estrogen-treated patients than in the non-treated patients. For seven or more years of treatment, the risk of cancer was nearly

14 times greater in the treated patients! There is little doubt that estrogen treatments increase the risk of cancer of both the uterus and the ovaries.[137] [138] [139]

Does progesterone make estrogen therapy safe?

The addition of progesterone to estrogen treatments has been shown to reduce the risk of uterine cancer,[140] but such treatment may considerably increase the risk of breast cancer.

A recent review of 16 studies reported in the *Journal of the American Medical Association* showed some interesting relationships. After 15 years of estrogen use, the rate of breast cancer increased by 30%.[141] Postmenopausal women who had a familial history of breast cancer, however, had a risk increase of 240%. Risk for premenopausal women on estrogen for 15 years increased by 100%. Other studies conducted on Seventh-day Adventist women showed a 70% increase in breast-cancer rate after nine years of estrogen use.[142] When estrogen is given in combination with progesterone for more than six years, however, the risk of breast cancer is increased by 440%![143]

It is also worthy of note that progesterone treatment negates much of the beneficial effect of estrogen for prevention of heart disease. Estrogen increases "good" HDL cholesterol and decreases "bad" LDL cholesterol. The addition of progesterone, however, does exactly the opposite, making a woman more susceptible to heart disease.[144] (For a full discussion of cholesterol, HDL and LDL, see the chapter on heart disease.)

Estrogens used in oral contraceptives relate to a doubling of the breast cancer risk when the "pill" has been used for more than eight years.[145]

In commenting on the use of estrogen treatment,[146] one physician made the observation that estrogen therapy could at best prevent about ten hip fractures per 1000 women if one accepts the estimated protective effects. The increase in endometrial cancer from the same treatments would be 40 to 50 per 1000 women. Thus, estrogen therapy for bones hardly seems like a good investment in the overall health of the postmenopausal women! It is also expensive and may damage not only the physical health but also the financial health of whole generations of retired people. Paying for drugs, calcium and estrogen may create an incubus which exceeds the financial capacities of elderly women. Worse yet, they are paying for products that may be either useless or detrimental to health.

Gallbladder disease, pulmonary embolism, diabetes and hypertension all increase with estrogen use.[147] In addition, we have observed another adverse influence of estrogen treatments which should make women consider other alternatives. . .weight gain. In working with thousands of overweight individuals at National Institute of Fitness, we have seldom talked to a woman who has not added body weight after starting estrogen therapy.

Compounding the deleterious influence of estrogen treatments is the fact that if the treatment is to produce anything worthwhile in terms of saving bone, it must be carried on forever. When estrogen treatments are discontinued, any bone retained by the treatments is quickly lost.[148] [149] The woman so treated, then, is no better off in terms of bone strength than if she had never taken the treatment. The problem does not stop there, however. Some research shows that although estrogen therapy initially saves bone, skeletal deterioration critically increases after a few months to a few years.[150] In view of these facts, it hardly seems reasonable to risk the potential side effects that relate to this treatment.

It is a mistake to alter the hormone balances with which nature has endowed woman. To do so assumes that God made some mistakes in the physiology of the human body and that these mistakes require a little fixing by the chemical lab. These manipulations may exact a terrible price.

Fluoride therapy may cause soft bones.

Sodium fluoride treatment has been used for many years to prevent bone loss. Fluoride treatment can indeed stimulate new bone growth. In some cases it appears that fracture rates have been significantly decreased by its use.[151] [152] A recent study, however, shows quite the opposite.[153] Whereas fluoride treatment significantly increased the bone density of the vertebrae and upper leg bones, it did not reduce the risk of fracture. The rate of fracture among those treated with fluoride was 3.2 times that of those not receiving the treatment. The authors of this study concluded that the use of fluorides should be discouraged.

It appears that fluoride treatment increases bone mass, but the bone produced is of inferior strength, thus rendering it susceptible to fracture. Overall, fluoride has proved to be a disappointment.[154] [155] Of further concern, this mineral has been indicted as a cause of synovitis (inflammation of joint membranes), gastric disorders (including vomiting and bleeding ulcers), and problems with connective tissue of the feet.[156] [157] Sodium fluoride can be a very toxic substance that may have no value in strengthening bone.

Other drug treatments

There are two other drugs used as therapy for osteoporosis: etidronate disodium and calcitonin. Etidronate disodium inhibits bone resorption (breaking down of bone material) and shows promise in helping the body to add new bone material.[158] [159] The question is, will it be proven to be toxic or harmful in the future?

Calcitonin is a fish-derived hormone that moves calcium from the blood to the bones. This drug has been shown to significantly increase bone mineral content when used for one year.[160] It also decreases loss of bone mineral in some studies.[161] At a cost of $10 per day, however, and with the need for daily injections, it is probably not practical therapy for bone loss.[162] As with etidronate disodium, long-term studies have not established its safety.

In the previously quoted research on disuse osteoporosis,[107] either etidronate disodium nor calcitonin were effective in slowing the extreme loss of calcium in volunteers who subjected themselves to extended bed rest. Exercise, especially weight-bearing exercise, is the preeminent method for retention and increase of bone mineral. All other treatments are ancillary and can have a positive influence only in the presence of some stress to the bones.

OTHER CONSIDERATIONS

Factors such as alcohol, smoking, certain steroid drugs, excessive salt, caffeine, diuretics, antibiotics, antacids, lack of obesity, and soft drinks may accelerate osteoporosis.[163] Let's consider a few of the most important.

Alcohol

Alcohol abuse contributes to loss of bone mass in various areas of the body.[164] [165] [166] [167] [168] [169] [170] Vertebral bone mass in alcoholics who had abused alcohol for at least ten years is only 58% of normal![169] The exact mechanism by which alcohol contributes to bone loss is not known, but suffice it to say that alcohol consumption and good bone health do not mix.

Smoking

Smoking contributes to bone loss to a great degree.[169] [171] [172] One researcher, commenting on the studies done on smoking and osteoporosis, made the following comment: "These studies demonstrate a striking association between the early presence of osteoporosis and both postmenopausal cigarette smoking and postmenopausal lack of obesity."[171]

Smoking may bring on an early menopause by shutting down a woman's natural estrogen supply. This in turn would cause a loss of bone. Such a scenario would be very important to the inactive, high-protein-consuming woman. But, as we have already established, it would be of little importance to the active, low-protein-consuming woman, since good bone health can be maintained on lower levels of estrogen. It is unlikely, though, that many cigarette smokers in our country have a very high level of physical activity or that they eat a low-protein diet. We can, therefore, add osteoporosis to the list of diseases that are either accelerated or caused by smoking.

Obesity as therapy?

In the studies of smoking and osteoporosis, all the women who were studied lost bone rapidly, whether they were obese, slender or non-smokers. Smoking accelerated bone loss, and interestingly enough, obesity retarded the loss.[169] [171] [172] Obese people produce more estrogen and are forced to exert a greater effort to move their bodies, which probably stimulates the bone to stay stronger. We might call this "exercise by default." Slender, sedentary people who smoked would not have the "advantage" of the exercise gained by being obese.

Obese people also have higher levels of estrogen than slender people, which could explain some of the differences in the rates of bone loss. As discussed earlier, estrogen retards bone loss in postmenopausal women. This primary female hormone is synthesized from the male hormone androgen.[173] Fat assists in this conversion; therefore, fatter females produce more estrogen and consequently have stronger bones, provided, of course, that all else is equal. Obesity is not a desirable condition in any case and can hardly be considered therapy for deteriorating bones. A good program of vigorous exercise for the slender woman, coupled with a low-protein nutrition program, will more than compensate for the "advantage" of obesity.

Steroids

Steroid drugs known as a glucocorticoids cause a rapid loss of bone mineral.[174] These drugs are similar to the body's own cortisone and are in wide use today to treat a variety of ailments, from lupus erythematosis to skin rashes. They can produce a loss of as much as 20% of the bone mineral in the ribs and vertebrae in one year![131] Prolonged use can obviously be devastating.

It appears that cortisone drugs do their damage in several ways.[175] They decrease the number of bone-forming cells (osteoblasts). They increase bone resorption (dissolving of old bone). They increase calcium excretion through the kidneys. They decrease intestinal absorption of dietary calcium. This is but one more example of the disappointing effects of drugs, which, although they may lead to some improvement of a diagnosed condition, invariably prove to have potentially fatal or harmful side effects when used for an extended period.

The use of these drugs for a variety of diseases should be seriously studied in terms of their potential for accelerating the osteoporotic process. Corticosteroids should also be evaluated in terms of their tendency to break down protein structures.[175] [176] Patients using these drugs are known to increase negative nitrogen balance by more than six-fold.[177]

Negative nitrogen balance indicates a breakdown of muscle and other protein structures in the same manner that negative calcium balance indicates a loss of bone. Glucocorticoids were called "wonder drugs" when they were first introduced. They certainly are. It is a wonder that anyone survives them.

Caffeine

Caffeine greatly increases urinary calcium excretion.[178] [179] [180] It is not known exactly how this occurs, but a dose of 5 milligrams per kilogram (2.2 pounds) of body weight triples urinary calcium loss![181] A person who weighs 160 pounds would need only about three cups of coffee to consume 5 milligrams of caffeine per kilogram of weight. Could this drug be as detrimental in causing negative calcium balance as animal proteins? Certainly it is a major addiction in much of the "developed" world, where osteoporosis is most prevalent.

Aluminum

Aluminum-containing antacids also cause large losses of calcium and extensive demineralization of bone.[182] These antacids cause a considerable increase in calcium lost through the urine and feces and are capable of accelerating already existing bone loss in elderly women or in people who are alcoholics.[183]

Soft drinks, soft bones

In the past 30 years, the consumption of carbonated beverages has tripled. Women over the age of 40, who consume these beverages regularly, have twice the risk of osteoporosis as those who do not.[184] Researchers feel that the high phosphoric acid content of carbonated beverages, especially cola drinks, may increase the acidity of the blood and thereby cause bone loss. Many soft drinks contain caffeine, which may also be an important factor.

We should bear in mind that for the vast majority, animal proteins and sedentary living are the preeminent causes of osteoporosis. The rest are important but form only the tip of the iceberg, the possible exception being caffeine. Aging and lack of calcium are not important causes of osteoporosis, and the disease is certainly not inevitable.

WHAT HAVE WE LEARNED?

1. Avoid all animal products. They are the primary cause of the osteoporosis epidemic.

2. Consumption of dairy products for calcium is not necessary. There is ample calcium for good health in vegetables, grains, legumes and fruits. These foods do not cause osteo- porosis and may protect against bone loss due to their naturally high content of boron. Eat freely of these foods.

3. Avoid smoking, alcohol, soft drinks, diuretics, and excessive intake of salt. All of these may contribute to bone decalcification.

4. Fitness is a key to maintaining strong bones and rebuilding weakened bones. One who maintains a high level of fitness at any age, and who does not eat animal products, can expect to halt or reverse osteoporosis. Gains in bone mass can occur with regular exercise.

   Recommendations for exercise are for 30-60 minutes or more of brisk walking per day or the equivalent in some other activity. Weight training for the entire body is also an excellent idea and will ensure that all the bones receive equal treatment. A program that stimulates the major muscle groups three times weekly can be done in just 20 total minutes per week.

   Consult a physician before beginning an exercise

program, especially if there are signs of weakened bones! He or she, with the help of a physical therapist, will be able to advise the person with osteoporosis as to the safest and most effective method of exercise.

5.   Remember that calcium saturation has virtually no effect in treating osteoporosis. And, it cannot increase bone mass unless accompanied by sex-hormone treatment, which may be dangerous indeed. Calcium supplementation may also contribute to kidney stones and iron deficiency anemia, inhibit bone remodeling, and cause a financial burden.

6.   Estrogen therapy reduces bone loss for a time but must be carried on for a lifetime if the results are to last. Some research indicates that the beneficial effects on bone are lost with extended use of estrogen. This therapy is fattening and increases the potential to contract several forms of cancer. (In my opinion, it is unnatural and unwise therapy for most women unless the ovaries have been removed.) A physician should be consulted before making any changes in therapy.

A parting thought

Primitive man, although he occasionally ate meat, could not have been a milk drinker—except perhaps for the last few thousand years of his development. He was obviously able to develop strong bones (the bones studied by anthropologists) without using any type of dairy product. And, we can state with certainty that calcium carbonate and calcium chloride pills were not available. Meat, by the way, is virtually depleted of calcium. It is highly unlikely that primitive man ate bones, except perhaps some fish bones in isolated societies. This lack of animal calcium left him with but one source for the calcium needed for health: vegetation. Many societies today, as previously mentioned, have never learned to use dairy products. Their bone strength is far superior to meat-eating, milk-drinking people.

There may be a few who detest exercise and who insist that calcium supplements and dairy products are the answers to preventing osteoporosis. This is understandable—it is easier to pop a pill or drink a glass of milk than to take a walk or visit a gym. Abstinence from some of the vices such as meat, soda pop, alcohol and smoking is a bitter pill for some individuals, who therefore invent excuses to continue on their self-destructive lifestyles. Pay no attention to these negative influences. Consult your physician and get started today on a bone-building program of sound nutrition and physical activity!

REFERENCES

[1]Hegsted, D. Calcium and osteoporosis. J Nutr 1986; 116:2316-2319.

[2]*The Human Body.* Arch Cape Press, 1989, p. 32.

[3]MacKinnon, J. Osteoporosis: A review. Phys Ther 1988; 68:1533-1538.

[4]Heaney, R. Nutritional factors in bone health in elderly subjects: Methodological and contextual problems. Am J Clin Nutr 1989; 50:1182-1189.

[5]Kolata, G. How important is dietary calcium in prevention of osteoporosis? Science 1986; 233:519-520.

[6]Meulman, J. Beliefs about osteoporosis. Arch Intern Med 1987; 147:762-765.

[7]Recker, R. The effect of milk supplements on calcium metabolism, bone metabolism, and calcium balance. Am J Clin Nutr 1985; 41:254-263.

[8]McDougall, J. *McDougall's Medicine: A Challenging Second Opinion.* New Century, publishers, Piscataway, NJ, 1985, p. 68.

[9]Hegsted, D. Relationships between nutrition in early life and late outcomes, including osteoporosis. *In* Nutrition and Aging. Alan R. Liss, publisher, 1990, pp. 73-87.

[10]Garn, S. Calcium intake and bone quality in the elderly. Ecol Food Nutr 1981; 10:131-133.

[11]Solomon, L. Osteoporosis and fracture of the femoral neck in the South African Bantu. J Bone and Joint Surg 1968; 50B:2-13.

[12]Walker, A. The influence of numerous pregnancies and lactations on bone dimensions in South African Bantu and Caucasian mothers. Clin Sci 1972; 42:189-196.

[13]McDougall, J. *McDougall's Medicine: A Challenging Second Opinion.* New Century, publishers, Piscataway, NJ, p. 71.

[14]Smith, R. Epidemiologic studies of osteoporosis in women of Puerto Rico and Southeastern Michigan with special reference to age, race, national origin and to related and associated findings. Clin Orthop 1966; 45:31-48.

[15]Cohn, S. Comparative skeletal mass and radial bone mineral content in Black and White women. Metabolism 1977; 26:171-178.

[16]Gilat, T. Lactase deficiency: The world pattern today. Israel J Med Sci 1979; 15:369-373.

[17]Campbell, T. A study on diet, nutrition and disease in the People's Republic of China. Part II. Division of Nutritional Sciences, Cornell University, Ithica, New York, 14085.

[18]Ettinger, B. Postmenopausal bone loss is prevented by treatment with low-dosage estrogen with calcium. Ann Intern Med 1987; 106:40-45.

[19]Kanis, J. Calcium supplementation of the diet-1: Not justified by present evidence. Brit Med J 1989; 298:137-149.

[20]Kanis, J. Calcium supplementation of the diet-2: Not justified by present evidence. Brit Med J 1989; 298:205-208.

[21]Nilas, L. Calcium supplementation and postmenopausal bone loss. Br Med J 1984; 289:1103-1106.

[22]Hegsted, D. Relationships between nutrition in early life and late outcomes, including osteoporosis. In Nutrition and Aging. Alan R. Liss, publisher, 1990, pp. 73-87.

[23]Riis, B. Does calcium supplementation prevent postmenopausal bone loss? N Engl J Med 1987; 316:173-177.

[24]Cook, J. Calcium supplementation: Effect on iron absorption. Am J Clin Nutr 1991; 53:106-111.

[25]Hallberg, L. Calcium: Effect of different amounts on nonheme- and heme-iron absorption in humans. Am J Clin Nutr 1991; 53:112-119.

[26]Seligman, P. Measurements of iron absorption from prenatal multivitamin supplements. Obstet Gynecol 1983; 61:356-362.

[27]Dawson Hughes, B. Effects of calcium carbonate and hydroxapatite on zinc and iron retention in post-menopausal women. Am J Clin Nutr 1986; 44:83-88.

[28]Dunn, J. The effects of dietary calcium salts and fat on iron absorption in the rat. S Afr J Med Sci 1968; 33:65-70.

[29]Barton, J. Calcium inhibition of inorganic iron absorption in rats. Gastroenterology 1983; 84:90-91.

[30]Heaney, R. Menopausal changes in calcium balance performance. J Lab Clin Med 1978; 92:953-963.

[31]Recker, R. Effect of estrogens and calcium carbonate on bone loss in post-menopausal women. Ann Intern Med 1977; 87:649-655.

[32]Nilas, L. Calcium supplementation and postmenopausal bone loss. Brit Med J 1984; 289:1103-1105.

[33]Orwoll, E. The rate of bone-mineral loss in normal men and the effects of calcium and cholecalciferol supplementation. Ann Intern Med 1990; 112:29-34.

[34]Riis, B. Does calcium supplementation prevent postmenopausal bone loss? N Engl J Med 1987; 316:173-177.

[35]Christensen, C. Quoted in Kolata, G. How important is dietary calcium in preventing osteoporosis? Science 1986; 233:519-520.

[36]Kanis, J. Calcium supplementation of the diet-1: Not justified by present evidence. Brit Med J 1989; 298:137-140.

[37]Kanis, J. Calcium supplementation of the diet-2: Not justified by present evidence. Brit Med J 1989; 298:205-208.

[38]Walker, A. Osteoporosis and calcium deficiency. Am J Clin Nutr 1965; 16:327-336.

[39]Marsh, A. Cortical bone density of adult lacto-ovo vegetarian and omnivorous women. J Am Diet Assn 1980; 76:148-151.

[40]Schultz, T. Nutrient intake and hormonal status of premenopausal vegetarian Seventh-day Adventist and premenopausal nonvegetarians. Nutr Cancer 1983; 4:247-259.

[41]Goldin, B. Estrogen excretion patterns and plasma levels in vegetarian and omnivorous women. N Engl J Med 1092; 308:1542-1547.

[42]Armstrong, B. Diet and reproductive hormones: A study of vegetarian and nonvegetarian postmenopausal women. JNCI 1981; 67:761-767.

[43]Marsh, A. Cortical bone density of adult lacto-ovo vegetarian and omnivorous women. J Am Diet Assn 1980; 76:148-151.

[44]Langley, G. *Vegan Nutrition.* The Vegan Society Ltd., publishers, Oxford, England, 1988, p. 5.

[45]Sanders, T. An anthropometric and dietary assessment of the nutritional status of vegan pre-school children. J Hum Nutr 1981; 34:349-357.

[46]Fulton, J. Pre-school vegetarian children. J Am Diet Assn 1980; 76:360-365.

[47]Mazess, R. Bone-mineral content of North American Eskimos. Am J Clin Nutr 1980; 27:916-925.

[48]Riggs, B. Dietary calcium intakes and rates of bone loss in women. J Clin Invest 1987; 80:979-982.

[49]Riggs, B. Quoted in Kolata, G. How important is dietary calcium in preventing osteoporosis? Science 1986; 233:519-520.

[50]Robertson, W. Dietary changes and the incidence of urinary caliculi in the U.K. between 1958 and 1976. J Chron Dis 1979; 32:469-476.

[51]Kolata, G. How important is dietary calcium in prevention of osteoporosis? Science 1986; 233:519-520.

[52]Orwoll, E. The rate of bone-mineral loss in normal men and the effects of calcium and cholecalciferol supplementation. Ann Intern Med 1990; 112:29-34.

[53]Stevenson, J. Dietary intake of calcium and postmenopausal bone loss. Brit Med J 1988; 297:15-17.

[54]Matkovic, V. Bone status and fracture rates in two regions of Yugoslavia. Am J Clin Nutr 1979; 32:540-549.

[55]Sandler, R. Postmenopausal bone density and milk consumption in childhood and adolescence. Am J Clin Nutr 1985; 42:270-274.

[56]Baran, D. Dietary modification with diary products for preventing vertebral bone loss in premenopausal women: A three-year prospective study. J Clin Endocrinol and Metab 1989; 70:264-270.

[57]Garn, S. Calcium intake and bone quality in the elderly. Ecol Food Nutr 1981; 10:131-133.

[58]Guyton, A. *Textbook of Medical Physiology.* W.B. Saunders, publishers, Philadelphia, PA, pp. 979-980.

[59]Allen, L. Protein-induced hypercalciuria: A longer-term study. Am J Clin Nutr 1979; 32:741-749.

[60]Licata, A. Acute effects of dietary protein on calcium metabolism in patients with osteoporosis. J Gerontol 1982; 36:14-19.

[61]Sherman, H. Calcium requirements of maintenance in man. J Biol Chem 1920; 44:21-27.

[62]Fuhrman, J. Osteoporosis: Why more calcium is not the answer. Mothering Magazine, Winter 1988, pp. 36-37.

[63]Zemel, M. Calcium utilization: Effect of varying level and source of dietary protein. Am J Clin Nutr 1988; 48:880-883.

[64]Schuette, S. Studies on the mechanism of protein-induced hypercalciuria in older men and women. J Nutr 1980; 110:305-315.

[65]Whiting, S. The role of sulfate in the calciuria of high-protein diets in adult rats. J Nutr 1980; 110:212-222.

[66]Zemel, M. Role of the sulphur-containing amino acids in protein-induced hypercalciuria in men. J Nutr 1981; 111:2106-2116.

[67]Tschope, W. Sulfur-containing amino acids are a major determinant of urinary calcium. Miner Electrolyte Metab 1985; 11:137-139.

[68]Hegsted, M. Urinary calcium and calcium balance in young men as affected by level of protein and phosphorus intake. J Nutr 1981; 111:553-562.

[69]Hegsted, M. Long-term effects of level of protein intake on calcium metabolism in young adult women. J Nutr 1981; 111:244-251.

[70]Chu, J. Studies in calcium metabolism II. Effects of low calcium and variable protein intake on human calcium metabolism. Am J Clin Nutr 1975; 28:1028-1035.

[71]Kim, Y. Effect of level of protein intake on calcium metabolism and on parathyroid and renal function in the adult human male. J Nutr 1979; 109:1399-1404.

[72]Zemel, M. Role of the sulfur-containing amino acids in protein-induced hypercalciuria in men. J Nutr 1981; 111:545-552.

[73]Hostetter, T. Human renal response to a meat meal. Am J Physiol 1986; 250:F613-F618.

[74]Zemel, M. Role of the sulfur-containing amino acids in protein-induced hypercalciuria in men. J Nutr 1981; 111:545-552.

[75]Mead, M. Boning up on osteoporosis. East West Journal, June 1989, p. 38.

[76]Food and Nutrition Board, U.S. National Academy of Sciences, 1980. Recommended allowances (9th edition).

[77]Linkswiler, H. Protein induced hypercalciuria. Fed Proc 1981; 40:2429-2433.

[78]Spencer, H. Do protein and phosphorus cause calcium loss? J Nutr 1988; 118:657-660.

[79]Spencer, H. Effect of a high-protein (meat) intake on calcium metabolism in man. Am J Clin Nutr 1978; 31:2167-2180.

[80]Spencer, H. Further studies of the effect of a high-protein diet as meat on calcium metabolism. Am J Clin Nutr 1983; 37:924-929.

[81]Marcus, R. The relationship of dietary calcium to the maintenance of skeletal integrity in man—An interface of endocrinology and nutrition. Metabolism 1982; 31:93-96.

[82]Kerstetter, J. Letter, J Nutr 1991; 121:152.

[83]Koop, C. 1988 Surgeon General's Report on Nutrition and Health.

[84]Breslau, N. Relationships of animal-protein-rich diet to kidney stone formation and calcium metabolism. J Clin Endocrin and Metab 1988; 66:140-146.

[85]Zemel, M. Calcium utilization: Effect of varying level and source of dietary protein. Am J Clin Nutr 1988; 48:880-883.

[86]Nielsen, G. Effect of dietary boron on mineral, estrogen, and testosterone metabolism in postmenopausal women. FASEB J 1987; 1:394-397.

[87]Nielsen, F. Boron—An overlooked element of potential nutritional importance. Nutrition Today, Jan-Feb 1988; 4-7.

[88]Rose, W. The amino-acid requirements of adult man. Nutrition Abstracts and Reviews 1957; 27:631-637.

[89]McDougall, J. The McDougall Plan. New Century, publishers, Piscataway, NJ 1983, pp. 98-101.

[90]Nutritive Value of American Foods in Common Units. Agriculture Handbook No. 456.

[91]Linkswiler, H. Protein induced hypercalciuria. Fed Proc 1981; 40:2429-2433.

[92]Hegsted, D. Calcium and osteoporosis. J Nutr 1986; 116:2316-2319.

[93]Robertson, W. The effect of high animal protein intake on the risk of calcium stone formation in the urinary tract. Clin Sci 1979; 57:285-288.

[94]Robertson, W. The pattern of urinary stone disease in Leeds and in the United Kingdom in relation to animal protein intake during the period 1960-1980. Urol Int 1982; 37:394-399.

[95]Brockis, J. The effects of vegetable and animal protein diets on calcium, urate and oxalate excretion. Br J Urol 1982; 54:590-593.

[96]Iguchi, M. Nutritional risk factors in calcium stone disease in Japan. Urol Int 1984; 39:32-35.

[97]Breslau, N. Relationship of animal protein-rich diet to kidney stone formation and calcium retention. J Clin Endocrinol Metab 1988; 66:140-146.

[98]Finalyson, B. Renal lithiasis in review. Urologic Clin N Am 1974; 1:181-212.

[99]Prien, E. The riddle of urinary stone disease. JAMA 1971; 216:503-507.

[100]Clinical Nutrition. Urinary calcium and dietary protein. Nutrition Reviews 1980; 38:9-10.

[101]Lewis, C. *Osteoporosis Exercise Book.* Aspen Publishers, 1987, p. 2.

[102]Donaldson, C. Effect of prolonged bed rest on bone mineral. Metabolism 1970; 19:1071-1084.

[103]Kaplan, F. Osteoporosis, pathology and prevention. Ciba-Geigy, Clinical Symposia 39 1987; 1:2-32.

[104]Rambeaut, P. Skeletal changes during space flight. Lancet 1985; ii:1050-1052.

[105]Issekutz, B. Effect of prolonged bed rest on urinary calcium output. J Appl Physiol 1966; 21:1013-1020.

[106]Krolner, B. Vertebral bone loss: An unheeded side effect of therapeutic bed rest. Clin Sci 1983; 64:537-540.

[107]Schneider, V. Skeletal calcium homeostasis and countermeasures to prevent disuse osteoporosis. Calcif Tissue Int 1984; 36:151-154.

[108]Centers for Disease Control. Progress toward achieving the 1990 national objectives for physical fitness and exercise. MMWR 1989; 38:450-453.

[109]Aloia, J. Prevention of involutional bone loss by exercise. Ann Intern Med 1978; 89:356-358.

[110]Cohn, S. Comparative skeletal mass and radial bone-mineral content in Black and White women. Metabolism 1977; 26:171-178.

[111]Saville, P. Muscle and bone hypertrophy: Positive effect of running exercise in the rat. Clin Orthop 1969; 65:81-88.

[112]Wolff, J. Das Gesetz der Transformation der Knochen. Berlin: Hirschwald, 1892.

[113] Jones, H. Humeral hypertrophy in response to exercise. J Bone Joint Surg 1977; 59A:204-208.

[114] Nilsson, B. Bone density in athletes. Clin Orthop 1971; 77:170-182.

[115] Drinkwater, B. Bone mineral content of amenorrheic and eumenorrheic athletes. N Engl J Med 1984; 311:277-281.

[116] Marcus, R. Menstrual function and bone mass in elite women distance runners. Ann Intern Med 1985; 102:158-163.

[117] Kanders, B. Interaction of calcium nutrition and physical activity on bone mass in young women. J Bone Mineral Res 1988; 3:145-149.

[118] Wilford, J. Skeletons record the burdens of work. New York Times, Oct. 27, 1987, pp. c1, c9.

[119] Dalsky, G. The role of exercise in the prevention of osteoporosis. Comp Ther 1989; 15:30-37.

[120] Drinkwater, B. Reported in In Health Magazine, May/June 1990, pp. 11-14.

[121] Lane, N. Long-distance running, bone density, and osteoarthritis. JAMA 1986; 255:1147-1151.

[122] Aloia, J. Skeletal mass and body composition in marathon runners. Metabolism 1978; 27:1793-1796.

[123] Personal communication. Department of Bone-Mineral Research, Tufts University, March 1990.

[124] Chow, R. Effect of two randomized exercise programs on bone mass of healthy postmenopausal women. Br Med J 1987; 295:1441-1444.

[125] Dalsky, G. Weight-bearing exercise training and lumbar bone mineral content in postmenopausal women. Ann Intern Med 1988; 108:824-838.

[126] Kanis, J. Calcium supplementation of the diet-2: Not justified by present evidence. Brit Med J 1989; 298:205-208.

[127] Smith, E. Physical activity and calcium modalities for bone-mineral increase in aged women. Med Sci Sports Exerc 1981; 13:60-64.

[128] Krolner, B. Physical exercise as prophylaxis against involutional vertebral bone loss: A controlled trial. Clin Sci 1983; 64:541-546.

[129] Beverly, M. Local bone mineral response to brief exercise that stresses the skeleton. Brit Med J 1989; 299:233-235.

[130] Smith, E. Bone involutional decrease in exercising middle-aged women. Calcif Tissue Int 1984; 36:129-138.

[131] Wickham, C. Dietary calcium, physical activity and risk of hip fracture: A prospective study. Brit Med J 1989; 299:889-892.

[132] Ettinger, B. Postmenopausal bone loss is prevented by treatment with low-dosage estrogen with calcium. Ann Intern Med 1987; 106:40-45.

[133] Cook, J. Sex hormones and cancer-producing compounds. Nature 1933; 131:205-206.

[134]Perry, I. The development of tumors in female mice treated with 1:2:5:6-dibenzanthracene and theelin. Am J Cancer 1937; 29:680-684.

[135]Gardner, W. Tumors in experimental animals receiving steroid hormones. Surgery 1944; 16:8-32.

[136]Ziel, H. Increased risk of endometrial carcinoma among users of conjugated estrogens. N Engl J Med 1975; 293:1167-1170.

[137]Smith, D. Association of exogenous estrogen and endometrial carcinoma. N Engl J Med 1975; 293:1164-1167.

[138]Mack, T. Estrogens and endometrial cancer in a retirement community. N Engl J Med 1976; 294:1262-1267.

[139]Hoover, R. Stilboesterol (diethylstilbesterol) and the risk of ovarian cancer. Lancet 1977; 533-534.

[140]Whitehead, M. Effects of estrogens and progestins on the biochemistry and morphology of the postmenopausal endometrium. N Engl J Med 1981; 305:1599-1605.

[141]Steinberg, K. A meta-analysis of the effect of estrogen-replacement therapy on the risk of breast cancer. JAMA 1991; 265:1985-1990.

[142]Mills, P. Prospective study of exogenous hormone use and breast cancer in Seventh-day Adventists. Cancer 1989; 64:591-597.

[143]Bergkvist, L. The risk of breast cancer after estrogen and estrogen-progestin replacement. N Engl J Med 1989; 321:293-297.

[144]Miller, V. Effects of conjugated equine estrogen with and without three different progestins on lipoproteins, high-density lipoprotein subfractions, and apolipoprotein A-1. Obstet Gynecol 1991; 77:235-240.

[145]U.K. National case-control study group. Oral contraceptive use and breast cancer risk in young women. Lancet 1989; 1:973-982.

[146]Ljunghall, S. Postmenopausal osteoporosis. Letter to the editor. Brit Med J 1982; 285:1504.

[147]McDougall, J. *McDougall's Medicine: A Challenging Second Opinion.* New Century, publishers, Piscataway, NJ, 1985, p. 81.

[148]Lindsay, R. Bone response to termination of estrogen treatment. Lancet 1978; 1:1325-1327.

[149]Horsman, A. Letter to the editor, Effect on bone of withdrawal of estrogen therapy. Lancet 1979; ii:33.

[150]Riggs, B. Short- and long-term effects of estrogen and synthetic anabolic hormone in postmenopausal osteoporosis. J Clin Invest 1972; 51:1659-1663.

[151]Vose, G. Effects of sodium fluoride, inorganic phosphate, and oxymethoione therapies in osteoporosis: A six-year progress study. J Gerontol 1978; 33:204-212.

[152]Riggs, B. Involutional osteoporosis. N Engl J Med 1986; 315:1676-1684.

[153]Riggs, B. Effect of fluoride treatment on the fracture rate in postmenopausal women with osteoporosis. N Engl J Med 1990; 322:802-809.

[154]Christensen, C. Prevention of early postmenopausal bone loss: Controlled two-year study in 315 normal females. Eur J Clin Invest 1980; 10:273-279.

[155]Editorial: Fluoride and the treatment of osteoporosis. Lancet 1984; 1:547.

[156]Lukert, B. Osteoporosis: A review and update. Arch Phys Med Rehab 1982; 63:480-487.

[157]Riggs, B. Effect of the fluoride/calcium regimen on vertebral fracture occurrence in postmenopausal osteoporosis. Comparison with conventional therapy. N Engl J Med 1982; 306:446-450.

[158]New treatment offers hope for osteoporosis patients. P.T. Bulletin 1987; 2:2.

[159]Storm, T. Effect of intermittent cyclical etidronate therapy on bone mass and fracture rate in women with postmenopausal osteoporosis. N Engl J Med 1990; 322:1265-1271.

[160]Mazzuoli, G. Effects of salmon calcitonin in postmenopausal steoporosis: A controlled double-blind clinical study. Calcif Tissue Int 1986; 38:3-8.

[161]Synthetic calcitonin for postmenopausal osteoporosis. Med Lett Drug Ther 1985; 27:53-54.

[162]McDougall, J. *McDougall's Medicine: A Challenging Second Opinion.* New Century, publishers, 1985, p. 86.

[163]Spencer, H. NIH Consensus Conference—Osteoporosis: Factors contributing to osteoporosis. J Nutr 1986; 116:316-319.

[164]Saville, P. Changes in bone mass with age and alcoholism. J Bone Joint Surg 1965; 47A:492-498.

[165]Nilsson, B. Serum density in alcoholism and after gastrectomy. Calcif Tissue Rev 1972; 10:167-170.

[166]Nilsson, B. Changes in bone mass in alcoholics. Clin Orthop 1973; 90:229-232.

[167]Nilsson, B. Conditions contributing to fracture of the femoral neck. Acta Chir Scand 1970; 136:383-384.

[168]Dalen, N. Osteopenia in alcoholism. Clin Orthop 1974; 99:201-202.

[169]Seeman, E. Risk factors for spinal osteoporosis in men. Am J Med 1983; 75:977-983.

[170]Bikle, D. Bone disease in alcohol abuse. Ann Intern Med 1985; 103:42-48.

[171]Daniell, H. Osteoporosis and the slender smoker. Arch Intern Med 1976; 136:298-304.

[172]Aloia, J. Risk factors for postmenopausal osteoporosis. Am J Med 1985; 78:95.

[173]MacDonald, P. Effect of obesity on conversion of plasma androstenedione to estrone in postmenopausal women with and without endometrial cancer. Am J Obstet Gynecol 1978; 130:448-455.

[174]Bockman, R. Steroid-induced osteoporosis. Orthopedic Clin N Am 1990; 21:97-107.

[175]Baxter, J. Tissue effects of glucocorticoids. Am J Med 1972; 53:573-589.

[176]Sapir, D. The role of ananine and glutamine in steroid-induced nitrogen wasting in man. Clin Sci Mol Med 1977; 53:215-220.

[177]Roubenoff, R. Catabolic effects of high-dose corticosteroids persist despite therapeutic benefit in rheumatoid arthritis. Am J Clin Nutr 1990; 52:1113-1117.

[178]Heaney, R. Effects of nitrogen, phosphorous, and caffeine on calcium balance in women. J Lab Clin Med 1982; 99:46-55.

[179]Whiting, S. Effect of dietary caffeine and theophylline on urinary calcium excretion in the adult rat. J Nutr 1987; 117:1224-1228.

[180]Massey, L. The effect of dietary caffeine on urinary excretion of calcium, magnesium, sodium, and potassium in healthy young females. Nutr Res 1984; 4:43-50.

[181]Whiting, S. Effect of prostaglandin inhibition on caffeine-induced hypercalciuria in healthy women. J Nutr Biochem 1990; 1:201-205.

[182]Spencer, H. Effect of small doses of aluminum-containing antacids on calcium and phosphorous metabolism. Am J Clin Nutr 1982; 36:32-40.

[183]Spencer, H. NIH Consensus Conference—Osteoporosis: Factors contributing to osteoporosis. J Nutr 1986; 116:316-319.

[184]Harvard University Study. Quoted in Longevity Magazine, October 1989.

5.

The Cancer Connection

5. *The Cancer Connection*

*In 1990, for the first time, lung cancer surpassed breast cancer as the number 1 cause of cancer deaths among women. This happened despite the fact that breast cancer deaths, already epidemic, increased rapidly in the past decade and are still accelerating. Contrary to the slogan used by the good people who produce Virginia Slims, **you have not come a long way, Baby!***

Perhaps the most feared of all diseases is cancer. Heart disease kills far more people, but it is often a silent killer, causing little pain until it delivers its death-dealing blows. Cancer, however, is not so "kind" to its victims. It is often associated with severe pain, and death is more likely to be lingering than quick. Therefore, most people dread cancer.

Heart disease is declining as a cause of death,[1] but cancer death is increasing.[2] It is expected that by the turn of the century, cancer will become the number-one killer.[2.1] One in four Americans will contract cancer, and the disease will strike two of three families.[3]

HOW DOES CANCER KILL?

Cancer is comprised of a large group of diseases that are characterized by uncontrolled growth and spread of abnormal cells.[4] When these cells have developed, their behavior is totally different from normal cells. They do not respect growth limits and in addition, are not restrained by their surrounding cells. This enables them to travel by way of the blood to other tissues where they can act as stimulators of new cancerous growth.[5]

Cancer kills by competing with normal tissue for nutrients. The uncontrolled proliferation of cancer cells demands much energy.

When a cancerous mass has grown sufficiently, it will demand most of the nutrition available to that particular area, leaving the normal tissue to suffer nutritive death.[5] This disease is one of the most difficult to retard and prevent, and the billions of dollars spent to wage war against it have largely been a waste of money.

THE CANCER WAR—
A DISASTROUS DEFEAT

The war against cancer has been a multi-billion dollar disaster. To illustrate how badly cancer is beating the "best" efforts at treatment and prevention, consider that the total of all cancers combined was up 14% between 1972 and 1987. The death rate from cancer was up 5%.[2] In addition, melanoma (severe skin cancer) increased by 83%, lung cancer by 31%, prostate cancer by 46% and colon and rectal cancer by 6%. Breast cancer rates have increased steadily since the early 1970s, but between 1980 and 1986 that increase was a staggering 24%![4]

On the positive side, the incidence of some cancers is decreasing, including leukemia (down 10%), stomach cancer (down 21%), uterine cancer (down 26%), and cervical cancer (down 36%). This is good news, but those cancers comprise only a small fraction of all cancer cases and are far outbalanced by the dramatic increases in other cancers.

A review by Dr. John Bailar in the *New England Journal of Medicine* entitled "Progress Against Cancer?" assessed the death rate for all cancers combined. "According to this measure," Dr. Bailar stated, "we are losing the war against cancer, notwithstanding progress against several uncommon forms of the disease, improvements in palliation, and extension of the productive years of life. A shift in research emphasis, from research on treatment to research on prevention, seems necessary if substantial progress against cancer is to be forthcoming."

Dr. Bailar was formerly editor and chief for the *Journal of the National Cancer Institute.* As will be seen in the remainder of this chapter, an ounce of prevention may indeed be worth a ton of cure. Treatment has been a debacle in terms of the epidemic cancers of the lung, colon, breast, prostate and pancreas.

All diseases have causes. The causes of cancer are not as clearly definable and certain as the causes of heart disease, but there are certainly some lifestyle changes that can dramatically decrease the odds of succumbing to this most-feared disease. Let's consider the most important cancers and how they are affected by nutrition, exercise and other habits.

LUNG CANCER: IS IT CAUSED BY CIGARETTE SMOKE OR FAT AND CHOLESTEROL?

Lung cancer is the most common cancer in the United States with the exception of common skin cancer, which is not nearly so deadly. There are about 157,000 new cases of lung cancer per year and 142,000 deaths. Between 1973 and 1987, the rate of lung cancer rose by 31%. All the increase was due to increased rates among women.[4] The rate for men has declined during the same period.

Lung cancer is now the *major* cause of cancer death in women. It surpassed breast cancer for the first time in 1990.[4] It is well established that lung cancer is caused primarily by smoking and that the percentage of men who smoke has declined, whereas the percentage of women who smoke has increased in the past 20 years.

Fat, cholesterol, smoking, and lung cancer

The American Cancer Society (ACS) lists the following risk factors for lung cancer:[4]

1. cigarette smoking
2. exposure to arsenic, asbestos and other industrial carcinogens

3. radiation

4. residential radon exposure

What the ACS fails to mention is the fact that in people who consume fewer animal products, the incidence of lung cancer is much lower than would be expected, even when the rate of smoking is very high.[7] [8] When weekly dietary cholesterol consumption exceeds 3500 milligrams, the lung cancer rate increases by 3½ times compared to the person who consumes less than 1000 milligrams per week! Three thousand five hundred milligrams of cholesterol is approximately the quantity of cholesterol that the typical American consumes weekly, which indicates, for the smoker, a much greater risk of lung cancer than would be produced by cigarettes alone. Figure 1 depicts the relationship of dietary cholesterol to the risk of lung cancer when all other risk factors for lung cancer are equal.

There is an absolute dose-response relationship between dietary cholesterol and lung cancer. The greater the consumption of cholesterol, the greater the risk of the disease.[7] [9] This is not indicative that cholesterol is the cause of lung cancer. Smoking is still the culprit. It points out, however, that cholesterol may create an ideal environment in which cancer can develop and grow. In other words, it may act as a co-carcinogen (a substance that supports the development of cancer when the cancer-causing agent is present).[10] Some of the cancer-causing agents in cigarette smoke require activation by other "secondary" chemicals before they can wreak their havoc in the lungs.[11] These chemicals may be produced as a consequence of the high-fat diet.[10]

If you eat a high fat diet, forget about help from your immune system.

Another method by which fats influence tumor growth is suppression of the body's immune system.[12] This supression decreases the ability of the body to destroy new cancer growths.[10] Whatever the method, high-fat diets do exert a strong influence in promoting lung cancer. This influence has been confirmed in animal studies,[13] [14] and different human

FIGURE 1:
Relationship of Cholesterol Intake
To Risk of Lung Cancer

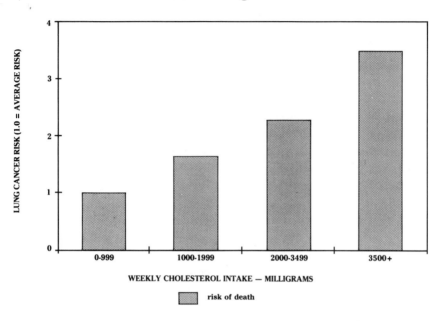

WEEKLY CHOLESTEROL INTAKE — MILLIGRAMS

risk of death

populations show profound variations in lung cancer rates according to their consumptions of fat. Those who smoke heavily have a much higher rate of lung cancer when they also consume a high-fat diet.[15] [16]

A cell known as a natural killer cell is a part of the immune system that can seek out and destroy cancer cells before they can be established. Low-fat diets dramatically increase the action of these cancer killers.[16.1]

Conversely, all fats, including fish fats and vegetable oils dramatically reduce the action of both killer cells and white blood cells, thereby imparing the function of the immune system.[16.2] [16.3] [16.4] [16.5] In reviewing the influence of the high-fat diet on the immune system, Dr. Neal Barnard (president of the Physician's Committee for Responsible Medicine) cites research which shows that vegetarians have twice the natural-killer-cell activity of non-vegetarians.[16.5] [16.6] Dr. Barnard attributes this difference not only to the lower fat content of vegetarian diets but also to the higher consumption of antioxidants such as beta carotene and vitamin C.

The cause of lung cancer, make no mistake, is the breathing of fouled air, usually by smoking, but also by breathing pollution of other sorts. However, the chance of contracting this disease can be greatly increased by making the wrong nutritional choices; namely, animal products and fats.

Dr. Ernst Wynder, in a study reported in the *Journal of the National Cancer Institute,*[10] stated that "calories from dietary fat were highly significantly correlated with lung cancer mortality." His research showed that *the association of fat intake to death from lung cancer was stronger by far than the association to smoking.* When the cancer-causing substance (tobacco smoke) has been introduced, dietary fat consumption becomes a stronger promoter of lung cancer than the tobacco smoke itself.

Vegetarian smokers have a lower rate of lung cancer than meat-eating smokers,[17] and high blood-cholesterol levels among all smokers relate to a higher incidence of lung cancer.[18] Both smoking and high-fat, high-cholesterol diets are killers and diametrically opposed to cancer prevention.

COLON AND RECTAL CANCER, FAT, AND BOWEL MOVEMENTS: WHAT IS THE RELATIONSHIP?

Low-fiber, high-fat nutrition habits are prime factors in the development of colon and rectal cancer. Fats are also adept at supporting the growth of these cancers.[19 20 21 22 23 24 25 26] There are 155,000 new cases per year and approximately 61,000 deaths, making colon and rectal cancer the second most deadly type of cancer.[4] Those populations that consume large quantities of refined foods, fats and animal products develop much more colon cancer than those populations where the basic nutrition consists of vegetables, grains and fruits.[27]

One of the mechanisms by which high-fat diets promote colon cancer is to cause the body to produce excessive bile acids, which are dumped into the colon. In the colon, these acids become strong carcinogens (cancer promoters) in both animals and humans.[28] [29] [30] [31] [32] [33]

In one experiment, three different diets were given to 12 men during three 20-day periods:[34] A mixed diet, a lacto-vegetarian diet, and a vegan diet (no animal products). Fecal levels of cholesterol and bile acids were highest on mixed diet. Levels of these carcinogens were lowest on the vegan diet. In view of that fact, it would certainly be expected that those who consume a high-fat diet are susceptible to colon and rectal cancers. This is borne out in population studies that show nearly a straight line increase in colon cancer as the consumption of fat increases country by country.

Figure 2 portrays the influence of fat consumption among various countries to death rates from colon cancer.[35]

Eat the meat, destroy the colon.

There is one risk factor for colon cancer that is perhaps more potent than the consumption of fats per se and that is the consumption of meat. The consumption of beef, chicken and pork correlates so closely to the rate of colon cancer that researchers have concluded that there is a dose-response relationship.[36] The same holds true for animal products per se.[37] [38] [39] [40] [41] In a recent report in the *New England Journal of Medicine* it was stated that women who ate beef, pork or lamb daily had 2.5 times the rate of colon cancer as those who ate these products once per month or less.

Change the lifestyle, change the risk.

What occurs when the Chinese move to North America and adopt a high-fat, high-meat diet? The rate of colon cancer increases dramatically.[43] Chinese-American women have a four times greater rate of colon and rectal cancer than their Chinese counterparts. For men, the rate is seven times greater. Dr. Alice Whittemore, who conducted a study on the Chinese in each country, noted a profound difference in colon cancer rates based on the consumption of saturated fats *and* the amount of physical

FIGURE 2:
Relationship of Dietary Fat Intake
To Death from Colon Cancer

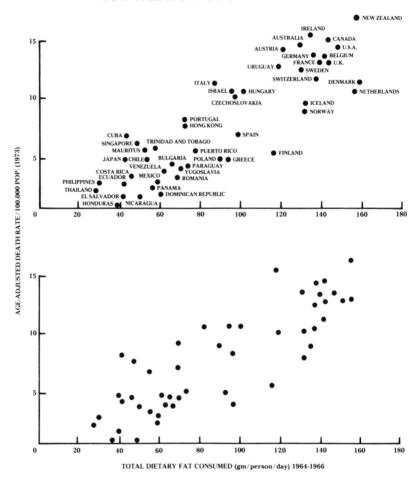

TOTAL DIETARY FAT CONSUMED (gm/person/day) 1964-1966

activity in which each group participated.

Dr. Whittemore concluded that saturated fat intake of more than ten grams per day could account for 60% of colon and rectal cancer among Chinese-American men and 40% among women.[35] Ten grams of fat per day is a very small amount—only 90 calories of fat. Most saturated fat, of course, is consumed in animal products. Other research confirms the profound influence of saturated fats on colon cancer.[44] [45] [46] When will we learn?

Dr. Whittemore's research also determined that among the most sedentary people, colon and rectal cancers increased more than 400% with increasing saturated fat consumption.

Exercise: A protection against potential colon cancer

In both North America and China, according to Dr. Whittemore, colon cancer increased with the amount of time spent sitting! In view of the data presented in the fitness chapter, this is not surprising. A major study reported in September 1991 in the *Journal of the National Cancer Institute*[43 · 1] showed that men who were very active (using at least 2500 calories per week in activity) had only half the chance of developing colon cancer as those who were inactive (using less than 1000 calories per week in activity).

Cholesterol does more than cause heart disease.

The intake of dietary cholesterol may also promote colon cancer.[21] [47] It is suspected that cholesterol acts as a co-carcinogen in the disease process.[21] This means that once the primary cause of the cancer is present, the cholesterol in the colon will stimulate the cancer to develop. Or, that it will greatly accelerate cancer growth. When rats have been given carcinogens and then "deprived" of dietary cholesterol, the rate of colon cancer is reduced, and the survival of the animals is prolonged.[47]

Of particular interest is the fact that in high-fat-consuming countries, colon cancer is sometimes more prevalent in those who have lower blood-cholesterol levels. This does not mean that low cholesterol levels cause colon cancer—quite the opposite. Colon cancer, once established, is capable of lowering cholesterol levels.

It can be stated with certainty that in societies on low-fat diets, those who consume more dietary cholesterol also have a higher rate of colon cancer. This higher rate is independent of serum-cholesterol levels. And, within societies such as the

Chinese, colon cancer decreases as blood cholesterol levels decrease. (See the chapter on heart disease for a complete discussion of blood cholesterol, dietary cholesterol and colon cancer.)

Polyunsaturates may contribute to colon cancer.

It is currently in vogue to increase the quantity of polyunsaturated fats in the diet to lower cholesterol and thereby reduce the chance of heart disease. This is unwise therapy, since such manipulation has lowered the incidence of heart disease but has probably increased the incidence of cancer.

When experimental animals are switched from a diet high in cholesterol and saturated fats to a diet high in cholesterol and polyunsaturates, greater numbers of cancerous tumors are produced.[48] It appears that polyunsaturates may lower blood cholesterol by forcing more cholesterol into the intestine, where it becomes the co-carcinogen previously described.

Concentrated polyunsaturates may or may not have some positive influence on heart disease. However, they should not be used as medicine, since their role in producing cancer is well established. It is not enough to reduce the quantity of animal products and saturated fats in one's diet. All excess fat should be eliminated. There is ample fat for good health in vegetables, grains, legumes and fruit. Excessive fat is dangerous, and a combination of sugar and fat, such as in pastries and candies, may be even more so.[49]

Fabulous fiber

The rate of colon cancer diminishes on a diet that is high in fiber.[50] [51] [52] [53] [54] Naturally-occurring high-fiber diets are also those which contain a very small portion of their calories in fat; therefore, it is difficult to determine whether it is fiber or lack of dietary fat that is responsible for lessened risk from colon cancer. It really doesn't matter, of course, since those who consume large quantities of unrefined grains, vegetables, and fruits (without added fats) will automatically receive the best of both nutritional recommendations.

Colon cancer and regularity—
Three movements per day keeps the doctor away.

Fiber consumption increases the number of bowel movements. In populations where the number of bowel movements per person per day is more than two, colon cancer is virtually unknown.[55] In "developed" Western societies where colon cancer is epidemic, 63-85% of the population have bowel movements once per day or less.[56] It is theorized that the increased fecal mass dilutes the carcinogens in the intestine and transports them out of the body before they have had time to make prolonged contact with the colon and rectum. Equally important is the fact that high-fiber diets generally contain fewer carcinogens to begin with, since they are usually low in fat and animal proteins.

High-fiber diets are good for colon health; therefore, adding concentrated fiber to cancer-causing foods such as meat and fat may effect a positive influence on colon cancer. However, if one wishes to most dramatically reduce the risk of colon cancer, then he or she should also eat as little of the carcinogen as possible. We should mimic the eating patterns of populations which have very little cancer. None of these societies add fiber as a therapy. They simply eat the nutrition-rich plant foods which are available and thereby reap the benefits of both high fiber and low fat.

Research shows conclusively that colon cancer is either caused or promoted by high-cholesterol, high-fat diets. Why, then, is so much money being spent to find a drug that will cure cancer while ignoring the education of the American public? The billions of dollars spent on drug research could be better spent in placing educational materials in the hands of every man, woman and child in the country.

The answer is quite simple. No one makes money by educating the public to the hazards of meat and fat. The pharmaceutical companies make no profit; the beef, chicken and fish industries don't profit, and the dairy industry doesn't profit. The only people who could profit from such action are the marked multitudes whose lives could be freed of the pain and disability.

As with heart disease, osteoporosis, diabetes, gallbladder

disease, kidney disease and others, we will not find a cure in the pill bottle nor in the hypodermic needle. At best, the pharmaceutical companies are looking for an antidote for the dietary toxins. Cures are better accomplished by removing the causes rather than trying to reverse the damage.

For the responsible individual determined to reduce his chances of colon cancer, the expedient of eliminating the carcinogens should be the first action taken. Since there are indeed dose-response relationships between both animal product and fat consumption to the development of colon and rectal cancers, he or she should consume the least possible quantity of these products. What an unusual idea!

BREAST CANCER—HOW MANY WOMEN WILL DIE NEEDLESSLY?

The increase in breast cancer in the past few years is astonishing. There has been an increase of 24% in the breast-cancer rate between 1980 and 1986,[4] and the disease shows no signs of abating. In 1990, the odds of a woman contracting breast cancer were 1-in-10. The report from the American Cancer Society for 1991, however, shows a 1-in-9 risk.[57]

This cancer is one of a group of cancers which is hormone-dependent. It is influenced primarily by three factors: (1) estrogen and progesterone, either naturally produced or ingested orally; (2) high-fat nutrition; (3) lack of physical fitness. The three factors are inextricably linked, however, and a good program of prevention will include alterations in all three for most American women.

Too much estrogen causes breast cancer.

A hormone-dependent cancer develops only in the presence of a particular hormone. In the case of breast cancer, the primary hormone is estrogen,[58] [59] although progesterone may come into play. To illustrate the importance of estrogen, we can consider women who never produce estrogen due to lack of ovarian function. These women *do not* incur breast cancer. The direct effect of estrogen is also seen in the fact that of the estimated 44,300 deaths from breast cancer in 1990, 44,000 occurred in women and only 300 in men.[4] Women, of course, produce more estrogen than men. The greater the amount of estrogen production, the greater is the risk that breast cancer will develop; and, once developed, the greater the estrogen availability, the faster the cancer will grow.[59]

This is not to say that "normal" estrogen levels should be considered dangerous. But, when the hormone is over-produced, the risk of the cancer is certainly increased. Further influences of estrogen on breast cancer are seen in the fact that when estrogen pills or any other type of artificial estrogen are taken, the risk of breast cancer increases considerably.[60] [61] [62]

Nutrition determines how much estrogen is produced.

What we eat has a profound influence on the production and elimination of sex hormones. When comparisons of the blood levels of estrogen and other sex hormones are made between vegetarian women and meat eaters, it is found that meat eaters have significantly higher levels.[63] Even a temporary change to a vegetarian diet can drop the levels of estrogen significantly.[64] Excessive estrogens are excreted through the feces, and there is an inverse relationship between blood estrogen levels and the fecal estrogen levels.[65] Vegetarians produce twice the fecal bulk as omnivorous women and excrete much more estrogen in that bulk.[63] It makes sense that if estrogens are carried out in the feces, they cannot be reabsorbed into the blood, where they can contribute to breast cancer.

When comparisons are made between vegetarians and omnivorous women, vegetarians show much *lower* levels of urinary estrogen.[66] A high level of urinary estrogen is correlated with a high incidence of breast cancer.[67]

As with colon cancer, there is a compelling correlation between breast cancer and the intake of dietary fats. The more fats consumed, the greater the incidence of the cancer.[68] [69] [70] [71] [72] [73] [74] [75] The same relationship exists between fat consumption and the level of estrogen in the blood,[76] indicating that high-fat diets cause high levels of estrogen in women, which in turn induce breast cancer.

Conversely, when women switch to "low-fat" diets, there is a precipitous drop in the levels of cancer-causing estrogens.[77] [78] [79] [80] This decrease can be as much as by 36% in a period of only 8-10 weeks.[77] This is accomplished by reducing consumption of fat to 25% of total calories, which can hardly be considered a low-fat diet. It is, however, considerably lower in fat than the 36-40% fat diet typical of American consumption. A much bigger drop in estrogen levels might be achieved by using a "real" low-fat diet, consisting of about 10% of total calories in fat.

Figure 3 illustrates the association between fat consumption and breast cancer in various countries.

Why do estrogen levels increase on high-fat diets?

There are two reasons for the exceptionally high blood-estrogen levels and low fecal-estrogen levels in women consuming a high-fat diet. Estrogens, after exerting influence on their target organs, are usually excreted into the intestine to be carried away. In the intestine they combine with nonabsorbable "carrier" substances that escort them out of the body by way of the feces. If this process does not take place, estrogens are reabsorbed into the blood where they build up in excessive amounts.[58] [65] [80]

A second reason for the high levels of estrogen in many women is obesity. Fat converts androgens (male hormones occurring in both sexes) to estrogens.[81] This is accomplished by the enzyme aromatase, which is present in fat tissue. In women who are obese, there is an elevated level of aromatase, meaning that they will produce more estrogens.[82] [83] These estrogens add to the now-excessive estrogen build-up in the blood.

Androgens, the raw material for estrogen production, are also much higher in meat-eating women than in vegetarians. This difference is primarily due to the increased consumption of animal proteins and fats. Lower androgen levels are associated with an increased consumption of carbohydrates, grains and fiber.[84]

FIGURE 3:
Relationship of Dietary Fat Consumption
To Death from Breast Cancer

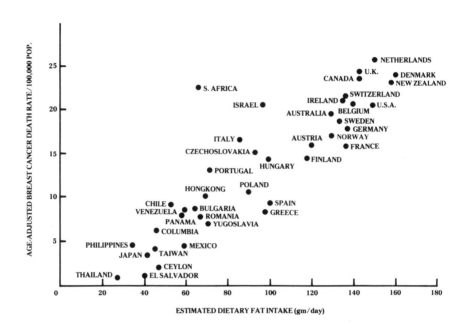

Those who consume a high-fat diet not only become more obese, but because of that obesity, convert more of their excessive androgens to estrogens and have a greater supply of androgens to convert!

HIGH-FAT DIETS = OBESITY =
MORE ANDROGENS + MORE AROMATASE =
MORE ESTROGEN = MORE BREAST CANCER

It is well known that obesity is associated with high levels of breast cancer.[85][86]

Another method of increasing the estrogen levels in women is to use oral contraceptives. The use of the "pill" for more than eight years has been shown in recent research to increase the incidence of breast cancer by 200%.[87]

Early menses is an international tragedy. Should girls be sexually mature at 12?

Perhaps the most shocking result of increasing estrogen levels is the decreasing age of menarche. Good examples are Oriental societies who have adopted American-style nutrition. In Japan, for instance, the age of menarche in 1875 was about 16.2 years of age. By 1950, that age had decreased to 15.2 years; by 1960, 13.0 years; by 1970, 12.5 years, and by 1974, 12.2 years.[88 89]

It is interesting that as these changes took place, they were accompanied by increases in the rates of several major cancers. During the same period, there was an accompanying surge in fat consumption and in the rates for cancers of the colon, breast and lung.[89]

In Chinese societies, the intake of fat is very low and the intake of calories from starch (complex carbohydrate) very high. The age of menarche ranges between 15.2 and 18.9 years, and there is a low rate of breast cancer.[90]

There is ample research to confirm the relationship of early menarche with a greatly increased rate of breast cancer.[91 92] It is a fact that girls who menstruate for the first time at an age younger than 13 have four times the rate of breast cancer as those who start after they are 17.[93]

As this is being written, my wife Vicki informs me that she has been watching an aerobic exercise program in which the instructor suggests that mothers should be concerned if their daughters have not menstruated by age of 12. She suggests that the family doctors should give them estrogen to compensate for this "abnormality." "It is not normal to wait until 15 years of age to menstruate," the instructor says. Somehow, she and I must have been reading different literature. How many cases of breast and uterine cancer will result from this remark to a nationwide television audience?

Mental health of young women is also negatively influenced by precocious sexuality. Girls between the ages of nine and 15 are not ready to cope with the physiological and anatomical changes that make them capable of reproductive activity. Should little girls have to endure the monthly period? Should a young lady of 12 need to be plagued by sexual urges that she is not emotionally mature enough to handle—possessing a 16- to 18-year-old body and a 12-year-old mind?

Should she be forced into an increased risk of venereal disease, unwanted pregnancy and reproductive cancer? These things are, to a great extent, caused by unwise nutritional choices—choices that are taught to her by family, TV and peers.

Girls at the age of 16 are ready to start dating and to have young men notice them. Before that, they should be free to enjoy childhood rather than being thrown into the adult world of man-woman relationships.

In their book, *The Day America Told the Truth,*[93.1] James Patterson and Peter Kim note the following frightening statistics:

1.   One in five children have lost their virtue by age 13.

2.   Almost ⅔ have lost their virtue by the age of 16.

It is no wonder that we have a problem with teen-age pregnancy, abortions and social diseases that threaten the fiber of our country. These problems could be dramatically reduced through feeding children properly during their formative years. This, along with strong moral training and example from parents and guardians, could remove a multitude of problems that beset our "oversexed" youth.

Late menopause: Another breast cancer risk factor

Not only do excessive fats bring on early menarche, but they also cause late menopause, which is associated with an increased breast cancer rate.[58 94 95 96 97] When women menstruate for the first time, the levels of estrogen they produce are greatly increased. Those on a high-fat diet produce far more estrogen than those on a low-fat diet. Not only do they start the large flow of estrogen four years earlier, but they experience menopause four years later, meaning that they add eight years of high estrogen activity to their lives. Since breast cancer is a hormone-dependent cancer, is it any wonder that these women have such high death rates from that disease?

"Death by fried chicken"

Within Japan, those women who consume the most fat have the highest level of cancer.[93] Japanese-American women also have rates of breast cancer equal to their Caucasian counterparts.[98] [99] [100] This is conclusive proof that the variations in breast cancer rates between Japan and America is not due to ethnic nor genetic differences.

A recent article in *Newsweek Magazine* called the Japanese increase in breast cancer and other "Western" diseases, "Death by Fried Chicken."[101] Such a title is an apt description of the nutritional hari kari being committed in Japan now that America has endowed the Japanese with its "fast-fat" franchises.

Nishamaru Shinuya, author of a best-selling book in Japan, is quoted in the *Newsweek* article as saying he believes that half of the Japanese who were born after 1959 will die before they are 41 years old.[86] He predicts that only 1/5 of the remainder will be around for ten years after that.

This is an interesting speculation in view of the fact that the average age at death is about 80 years—the highest life expectancy of any nation in the world. In 1988, however, there were 42,000 more deaths in Japan than in 1987—the first time in a decade in which deaths had not shown a decline. Shinuya's words may indeed be prophetic.

To reduce breast cancer risk, get the fat out!

There are those who question the role of dietary fat as a cause of breast cancer. Part of this skepticism is due to research which found no significant difference in breast cancer and colon cancer rates in women when fat consumption ranged from 32% to 44% of total calories.[102] [103] This was also true of prostate and colon cancer rates in men. This is not surprising, since 32% of total calories can hardly be considered a low-fat diet! Other studies indicate that there is a threshold level of fat at which breast cancer rates start to diminish, and that level is between 25 and 30%.[104]

One researcher indicated that women who consumed less than 30% of calories from fat had only half the normal rate of breast cancer.[105] It is no wonder that comparing intakes of 32% to intakes of 44% usually shows little in the way of a protective effect with a "low-fat" diet.

One piece of research, however, shows that breast cancer rates increase with increasing fat consumption—even when that consumption increases from 30% of calories to over 40%.[106] The reason for the discrepancy is unknown.

But will a low-fat diet actually decrease the risk of breast cancer?

It certainly makes sense that changing to a low-fat diet would decrease the risk of breast cancer, but until lately, it has not been proven to do so. There are those who agree that populations that eat a low-fat diet have a lesser degree of cancer. They are not convinced, however, that a switch to a low-fat diet will do any good for a person who has been on a high-fat diet. In other words, once the damage of the high-fat diet has been done, they believe that a change will probably do little good.

Recent evidence indicates that reducing the dietary fat can make a considerable difference in the rate of breast cancer and other cancers.[106.1] Women who had switched to a low-fat (20% of calories from fat) diet from a typical American diet had only a bout ⅔ the rate of cancers as did those who continued to eat the fatty American diet. The study continued for a three-year period, indicating that a dramatic decrease in cancer incidence can be achieved in a short period of time by reducing fat in the diet. It is my opinion that the results would have been much more dramatic if the fat content of the diet had been reduced to 10% or less.

The salient point is that population studies show conclusively that increasing fat consumption relates closely to the incidence of breast cancer at consumption rates less than 30% of total calories.

Since the "Westernization" of Japan, there has been an

increase in fat consumption from 7.5% to 28% of total calories. There has also been a concomitant rise in breast cancer rates.[104] This attests that 28% of total calories in fat may be much too high. However, the breast cancer rate for Japanese women is still much lower than the rate for Americans, either Japanese or Caucasian. It appears that a diet that is about 10% or less of total calories in fat is most protective against breast cancer.

In both China and Japan, the lowest fat consumption (6-7%) predicts the lowest cancer rate. There is little doubt that dietary fat is the primary factor in promoting breast cancer.[107]

Below a consumption of 30% of total calories in fat, *every 10% increase predicts a 30% increase in the incidence of the disease.*[108] Of particular concern are saturated fats, which seem to have the most profound relationship to incidence of breast cancer.[109] [110] [111] [112] [113] All fats, however, should be kept to a minimum, including monounsaturates. Total dietary fats relate very highly to breast cancer, even when most of the fat is monounsaturated.[114]

Eat animals, get breast cancer.

There are also compelling correlations between breast cancer and the consumption of animal products.[93] [113] These products, of course, are usually replete with fat and cholesterol, so the association is not surprising. The animal proteins contained in these products, however, may exert their influences independently of fat and cholesterol.

An interesting piece of research was conducted at Cornell University[115] in which rats were given aflotoxin, a carcinogen that promotes liver cancer in animals. When the rats were given a high-protein diet, the liver cancer developed quite rapidly. When put on a low-protein diet, the development of the cancers abruptly stopped. When the high-protein diet was again used, the cancers again began to grow.

It was also noted that when the diet was switched from a high-animal-protein diet to a diet high in vegetable protein, the cancers developed at much slower rates. An interesting facet of this study was the finding that when the vegetable protein used in the study (wheat) was altered to more closely resemble an animal protein, the cancer-producing influences became equal to those of the animal proteins. It is also well to note that the cancer-promoting animal protein in this experiment was casein, which is derived from milk.

It is probable that there are some of the same underlying causes for many of the different forms of cancer. There are, of course, three potential carcinogens (or co-carcinogens) in many animal products: fat, animal protein, and cholesterol.

Grow tall, die young.

The hormones that cause breast cancer also stimulate growth. It was previously disclosed that there was a close correlation between obesity and breast cancer. We might expect that women who are tall and those who are heavy are at higher risk for breast cancer. *This is exactly the case. Tall and heavy women in Japan have a rate of breast cancer which is 11.5 times higher than those who are small.*[93]

Women in the U.S. also show considerably increased risk for breast cancer with increasing body size.[116] There is no doubt that as the quantity of fat and meat consumption has increased in both the U.S. and Japan, there has been an increase in the physical stature of the people. High-fat diets produce excessive sex hormones, which produce both large bodies and cancer. We pay a dear price for the increase in stature. In the case of cancer, bigger is certainly not better!

Let's get fit!

Cancer rates are dramatically lower in those who keep themselves fit. (See the chapter on fitness.) Physical fitness acts primarily as a prophylactic against the ravages of the American diet. Therefore, it is wise to include regular daily exercise in any program of cancer prevention, and it is absolutely imperative for the person who refuses to eat correctly.

A little surprise about calorie consumption and cancer. The fewer calories you eat, the more likely you are to contract breast cancer.

In the chapter on obesity, research is presented which shows that obese people eat fewer total calories and far fewer calories per pound of body weight than thin people. Eating more calories—in other words, a higher energy intake—might protect against breast cancer, since obesity is a risk factor for that cancer.

A recent study reported in the *American Journal of Clinical Nutrition*[117] confirmed that opinion. Women who consumed more than 2335 calories per day had only 58% of the number of breast cancer cases as those who consumed less than 1792 calories per day! The same study showed a strong inverse correlation between carbohydrate consumption and breast cancer rate, meaning that the extra calories were coming from carbohydrates. Just what the doctor ordered!

Do low calorie diets contribute to breast cancer?

We have shown that as fat cells become larger, they become more efficient at converting androgens to estrogens and that more estrogens are produced by fatter bodies. We have also firmly established in the chapter on obesity that calorie-restricted dieting is a very potent producer of fat bodies. If, year by year, an increasing number of women joins the ranks of the dieters, then we would expect to see the female population becoming fatter. We would also expect fatter bodies to produce higher levels of estrogen, thereby increasing the rate of breast cancer.

Although we have no statistics on the increase in dieting among adults, we know that since 1970, the percentage of teenage girls who are on a diet on any given day has increased from 30% to an amazing 63%![118] It is likely that this increase holds for other segments of the female population. Research presented in the obesity chapter shows that the female population is still getting fatter. It is my opinion that the quick, upward trajectory of breast cancer cases is due in part to increased dieting among women. The number of dieters is increasing, the number of fat women is increasing, and breast cancer is increasing at an alarming rate.

The relationship of dieting to breast cancer has not been scientifically proven, but it is quite plausible and certainly furnishes a better explanation for the proliferation of breast cancer than anything else that has been put forth. Since most cancers take years to develop to the point that they are detectable, it is unlikely that the increase in breast cancer cases has peaked, nor will it peak if women continue their "starve and binge" programs.

Menopausal estrogen treatments promote breast cancer.

One of the more frightening trends in the field of medicine is the almost universal practice of prescribing estrogen to post-menopausal women to prevent osteoporosis and to protect against heart disease. This is known as *estrogen replacement therapy* and is a dangerous practice indeed.

A review of all valid research conducted on the relationship of menopausal estrogen use to the risk of breast cancer was reported recently in the *Journal of the American Medical Association*. The authors found a direct relationship between the duration of estrogen use and the risk of development of breast cancer.[62] If women used estrogen replacement therapy for 15 years, the risk of breast cancer increased by 30%. Approximately three million women use this therapy. The authors further point out that the therapy may cause approximately 4708 new cases of breast cancer per year and 1,468 deaths.

Of further importance is the fact that with 25 years of estrogen use, the increase in risk of breast cancer is 50%.[62] Twenty-five years of estrogen treatment is a goal which many doctors are suggesting to their patients.

The authors reviewed all of the studies for quality of experimental design and validity of research. When analyzing only the studies that were deemed to be of the highest quality, the picture became more bleak. Fifteen-year estrogen use would increase breast cancer risk by 60%. Twenty-five years would increase risk by 100%. This extrapolates to 10,000 new (and unnecessary) cases of breast cancer per year and 3000 deaths!

In commenting on this opinion, Dr. Sidney Wolfe, editor of the *Public Citizen Health Research Group Health Letter*, states that, "in the meantime, the FDA should move to force American Home Products and other companies manufacturing estrogens to update the labeling, which grossly understates the clear risk of breast cancer."[118.1]

We firmly established in the osteoporosis chapter that estrogen therapy is totally unnecessary as a method to prevent bone loss. We also showed that nutrition free from animal proteins, plus an exercise program, could prevent—and to an extent reverse—osteoporosis. Therefore, one of the prime reasons for the use of these dangerous hormones is null and void.

A second reason for the use of these hormones is the belief that they will prevent heart disease. However, some studies indicate that estrogen treatments may increase the risk of the disease.[118.1] One physician indicates that the reduction in death from heart disease may be due to the fact that leaner, more educated, wealthier women are more likely to take the hormones (due to the belief that they are good for health) than poorer, heavier women. Thinner, wealthier, educated women, of course, are already at a decreased risk for heart disease. When compared to the poorer, heavier women, they will show a decreased risk regardless of whether they take hormone treatments.[118.2]

DNA damage by the high-fat diet

DNA, a chemical that determines genetic characteristics, is a constituent of all living cells. When oxygen combines with DNA, it causes damage which may promote cancerous tumors.[118.3] Such damage is thought to be an intermediate indication of breast cancer risk.[118.4]

A 1991 study in the *Journal of the National Cancer Institute* showed the results of a low- versus high-fat diet on the level of oxidative damage to DNA among women at high risk for breast cancer.[118.4] Women who were placed on the high-fat diet had three times the level of oxidative damage as those on the low-fat diet. It is not known whether the damage was caused by excessive estrogens or by the fat itself. It is, however, another indication of the unnecessary havoc wrought by a high-fat diet.

UTERINE CANCER

Uterine cancer afflicts another 46,500 women per year, which results in approximately 10,000 deaths.[4] The ACS lists the risk factors for this disease (which includes cancers of both the cervix and endometrium) as early age at first sexual intercourse, multiple sex partners, cigarette smoking, history of infertility, failure to ovulate, prolonged estrogen therapy, and obesity.

The ACS again fails to mention the close relationship between consumption of fat and uterine cancer. If early intercourse is a risk factor for uterine cancer, who is apt to have intercourse earlier—a girl who is precociously sexual or one who is not? We have already established that the high-fat diet causes young women to become sexually mature years earlier than nature intended.

Excessive estrogen strikes again.

Estrogen is also a risk-factor for uterine cancer.[119] [120] [121] It is necessary to repeat for emphasis at this point that progesterone treatments are often combined with estrogen treatments to reduce the risk of uterine cancer. *These treatments have been shown to increase the rate of breast cancer by 440%.*[122] Obesity, which increases the quantity of estrogens (see breast cancer) is also associated with increased rates of uterine cancer.[123]

The high-fat diet, as previously noted, is very effective at producing high levels of estrogen. The best prevention and therapy is to eat a low-fat diet and, on a physician's advice, consider giving up estrogen therapy. Remember: Bone loss will not be a problem when proper nutrition is used. (See the chapter on osteoporosis.) If we look back at Figure 3 (Breast Cancer and Fat Consumption), we can substitute uterine cancer for breast cancer and see an almost identical relationship.

OVARIAN CANCER

Ovarian cancer is less common than uterine cancer but far more deadly. Twenty thousand five hundred new cases were estimated for 1990, along with 12,400 deaths.[4] As with uterine and breast cancer, estrogen greatly increases the risk. Estrogen treatments cause ovarian cancer in animals, and the drug Premarin, an estrogen used to alleviate menopausal symptoms, can increase the incidence of ovarian cancer 2-3 fold.[124]

In experiments on dogs, hormone treatments produced cancers in 75-80% of the dogs treated.[124] When the hormones were withdrawn, it took only a few months for the cancers to begin to regress. Ovarian cancer is another hormone-dependent cancer, and it probably matters little whether the hormones are taken in the form of a drug or produced by the high-fat diet of the typical American woman.

It is a bit surprising that the correlation of sex hormones as a cause of various cancers is not more widely addressed and that the information is not distributed to potential victims. It has been known for nearly 60 years that sex hormones cause cancer in laboratory animals.[125] [126] [127] We have already discussed the mechanisms by which the high-fat diet increases blood estrogen levels. We should then expect a high-fat diet to relate closely to the incidence of ovarian cancer, since it is hormone dependent. At least one study confirms this relationship.[128]

Is yogurt a health food?

Ovarian cancer may also be influenced by particular types of dairy products; namely, those prepared from cultured milk. Women who consume one or more helpings of cottage cheese per month increase the risk of ovarian cancer by 40% when compared to those who eat these products less than once per month.[129] Those who consume one or more helpings of yogurt per month increase the chance of ovarian cancer by 70%.

It appears that the breakdown of lactose by the "culture" bacteria produces a chemical that acts as a co-carcinogen for ovarian cancer. It is surprising that people believe that a harmful food such as cow's milk can be rotted with bacteria and thereby turned into a health food! *We need to think.*

PROSTATE CANCER

There are approximately 106,000 new cases of prostate cancer per year in the U.S. Thirty thousand deaths per year result from the disease.[4] Among all cancers, only lung cancer kills more men.

Dietary fat: A primary cause once again

As with the other cancers thus far considered, prostate cancer relates very closely to eating patterns, and fat consumption again emerges as a primary culprit.[130] Japanese men, who consume far less fat than Americans, have only about 1/40 the rate of prostate cancer as American Blacks, who have the highest rate in the world.[131] [132] Japanese men whose families migrated generations earlier to the U.S., however, have a very high rate of fatal prostate cancer compared to men living in Japan.[132.1]

However, as fat consumption has increased in Japan, there has been a concurrent increase in the rate of prostate cancer.[133] Rates of prostate cancer correlate closely to fat consumption when countries are compared to each other,[134] [135] when ethnic groups are compared,[136] and when people from different counties or from different geographical areas in the same country are compared.[137]

Those men who are prostate-cancer patients consume a diet higher in fat than those who do not have prostate cancer.[138] Those who consume larger quantities of saturated fat per se are also at greater risk.[139] (See Figure 4.) Again, fats from animal products, or perhaps even animal proteins, are the main causative factors.

When animal product consumption is compared to the rates of death, it is found that the consumption of meat and dairy products correlate very closely with the death rate.[140] [141] [142] [143] [144]

FIGURE 4:
Relationship of Dietary Fat Consumption
To Death from Prostate Cancer

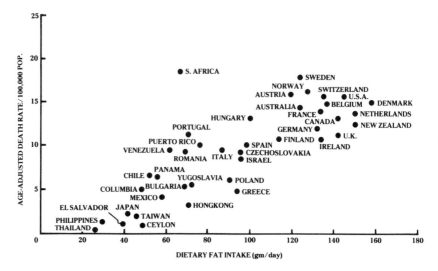

Obese men also have a death rate from prostate cancer much higher than non-obese men.[144]

We have established the effect of dietary fats on hormone production. Prostate cancer is influenced by hormones to as great an extent as breast and uterine cancer.[145] [146] [147] [148] And, like breast and uterine cancer, prostate cancer is hormone dependent.[149] [150]

Men: Eat a high fat diet and later in life you may not be able to urinate!

A disorder that may relate to prostate cancer is known as benign prostatic hyperplasia, a swelling of the prostate that usually occurs in later life. The swelling puts pressure on the urethra and sometimes makes urination difficult, painful or impossible. The development of this disease is also dependent on sex hormones, as evinced by the fact that it develops only in men who have intact testes. The process is dependent on testosterone and accelerated by estrogen.[151] Obese people, as established, produce more sex hormones than the non-obese. We would therefore expect a relationship between obesity and prostatic hyperplasia.

A vegetarian diet produces a decrease in levels of testosterone.[152] A low-fat diet does the same.[153] As with the other cancers, prevention depends on making proper nutritional choices. An important note: Men should not worry about decreased libido due to decreased testosterone levels. Many primitive societies who consume near-vegetarian diets are known for large families. And, as mentioned in the chapter on heart disease, the high-fat diet causes impotence.

PANCREATIC CANCER

Pancreatic cancer is the fifth leading cause of cancer death in the U.S., taking the lives of 25,000 people per year. This is a cancer which has a very poor survival rate, with only 3% of patients alive five years after diagnosis. It is a "silent" disease which shows no symptoms until it has progressed to advanced stages.[4] At the risk of sounding like a broken record, the statement that needs to be made about pancreatic cancer is that it occurs much more frequently in countries where fat consumption and/or animal product consumption is high.[4 154 155]

There is no doubt that the relationship of dietary-fat and animal-product consumption to the major cancers is absolutely monotonous. The same monotonous relationship exists between these dietary factors and heart disease, diabetes, kidney disease, gallbladder disease, osteoporosis, diverticular disease and who knows how many other infirmities. Perhaps if we keep belaboring the point, someone will listen. Anyone who states that these maladies are not due in great part to poor nutritional choices is engaging in wishful thinking. He is unable (or unwilling) to believe that he may be forced to make a choice between his addictions and his health.

EAT THOSE VEGIES!

Vegetable consumption protects against breast cancer and many other cancers. Women who consume the greatest quantity of vegetables have only 10% of the number of breast cancer cases as those who consume the least.[156] The most important vegetables may be those which contain vitamin A or its precursor, known as beta-carotene.[157] [158] [159] Those who have low levels of beta-carotene in their blood are at definite increased risk for breast cancer.[160] Recently, research has been reported which confirms that cancer of the larynx is 2½ times higher among those who consume the most fat as compared the those with the lowest fat intake. Cancer of the larynx is also twice as prevalent in those who consume the least beta-carotene.

Cruciferous vegetables such as brussel sprouts, cauliflower, and cabbage are very protective against colon cancer,[161] [162] and the consumption of vegetables and fruit in general correlates to lowered incidence of cancers such as colon,[163] [164] breast,[165] and lung.[166] There is also a protective influence of grain intake against these common cancers.[167] [168]

OTHER CANCERS

Cancers of the mouth, larynx, throat, and esophagus occur more frequently among those who drink alcohol or who use smokeless tobacco.[4] Liver cancer is increased by alcohol consumption. Foods that have been salt-cured, smoked and/or nitrite cured are linked to cancer of the stomach.[4] Vegetable consumption, however, is protective against stomach cancer.[35] Renal (kidney) cancer rates are increased by animal-protein consumption.[15]

Skin cancer, of course, is related to sun exposure, but I am not convinced that the prime cause of skin cancer is not the high-fat diet. Sunlight may act primarily as an activator. It is definitely not wise to overexpose, since the healthful effects of sun can be obtained in only a few minutes of daily exposure.

There are dozens of other cancers that may have varying

causes, but they comprise a small portion of the total—probably less than 10%. This means that cancer is, in most cases, preventable by altering environmental influences.

In the future, I believe research will show that nearly all cancers are related to controllable environmental factors. It is nonsense to assume that cancer is inevitable for a certain percentage of the population. The war on cancer will continue to be a farce until we remove the causes of the disease. Until that time, we are looking for an antidote, not a cure.

WHAT HAVE WE LEARNED?

1. Most cancers, and particularly the epidemic cancers of the lung, breast, colon, prostate, and uterus, can be prevented by a change in dietary habits.

2. Fat and animal-product consumptions are the environmental variables that relate most closely to these cancers. Other dietary factors that appear to increase some cancers include alcohol, nitrites and salt.

3. Fiber consumption and vegetable consumption are associated with a decreased risk of most cancers.

4. As with most other diseases, higher levels of physical fitness are associated with lessened risk of cancer, especially cancer of the breast and colon.

5. Recommendations are for a low-fat, high-fiber, low-animal-protein diet, along with exercise as delineated in the chapter on fitness. Always consult a physician before making changes in either diet or activity level.

Remember that an ounce of prevention may indeed be worth tons of cure, since conventional treatment, thus far, has been a debacle for most of the epidemic cancers.

REFERENCES

[1]Goldman, L. The decline in eschemic heart disease mortality rates. An analysis of the comparative effects of medical interventions and changes in lifestyle. Ann Intern Med 1984; 191:825-836.

[2]National Cancer Institute. Annual Update, 1990.

[2 1]American Hospital Association Report. Meditrends 1991-1992.

[3]Hopkins, G. Role of diet in cancer prevention. J Environ Toxicol Oncol 1985; 5:279-298.

[4]American Cancer Society. Cancer facts and figures, 1990, p. 1-22.

[5]Guyton, A. *Textbook of Medical Physiology.* W.B. Saunders, publishers, Philadelphia, PA 1981, p. 39.

[6]Bailar, J. Progress against cancer? N Engl J Med 1986; 314:1226-1232.

[7]Hinds, M. Dietary cholesterol and lung-cancer risk among men in Hawaii. Am J Clin Nutr 1983; 37:192-193.

[8]Kolonel, L. Nutrient intakes in relation to cancer incidence in Hawaii. Br J Cancer 1981; 44:332-339.

[9]Jain, M. Dietary factors and the risk of lung cancer: Results from a case-control study, Toronto, 1981-1985. Int J Cancer 1990; 45:287-293.

[10]Wynder, E. Association of dietary fat and lung cancer. JNCI 1987; 79:631.

[11]Gelboin, H. Benzo(a)pyrene metabolism, activation and carcinogenesis: Role of the regulation of mixed function oxidases and related enzymes. Physiol Rev 1980; 60:1107.

[12]Hall, T. Inhibition of human natural-killer-cell activity by prostaglandin D-2. Immunol Lett 1983; 7:141-144.

[13]Beems, R. Modifying effect of dietary fat on benzo(a)pyrene-induced respiratory tract tumors in hamsters. Carcinogenesis 1984; 5:413-417.

[14]Kroes, R. Nutritional factors in lung, colon, and prostate carcinogenesis in animal models. Fed Proc 1986; 45:136-141.

[15]Armstrong, B. Environmental factors and cancer incidence and mortality in different countries, with special reference to dietary practices. Int J Cancer 1975; 15:617-631.

[16]Carroll, K. Dietary fat in relation to tumorigenesis. Prog Biochem Pharamcol 1975; 10:308-353.

[16 1]Barone, J. Dietary fat and natural-killer-cell activity. Am J Clin Nutr 1989; 50:861-867.

[16 2]Endres, S. The effect of dietary supplementation with n-3 polyunsaturated fatty acids on the synthesis of interlukin-1 and tumor necrosis factor by mononuclear cells. N Engl J Med 1989; 320:265-271.

[16.3]Kelley, D. Dietary alpha-linoleic acid and immunocompetence in humans. Am J Clin Nutr 1991; 53:40-46.

[16.4]Hawley, H. The effects of long-chain free fatty acids on human neutrophil function and structure. Lab Invest 1976; 34:216-222.

[16.5]Nordenstrom, J. Decreased chemotaxic and random migration of leukocytes during intralipid infusion. Am J Clin Nutr 1979; 32:2416-2422.

[16.6]Barnard, Neal. Foods and immunity. Guide to healthy eating, July/August 1991, pp. 3-5, 15.

[16.7]Malter, M. Natural killer cells, vitamins, and other blood components of vegetarian and omnivorous men. Nutr Cancer 1989; 12:271-278.

[17]Lemon, F. Death from respiratory system disease in Seventh-day Adventist men. JAMA 1966; 198:137-146.

[18]Stamler, J. Elevated cholesterol may increase lung-cancer risk in smokers. Heart Res J Lett 1969; 14:2.

[19]Carroll, K. Experimental evidence of dietary factors and hormone-dependent cancers. Cancer Res 1975; 15:617-631.

[20]Walker, A. Colon cancer and diet, with special reference to intakes of fat and fiber. Am J Clin Nutr 1976; 29:1417-1426.

[21]Cruse, P. Dietary cholesterol is co-carcinogenic for human colon cancer. Lancet 1979; 1:752-755.

[22]Reddy, B. Effect of a diet with high levels of protein and fat on colon carcinogenesis in F344 rats treated with 1,2-dimethylhydrazine. JNCI 1976; 57:568-569.

[23]West, D. Dietary intake and colon cancer: Sex and anatomic site-specific associations. Am J Epidemiol 1989; 130:883-894.

[24]Vogel, V. Dietary epidemiology of colon cancer. Hematology/Oncology clinics of North America 1989; 3:35-63.

[25]Fruedenheim, J. A case-control study of diet and rectal cancer in western new York. Am J Epidemiol 1990; 131:612-624.

[26]Shike, M. Primary prevention of colorectal cancer. The WHO Collaborating Centre for the Prevention of Colorectal Cancer. Bull WHO 1990; 68:377-385.

[27]McDougall, J. *The McDougall Program. Twelve Days to Dynamic Health.* NAL Books, publishers, 1990, p. 327.

[28]Hill, M. Bacteria and aetiology of cancer of the large bowel. Lancet 1971; 1:95-100.

[29]Narisawa, T. Promoting effect of bile acids on colon carcinogenesis after intrarectal installation of N-Methyl-Nitro-Nitrosoguanidine in rats. JNCI 1974; 53:1093-1097.

[30]Chomchai, C. The effect of bile on the induction of experimental intestinal tumors in rats. Dis Colon Rectum 1974; 17:310-312.

[31]Galloway, D. Experimental colorectal cancer: The relationship of diet and faecal bile acid concentration to tumor induction. Br J Surg 1986; 73:233-237.

[32]Reddy, B. Dietary fat and its relationship to large bowel cancer. Cancer Res 1981; 41:3700-3705.

[33]Reddy, B. Metabolic epidemiology of colon cancer: Faecal bile acids and neutral sterols in colon cancer patients and patients with adenomatous polyps. Cancer 1977; 39:2533-2539.

[34]Van Fassen, A. Bile acids, neutral steroids and bacteria in feces as affected by a mixed, a lacto-vegetarian and a vegan diet. Am J Clin Nutr 1987; 46:962-967.

[35]Reddy, B. Nutrition and its relationship to cancer. Adv Cancer Res 1980; 12:237-345.

[36]Berg, J. Quoted in Robbins, *J Diet for A New America*. Stillpoint Publishing 1987, p. 254.

[37]Lee, H. Colorectal cancer and diet in an Asian population—A case control study among Singapore Chinese. Int J Cancer 1989; 43:1007-1016.

[38]Benito, E. A population-based case-control study of colorectal cancer in Majorca. Int J Cancer 1990; 45:69-76.

[39]West, D. Dietary intake and colon cancer. Sex and anatomic site-specific associations. Am J Epidemiol 1989; 130:883-894.

[40]Campbell, T. A study on diet, nutrition and disease in the People's Republic of China, Part II. Division of Nutritional Sciences, Cornell University, Ithaca, NY, November 1989.

[41]Campbell, T. Personal communication, May 1990.

[42]Willet, W. Relation of meat, fat, and fiber intake to the risk of colon cancer in a prospective study among women. N Engl J Med 1990; 323:1664-1672.

[43]Whittemore, A. Diet, physical activity and colorectal cancer among Chinese in North America and China. JNCI 1990; 82:915-926.

[43.1]Lee, I. Physical activity and risk of developing colorectal cancer among college alumni. JNCI 1991; 83:1324-1329.

[44]Berrino, F. Mediterranean diet and cancer. Europe J Clin Nutr 1989; 43 (supp 2):49-55.

[45]Benito, E. A population-based case-control study of colorectal cancer in Majorca. Int J Cancer 1990; 45:69-76.

[46]Willett, W. The search for the causes of breast and colon cancer. Nature 1989; 338:389-394.

[47]Cruse, J. Dietary cholesterol deprivation improves survival and reduces incidence of metastatic colon cancer in dimethylhydrazine-pretreated rats. Gut 1982; 23:594-599.

[48]Broitman, S. Polyunsaturated fat, cholesterol, and large-bowel tumorigenesis. Cancer 1977; 40:2455-2463.

[49]Bristol, J. Sugar, fat and the risk of colorectal cancer. Br Med J 1985; 291:1467-1470.

[50]Cummings, J. Dietary fibre and large bowel cancer. Proc Nutr Soc 1981; 40:7-14.

[51]Burkitt, D. Colon-rectal cancer: Fiber and other dietary factors. Am J Clin Nutr 1978; 31:558-564.

[52]Reddy, B. Nutrition and its relationship to cancer. Adv Cancer Res 1980; 32:237-245.

[53]Nigro, N. Effect of dietary fiber on azoxymethane-induced intestinal carcinogenesis in rats. JNCI 1979; 62:1097-1102.

[54]Freeman, H. Dietary fibre and colonic neoplasia. Can Med Assoc J 1979; 121:291-296.

[55]Walker, A. Colon cancer and diet, with special reference to intakes of fat and fiber. Am J Clin Nutr 1976; 29:1417-1426.

[56]Connel, A. Variation in bowel habits in two population samples. Brit Med J 1965; 2:1095-1099.

[57]Friend, T. New breast cancer odds: 1-in-9 risk. USA Today, January 20, 1991.

[58]McDougall, J. *McDougall's Medicine: A Challenging Second Opinion.* New Century, publishers, 1985, pp. 19-23.

[59]Kirschner, M. The role of hormones in the etiology of human breast cancer. Cancer 1977; 39:2716-2726.

[60]Judd, H. Estrogen replacement therapy: Indications and complications. Ann Intern Med 1983; 98:195-205.

[61]Mills, P. Prospective study of exogenous homrone use and breast cancer in Seventh-day Adventists. Cancer 1989; 64:591-597.

[62]Steinberg, K. A meta-analysis of the effects of estrogen-replacement therapy on the risk of breast cancer. JAMA 1991; 265:1985-1990.

[63]Schultz, T. Nutrient intake and hormonal status of premenopausal vegetarian Seventh-day Adventist and premenopausal nonvegetarians. Nutr Cancer 1983; 4:247-259.

[64]Bennet, F. Diet and sex-hormone concentrations: An intervention study for the type of fat consumed. Am J Clin Nutr 1990; 52:808-812.

[65]Goldin, B. Estrogen excretion patterns and plasma levels in vegetarian and omnivorous women. N Engl J Med 1982; 307:1542-1547.

[66]Armstrong, B. Diet and reproductive hormones: A study of vegetarian and nonvegetarian postmenopausal women. JNCI 1981; 67:761-767.

[67]Morreal, C. Urinary excretion of estrone, estradiol, and estriol in post-menopausal women with primary breast cancer and in normal controls. JNCI 1979; 63:1171-1174.

[68]Lea, A. Dietary factors associated with death rates from certain neoplasms in man. Lancet 1966; 2:332-333.

[69]Carroll, K. Experimental evidence of dietary factors and hormone-dependent cancers. Cancer Res 1975; 35:3374-3383.

[70]Drasar, B. Environmental factors and cancer of the colon and breast. Br J Cancer 1973; 27:167-172.

[71]Armstrong, B. Environmental factors and cancer incidence and mortality in different countries with special reference to dietary practices. Int J Cancer 1975; 15:617-623.

[72]Knox, E. Foods and diseases. Br J Coc Prev Med 1977; 31:61-80.

[73]Hiryama, T. Epidemiology of breast cancer with special reference to the role of diet. Prev Med 1978; 7:173-195.

[74]Gray, G. Breast cancer incidence and mortality rates in different countries in relation to known factors and dietary practices. Br J Cancer 1979; 39:1-7.

[75]Hems, G. The contributions of diet and childbearing to breast cancer. Br J Cancer 1978; 37:974-982.

[76]Goldin, B. The relationship between estrogen levels and diets of caucasian-American and oriental-immigrant women. Am J Clin Nutr 1986; 44:945-953.

[77]Woods, M. Low-fat, high-fiber diet and serum estrone sulfate in premenopausal women. Am J Clin Nutr 1989; 49:1179-1183.

[78]Rose, D. Effect of a low-fat diet on hormone levels in women with cystic breast disease. I. Serum steroids and gonadotropins. JNCI 1987; 78:623-626.

[79]Rose, D. Effect of a low-fat diet on hormone levels in women with cystic breast disease. II. Serum radioimmunoassayable prolactin and growth hormone and bioactive lactogenic hormones. JNCI 1987; 78:627-631.

[80]Gorbach, S. Estrogens, breast cancer and intestinal flora. Rev Infect Des 1984; 6:supplement 1:S85-S89.

[81]Schindler, A. Conversion of androstenedione to estrone by human fat tissue. J Endocrinol Metab 1972; 35:627-630.

[82]MacDonald, P. Effect of obesity on conversion of plasma androstenedione to estrone in postmenopausal women with and without endometrial cancer. Am J Obstet Gynecol 1978; 130:448-455.

[83]McKenna, T. Pathogenesis and treatment of polycystic ovary syndrome. N Engl J Med 1988; 318:558-562.

[84]Aldercreutz, H. Diet and plasma androgens in postmenopausal vegetarian women with breast cancer. Am J Clin Nutr 1989; 49:433-442.

[85]Health Implications of Obesity. National Institutes of Health Consensus Development Conference Statement. 1990; 5(9):1-7.

[86]de Waard, F. Dietary fat and mammary cancer. Nutr and Cancer 1986; 8:5-8.

[87]U.K. national case-control study group. Oral contraceptives use and breast cancer risk in young women. Lancet 1989; i:973-982.

[88]Robbins, J. *Diet for A New America.* Stillpoint, publishers, Walpole, NH 1987, pp. 266-267.

[89]Kagawa, Y. Impact of westernization on the nutrition of the Japanese: Changes in physique, cancer, longevity and centenarians. Prev Med 1978; 7:205-217.

[90]Campbell, T. A study on diet, nutrition and disease in the People's Republic of China. Division of nutritional sciences, Cornell University, Ithaca, NY, p. 5.

[91]Staszewski, J. Age at menarche and breast cancer. JNCI 1971; 47:935-940.

[92]Hill, P. Diet, life style and menstrual activity. Am J Clin Nutr 1980; 33:1192-1198.

[93]Hirayama, T. Epidemiology of breast cancer with special reference to the role of diet. Prev Med 1978; 7:73-75.

[93 1]Patterson, J. The Day America Told the Truth. Prentice Hall, publishers, 1991.

[94]Frommer, D. Changing age of menopause. Br Med J 1964; 2:349-351.

[95]Trichopoulos, D. Menopause and breast-cancer risk. JNCI 1972; 48:605-613.

[96]Armstrong, B. Diet and reproductive hormones, a study of vegetarian and non-vegetarian postmenopausal women. JNCI 1981; 67:761-767.

[97]Hill, P. Environmental factors of breast and prostatic cancer. Cancer Res 1981; 41:3817-3818.

[98]Haenzel, W. Studies of Japanese migrants, 1. Mortality from cancer and other diseases among Japanese in the U.S. JNCI 1968; 40:43-51.

[99]Kolonel, L. Nutrient intakes in relation to cancer incidence in Hawaii. Br J Cancer 1981; 44:332-339.

[100]Buell, P. Changing incidence of breast cancer in Japanese-American women. JNCI 1973; 51:1479-1483.

[101]Powell, B. Death by fried chicken. Newsweek, September 24, 1990, p. 36.

[102]Willet, W. Dietary fat and the risk of breast cancer. N Engl J Med 1987; 316:22-28.

[103]Ezell, C. A little less fat won't cut cancer risk. Science News 1991; 139:260.

[104]Wynder, E. Strategies toward the primary prevention of cancer. Arch Surg 1990; 125:163-169.

[105]Science News, 1989, p. 102.

[106]Howe, G. A cohort study of fat intake and risk of breast cancer. JNCI 1991; 83:336-340.

[106 1]Henderson, M. Cancer incidence in Seattle Women's Health Trial participants by group and time since randomization. JNCI 1991; 83:1260-1261.

[107]Yu, S. A case-control study of dietary and non-dietary risk factors for breast cancer in Shanghai. Cancer Research 1990; 50:5017-5021.

[108]Van't Veer, P. Dietary fat and the risk of breast cancer. Int J Epidemiol 1990; 19:12-18.

[109]Willet, W. The search for the causes of breast and colon cancer. Nature 1989; 338:389-394.

[110]Berrino, F. Mediterranean diet and cancer. Europ J Clin Nutr 1989; 43 (supp 2):49-55.

[111]Howe, G. Dietary factors and risk of breast cancer: Combined analysis of 12 case-control studies. JNCI 1990; 82:561-569.

[112]Brisson, J. Diet, mammographic features of breast tissue, and breast-cancer risk. Am J Epidemiol 1989; 130:14-24.

[113]Toniolo, P. Calorie-providing nutrients and risk of breast cancer. JNCI 1989; 81:278-286.

[114]Yu, S. A case-control study of dietary and non-dietary risk factors for breast cancer in Shanghai. Cancer Research 1990; 50:5017-5021.

[115]Schulsinger, D. Effect of dietary protein quality on development of aflotoxin B-induced hepatic prenoplastic lesions. JNCI 1989; 81:1241-1245.

[116]de Waard, F. Breast cancer incidence and nutritional status with particular reference to body weight and height. Cancer Res 1975; 35:3351-3356.

[117]Knekt, P. Dietary fat and the risk of breast cancer. Am J Clin Nutr 1990; 52:903-908.

[118]Rosen, J. Prevalence of weight reducing and weight gaining in adolescent girls and boys. Health Psychology 1987; 6:131-147.

[118.1]Wolfe, S. New evidence that menopausal estrogens cause breast cancer: Further doubts about the prevention of heart disease. Public Citizen Health Research Group Health Letter 1991; 7:4-6.

[118.2]Vandenbroucke, J. Postmenopausal oestrogen and cardioprotection. Lancet 1991; 337:833-834.

[118.3]Cerutti, P. Prooxidant states and tumor production. Science 1985; 227:375-381.

[118.4]Djuric, Z. Effects of a low-fat diet on levels of oxidative damage to DNA in human peripheral nucleated blood cells. JNCI 1991; 83:766-769.

[119]Ziel, H. Increased risk of endometrial carcinoma among users of conjugated estrogens. N Engl J Med 1975; 293:1167-1170.

[120]Smith, D. Association of exogenous estrogen and endometrial carcinoma. N Engl J Med 1975; 293:1164-1167.

[121]Mack, T. Estrogens and endometrial cancer in a retirement community. N Engl J Med 1976; 294:1262-1267.

[122]Bergkvist, L. The risk of breast cancer after estrogen and estrogen-progestin replacement. N Engl J Med 1989; 321:293-297.

[123]Nisker, J. Serum sex-hormone-binding globulin capacity and the percentage of free estradiol in postmenopausal women with and without endometrial carcinoma: A new biological basis for the association between obesity and endometrial carcinoma. Am J Obstet Gynecol 1988; 138:637-642.

[124]Hoover, R. Stilboesterol (diethylstilbesterol) and the risk of ovarian cancer. Lancet 1977; 533-534.

[125]Cook, J. Sex hormones and cancer-producing compounds. Nature 1933; 131:205-206.

[126]Perry, I. The development of tumors in female mice treated with 1;2;5;6 = dibenzanthracene and theelin. Am J Cancer 1937; 29:680-684.

[127]Gardner, W. Tumors in experimental animals receiving steroid hormones. Surgery 1944; 16:18-32.

[128]Shu, X. Dietary factors and epithelial ovarian cancer. Br J Cancer 1989; 59:92-96.

[129]Cramer, D. Galactose consumption and metabolism in relation to the risk of ovarian cancer. Lancet 1989; II:66-71.

[130]Miller, A.B. Diet and cancer: A review. Acta Oncologica 1990; 29:87-95.

[131]Doll, R. Geographic variation in cancer incidence: A clue to causation. World J Surg 1978; 2:595-602.

[132]Hutchinson, G. Epidemiology of prostate cancer. Semin Oncol 1976; 3:151-159.

[132.1]Lange, P. Early detection for prostate cancer? JNCI 1991; 83:1199-1201.

[133]Hirayama, T. Epidemiology of prostate cancer with special reference to the role of the diet. JNCI Monogr 1979; 53:149-155.

[134]Reddy, B. Nutrition and its relationship to cancer. Adv Cancer Res 1980; 32:237-345.

[135]Armstrong, B. Environmental factors and cancer incidence and mortality in different countries, with special reference to dietary practices. Int J Cancer 1975; 15:617-631.

[136]Kolonel, L. Nutrient intakes in relation to cancer incidence in Hawaii. Br J Cancer 1981; 44:332-339.

[137]Blair, A. Geographic patterns of prostate cancer in the United States. JNCI 1978; 61:1369-1384.

[138]Rotkin, I. Studies in the epidemiology of prostatic cancer; expanded sampling. Cancer Treat Rep 1977; 61:173-180.

[139]Slattery, M. Food consumption trends between adolescent and adult years and subsequent risk of prostate cancer. Am J Clin Nutr 1990; 52:752-757.

[140]Talamini, R. Nutrition, social factors and prostatic cancer in a Northern Italian population. Br J Cancer 1986; 53:817-821.

[141]Lew, E. Variations in mortality by weight among 750,000 men and women. J Chron Dis 1979; 32:563-576.

[142]Graham, S. Diet and the epidemiology of carcinoma of the prostate galdn. JNCI 1983; 70:687-692.

[143]Snowdon, D. Diet, obesity and the risk of fatal prostate cancer. Am J Epidemiol 1984; 120:244-250.

[144]Mills, P.K. Cohort study of diet, lifestyle, and prostate cancer in Adventist men. Cancer 1989; 64:598-604.

[145]Hill, P. Diet and urinary steroids in Black and White North American men and Black South African men. Cancer Res 1979; 39:5101-5105.

[146]Hill, P. Environmental factors and breast and prostatic cancer. Cancer Res 1981; 41:3817-3818.

[147]Hill, P. Response to leutenizing releasing hormone, thyrotropic hormone and human chorionec gonadotropin administration in healthy men at different risks of prostate cancer and in prostatic cancer patients. Cancer Res 1982; 42:1074-2080.

[148]Rose, D. The biochemical epidemiology of prostate carcinoma. In Ip, C. *Dietary Fat and Cancer.* Liss, publishers, New York, pp. 43-68.

[149]Huggins, C. Studies in prostatic cancer, I. The effect of castration, of estrogen and of androgen on serum phosphatases in metatastic carcinoma of the prostate. Cancer Res 1941; 1:293-297.

[150]Shearer, R. Plasma testosterone: An accurate monitor of hormone treatment in prostatic cancer. Br J Urol 1973; 45:668-675.

[151]Wilson, J. The pathogenesis of benign prostatic hyperplasia. Am J Med 1980; 68:745-756.

[152]Hill, P. Plasma hormones and lipids in men at different risk for coronary heart disease. Am J Clin Nutr 1980; 33:1010-1018.

[153]Hamalainen, E. Diet and serum sex hormones in healthy men. J Steroid Biochem 1984; 20:459-464.

[154]Olsen, G. A case-control study of pancreatic cancer and cigarettes, alcohol, coffee and diet. Am J Pub Health 1989; 79:1016-1019.

[155]Farrow, D. Diet and the risk of pancreatic cancer in men. Am J Epidemiol 1990; 132:423-431.

[156]Katsuoyanni, K. Diet and breast cancer: A case-control study in Greece. Int J Cancer 1986; 38:815-820.

[157]Graham, S. Diet in the epidemiology of breast cancer. Am J Epidemiol 1982; 116:68-75.

[158]Rettura, G. Dimethylbenz(a)anthracene (DMBA) induced tumors: Prevention by supplemental b-carotene (BC). Fed Proc 1983; 42:786.

[159]Rohan, T. A population-based case-control study of diet and breast cancer in Australia. Am J Epidemiol 1988; 128:478-489.

[160]Potischam, N. Breast cancer and dietary and plasma concentrations of carotenoids and vitamin A. Am J Clin Nutr 1990; 52:909-915.

[160.1]Study shows diet may affect occurrence of laryngeal cancer. Obesity Update, July/August 1991, p. 2.

[161]Lee, H. Colorectal cancer and diet in an Asian population: A case-control study among Singapore Chinese. Int J Cancer 1989; 43:1007-1016.

[162]Benito, E. A population-based case-control study of colorectal cancer in Majorca. Int J Cancer 1990; 45:69-76.

[163]Miller, A.B. Diet and cancer: A review. Acta Oncologica 1990; 29:87-95.

[164]West, D. Dietary intake and colon cancer: Sex and anatomic site-specific associations. Am J Epidemiol 1989; 139:883-894.

[165]Howe, G. Dietary factors and risk of breast cancer: Combined analysis of 12 case-control studies. JNCI 1990; 82:561-569.

[166]Willet, W. Vitamin A and lung cancer. Nutrition Reviews 1990; 48:201-211.

[167]Kodama, M. Interrelation between Western type cancers and non-Western type cancers as regards their risk variations in time and space. II. Nutrition and cancer risk. Anticancer Research 1990; 10:1043-1049.

[168]Van't Veer, P. Dietary fiber, beta carotene and breast cancer: Results from a case-control study. Int J Cancer 1990; 34:825-828.

6.

A Potpourri of "Affluent" Diseases

6. *A Potpourri of "Affluent" Diseases*

> *"The doctor of the future will give no medicine, but instead will interest his patients in the care of the human frame, in diet, and in the cause and prevention of disease."*
>
> —Thomas Edison

We have discussed four of the most deadly diseases as well as the number one cosmetic problem, obesity. We will now consider a few more of our more familiar diseases and their relationships to food habits.

It would be impossible within the scope of this book to expound on the entire range of maladies from hangnails to hemorrhoids. We have therefore selected a few of the more common infirmities that are influenced by our food choices in hopes that we may positively influence the health and well-being of the greatest number of people. It is by no means a complete list of diseases that are influenced by nutrition. It is likely that any chronic disease condition could be positively influenced by a change to a low-fat, high-starch, animal-free nutrition program. The very worst that can happen with such a change is that it will do no good. It is certain that it will do no harm. The best that can happen is the prevention of many years of illness.

ARTHRITIS

Arthritis, meaning inflammation of a joint, is America's number one crippling disease, affecting the lives of 37 million people or about one in every seven.[1] Another person develops arthritis every 33 seconds, and the resultant disability accounts for 500 million days of restricted activity and 27 million days lost from work each year. In fact, it is the leading cause of industrial absenteeism and second only to heart disease in expenditures on disability payments. Arthritis costs the public $8.6 billion annually in lost wages and medical bills.[1]

There are about 100 forms of arthritis, the most common of which are rheumatoid arthritis, gout, systemic lupus erythematosus and osteoarthritis.

There are many studies that indicate that proteins—particularly animal proteins—cause many of these arthritic diseases. When partially digested proteins are absorbed into the blood, they are perceived as foreign invaders or antigens. Antibodies are formed in response to this threat, and they combine with the antigens in order to neutralize them. This combination is called an antigen-antibody complex. These complexes are usually carried to the liver where they are broken down and eliminated. But, in the case of some types of arthritis, a few of them lodge in joint tissue and other tissues of the body, causing irritation and subsequent arthritic symptoms.

Cow's milk proteins and egg proteins are both adept at producing arthritic changes in the joints of experimental animals,[2] and the removal of all dairy products has proven to reduce or eliminate arthritic symptoms in some, but not all, humans.[3] Other foods such as fish, meat and chicken may also bring on arthritic attacks; and, in some cases, humans may experience arthritis after consuming specific vegetable foods such as wheat and rice.[4]

In a study reported in the *Arthritis and Rheumatism* journal, 14 arthritic patients were put on a complete fast for one week. All of them experienced considerable improvement in arthritic symptoms.[5] This obviously means that arthritis was being relieved by *not eating some specific food or group of foods*. We do not advocate fasting, except as a method of discovering which food is producing the arthritic symptoms. By re-introducing one specific food at a time after the fast and then observing the results, a person can discover which food or group of foods are causing the problem.

It is puzzling to note that one of the Arthritis Foundation's pamphlets suggests that we should be skeptical of those who advocate dietary therapy for arthritis. We should be especially wary, they say, of suggestions to eliminate any specific food group as a method of relieving arthritis.[6] Research, however, supports the idea that we may very well eliminate the group of foods that causes the disease.

Dietary fat is also implicated in arthritis and may either cause or exacerbate the disease. Although there may be other causes of arthritis, certainly nutrition is a prime factor. Let's take a look at some of the more common classifications of arthritis and a few of the research studies that support a strong relationship to eating habits.

Rheumatoid arthritis: Is it curable?

The Arthritis Foundation states boldly that food does not cause arthritis—a statement that is not true. For instance, researchers at the Wayne State University Department of Medicine fed very-low-fat diets to two patients with rheumatoid arthritis. The patients experienced remission of all joint pain within a few days.[7] After being totally free of arthritic symptoms for periods of nine and 14 months, these two patients were challenged with high-fat foods. Within 24 to 48 hours their symptoms returned. The researchers then observed four more arthritic patients who had been given a fat-free diet. All were totally free of symptoms in seven weeks, and all experienced relapse of the disease within 72 hours when fats were added into their diets.

Beef, chicken, cheese, safflower oil, and coconut oil were used in this study to determine whether there was a different response to different fats. All were equally adept at creating the arthritic symptoms.[7] After these observations, the researchers made this statement: "We conclude that dietary fats in amounts normally eaten in the American diet cause the inflammatory joint changes seen in rheumatoid arthritis."

Somehow, the Arthritis Foundation must have missed that piece of research.

Although dietary fat was studied in this research, it is possible that a reduction in animal proteins was also a factor in eliminating arthritic symptoms.

Whichever factor was responsible for curing the arthritis, it is safe to say that dietary treatment (which produced a 100% remission of the disease) is far superior to anything the drug companies have to offer. Drug treatments in many cases have been either ineffective or harmful.[8][9][10][11][12][13][14] In a study of the long-term outcome of arthritic drug treatments, one researcher concluded that the concept of "remission inducing" drugs is fallacious.[15] His research pointed out that after 20 years of drug treatments, 35% of those studied had died, many of them from rheumatoid arthritis. Another 19% were severely disabled.

Gout

Gout is a sudden and painful form of arthritis which comes and goes and often causes swelling of the joints, particularly the toes. It is nearly always accompanied by high blood levels of uric acid,[16] which are, in turn, a breakdown product of proteins. Uric acid crystals lodge in the joints where they irritate joint tissue and cause sudden and painful swelling.

The low-protein nutrition plan at National Institute of Fitness usually eliminates gout symptoms within a few days, since uric acid levels quickly normalize. Gout (and high uric acid levels) are uncommon among people who eat high-starch, low-protein diets.[17]

For instance, a study of Filipinos living in Honolulu showed them to have 68 times the rate of gout as those who lived in the Philippines![17] Filipinos living in other areas of the U.S have a high rate of gout and higher uric acid levels than Caucasians living in the U.S.[18] Yet, there is little problem with the disease in the Philippines.

Lupus Erythematosus

This disease, commonly known as lupus, is a disease attributed to antigen-antibody complexes.[19] Arthritis is only one symptom of this disease, since the complexes also settle in other tissues of the body, such as the skin, kidneys, brain and lungs.[19] A characteristic of the person who suffers from lupus is generally a darkened patch of skin across the nose and under the eyes, resembling a mask. Sensitivity to sunlight is also common. Lupus is often deadly since it can adversely affect so many different systems of the body.

As with most of the other diseases we have discussed, we find that lupus is a disease that occurs more frequently in societies that eat the fat-laden, high-protein diet.[20] [21] [22] In animal research, lupus improves quickly with a low-protein, low-fat diet.[23] In a review of dietary factors and their relationships to lupus, Dr. A. Steinberg cited several studies which indicated that a low-protein, low-fat diet lessened symptoms and decreased antigen-antibody complexes among animals and/or humans.[24]

Osteoarthritis

Osteoarthritis is commonly known as "wear and tear" arthritis, since it usually involves joints that are under constant use. Although heavy joint use may contribute to this malady, it is not, in itself, a primary cause. Runners between the ages of 50 and 70 for instance, have joint health which is at least as good, if not better, than those who do not run.[25] There is no doubt that the joints of the hips, knees, ankles and spine are used millions of times more in runners than non-runners. We can therefore state unequivocally that exercise in not a cause of osteoarthritis. "Developing" populations who engage in heavy labor have a much lesser incidence of arthritis than populations that are "developed" and engage in less labor.[26] Dietary habits favor a higher-fat, high-protein diet in developed societies, which may also contribute to osteoarthritis.

However, there may be factors other than diet in the cause of this disease. As Dr. John McDougall states, "Other theories may be proposed as we learn more about this common disease of affluent populations consuming rich foods."[27] We must wonder, however, if the fact that this disease occurs almost exclusively in such populations does not implicate the diet as the primary suspect.

We have observed many of our osteoarthritic guests regain full mobility of their joints shortly after beginning their program of exercise and low-fat, low-protein nutrition. Although x-rays show that the arthritis still exists, relief of symptoms is rapid in many cases.

A proper diet and non-traumatic aerobic exercise as described in the chapter on fitness are the therapies recommended for those suffering from arthritic diseases.

ASTHMA—A PRODUCT OF ANIMAL CONSUMPTION

Bronchial asthma, a disease that causes periods of breathing difficulty, is, in most cases, an allergic response to animal products. The drugs used to relieve symptoms of this disease frequently cause nervousness, insomnia, dizziness, nausea, irregular heartbeat, increased blood pressure, muscle weakness, water retention, yeast infections and severe mental disturbances, among others.[28] In the case of these drugs, the treatment may be worse than the disease!

A health movement in Sweden claims that a vegan diet (no animal products whatsoever) can improve or cure this malady.[29] In order to test this hypothesis, several doctors studied asthma patients who had been suffering from the disease for an average of 12 years. These patients were put on a vegan diet for one year. The results were published in the *Journal of Asthma* in 1985. At the end of the 12-month period, nearly all of the patients were free of medication, or their medication was dramatically reduced. Seventy-one percent of these patients improved within four months; 92% improved in one year.[29] The authors suggested that a favorable alternative for those who fear conventional medication is the vegan program and that such a program would help them to get well. Such a regimen seems a small price to pay to breathe freely—without the use of dangerous chemicals.

DIVERTICULAR DISEASE AND
OTHER DISEASES OF DIGESTION

If one regularly consumes a diet characteristic of industrialized societies, i.e., high in animal products and processed foods, there is a 50% chance that diverticular disease will develop by age 65. The colon will look like a blister pack! Pockets form on the large intestine as a result of excessive pressure acting on weakened areas of the colon wall, eventually ballooning outward to produce peninsula-like sacs that are attached to the gut by a narrow neck. These sacs are known as diverticula, and the condition is referred to as diverticular disease. The most common form, *diverticulosis*, is characterized by intact sacs with no infection, and often, no pain. However, if the diverticula become inflamed by marauding microorganisms carried into the pockets by fecal material, the disease then becomes known as *diverticulitis*—a condition which may have serious medical consequences. Some of those consequences may include sporadic abdominal pain, alternating constipation and diarrhea, flatulence, fever, blood and mucus in the stool, and frequent urination.[30]

Current data suggests that the risk of diverticular disease increases with age. One source indicates that 10% of those over age 45 may be afflicted,[31] while other authorities assert that 40% of all middle-aged Americans have the disease.[32] Data on older Americans indicate that 35-50% of those 60-65 years of age suffer from the condition;[33] [34] [35] yet, this disease was unknown at the turn of the century.[31] [35] Not coincidentally, the incidence of the disease has increased directly with the development of technology which transformed the local barrel-of-beans corner grocery store into today's outlet of boxed noodle products and thousands of other processed foods.

Improper diet causes diverticular disease,[34] specifically a diet devoid of fiber. This fact is substantiated by both animal[36] and human[37] [38] research. Further, in surveys of non-industrialized nations where the populace consumes a diet high in unprocessed plant foods, diverticular disease is virtually unknown.[34] [39] [40] Vegetarians in England, who consume larger volumes of fiber than non-vegetarians, experience only ⅓ the incidence of the disease compared to the general population.[32]

Diverticula develop due to the excessive colon pressure inherent to small, hard fecal masses resulting from a diet high in fat and low in fiber. Years of exposure to high pressure cause a progressive weakening of the colon wall which eventually balloons outward, forming pockets (diverticula).

Diet is the cause of the disease, and diet is also the cure. Pending approval of a qualified physician, the best treatment is a high-fiber, starch-based diet. Pain, constipation and other symptoms of diverticulitis are usually relieved quickly with such a regimen.[34 38 41 42 43] Adequate fiber ensures a soft and bulky stool which moves rapidly, and without excessive pressure, through the colon. Vegans, (those who eat no animal products) have a much faster transit time (passage of food through the digestive system) than those who eat a conventional diet.[44]

At any age, diverticular disease is far more common among meat eaters than vegetarians.[45] In our earlier discussion of cancer, we noted that colon cancer was nearly unknown among societies where bowel movement frequency exceeded two movements per day per person. These societies, of course, consume heavy quantities of fiber and eat little fat. Apparently, virtually all colon problems are related to diet.

Those who are unwilling to change nutritional habits may believe that frequency of defecation is more easily accomplished by laxative use. This is unwise therapy indeed. Laxatives may actually increase the amount of fluid feces forced into the diverticula, thereby intensifying the disease.

Constipation, Varicose Veins, Hemorrhoids, Hiatal Hernia and Appendicitis

Constipation often occurs concurrently with or as a by-product of diverticular disease. The hard, compacted fecal mass which results from fiber-deplete nutrition is hard to eliminate and requires a great deal of straining. The straining causes strong pressures on the veins of the legs, which ultimately injures them, causing varicose veins. Some of the veins most affected by the intense straining are those of the anus. These specialized varicose veins are known as hemorrhoids. *There is about 1000 times the rate of varicose veins and hemorrhoids in populations consuming a low-fiber, high-fat diet as in those that consume a high-fiber, low-fat diet.*[46] Yet, as people change from the high-fiber diet to the low-fiber diet, these diseases increase concomitantly.[46]

Excessive straining may also force a part of the stomach through the natural opening in the diaphragm, resulting in a condition known as hiatal hernia.[47] Population studies indicate a rare or non-existent occurrence of the condition among those who consume high-fiber, low-fat diets and a very high incidence among those on the typical "civilized" diet.[47] Dr. Denis Burkitt, a physician noted for research relating diet and disease, stated in an interview that, "We have never found any community in the world which passes large, soft stools and gets hiatus hernia."[48] The societies that have a very low prevalence of the disease have about three to four times the fecal mass of those who have a high prevalence; and, the stools of the former are soft, whereas the stools of the latter are firm and hard.[49]

Soft stools are easier to move, thereby requiring less straining. Hard stools and high pressure in the intestine may also block the appendix, resulting in the infection and inflammation known as appendicitis.[50] This condition is rarely seen among societies that consume low-fat, high-fiber diets; but, as these societies began to adopt a "Western" diet, the incidence of appendicitis increases dramatically.[50]

Ulcers

Many guests who attend our resort report having suffered from chronic acid indigestion for years. Nearly all of these people are free of indigestion within one week, some within only a day or two.

Excessive acid production may also cause ulcers in some individuals. Certain foods cause a higher stomach-acid secretion than others and should be avoided. Primary offenders in raising stomach acid are milk[51] [52] and coffee (both regular and decaffeinated).[53] Cigarette smoking is also closely associated with ulcers.[54] [55] [56] [57] As might be expected, a "fat-free" diet has been shown to be very effective in healing ulcers.[58]

All of these digestive-system disorders may be prevented, mitigated or cured by avoiding obviously harmful products such as coffee and cigarettes and by eating meals that do not turn digestive and excretory systems into cesspools; namely, meals containing high-fiber, low-fat, animal-product-free foods.

GALLBLADDER DISEASE

Those who have suffered from (or witnessed) a severe gallbladder attack realize that it is not medically insignificant. The attack may involve profuse sweating, excruciating pain in the abdomen, and agony. The pain is caused by stones formed in the gallbladder and is intensified when there is infection in the gallbladder and the adjoining bile ducts. Following an attack, there are such unpleasant after-effects as nausea, vomiting and constipation.[59]

The pain associated with this malady is so intense that 465,000-480,000 Americans per year opt to have their gallbladders removed to put a stop to their discomfort.[60] It is estimated that 15 million have gallstones, representing 20% and 10% of the female and male populace, respectively.[61] Those at greatest risk are the obese and diabetic. Postmenopausal women taking estrogen therapy also have 2-3 times the rate of gallbladder disease.[62] An even stronger relationship exists between gallbladder disease and nutrition.

Getting stoned

The gallbladder is a small sac-like organ whose purpose is to serve as a warehouse and dispensing agent of bile (gall) produced in the liver. Beginning from the body's chemical plant (liver), bile descends down the common bile duct and into the gallbladder for temporary storage. As food enters the intestinal tract, the gallbladder contracts, squeezing out bile into the cystic duct and finally back down the common bile duct where it combines with lipase (produced by the pancreas) at the entrance to the small intestine (duodenum).

Bile assists lipase in the breakdown of fats and also assists in the absorption of fats from the intestine. Bile contains components such as biliverdin and bilirubin (darkly pigmented waste products from broken-down red blood cells) and cholesterol. When heavily concentrated, these biliary components may precipitate out of solution and form crystals—the beginning of gallstones. These crystals may grow into full-blown gallstones, ranging in size from microscopic to one inch in diameter. A common cause of a gallbladder attack is the lodging of a large stone in the cystic duct or common bile duct. The rapid cessation of pain after an attack is likely the result of an impacted stone in the cystic duct moving back into the gallbladder.[59] If the stone becomes fixed in the common bile duct, jaundice occurs until it passes into the small intestine.[59]

When the walls of the gallbladder and/or the adjoining bile ducts become irritated and infected, a condition known as cholecystitus results. Most cases are associated with gallstones and begin with the movement of bacteria from the duodenum to the gallbladder area.

Faulty nutrition is likely the cause of most gallbladder disease. Here are a few of the clues which bring us to these conclusions:

1. Cholesterol is the main component in 90% of all gallstones.[63] [64]

2. Regular consumption of polyunsaturated fat forces stored cholesterol out of the body tissues, through the liver and gallbladder, and into the intestinal tract.[65]

3. Large quantities of cholesterol in the gallbladder favor gallstone formation.[66]

4. Relief of pain, in many cases, follows a switch to a low-fat diet.[67]

5. Wheat bran has been shown to increase cholesterol solubility, making it less apt to crystallize out of solution.[68]

6. Non-vegetarians have 150% more gallbladder disease than vegetarians.[69] [70]

7.   Gallbladder disease is rare in non-industrialized countries.[71]

It is quite obvious from the above list that nutrition is a primary factor in the development of gallbladder disease, particularly the high-fat, low-fiber diet of America and other "developed" nations. Dietary cholesterol and polyunsaturated fats promote gallstone formation, whereas high fiber intake favors prevention.

It is important to know that women who have their gallbladders removed are at a 70% greater risk of developing colon cancer[72] and that men who have gallstones are at three times the risk of gallbladder cancer.[61]

HEADACHES

As early as 1913, it was proposed that migraines might be due to an allergic response to certain foods.[73] Migraine attacks are brought on most frequently by cow's milk, eggs, chocolate, oranges and wheat, although almost any food can cause an allergic response and subsequent headache in a specific individual.[74]

Finding the offending food is usually not hard to do. Dr. McDougall suggests the elimination of all animal products, chocolate and nuts. If the allergy still persists, he suggests the elimination of wheat, corn, citrus fruits, tomatoes, and strawberries (which are the most common allergens among vegetable products). The headache or other allergy will then usually go away. Then, one vegetable food at a time can be added into the diet until the one is found that causes the allergy. The food should be eaten in large quantities for about three days. If it causes no reaction, then another food can be introduced for three days, etc. For more information on the elimination diet, read *The McDougall Program: Twelve Days to Dynamic Health.*

We have observed that many of our guests become free of migraines and other headaches within four weeks on our program. This indicates that a low-fat, low-protein diet may be beneficial. There is, however, one notable exception to their success. Many of them who have been consuming coffee or other caffeinated foods have severe withdrawal headaches when they give up these products.

This observation is substantiated in the professional literature; withdrawal headaches are common among those who give up the habit of caffeinated beverages.[75] In these cases, it is often necessary to allow them a small amount of caffeine for a day or two in order to tolerate the headaches. They are usually able to completely eliminate caffeine within a week with no adverse effects.

IRON-DEFICIENCY ANEMIA

There is some concern that the high content of phytates and oxylates in a high-fiber diet may decrease the absorption of iron from food, creating the potential for anemia—a disorder characterized by low levels of iron in the blood. This condition can bring on lethargy and general fatigue as well as a lack of physical endurance.

The iron in meat is supposedly more easily absorbed than that in vegetable foods, and well it may be, but the body adjusts the amount of iron absorbed according to its *needs*.[76] Vitamin C, which is generally consumed in much greater quantities in vegan diets, causes an increase in iron absorption from foods—an increase which negates any negative influence of phytates and oxylates.

High-fiber diets do not interfere with adequate iron absorption. If they did, we would expect to see vegetarian and vegan societies suffering from low blood-iron levels. The fact is that iron-deficiency anemia is rare in vegetarians and vegans, with most studies showing them to have iron levels at least as high or higher than those who eat meat and other animal flesh.[77] [78 79 80]

As to dietary intake of iron, vegans usually ingest at least twice the recommended daily allowance.[81]

The Chinese consume a very high-fiber diet. Results of

studies show that the Chinese have far greater blood-iron levels and consume three times more dietary fiber than people living in the U.S.[82][83] There is, in fact, a very strong association between iron levels and dietary fiber. The higher the fiber intake among Chinese, the greater the level of iron in the blood.[83]

Loss of blood can also produce anemia. Hemorrhoids, diverticular disease and ulcers can increase blood loss as can a heavy menstrual flow in women.[76] As we have discussed in the chapter on cancer, the high-fat diet causes a dramatic increase in estrogen production. This in turn thickens the endometrial tissues, which causes much heavier bleeding during the menstrual period.[76]

In addition, cow's milk products irritate the intestinal tract in some individuals, causing a loss of blood in the stool, especially in infants.[84][85][86] A recent study reported in the *Journal of Pediatrics* showed that infants fed cow's milk had five times the loss of hemoglobin (an iron carrying substance) in the stool as those fed formula.[87] Breast milk is probably far superior to either, although at present I know of no research that compares formula to breast milk feeding in terms of iron loss.

Although there have been few studies on adults with anemia, it is likely that some adults may also become anemic from drinking milk. Dr. McDougall states, "I believe that someday dairy products will be recognized as the main cause of iron-deficiency anemia in adult women."[76] Milk, of course, is for baby cows, not human beings.

Another factor which may influence iron-deficiency anemia is calcium supplementation, which dramatically reduces iron absorption.[88][89] In fact, 165 milligrams of calcium taken as milk, cheese, or calcium chloride will reduce iron absorption by 50-60%![89] The calcium mania discussed in the chapter on osteoporosis may be responsible for more than a little of the anemia which is so prevalent among young women.

MULTIPLE SCLEROSIS (M.S.)

This disease, a crippler of young adults, is a nerve affliction that may lead to paralysis, loss of vision and other disorders. Although many health professionals dismiss any connection between the disease and nutrition,[90] the correlation to nutritional habits is incontrovertible. A primary culprit, as might be expected, is animal fat. The geographical distribution of the disease shows that the highest rates of M.S. follow the highest consumption of animal fats world wide.[91] The same correlation exists between M.S. and milk consumption.[92]

Dr. Roy Swank, head of the Department of Neurology at Oregon Medical School, has proven the efficacy of the low-fat diet in treating M.S. His M.S. patients treated with a low-fat diet (less than 20 grams of fat per day) had a 31% death rate from all causes. Those who consumed 25 grams per day had death rates of 79%, and those who consumed 41 grams or more had death rates of 81%.[93] His patients who participated in the low-fat diet also lived about three times as long after diagnosis as those who consumed a high-fat diet. Dr. Swank noted that when the disease is diagnosed early and the victim placed on a low-fat diet, there is a 95% chance that the victim will either maintain status quo or improve over the next 20 years.[94] [95]

As with other degenerative diseases, when people move from countries of low-fat consumption to high-fat consumption, they adopt the habits and inherit the illnesses of their new homelands. For instance, West Indies natives have only 1/8 the chance of being diagnosed with M.S. compared to children of West Indians born and raised in London.[96]

Animal fats and/or milk products may damage the nervous systems of young people, which may in turn contribute to M.S. Whatever the mechanism, the relationship of M.S. to animal products, milk and fat is clear. M.S. is one more disaster resulting from improper nutrition.

Remember that almost everyone will benefit from the low-fat, high-fiber nutrition that we advocate. Consult your physician (be sure to give him a copy of this book to read first) for his recommendations and look forward to a happier and healthier future.

REFERENCES

[1] Arthritis Foundation. Demographic and Economic Facts, 1990.

[2] Welsh, C. Comparison of the arthritogenic properties of dietary cow's milk, egg albumin and soya milk in experimental animals. Int Archs Allergy Appl Immun 1986; 80:192-199.

[3] Ratner, D. Does milk intolerance affect seronegative arthritis in lactase-deficient women? Isr J Med Sci 1985; 21:532-534.

[4] Beri, D. Effect of dietary restrictions on disease activity in rheumatoid arthritis. Ann Rheum Dis 1988; 47:69-72.

[5] Hafstrom, I. Effects of fasting on disease activity, neutrophil function, fatty acid composition, and leukotriene biosynthesis in patients with rheumatoid arthritis. Arthr Rheum 1988; 31:585-592.

[6] Arthritis Foundation. Diet guidelines and research, 1987. p. 17.

[7] Lucas, C. Dietary fat aggravates rheumatoid arthritis. Clin Res 1981; 29:754A.

[8] Richter, J. Analysis of treatment terminations with gold and antimalarial compounds in rheumatoid arthritis. J Rheumatol 1980; 7:153-159.

[9] Husain, Z. Treatment complications of rheumatoid arthritis with gold, hydroxycholoroquine, D-penicillamine and levamisole. J Rheumatol 1980; 7:825-830.

[10] Rothermich, N. Clinical trial of penicillamine in rheumatoid arthritis. Arthr Rheum 1981; 24:1473-1478.

[11] Grindulis, K. Outcome of attempts to treat rheumatoid arthritis with gold, penicillamine, sulphasalazine or dapsone. Ann Rheum Dis 1984; 43:398-401.

[12] Thompson, P. Practical results of treatment with disease-modifying antirheumatoid drugs. Br J Rheumatol 1985; 24:167-175.

[13] Situnayake, R. Long-term treatment of rheumatoid arthritis with sulphasalazine, gold, or penicillamine: A comparison using life-table methods. Ann Rheum Dis 1987; 46:177-183.

[14] Kushner, I. Does aggressive therapy of rheumatoid arthritis affect outcome? J Rheumatol 1989; 16:1-4.

[15] Scott, D. Long-term outcome of treating rheumatoid arthritis: Results after 20 years. Lancet 1987; 1:1108-1111.

[16] McDougall, J. McDougall's Medicine: A Challenging Second Opinion. New Century, publishers, Piscataway, NJ 1985, p. 234.

[17] Healey, L. Hyperuricemia in Filipinos: Interaction of heredity and environment. Am J Hum Genetics 1967; 19:81-85.

[18] Decker, J. Gouty arthritis in Filipinos. N Engl J Med 1959; 261:805-806.

[19]McDougall, J. *McDougall's Medicine: A Challenging Second Opinion.* New Century, publishers, Piscataway, NJ 1985, p. 246-247.

[20]Chang, N. Rheumatic diseases in China. J Rheumatol 1983; 10 (suppl 10):41-45.

[21]Serdula, M. Frequency of systemic lupus erythematosus in different ethnic groups in Hawaii. Arthr Rheum 1979; 22:328-333.

[22]Taylor, H. Systemic lupus erythematosis in Zimbabwe. Ann Rheum Dis 1986; 45:645-648.

[23]Izui, S. Low-calorie diet selectively reduces expression of retroviral envelope glycoprotein gp70 in sera of NZBxNZW F1 hybrid mice. J Exp Med 1981; 154:1116.

[24]Steinberg, A. Systemic lupus erythematosus: Insights from animal models. Ann Intern Med 1984; 100:714-727.

[25]Lane, N. Long-distance running, bone density, and osteoarthritis. JAMA 1986; 255:1147-1151.

[26]Valkenburg, H. Osteoarthritis in some developing countries. J Rheumatol 1983; 10 (suppl 10):20-22.

[27]McDougall, J. *McDougall's Medicine: A Challenging Second Opinion.* New Century, publishers, 1985, p. 239.

[28]DeSilver, D. Powerful drugs, disturbing effects. Vegetarian Times, August 1989, p. 24.

[29]Lindahl, O. Vegan regimen with reduced medication in the treatment of bronchial asthma. Journal of Asthma 1985; 22:45-55.

[30]Almy, T. Diverticular disease of the colon. N Engl J Med 1980; 302:324-333.

[31]Condon, E. *The Concise Home Medical Guide.* Modern Promotions, Unisystems, Inc., publisher, New York, pp. 230-231.

[32]Brody, J. *Jane Brody's Nutrition Book.* W.W. Norton, publishers, New York, p. 148.

[33]—Keep taking your bran. Editorial. Lancet 1979; 1:1175.

[34]Mcdougall, J. *The McDougall Program.* NAL Books, publishers, New York, p. 340.

[35]Lamb, L. Colon disorder prompts many questions. Syndicated column: Ask Dr. Lamb, January, 1991.

[36]*Cello, J. Diverticular disease of the colon. West J Med 1981; 134:515-523.*

[37]Burkitt, D. Dietary fiber and disease. JAMA 1974; 229:1068-1074.

[38]Painter, N. Diverticular disease of the colon. *In* Trowel, H. (ed) *Dietary Fibre, Fibre-depleted Foods, and Disease.* Academic Press, publishers, New York, pp. 145-160.

[39]McDougall, J. *The McDougall Plan*. New Century, publishers, Piscataway, New York, p. 118.

[40]Mendelhoff, A. Thoughts on the epidemiology of diverticular disease. Clin Gastroenterol 1986; 15:855-877.

[41]Burkitt, D. Some diseases characteristic of modern Western civilization. Br Med J 1973; 1:274-278.

[42]Painter, N. The high-fiber diet in the treatment of diverticular disease of the colon. Postgrad Med 1974; 50:629-632.

[43]U.S. Department of Health and Human Services. Surgeon General's Report on Nutrition and Health. Publication # 88-50210. Superintendent of Documents. Washington, D.C., pp. 415-416.

[44]Davies, G. Bowel function measurements of individuals with different eating patterns. Gut 1986; 27:164-169.

[45]Gear, J. Symptomless diverticular disease and intake of dietary fibre. Lancet 1979; 1:511-514.

[46]Burkitt, D. Varicose veins, deep vein thrombosis, and haemorrhoids: Epidemiology and suggested aetiology. Br Med J 1972; 2:556-561.

[47]Burkitt, D. Hiatus hernia: Is it preventable? Am J Clin Nutr 1981; 34:428-431.

[48]Burkitt, D. Quoted in Barnard, N. *The Power of Your Plate*. Book Publishing Company, publishers, Summertown, Tennessee, 1990, p. 123.

[49]Burkitt, D. Effect of dietary fiber on stools and transit times and its role in the causation of disease. Lancet 1972; 2:1408-1412.

[50]Burkitt, D. *Refined Carbohydrate Foods and Disease*. Academic Press, publishers, New York, 1978, p. 87.

[51]Ippoliti, A. The effect of various forms of milk on gastric-acid secretion. Ann Intern Med 1976; 84:286-289.

[52]Kumar, N. Effect of milk on patients with duodenal ulcers. Br Med J 1986; 293:666

[53]Cohen, S. Gastric-acid secretion and lower-esophageal-sphincter pressure in response to coffee and caffeine. N Engl J Med 1975; 293:897-899.

[54]Paffenbarger, R. Chronic disease in former college students. XIII. Earlier precursors of peptic ulcer. Am J Epidemiol 1974; 100:307-315.

[55]Friedman, G. Cigarettes, alcohol, coffee and peptic ulcer. N Engl J Med 1974; 290:469-473.

[56]Gugler, R. Effect of smoking on duodenal ulcer healing with cimetidine and oxmetidine. Gut 1982; 23:866-871.

[57]Sontag, S. Cimetidine, cigarette smoking, and recurrence of duodenal ulcer. N Engl J Med 1984; 311:689-693.

[58]Childs, P. Peptic ulcer, pyloroplasty, and dietary fat. Ann Roy Coll Surg Engl 1977; 59:143-147.

[59]Condon, E. *The Concise Home Medical Guide.* Ottenheimer Publishers, Inc., Canada, 1980, pp. 237-239.

[60]Ransohoff, D. Prophylactic cholecystectomy or expectant management of silent gallstones. Ann Intern Med 1983; 99:199-204.

[61]Maringhini, A. Gallstones, gallbladder cancer and other gastrointestinal malignancies. Ann Intern Med 1987; 107:30-40.

[62]Boston Collaborative Drug Surveillance Program. Surgically confined gallbladder disease, venous thromboembolism, and breast tumors in relation to post-menopausal estrogen therapy. N Engl J Med 1974; 290:15-19.

[63]McDougall, J. *The McDougall Plan.* New Century, publishers, Piscataway, N.J., 1983, p. 63.

[64]DenBesten, I. The effect of dietary cholesterol on the composition of human bile. Surgery 1973; 73:266-271.

[65]Nestel, P. Lowering of plasma cholesterol and enhanced sterol excretion with the consumption of polyunsaturated ruminant fats. N Engl J Med 1973; 288:379-383.

[66]Bennion, L. Risk factors for the development of cholelithiasis in man, II. N Engl J Med 1978; 299:1221-1227.

[67]Goodhart, R. *Modern Nutrition in Health and Disease.* Lea and Febiger, publishers, Philadelphia, 1980, p. 974.

[68]Pomare, E. The effect of wheat bran upon bile salt metabolism and upon lipid composition of bile in gallstone patients. Am J Digest Dis 1976; 21:521-526.

[69]Pixley, F. Effect of vegetarianism on development of gallstones in women. Br Med J 1985; 291:11-15.

[70]Pixley, F. Dietary factors in the aetiology of gallstones: A case contract study. Gut 1988; 29:1511-1515.

[71]Johnson, L. The natural history of cholelithiasis: The National Cooperative Gallstone Study. Ann Intern Med 1984; 101:171.

[72]Linos, D. Cholecystectomy and carcinoma of the colon. Lancet 1981; 2:379-382.

[73]Mansfield, L. Food allergy and adult migraine: Double blind and mediator confirmation of an allergic etiology. Ann Allergy 1985; 55:126-129.

[74]Egger, J. Is migraine food allergy? A double-blind controlled trial of oligoantigenic diet treatment. Lancet 1983; 2:865-869.

[75]Smith, R. Caffeine withdrawal headache. J Clin Pharm Ther 1987; 12:53-58.

[76]McDougall, J. *The McDougall Program.* NAL Books, publishers, New York, 1990, pp. 307-308.

[77] Abdulla, M. Nutrient intake and health status of vegans. Chemical analyses of diets using the duplicate portion sampling technique. Am J Clin Nutr 1981; 34:2464-2477.

[78] Ellis, F. Veganism, clinical findings and investigations. Am J Clin Nutr 1970; 23:249-255.

[79] Sanders, T. Haematological studies on vegans. Br J Nutr 1978; 40:9-15.

[80] Anderson, B. The iron and zinc status of long-term vegetarian women. Am J Clin Nutr 1981; 34:1042-1048.

[81] Langley, G. *Vegan Nutrition. A Survey of Research.* The Vegan Society, Ltd., publishers, Oxford, England, p. 83.

[82] Brody, J. Huge study indicts fat and meat. New York Times, May 8 1990, p. c-14.

[83] Campbell, T. A study on diet, nutrition and disease in the People's Republic of China, Part II. Division of Nutritional Sciences, Cornell University, Ithaca, New York, 1989, p. 3.

[84] Woodruff, C. The role of fresh cow's milk in iron deficiency. Am J Dis Child 1972; 124:26-30.

[85] Wilson, J. Studies on iron metabolism. V. Further observations on cow's milk-induced gastrointestinal bleeding in infants with iron-deficiency anemia. J Pediatr 1974; 84:335-344.

[86] Fomon, S. Cow milk feeding in infancy: Gastrointestinal blood loss and iron-deficiency anemia. J Pediatr 1981; 98:540-545.

[87] Ziegler, E. Cow milk feeding in infancy: Further observation on blood loss from the gastrointestinal tract. J Pediatr 1990; 116:11-18.

[88] Cook, J. Calcium supplementation: Effect on iron absorption. Am J Clin Nutr 1991; 53:106-111.

[89] Hallberg, L. Calcium: Effect of different amounts on nonheme- and heme-iron absorption in humans. Am J Clin Nutr 1991; 53:112-119.

[90] McDougall, J. *The McDougall Program.* NAL Books, publishers, New York, p. 376.

[91] Alter, M. Multiple Sclerosis and nutrition. Arch Neurol 1974; 31:267-272.

[92] Agranoff, B. Diet and the distribution of Multiple Sclerosis. Lancet 1974; 2:1061-1066.

[93] Swank, R. Multiple Sclerosis: The lipid relationship. Am J Clin Nutr 1988; 48:1387-1393.

[94] McDougall, J. *The McDougall Program.* NAL Books, publishers, New York, 1990, p. 378.

[95] Swank, R. Multiple Sclerosis: Twenty years on low-fat diet. Arch Neurol 1970; 23:460-474.

[96] Elian, M. Multiple Sclerosis among the United Kingdom-born children to immigrants from the West Indies. J Neurology, Neurosurgery, and Psychiatry 1987; 50:327-332.

7.

Herbivorous By Design

7. Herbivorous By Design

> *"Your greatest want is, you want much of meat.*
> *Why should you want? Behold the earth hath roots;*
> *Within this mile break forth a hundred sprigs;*
> *The oaks bear mast, the briers scarlet hips;*
> *The bounteous housewife nature on each bush*
> *Lays her full mess before you. Want? Why want?"*
>
> —Shakespeare

Unless you have been asleep while reading this book, you have sensed a recurrent theme: the importance of reducing the consumption of animal products and other high-fat foods. Like others, you may have reluctantly concluded that the epidemic of obesity and degenerative disease is a direct result of the failure to heed Mom's ever sensible advice to "cut back on rich foods if you want to be slim." When pressed for a definition of "rich foods," Mom reminded us that spare tires are made of chocolate bars, butterscotch sundaes and other "sweets." Somehow, though, home-made brownies, pot roasts, bacon and eggs, home-made ice cream and a few glasses of whole milk never seemed quite so threatening.

Mom was probably not a vegetarian; in fact, far from it. Endowed with the prevailing nutritional wisdom, love and an abiding spirit of maternal responsibility, she focused her meal planning around the sacred "four basic food groups." Consequently, Mom's offspring (you and I) were predisposed to an omnivorous philosophy at a young, impressionable age.

Commercial interests have perpetuated the myth. We have been taught to associate eggs for breakfast with country living, fresh air and health. Dairy Council ads depict athletes drinking milk. A young, intelligent-looking woman contemplates cheese for calcium, and macho James Garner (looking for all the world like the Marlboro man) tells us that "beef is *real* food for *real* people."

To their dismay, many of those who believe the ads have found that beef is real food for creating real disease. James Garner, for instance, had a *real* quadruple bypass operation. If the wimps of the world can't beat the meat eaters, at least they can outlast them (by several years, as established in the chapter on longevity).

At the other end of the spectrum, vegetarians have also been the product of stereotyping. They have either been portrayed as frail, nutrient-deplete humans resembling survivors of Auschwitz or as lingering hippies of the '60s—advocates of free love and spiritual harmony with the cosmos.

It may surprise many to find that vegetarians are neither weaklings nor freaklings. (Some of them are even registered Republicans.) Bill Pearl and Andreas Cahling are two of the most muscular bodybuilders in the world; Olympian Gayle Oline Kova, who sports the most amazingly muscular legs ever seen on a female athlete, is not a wimp; "Bionic Woman" Lindsay Wagner is hardly at Death's door; authors Dr. John McDougall and Mary McDougall, Dr. Michael Klaper, Dr. Neal Barnard, and John Robbins are all vibrantly healthy examples of the philosophies they espouse. These people eat no animal products. Dave Scott, the greatest triathlete the world has ever known, is also a vegetarian.

LET'S CREATE A WORLD

Let's assume that you have been given the power to create your own world. After reviewing the latest set of *Time-Life Books,* you've become impressed with the beauty of life, particularly plant life on a place called "Earth." The next day, endowed with enthusiasm and a "can do" attitude, you create your world, abounding with trillions of lush, beautiful plants, ranging in size from single-celled microflora to 500-foot redwoods. Not bad for a day's work.

A short time later, however, you notice something drastically wrong. Your once-beautiful creation is being overrun with plants. Because of the intense competition for sunlight, oxygen, and nutrients, many of your trees, shrubs and grasses have been annihilated, only to cause unprecedented increases in the microbial population. Your world is quickly becoming a wasteland of decaying sewage! Back to the *Time-Life Books.*

To solve the problem, you create and introduce plant-eating animals (herbivores) into your world. Animals such as horses, deer, sheep, cattle, antelope, etc., seem suitable, since they are obviously designed to thrive on vegetable matter. Unfortunately, the experiences of the first period of creation repeat themselves with the second, and your world becomes inundated with multitudes of starving animals, ferociously competing for a dwindling number of plants—not a pretty sight.

By now you understand what's happening and create the carnivore—an animal designed not only to eat the plant feeders but other carnivores as well! To your satisfaction, your world is now in balance.

Overseeing your creation, you recall with justifiable pride the foresight utilized in designing your latest world addition, the carnivore. Obviously, an animal constructed to feed off other animals has to be able to catch, overpower, and kill its prey. Thus, your carnivores, like those on earth, were built with the anticipated characteristics of a successful hunter—speed, strength, and exceptional sensory perception (smell, vision, hearing). In order for these animals to kill their victims and separate the flesh into smaller chunks, you endow them with claws and fangs. Naturally, the internal and biochemical design of your carnivorous species would, by necessity of the food consumed, vary greatly from that of herbivores.

On your fourth day of creation, you opt to tackle your biggest creative challenge: *Homo sapiens.* However, upon examination of your model prototypes (Earth men and women), you are faced with a frustrating enigma. Was man designed to thrive best on animal or plant food? At first glance these earth creatures have all the apparent characteristics of herbivores. However, all of your references are replete with pictures of "Double Whoppers with Cheese," tacos, and meat as the foods focused on at mealtimes. Something seems to be wrong.

Being a benevolent creator, you decide to postpone your work, pending the results of further research. After all, you need assurances that your ultimate creation, man, will enjoy a maximum nutrition advantage necessary in an uncivilized but beautiful world. . .a world devoid of "Beef and Cheddars," "Pizza Supremes," and extra crispy fried chicken.

THE "FIRST" MAN WANTS A STEAK.

Now let's observe the meat-eating dilemma from another point of view—that of the "first" man to exist on earth—a man who has not yet invented weapons nor learned to use fire. Here he is, sitting in front of his shelter, not having eaten for several hours. Suddenly he has an insatiable desire for a steak. As he peers into the distance, he sees a water buffalo drinking by the bank of the river.

There is his steak, still on the hoof. He decides to run after his prey, but alas, finds that the buffalo is considerably faster than himself. But as luck would have it, the buffalo, in its excitement, falls down an embankment and injures one of its legs, rendering it incapable of flight. Our hunter now approaches his quarry. Without a weapon he must use his own physical capabilities to dispatch this luscious beast. Perhaps he will "take the bull by the horns" and break its neck.

On attempting to grasp the buffalo, he finds to his dismay (as he is tossed through the air for 20 feet) that the horns and neck of the animal are quite strong. He then opts for the method used by most carnivores: he leaps onto the buffalo's back, attempts to sink his teeth into its neck and again tries to break the neck of the animal. Problems again. His teeth will not do the job, and somehow, the buffalo does not take kindly to the attempt. Battered and torn, the "hunter" pulls himself away from his injured adversary and tries to think of a better way.

Help arrives in the form of a lion, who quickly dispatches the buffalo, opens its stomach cavity and eats his fill. The lion then departs, leaving most of the carcass behind. The man, seeing his chance, goes to the carcass and settles down to eat his steak. He finds that much of the carcass is still covered with hide, making it impossible to get to the meat. On finding an area where the hide has been ripped away by the lion, however, he attempts to eat. Somehow, without being cooked, the flesh is quite tough, and his task seems impossible. Perhaps he can wait a few days until the meat has lain in the sun and been tenderized by the action of bacteria. Sounds delicious, doesn't it? If he does return to eat such a delicacy, he will probably respond to the meal in about the same manner that you and I would respond. The first man may also be the last, since he will probably die of food poisoning.

Our hypothetical man, unsuccessful in his attempt at procuring a steak, then seeks smaller animals but finds that they are faster, more agile, or meaner than himself. His hunger is now intense, and he notices that there is a plant growing near his cave. He extirpates it and sees a rounded root—a potato. It does not scratch, stomp, nor outrun him. His hand fits around it beautifully. He has found the perfect meal for man.

Yes, men were hunters and gatherers during most of their development. Their superior intellects enabled them to control fire and to use weapons. The eventual change to killing, cooking and eating animals, however, was a detriment to the health of man. The first men were herbivorous by necessity. Subsequent men should be herbivorous by choice.

Let's look at some facts.

ANATOMICAL ENGINEERING FOR SPECIFIC FOOD

One can correctly assume that, as a group, plant-eating animals possess several unique characteristics. By comparing these traits to those existent, modified, or absent in *Homo sapiens,* we can begin to speculate as to the appropriate food choice(s).

In a publication entitled "What's Wrong With Eating Meat,"[1] the author, Vistara Parham, points out several differences between herbivores and meat-eating animals. Also discussed is the uncanny similarity between the plant-feeding species and human beings. A condensed version of that information is the subject of Table 1.

Unless you had ancestors from Transylvania, you probably

TABLE 1

Similarities and Differences Between Carnivores, Herbivores, and Man[1]

Carnivores	Herbivores	Man
Has claws	No claws	No claws
Has sharp pointed front teeth	No sharp pointed front teeth	No sharp pointed front teeth
No flat back molar teeth	Has flat back molar teeth	Has flat bac molar teeth
No pores on skin	Pores on skin	Pores on skin
Small salivary glands	Well-developed salivary glands	Well-developed salivary glands
Acid saliva	Alkaline saliva	Alkaline saliva
No ptyalin in saliva	Ptyalin in saliva	Ptyalin in saliva
Much hydrochloric acid in stomach	Hydrochloric acid in stomach 1/20th as strong as meat eaters	Hydrochloric acid in stomach 1/20th as strong as meat eaters
Short intestinal tract—3 times trunk length	Long intestinal tract—10 to 12 times trunk length	Long intestinal tract—12 times trunk length

do not have fangs. Sharp front incisors and canine teeth combined with an exceptionally strong jaw are found in carnivorous species, and they are there for a purpose: to kill and rip flesh. Herbivores and man, on the other hand, possess well-developed flat back molars for grinding food.

In addition, humans and most plant-eating animals, unlike the meat eaters, have well-developed salivary glands, alkaline saliva, and secrete a starch-splitting enzyme in the saliva known as ptyalin. This "design" is perfectly suited for pre-digesting grains, tubers, and other vegetable matter. Because cats and other carnivores do not have grinding teeth (flat back molars), large pieces of non-predigested flesh will enter the stomach. This may explain why the stomach hydrochloric acid in carnivores is 10 to 20 times stronger than in herbivores; quite effective for breaking down fibers of connective tissue and muscle. Perhaps not coincidentally, man, like the plant eaters, produces only weak amounts of stomach acidity.

Claws, another carnivorous characteristic, are not found in herbivores or man. As is true of the razor-like incisor and canine teeth, claws are an asset to the meat-eating hunter.

And the list continues. Carnivorous animals do not possess skin pores for the release of body heat. Anyone who has ever watched a cat panting on a warm summer day realizes that meat eaters perspire through their mouths. Herbivores, however, such as zebras, sheep, horses (and man?) utilize millions of porous openings on the surface of the skin for perspiring.

Perhaps the most striking difference between the flesh eaters and plant consumers is intestinal tract length. Herbivores and man, as shown, have decidedly longer intestinal tracts (10 to 12 times trunk length) than carnivores (three times trunk length). It has been speculated that flesh is readily catabolized by digestive microflora. Thus, putrefaction and possible resultant illness are kept "at bay" by a shorter digestive tract.

Longer tracts, on the other hand, as possessed by plant eaters and humans, are more ideally suited for plant food breakdown since vegetable matter is somewhat more resistant to catabolic processes. It is also hypothesized that since the material in the gut moves much more slowly when that material is composed of animal foods (ask any constipated meat eater), a short intestinal tract is ideal for the flesh eater. A herbivore, however, needs more transit time to absorb nutrients from the rapidly moving, fiber-filled plant foods. Thus, the long intestinal tract would be ideal for the plant eater.

One asset of a good natural hunter is speed. Obviously, if all carnivores were faster (and had more endurance) than herbivores, ecology would quickly be in turmoil. Thus, one would expect a balance in ability to avoid harm or pursue a dinner as indicated in Table 2. Included in this random sampling of animal speed data is *Homo sapiens* (man)—not exactly Speedy Gonzales and unimpressively added to the bottom quarter of the list.

Obviously, this chart does little to convince us that natural law produced a 20th Century human being designed primarily for carnivorism or herbivorism. We can say, however, that man is relatively slow—and being slow would, by necessity, require additional skills and attributes to be a successful hunter.

Unless you've been training with the Tarahumara Indians, you may find it difficult to run down a deer for tonight's dinner. The ability to endure may serve the slower hunter well. Stealth, yet another trait of a thriving carnivore, may produce nourishment from a successful ambush. A lion, for example, capable of running 50 mph, may cut his work short by surprising a resting, relaxed, but equally fast wildebeest.

Enhanced sensory perception is an attribute inherent in many carnivores (and herbivores). Most hunters have good night sight and up to a 250 degree field of vision. By contrast, man has a 180 degree field of vision and relatively poor night sight.

Most meat eaters also enjoy a heightened sense of smell. Dogs, for example, have 125 to 200 million ethmoidal cells responsible for their exceptional olfaction. (By contrast, man has approximately 5 million ethmoidal cells.) In controlled studies, man's best friend has been able to detect by smell one drop of blood in five quarts of water[2] Dogs and other carnivorous hunters significantly increase their ability to smell fatty acids (from other animals) when deprived of food for an extended period. How auspicious. The hunter has been granted a decisive self-preservation mechanism. When he becomes hungry, his ability to smell food improves.

Many carnivores (and some herbivores) have exceptional

TABLE 2
Speed of Animals, Including Man[14]

Animal	Speed	Primarily A Carnivore Or Herbivore	
Cheetah	70 mph	Carnivore	
Pronghorn Antelope	61 mph		Herbivore
Wildebeest	50 mph		Herbivore
Lion	50 mph	Carnivore	
Thomson's Gazelle	50 mph		Herbivore
Quarter Horse	47.5 mph		Herbivore
Elk	45 mph		Herbivore
Cape Hunting Dog	45 mph	Carnivore	
Coyote	43 mph	Carnivore	
Gray Fox	42 mph	Carnivore	
Hyena	40 mph	Carnivore	
Zebra	40 mph		Herbivore
Mongolian Wild Ass	40 mph		Herbivore
Greyhound	39.35 mph	Carnivore	
Whippet	35.5 mph	Carnivore	
Rabbit	35 mph		Herbivore
Mule Deer	35 mph		Herbivore
Jackal	35 mph	Carnivore	
Reindeer	32 mph		Herbivore
Giraffe	32 mph		Herbivore
White-Tailed Deer	30 mph		Herbivore
Wart Hog	30 mph		Herbivore
Grizzly Bear	30 mph	Carnivore	
Cat (Domestic)	30 mph	Carnivore	
MAN	27.89 mph	? ? ? ? ?	? ? ? ? ?
Elephant	25 mph		Herbivore
Black Mamba Snake	20 mph	Carnivore	
Six-Lined Race Runner	18 mph	Carnivore	
Wild Turkey	15 mph	Carnivore	
Squirrel	12 mph		Herbivore
Pig (Domestic)	11 mph		Herbivore
Chicken	9 mph	Carnivore	

hearing ability, capable of detecting frequencies exceeding 100,000 cycles per second. Humans, on the other hand, hear up to 30,000 cycles per second.

If man were meant to eat other animals, it would appear that the human race has been the unfortunate recipient of some serious engineering flaws. Our bodies are simply ill-suited for meat eating. I suspect the first person on earth would have quickly discovered that harvesting berries was much easier than chasing an antelope.

But wait. We've been negligent in not discussing perhaps the most significant factor of all: the human brain. With all that grey matter upstairs maybe we don't need claws and fangs to "bring home the bacon." True—but is it to our healthful advantage? Has mankind consistently utilized his superior intellect to further personal wellness? If so, then we could realistically presume (but still question) the appropriateness of flesh on the dinner plate. However, despite the enormous benefits enjoyed from our ever-accelerating technology, harmful impediments to man's "best shot" at health have also surfaced. Witness air pollution, water pollution, asbestos insulation, fast automobiles, agent orange, "fast" burgers and fries, etc.

Thus, technology's track record, serving both mankind's betterment and shame, would render any deductive pro-carnivorism argument invalid (but not disproven). Science has created more than a few monsters as direct or indirect offshoots of its inspired work. A consumer of the '90s, for example, has justifiable confidence in the immediate safety and aesthetic value of a can of green beans. Yet, he or she may begin to wonder why, in that same can, there are over 1000 milligrams of sodium.

A BRIEF COMPARISON OF THE "FUELS"

Hopefully, after reading the previous section, you have begun to question the suitability of animal foods for human fuel. Do they serve like a high-octane fuel in a high-compression engine? Or are they more like kerosene, causing sludging and poor performance? First, we must agree that foods originating from animals differ in composition from those of plant origin. All biological materials are not the same.

Table 3 compares caloric and nutrient contents of three typical animal foods (beef, milk, eggs) to three common plant foods (corn, potatoes, collard greens). Our purpose is not to speculate as to which (all, some, or none) are advantageous to the human. We simply wish to point out that there are distinct differences between popular foods originating from animals and those derived from plants. One would suspect, for example, that an animal needing an energy rich diet (high in fat) would be best served by eating other animals, whereas species who thrive best on carbohydrate and fiber would prosper via plant consumption. Table 3 is meant to represent many (but certainly not all) foods within a particular group. There are a few exceptions.

However, if we were to compare a multitude of unprocessed foods, a few eternal truths would soon evolve, such as,

Animal foods are:
1. higher in calories
2. higher in fat
3. higher in protein
4. lower in complex carbohydrates
5. cholesterol-laden
6. void of fiber

Unprocessed plant foods are:
1. lower in calories
2. lower in fat
3. lower in protein
4. higher in complex carbohydrates
5. void of cholesterol
6. fiber-laden

Now let's compare the nutrient requirements of carnivores, herbivores, and man to determine which "fuel group" best serves health.

TABLE 3

A Comparison of the Composition of One-Pound Samples of Typical Unprocessed Animal and Plant Foods[15]

| | ANIMAL FOODS | | |
FACTOR	Beef Chuck	Cow's Milk	Chicken Egg
Calories	1166	299	658
Carbohydrate	- - -	22.2 g	3.6 g
Protein	84.8 g	15.9 g	52.1 g
Fat	88.9 g	16.8 g	46.4 g
% Fat Calories	69%	51%	63%
Vitamin A	180 IU	690 IU	4760 IU
Thiamine	0.36 mg	0.15 mg	0.42 mg
Riboflavin	0.75 mg	0.78 mg	1.20 mg
Niacin	20.4 mg	0.3 mg	0.2 mg
Vitamin C	- - -	5.0 mg	- - -
Calcium	50 mg	531 mg	218 mg
Phosphorous	853 mg	417 mg	828 mg
Iron	12.7 mg	0.2 mg	9.3 mg
Sodium	- - -	227 mg	493 mg
Potassium	- - -	635 mg	521 mg
Cholesterol	320 mg	50 mg	2200 mg
Fiber	- - -	- - -	- - -

TABLE 3

A Comparison of the Composition of One-Pound Samples of Typical Unprocessed Animal and Plant Foods[15]

	PLANT FOODS		
FACTOR	Corn	Potato	Collard Greens
Calories	240	279	139
Carbohydrate	55.1 g	62.8 g	23.1 g
Protein	8.7 g	7.7 g	14.8 g
Fat	2.5 g	0.4 g	2.5 g
% Fat Calories	9%	1%	16%
Vitamin A	1000 IU	- - -	28,680 IU
Thiamine	0.37 mg	0.39 mg	0.48 mg
Riboflavin	0.29 mg	0.14 mg	0.97 mg
Niacin	4.2 mg	5.4 mg	5.1 mg
Vitamin C	31 mg	73 mg	469 mg
Calcium	7 mg	26 mg	771 mg
Phosphorous	277 mg	195 mg	253 mg
Iron	4.7 mg	2.2 mg	4.6 mg
Sodium	- - -	11 mg	- - -
Potassium	699 mg	1495 mg	1388 mg
Cholesterol	- - -	- - -	- - -
Fiber	3.2 g	2.3 g	3.7 g

NUTRIENT REQUIREMENTS: A COMPARISON OF A HERBIVORE, AN OMNIVORE, AND A CARNIVORE TO HOMO SAPIENS

In a previous section, we pointed out some unique characteristics shared by man and herbivorous animals, (alkaline saliva, ptyalin, low stomach acidity, long digestive tract, etc.). Some may argue that these are interesting similarities but not convincing of the need to graze for optimum health. If the foods normally consumed by a rabbit and cat were switched, for example, the rabbit would die and the cat would starve.

Perhaps, however, the inherent differences of food consumed by animals in nature may reflect unique differences in nutrient requirements between the hunters and their plant-eating prey. The National Academy of Sciences, in the past, has sanctioned research to determine nutrient requirements for a variety of animals, including dogs,[3] cats,[4] swine,[5] rabbits,[6] sheep,[7] minks and foxes,[8] horses,[9] laboratory animals,[10] non-human primates,[11] and others.

The Food and Nutrition Board of the National Research Council has developed similar recommendations for human beings called recommended daily allowances (RDAs).[12] Let's use this information to compare the energy and nutrient requirements of a representative carnivore, herbivore and man on a *per kilogram of body weight per day* basis. We may thus be able to determine:

1 Are there differences between meat and plant eaters and, if so,

2. Do man's RDAs more closely resemble those of a healthy carnivore or herbivore?

Table 4 makes the comparisons. For the sake of simplicity, a 70-kilogram adult male is compared to a single grazer (horse) and a well-known carnivore (cat). However, for the dedicated disciples of the "four basic food groups," a fourth member of the comparison group, the dog, is included. Fido, an acknowledged omnivore, can thrive equally well on either meat or formulated grain products.

By sheer logic, replete with past experience, one would expect tabulated information to yield some trends and some trendless inconsistencies. Table 4 reports only those 15 nutrient or calorie requirements where trends were apparent. Man's RDAs were judged to be similar to:

1. the herbivore, or
2. the herbivore and omnivore, or
3. the omnivore, or
4. the omnivore and carnivore, or
5. the carnivore.

These are the results:

Man similar to the herbivore . . . . 11 times
Man similar to the herbivore and omnivore . . . . . . 1 time
Man similar to the omnivore . . . . 2 times
Man similar to the omnivore and carnivore . . . . 1 time
Man similar to the carnivore . . . . 0 times

According to this simple comparison, man appears to heavily favor the herbivorous segment of the food chain. In fact, the only nutrient requirement which appears to favor pro-carnivorism is vitamin A. This may be an observation which is more reflective of an estimated four-fold human RDA safety factor than an inherent similarity to feline metabolism. These lopsided results, in addition to the herbivorous-by-anatomy analysis aired earlier, would leave many a pot-roast warrior grappling for rebuttal.

It is fascinating to observe how closely animal food and plant food appear to ideally suit the nutrient needs of carnivores and herbivores, respectively. A common house cat or a lion with relatively high requirements for calories, protein, vitamin A, thiamine, riboflavin, niacin, calcium, phosphorous, etc., could do no better than to consume beef, milk, and an occasional egg (Table 3). *Au contraire,* herbivores (such as the horse, you and me) who need to avoid fat and cholesterol and have only a fraction of the protein and energy requirements needed to

TABLE 4

Energy Needs and Healthful Daily Intakes of Select Nutrients for a Herbivore, Omnivore, Carnivore, and Man[3] [4] [9] [12]

FACTOR	Expressed As (a)	Herbivore Horse	Omnivore Dog	Carnivore Cat	MAN	Man Most Similar To:
Energy	KCal/Kg/Day	33	62	87	37(b)	Herbivore
Protein	g/Kg/Day	1.3	2.8	6.1	0.8	Herbivore
Vit. A.......	IU/Kg/Day	25	75	217	144	Omnivore/ Carnivore
Vit. D.......	IU/Kg/Day	4.1	8.0	21.7	3.3	Herbivore
Vit. E.......	IU/Kg/Day	0.22	0.50	1.73	0.15	Herbivore
Thiamin	mg/Kg/Day	0.04	0.02	0.11	0.02	Herbivore/ Omnivore
Riboflavin ...	mg/Kg/Day	0.03	0.05	0.11	0.02	Herbivore
Niacin	mg/Kg/Day	in vivo	0.23	0.98	0.25	Omnivore
Folacin	ug/Kg/Day	in vivo	4.0	21.6	6.5	Omnivore
B12	ug/Kg/Day	in vivo	0.50	0.43	0.05	Herbivore
Calcium.....	mg/Kg/Day	46	119	217	13	Herbivore
Phosphorous.	mg/Kg/Day	28	89	173	13	Herbivore
Iron	mg/Kg/Day	0.60	0.65	2.17	0.24	Herbivore
Zinc........	mg/Kg/Day	0.60	0.72	0.65	0.23	Herbivore
Iodine	ug/Kg/Day	1.5	12.0	21.7	2.4	Herbivore

(a) Each factor is expressed in terms of its concentration, i.e., Kcal, g, mg, ug, or International Units (IU), per kilogram of body weight per day.

(b) Estimated daily energy intake for a 70 kg adult male is 2600 calories, i.e., 37 calories/kg body weight/day.

sustain Elsa and Morris, would thrive best on roots, shoots and fruits.

THE OMNIVORE MYTH

Charts illustrating the "four basic food groups," as seen in most of our classrooms and as published by the National Dairy Council, have left an indelible impression on many minds. These ubiquitous charts grace the walls of elementary schools, physician's offices, and medical schools. Anyone daring to challenge the meat, poultry or dairy industries is not likely to be applauded by many apple-pie institutions. One belief premised on the "basic four" is that there exists an ideal blend of animal products and plant foods that supports optimum well-being. Any deviation from this ideal blend would lessen health. This prevalent concept is illustrated in Figure 1.

Why, then, are the facts in conflict with that belief? We have a nation of omnivores (not anatomically nor physiologically but by choice)—a nation of overweight, frequently ill omnivores. What are some of the favorite foods of an omnivore? How about chili, pizza, cheeseburgers, steak, and macaroni and cheese?

A partial truth of the presumed omnivorous advantage is that as consumption of animal products increases (away from the ideal blend), health diminishes. A wealth of research reported in this book will certainly serve as irrefutable corroboration. For example, we've repeatedly seen higher incidences of osteoporosis, heart disease, and other afflictions in select groups and entire societies that consume greater amounts of animal products.

What about the other end of the spectrum? An incorrect presumption of a pro-health meat-and-potatoes regimen is that ingestion of greater amounts of vegetable matter (again, away from the ideal blend) will ultimately result in increased sickliness. The sickliness, according to this incorrect presumption, would be caused by deficiencies of protein, vitamins, and other nutrients.

This reaction is understandable. After all, how can a healthy human being thrive on only two of the four basic food groups?

FIGURE 1:
Depiction of the "Presumed"
Health Benefits of Omnivorism

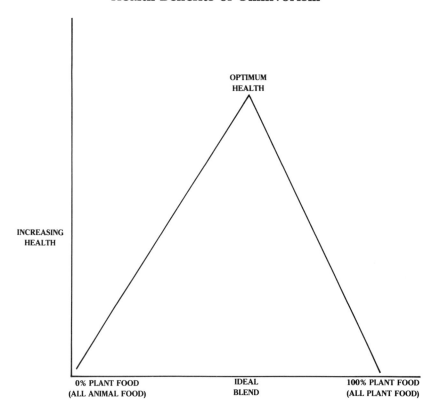

OPTIMUM
HEALTH

INCREASING
HEALTH

0% PLANT FOOD   IDEAL   100% PLANT FOOD
(ALL ANIMAL FOOD)   BLEND   (ALL PLANT FOOD)

Yet, as reported throughout this text, vegetarians suffer significantly less from all major degenerative diseases and live years longer than the rest of the population. Perhaps they have been doing something right. A more accurate depiction of health vs. animal/plant food consumption is best illustrated in Figure 2.

It is appropriate at this point to make what may seem to be a surprising statement in view of what we have been discussing: Primitive men, once they had developed weapons, occasionally ate meat. Meat could not have been a staple of their diets, but

FIGURE 2:
Depiction of the "Actual" Health
Benefits of Herbivorism

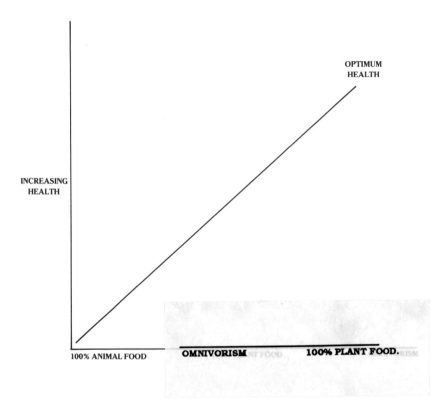

when it was available, it was eaten. Anthropological records leave little doubt as to this fact.

In times of famine, then as now, killing and eating animals may have been the only way to survive. As the human intellect developed, the ability to hunt became more developed. Feasts on meat became popular, although they were probably few and far between. For most of man's existence, he has been omnivorous, with the bulk of his food coming from the vegetable kingdom. We do have the ability to digest meat, and in hard times, this ability may have assured survival of the species. We are, however, primarily herbivorous by design and obviously thrive best on a pure vegetarian diet.

Though we may need to eat meat in cases of severe hunger, it is to our detriment to eat it in other circumstances. The studies in China referred to throughout this book show clearly that eating even small amounts of animal foods is more detrimental to the health than eating none at all. Without question, there is a dose-response relationship between the consumption of these products and the rate of degenerative diseases. The public should be educated to these facts.

And, the public is beginning to listen. Physicians who are alarmed at the health-destroying habits of typical Americans are becoming authors, and their books are moving up the best-seller lists. We have already mentioned Dr. Ornish, Dr. McDougall, Dr. Neal Barnard and Dr. Michael Klaper. We are on the threshold of a national dietary upheaval that promises a brighter future for those courageous souls not hampered by their old habits.

Something new is afoot in the medical arena. A new group known as the Physicians Committee for Responsible Medicine (PCRM), headed by Neal Barnard, M.D., is advocating a new four basic food groups: grains, legumes, fruits and vegetables. The current membership has reported its intentions[13] to furnish educational materials to schools, combined with a media push featuring vegetarian celebrities and respected physicians.

According to Dr. Barnard, "The basic dietary guidelines taught to us as children are wrong. The goal will be to get the public to recognize and accept the fact that we've turned the corner in nutrition. You don't alleviate diseases with a chicken or lean-meat diet but with a pure vegetarian diet. Research is now clear and sufficient enough to recommend this." He further states, "We're not saying that you can never have another Haagen Dazs, but the basis of a healthful diet is not meat, fish, or cheese."

Right on, Dr. Barnard. It is good to see courageous physicians stepping to the forefront to assure the most effective and humane treatment of their patients—treatment that will actually help their patients to get well.

REFERENCES

[1]Parham, V. *What's Wrong With Eating Meat?* PCAP Publications. Corona, New York, 1981, pp. 3-11.

[2]Mery, F. *The Life History and Magic of the Dog.* Madison Square Press, New York, NY, 1968, p. 143.

[3]National Research Council. *Nutrient Requirements of Dogs.* National Academy Press, Washington, D.C., 1985.

[4]National Research Council. *Nutrient Requirements of Cats.* National Academy Press, Washington, D.C., 1986.

[5]National Research Council. *Nutrient Requirements of Swine.* National Academy Press, Washington, D.C., 1988.

[6]National Research Council. *Nutrient Requirements of Rabbits.* National Academy Press, Washington, D.C., 1977.

[7]National Research Council. *Nutrient Requirements of Sheep.* National Academy Press, Washington, D.C., 1985.

[8]National Research Council. *Nutrient Requirements of Mink and Foxes.* National Academy Press, Washington, D.C., 1982.

[9]National Research Council. *Nutrient Requirements of Horses.* National Academy Press, Washington, D.C., 1978.

[10]National Research Council. *Nutrient Requirements of Laboratory Animals.* National Academy Press, Washington, D.C., 1978.

[11]National Research Council. *Nutrient Requirements of Non-human Primates.* National Academy Press, Washington, D.C., 1978.

[12]National Research Council. 6Recommended Dietary Allowances. Ninth rev. ed., National Academy Press, Washington, D.C., 1980.

[13]Wiley, C. Doctors push for a new basic four. Vegetarian Times, April 1991, pp. 14-15.

[14]The World Almanac and Book of Facts. Newspaper Enterprise Association, Inc., New York, New York, 1981, p. 804.

[15]Watt, B. Composition of Foods. Agriculture Handbook No. 8. Superintendent of Documents, Washington, D.C., 1963, pp. 72, 84, 85, 87, 96, 106, 146.

8.

Protein Mythology and Related Fables

8. Protein Mythology and Related Fables

> "Nothing will benefit human health and increase the chances for survival of life on earth as much as the evolution to a vegetarian diet."
>
> —Albert Einstein

Over the last two decades, there have been tens of thousands of misleading and frequently outlandish reports on food and health. Everything from cookies to cassava, margarine to Metamucil, has been touted as the pain-free way to lose weight, cure cancer, prevent stroke, etc. One tabloid recently proclaimed that arthritis could be cured by WD-40!

Fortunately, from within this thick cloud of blarney, truth is beginning to emerge. Americans are catching on and are especially aware that there are genuine health gains to be reaped by reducing cholesterol, fat, sugar and salt in the diet. Most recognize that there is something inherently beneficial about whole grain breads as opposed to their milled counterparts. Consumer surveys continue to reflect a growing dissatisfaction with "quasi-healthful" food products such as eggless mayonnaise (99% of calories from fat), "organic" high-fat cookies, and other foods intended to mislead the public. Both manufacturers and retailers are responding positively with hundreds of new, healthful foods that line the expanding shelf space of the supermarkets. This represents an ongoing change for the better.

There are, however, three issues that remain a bastion of resistance against a healthful diet; namely, the worries about protein, milk, and vitamin B-12.

PROTEIN—AN UNNECESSARY WORRY

As one local philosopher queried, "If you don't eat any meat or drink any milk, where in the heck are ya gonna get your protein . . . lettuce?" (Why do they always think that vegetarians live on lettuce?) Of course, we all know that proteins are the building blocks of muscle and many other tissues of the body and that animal products are concentrated sources. Thus, the meat proponents argue that to be strong and aggressive, like the tiger, we need to consume flesh. Somehow they fail to notice that apes, elephants, horses and rhinoceri seem to develop massive muscles while consuming their vegetarian diets. The next time you drive past the local burger emporium, you may want to count the number of sickly, overweight "tigers" you see through the plate glass windows.

The truth is, that as a society, *we are ingesting too much protein!* The typical American consumes 90 to 120 grams of this nitrogen-laden substance daily.[1] The current recommended RDA is 0.8 grams per kilogram of body weight,[2] which includes a large "safety" factor. This recommendation would suggest that a 70 kilogram (154 pound) man would need 56 grams of protein daily and that a 55 kilogram woman would need 44 grams. The typical American, therefore, is consuming in excess of the RDAs, which themselves are in excess of minimum daily requirements (MDRs).

The quantity of protein needed to maintain health is the amount that keeps the body in positive nitrogen balance—in other words, to ingest more nitrogen than is excreted in the feces and urine. Under controlled starvation conditions (fasting), urinary nitrogen losses will increase dramatically since the body will depend heavily on protein catabolism for energy. As cited in an article by William Harris, M.D.,[3] an adult male on a fast will excrete 4.32 grams of nitrogen per day. This is approximately equal to 27 grams of protein. In other words, only 27 grams of protein would be required to keep the body in a positive nitrogen balance under conditions of maximum bodily protein loss. We would expect, then, under non-starvation conditions, a greatly reduced protein requirement, since carbohydrate and fat would serve as the primary caloric substrates (sources).

The estimates for MDRs of protein vary. Research conducted between 1920 and 1946[4][5] estimated that 0.5 grams per kilogram of body weight would meet the minimum requirement, i.e., 35 grams for a 70 kilogram male and 27.5 grams for a 55 kilogram female. Other researchers put the minimum daily requirement at 30 grams for an average-weight man.[6] More recent research suggests an even lower MDR of about 20 grams per day.[7][8] Observations of healthy people thriving on approximately 20 grams of protein daily[9] would indicate that the MDR would be no more than 20 grams. It could be less. The work of Dr. William Rose[10] actually showed that young, healthy men would stay in positive nitrogen balance when only 2.5% of their total calories came from protein. At 3000 calories per day, that would indicate a requirement of only about 19 grams daily.

Dr. Rose's research certainly makes sense. An infant will double its weight in the first 180 days after birth. During that time, all the protein structures such as muscle and connective tissue will also approximately double in size. *It is obvious that the requirements for protein during this period will exceed anything he or she will ever need during the rest of a lifetime.* After all, there will never again be a doubling of size in a six-month period. It will take years before another doubling takes place.

Breast milk is obviously the perfect food for infants, containing sufficient protein for the rapid growth of the structures mentioned. Surprisingly, however, breast milk contains only 5% of its total calories in protein! Yet, this 5% is ample to support the tremendous growth in the first six months of life. *It follows that 5% of total calories will be more than enough protein for a slower-growing child and much more than enough for an adult who has ceased growing*—adding no size to his protein structures whatsoever. A glaring error was made in using rats to determine protein requirements for human beings. A mother rat's milk contains ten times the concentration of protein as does human breast milk. Yet, this is the animal whose nutrition we have sought to emulate.

How hard is it to get 2.5% or even 5% of our calories from protein by eating plant foods? Table 1, originally done by William Harris, M.D., displays the protein contents of various foods and should set to rest any lingering fears about developing protein deficiencies from a nutrition program devoid of animal products.[3] Most vegetable products have far more than enough protein for humans.

If life depended on it, a person could not develop a protein deficiency on a starch-based diet unless he or she lived on poi alone—provided, of course, that the normal number of calories was consumed. It would take a very careful selection of low-protein fruits and vegetables to approach anything less than the 2.5% minimum.

Many may recall the horrid pictures of third world children—small, hungry, and wasting away with the ravages of protein-deficiency (kwashiorkor). Those of us who have contributed to missionary work may have rightfully assumed our charitable dollars would aid in the purchasing of medical supplies and certainly food. The promise of alleviated suffering and restored health was often depicted in photos of these same children drinking an allotment of milk just handed them. Isn't it possible, then, that we may be inclined to associate stunted growth and lack of muscle development with a lack of animal foods, or at least milk?

Children (and adults) who suffer with kwashiorkor *are starving; they're simply not getting enough total food!* Consequently, they may also be deficient in other nutrients. Many reports have indicated that protein-deficient (starving) societies quickly regain their health when provided with more of their native vegetarian foods.[11] [12] [13] [14]

There's more to the story, however. Most of us are aware that protein is composed of substances called amino acids, of which there are 22 found in food. Through the painstaking work of Dr. Rose on men[15] and Dr. Leverton on women,[16] eight amino acids were determined to be necessary (essential) in the adult diet. Both researchers doubled the observed minimum requirements for what they called "safe levels." In later research, Dr. Rose[17] [18] noted that the presence of two non-essential amino acids, tyrosine and cystine, could reduce the requirement of phenylalanine (by 70% to 75%) and methionine (by 80% to 90%), respectively.

Based on these data, Dr. John McDougall[19] clearly showed a variety of single plant foods to be complete protein sources. A

TABLE 1

Percent of Calories from Protein in Vegetable Foods

VEGETABLES	% CALORIES FROM PROTEIN
Seaweed—spirulina, dried	79.3
Watercress—raw	78.0
Mustard greens—boiled, drained	60.2
Spinach—raw, chopped	53.3
Alfalfa seeds—sprouted, raw	52.8
Cabbage—white mustard, raw	46.7
Lettuce—romaine, raw, shredded	45.0
Broccoli—raw	43.7
Tofu—raw, firm	43.6
Chard—Swiss, raw	42.7
Asparagus—raw, boiled, spears	42.4
Soybeans—sprouted, steamed	41.9
Balsam pear—leafy tip, boiled	41.8
Natto-fermented soybeans	40.5
Lettuce—butterhead, head	39.8
Amaranth—boiled, drained	39.7
Benas—mung, sprouted, boiled	38.8
Bamboo shoots—raw	38.3
Tempeh—soybean products	38.1
Beet greens—boiled, drained	37.0
Soybeans—green, boiled, drained	34.7
Lentils—sprouted, raw	34.1
Cauliflower—raw, chopped	33.2
Cress—garden, raw	32.5
Mushrooms—raw, chopped	32.4
Chives—raw, chopped	32.0
Squash—zucchini, raw, sliced	31.6
Collards—raw, boiled, drained	31.1
Endive—raw, chopped	31.0
Lettuce—iceberg, raw leaves	30.8
Lentils—whole, cooked	30.5
Cabbage—celery, raw	30.3
Cowpeas—blackeye, raw, boiled	30.1
Cabbage—savoy, raw, shredded	29.5
Parsley—raw, chopped	29.3

TABLE 1 *continued*

Percent of Calories from Protein in Vegetable Foods

VEGETABLES	% CALORIES FROM PROTEIN
Chicory greens—raw, chopped	29.1
Onions—young green	27.8
Beans—black, cooked, boiled	26.8
Beans—navy pea, dried, cooked	26.8
Beans—great northern, dried, cooked	26.6
Peas—edible podded, raw	26.6
Brussel sprouts—raw, boiled	26.5
Beans—small white, boiled	25.5
Kohlrabi, raw	25.1
Kale—raw, boiled, drained	24.1
Dandelion greens—boiled	24.0
Okra—raw, boiled, drained	23.8
Beans—adzuki, boiled	23.5
Miso-fermented soybeans	23.1
Beans—garbanzo, dried, raw	22.8
Turnip greens, raw, boiled	22.6
Beans—lima, raw, boiled, drained	22.4
Beans—French, cooked, boiled	21.9
Beans—snap, wax, raw, boiled	21.5
Beans—snap, green, raw, boiled	21.5
Cabbage—common, raw, sliced	21.0
Artichokes—boiled, drained	20.8
Beans—green, frozen, French	20.4
Cabbage—red, raw, shredded	20.4
Peppers—hot chili, raw	20.0
Garlic—raw, clove	19.0
Lotus root—raw	18.7
Tomato—raw, red ripe	18.2
Squash—summer, boiled, sliced	18.1
Celery—pascal, raw stalk	17.3
Cucumber—raw, whole	16.7
Gourd—white flowered, boiled	16.0
Seaweed—kelp (kombu), raw	15.6
Pumpkin—raw, cubes	15.5
Radishes—raw	15.4

TABLE 1 *continued*

Percent of Calories from
Protein in Vegetable Foods

VEGETABLES	% CALORIES FROM PROTEIN
Shallots—raw	14.3
Peppers—sweet, raw	14.0
Onions—mature, raw, chopped	13.9
Beets—whole, boiled, drained	13.7
Rutabagas—boiled, drained	13.0
Corn—kernels from one ear	12.3
Eggplant—boiled, drained	11.9
Hummus	11.5
Jerusalem artichokes—raw	10.5
Ginger root—raw, sliced	9.9
Leeks—raw	9.8
Carrot—raw, whole, scraped	9.5
Burcock root—boiled, drained	9.5
Squash—butternut, baked	8.9
Potato skin—baked	8.7
Potato—baked, flesh and skin	8.4
Yam—mountain, Hawaii, steamed	8.4
Nuts—chestnuts, Chinese, raw	7.4
Sweet potato—baked, peeled	6.6
Parsnips—sliced, boiled, drained	6.5
Taro—raw, sliced	5.6
Water chestnuts—Chinese, raw	5.3
Poi	1.4

FRUITS	% CALORIES FROM PROTEIN
Lemons—raw, peeled	15.1
Melons—casaba, raw	13.6
Mulberries—raw	13.2
Pitanga—raw	12.0
Apricot—raw, without pit	11.7
Loganberries—frozen	11.1
Melons—cantaloupe, raw	9.8
Limes—raw	9.4

TABLE 1 *continued*

Percent of Calories from Protein in Vegetable Foods

FRUITS	% CALORIES FROM PROTEIN
Passion fruit—purple, raw	8.9
Boysenberries—frozen, unsweetened	8.8
Pummelo—raw, sections	8.1
Strawberries—raw, whole	8.1
Longans—raw	8.0
Oranges—raw, sections	8.0
Watermelon—raw	7.9
Gooseberries—raw	7.9
Roselle—raw	7.9
Nectarines—raw	7.6
Grapefruit—raw, pink and red	7.4
Raspberries—raw	7.3
Pricklypears—raw	7.1
Cherries—sweet, raw	6.7
Peaches—raw, whole	6.6
Guavas—common, raw	6.6
Carambola—raw	6.6
Kiwifruit—raw	6.5
Papayas—raw	6.4
Sapotes—raw	6.3
Soursop—raw, pulp	6.0
Plums—raw, Japanese hybrid	5.8
Tangerines—raw, peeled	5.7
Pomegranates—raw	5.7
Blackberries—raw	5.6
Cherimoya—raw	5.5
Lychees—raw	5.3
Melons—honeydew, raw	5.1
Tamarinds—raw	4.8
Avocado—raw, California	4.8
Blueberries—raw	4.7
Bananas—raw, peeled	4.5
Prunes—dried, uncooked	4.4
Raisins—seedless	4.3
Plantains—raw	4.3

TABLE 1 *continued*

Percent of Calories from
Protein in Vegetable Foods

FRUITS	% CALORIES FROM PROTEIN
Breadfruit—raw	4.2
Figs—raw	4.1
Grapes—raw, slip skin type	4.0
Grapes—raw, adherent skin	3.7
Elderberries—raw	3.6
Carissa—raw	3.3
Persimmons—raw, Japanese	3.3
Loquats—raw	3.2
Mangos—raw	3.1
Pineapple—raw, diced	3.1
Dates—natural, dried, whole	2.9
Quinces—raw	2.8
Pears—raw, bartlett, unpeeled	2.7
Sapodilla—raw	2.1
Apples—raw, unpeeled	1.3
Cranberry sauce—canned, sweetened	0.5

GRAINS	% CALORIES FROM PROTEIN
Flour—sesame, lowfat	60.1
Flour—soybean, lowfat	48.9
Flour—wheat, whole grain	16.1
Popcorn—popped, plain	16.0
Flour—buckwheat, whole, groat	15.0
Spaghetti—cooked, firm, hot	14.8
Bulgur—dried, commercial	14.3
Macaroni—cooked, firm, hot	13.5
Noodles—somen, wheat, dried	12.7
Flour—barley	11.4
Barley—pearled, uncooked	11.3
Tortilla—flour	10.5
Flour—carob	10.2
Matzo—meal	10.1

TABLE 1 *continued*

Percent of Calories from Protein in Vegetable Foods

GRAINS	% CALORIES FROM PROTEIN
Rice—brown, long grain, cooked	9.3
Cornmeal—whole grain, dried	9.0
Rice—white, parboiled, dried	7.3
Flour—rice, white	6.5

condensed and modified version of the McDougall chart is shown in Table 2. Included in the table are two parameters used to gauge the nutritional worth of the protein. One is the percentage of minimum total protein requirement. The other is the percentage of minimum requirement of the limiting essential amino acid (i.e., the amino acid closest, percent-wise, to the daily minimum as established by Rose).

Please note that all the plant foods listed have substantially more than adequate amounts of both total protein and essential amino acids. We may also be surprised to find that asparagus and broccoli are excellent sources of protein—providing 13 to 17 times the daily minimum requirements within 3000 total calories. (I'll bet you thought they were all water, fiber, and flavor.)

At National Institute of Fitness, we offer a nutrition program that is low in fat, sodium and cholesterol and high in fiber and starch. We also serve no caffeinated foods, alcohol, or diet sweeteners. Approximately one-third of our guest population opt for vegan meals. As you might expect, we are frequently asked if our strict vegetarian (vegan) nutrition program includes sufficient protein and essential amino acids. Table 3 provides an appropriate analysis of the food from a typical daily vegan meal plan. Although the total calories for the day were slightly more than 1400 (guests are required to ask for more food when they are hungry), the total protein and essential amino acid requirements were more than adequately met. For someone

TABLE 2

An Assessment of Protein Content Contained Within 3000 Calories of Various Foods[1]

Food	Total Protein	Total Protein: Percent of Minimum Requirement[2]	Limiting Essential Amino Acid: Percent of Minimum Requirement
Corn	109 grams	550%	260%
Brown Rice	64 grams	320%	260%
Wheat Flour	120 grams	600%	560%
White Beans	198 grams	990%	720%
Potatoes	82 grams	410%	320%
Broccoli	338 grams	1,690%	1,500%
Tomatoes	150 grams	750%	530%
Asparagus	330 grams	1,650%	1,320%
Club Steak	276 grams	1,380%	1,240%
Egg	238 grams	1,190%	1,520%
Milk	160 grams	800%	920%

[1]For an expanded table showing a breakdown of the eight essential amino acids, see *The McDougall Plan*, p. 99, by Dr. John A. McDougall and Mary A. McDougall, New Century Publishers, Inc., Piscataway, NJ, 1983.

[2]The minimum total protein requirement was considered to be 20 grams per person per day.

consuming a proportionally higher number of total calories (3000, for example), total protein and essential amino acids would, of course, more than double, providing additional reassurance.

And for the record . . . lettuce is deficient in five of the eight essential amino acids and contains less than one gram of protein per typical serving. Thus, a word to the wise (future vegans): plan on eating more than lettuce once you've parted company with the flesh, eggs, and milk. Seriously, by consuming a variety of foods and food products composed of fruits, vegetables, grains, and legumes, you will receive more than adequate amounts of essential nutrients, including protein.

UDDER NONSENSE

Although we have alluded to the harmful influence of milk throughout this book, perhaps it would be appropriate to state succinctly that milk is far from being the perfect food. Cow's milk is designed for calves, not humans. Breast milk is for babies. Neither is intended for use by children or adults, and cow's milk is certainly not intended for use by human infants.

We have mentioned the close correlation between milk consumption and osteoporosis internationally and have discussed the influence of milk on blood fats, multiple sclerosis, allergies and iron-deficiency anemia. Half the world's population is lactose intolerant. How fortunate for them! They cannot tolerate milk. Of course, we have now helped them with their "problem" by producing an enzyme that can be taken orally in pill form to digest the lactose. Now we can poison the other half. Ah, technology. . . . Where are you leading us?

Maybe you, like me, were misled into thinking that milk is essential for healthy growing children. After all, kids could use the extra protein provided by milk for their rapid muscle, bone, and organ development. This assumption, fueled by dairy industry advertising, is "udder nonsense." Children do not need the excess protein provided by milk.

The purpose of milk from any animal species is to provide

TABLE 3

Calories, Protein, and Essential Amino Acids of N.I.F. Vegan Meals For A One-Day Period[10] [16] [17] [18] [19]

	Calories	Protein Grams	Try	Thr	Iso	Leu	Lys	Met	Phe	Val
BREAKFAST:										
1 ounce raisins	54	0.6	2	8	3	6	7	10	6	8
2 pancakes	100	3.7	32	77	114	178	72	40	130	123
¾ cup oatmeal	105	4.5	61	158	207	345	184	75	247	264
¼ cup banana	26	0.3	4	10	10	20	14	3	11	14
¼ cup apple syrup	28	0.1	2	5	5	7	7	2	3	5
LUNCH:										
1 cup split pea soup	60	8.0	80	285	409	606	532	87	365	409
2 tomato slices	12	0.6	10	36	32	45	46	8	31	31
½ cucumber	20	0.8	4	14	16	23	22	5	12	17
3 mushrooms	2	0.2	4	- -	299	158	- -	95	- -	212
1 slice onion	10	0.3	3	3	3	5	9	2	6	4
1 Tbsp oil-free dressing	- -	- -	2	6	9	15	8	5	7	10
2 slices wheat bread	160	7.5	64	156	232	362	154	80	256	246
½ cup applesauce	53	0.2	2	7	7	12	12	2	6	10
DINNER:										
½ cup corn	80	2.0	10	65	60	175	60	30	90	100
1 corn tortilla	50	1.0	8	60	88	242	38	28	64	78
4 ounces pinto beans	67	8.5	69	168	445	669	577	73	429	476
1 ounce soy cheese	100	2.0	41	105	162	234	190	41	123	159
¼ cup tomato sauce	18	0.5	6	21	19	26	27	8	18	18
1 piece shortcake	100	2.7	16	38	60	101	30	17	71	56
½ cup strawberries	48	1.0	10	28	21	46	37	1	27	27
SNACKS:										
1 apple	81	0.3	3	10	11	17	17	3	7	12
2 potatoes	240	5.0	42	172	184	210	222	50	184	222
TOTALS	1414	49.8	475	1432	2396	3502	2265	665	2093	2501
Required for Men			250	500	700	1100	800	110	280	800
Required for Women			160	300	450	620	500	55	280	650
% Req. Obtained, Men			190	266	342	318	283	605	1037	313
% Req. Obtained, Women			297	444	532	565	453	1209	1037	385

[1] Try = Tryptophan   Trh = Threonine   Iso = Isoleucine   Leu = Leucine
Lys = Lysine   Met = Methionine   Phe = Phenylalanine   Val = Valine

nutrition for the *newborn of that species*. We shouldn't be surprised to find a difference in milk composition between species. For example, the protein content of cow's milk is 20% of total calories compared to 5% for humans. Moreover, the time for a baby calf to double in size after birth is 47 days as compared to 180 days for a human baby.

It appears that mother nature did her homework and provided extra protein for the faster growing creature. The six months required to double the body weight of the human baby is the fastest period of body growth we *Homo sapiens* will ever experience. And, that growth occurs on a natural food source which contains only about 5% of calories as protein. Thus, during *slower growth periods of our childhood, do we really need 20% calories as protein from the milk of another species* with all its saturated fat (50% calories from fat)? I think not.

Incidentally, the indirect relationship between protein content of mother's milk and time (days) to double in weight after birth appears to be consistent in nature. Using information provided by Bell[20] and reported by McDougall,[19] we can see this trend immediately by looking at the data in a somewhat different light. In Figure 1, a comparison of the species milk protein to rate of growth after birth is illustrated. In another chapter, we compared group characteristics of herbivores, omnivores and carnivores. Interestingly, Figure 1 provides us with two additional differences. Consumers of animal foods (dogs, cats, and rats) have much higher protein contents in their species milk (7.1% to 11.8%). Likewise, they also grow faster after birth (12.5% to 22.2% of newborn body weight per day). Our strict herbivores (horses, cows, and goats), however, have much lower protein in their milk (2.4% to 4.1%) and correspondingly grow at a slower rate (1.7% to 5.3% of newborn body weight per day).

What does this imply, then, for the appropriate food choices of *Homo sapiens* with the absolute lowest mother's milk protein (1.2%) and the slowest growth rate after birth (0.6% of birth weight per day)? If you believe that there are *right* foods by design for *Megahealth*, then you will have no choice but to question the suitability of milk and dairy products as adjuncts to wellness.

FIGURE 1

Relationship of Protein Content of Mother's Milk To Rate of Growth After Birth[20]

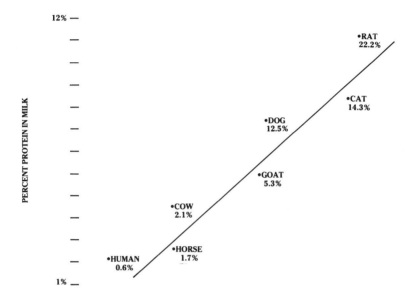

¹Rat's Milk = 11.8% protein. Rats double in size after birth in 4½ days (22.2% of body weight per day)

²Cat's Milk = 9.5% protein. Cats double in size after birth in 7 days (14.3% of body weight per day)

³Dog's Milk = 7.1% protein. Dougs double in size after birth in 8 days (12.5% of body weight per day)

⁴Goat's Milk = 4.1% protein. Goats double in size after birth in 19 days (5.3% of body weight per day)

⁵Cow's Milk = 3.3% protein. Cows double in size after birth in 47 days (2.1% of body weight per day)

⁶Horse's Milk = 2.4% protein. Horses double in size after birth in 60 days (1.7% of body weight per day)

⁷Human Milk = 1.2% protein. Humans double in size after birth in 180 days (0.6% of body weight per day)

Right after the turn of the century, rat research led investigators[21] to suggest that humans would be best served by consuming milk and eggs. The reason: rats grew extremely well on lactalbumin (a milk protein) and best on a mixture of egg proteins. In ranking the relative quality of several protein sources, these researchers assigned a very poor rating to plant proteins that supported the least amount of rat growth. These studies may be regarded as totally valid—*for rats only!*

People are not rats. Our physiology is different. We've seen that newborn rats grow nearly 40 times faster than human infants and are supported by the mother's milk which has ten times more protein. Obviously, significant metabolic differences exist . . . differences that would render this type of direct rat-to-man research invalid or at least off-target.

There are further reasons for placing milk (and other dairy products) on the healthy person's "most unwanted" list. Many milk-based foods are extremely high in fat. For example, look at the fat calories from these common dairy products:[22] [23]

Whole Milk:	50% Calories from Fat
Cream Cheese:	74% Calories from Fat
American Cheese:	74% Calories from Fat
Cottage Cheese (4% Fat):	38% Calories from Fat
Butter:	100% Calories from Fat
Cream:	97% Calories from Fat
Sour Cream:	88% Calories from Fat
Vanilla Ice Cream:	48% Calories from Fat

Consumption of foods such as these have been conclusively linked to an increased risk of heart attack and stroke. (See the chapter on heart disease.) They are inappropriate in the diets of those seeking long, healthy, productive lives.

Some will point out that we have failed to discuss the redeeming benefits of the relatively new "lite" line of dairy products, such as fat-free ice cream, low-fat cottage cheese, non-fat yogurt, skim and non-fat milk, etc. These products (and others) are concentrated sources of animal protein. One percent cottage cheese, for example, has 62% calories from protein, low-fat yogurt has 29% and skim milk 39% protein calories. We've already seen that the average American consumes 90 to 120 grams of protein per day—4½ to 6 times more than his or her body requires. As pointed out in the osteoporosis chapter, when we compare the dairy intake of different societies, there is a general upward trend in the disease as milk consumption increases. Surprising, but true. Any potential skeletal benefit of consuming a calcium-rich glass of milk (even low-fat or skim) is negated by the high-protein level.

There are other valid reasons for ceasing consumption of these high-fat, high-protein, fiberless foods. Consumption of excessive protein, fat, and cholesterol has been shown to cause and exacerbate kidney disease.[24] Casein (milk protein) has also been frequently linked to infections and allergies. In many cases, relief from the symptoms of recurrent bronchial infections, asthma, some skin rashes, rheumatoid arthritis, and other inflammations can be accomplished simply by eliminating dairy products from the diet.[24][25]

For those who wish to benefit from a change in nutrition, a word of advice is in order. Many seemingly harmless non-dairy foods may contain ingredients derived from milk (casein, lactose, skim milk, cream, whey, galactose, etc.). These ingredients find their "whey" into breads, soups, flavored noodle concoctions, and other formulated products. Thus, a good habit to develop (or nurture) for those in pursuit of Megahealth is to check the ingredients on each food product before purchasing. There is nothing that even begins to rival the profound affect on your weight and wellness as the composition of the "fuels" you put into your body daily. Be convinced. Study the food labels, buy wisely, and begin enjoying the priceless rewards of good health.

VITAMIN B-12: A UNIQUE CONCERN FOR THE HEALTHFULLY INCLINED

Cyanocobalamin . . . sounds ominous . . . not unlike a waste product from a nuclear reactor. You probably know it as 5,6-dimethylbenzimidazolyl cyanocomide (or perhaps as vitamin B-12). Whatever title you affix to it, in all of its various forms (hydroxycobalamin, cyanocobalamin, coenzyme B-12), this substance is undeniably essential for human health, albeit in small amounts.

Three nutrients (folacin, vitamin B-12, and zinc) are required for cell division within any tissues of the body. Since the role of B-12 is to render folic acid (folacin) available for key anabolic reactions, the deficiency symptoms of both folic acid and cobalamin are similar: anemia and accompanying paleness of skin. A severe B-12 deficit (extremely rare) may result in deterioration of nerve tissue in the spinal cord—symptoms being tingling and numbness in the toes and fingers, loss of balance, and weakness (and pain) in the arms and legs.

For anyone seriously contemplating the pros and cons of vegetarianism, then, the B-12 issue has the potential of throwing "cold water" on some otherwise worthwhile zeal. The reason: vitamin B-12, an essential nutrient, is found only in significant amounts in animal products. A brief explanation is in order. First, B-12 is produced only by bacteria and fungi, inherent to the soil. Good sources of this vitamin, for example, include activated sewage sludge, manure, and dried estuarine mud. As an animal consumes plants coated with dirt, it will invariably ingest the microflora that have synthesized the vitamin.

In the primitive, mostly-herbivorous chronology of man, much B-12 was likely assimilated in this fashion. This nutrient, unlike the other B vitamins, is readily stored in animals, including humans. Most plants, on the other hand, may have B-12 on adhering surface dirt but are unable to absorb and warehouse it. Thus, flesh, milk, and eggs are sources of cobalamin, whereas washed, cleaned, peeled, and/or trimmed plant foods are virtually depleted.

So, then, how do we provide ourselves with an adequate daily supply of this vitamin? In other words, what's for dinner tonight—a 12-ounce, medium rare T-bone or a lip-smacking, tastefully seasoned bowl of sewage? Fortunately, the answer is neither. The current Recommended Daily Dietary Allowance (RDA) for adults is relatively small, i.e., three micrograms per day.[26] Because we have the ability to store B-12, a typical American omnivore may have a 20 to 30-year supply in the body tissues.[27]

There have been only a few cases of B-12 deficiency among the tens of millions of vegetarians worldwide. It is suspected that the microbial populations within the mouth and intestines are actively at work producing sufficient healthful amounts. Regardless, responsible health authorities are advocating that strict vegetarians (vegans) consume a daily five microgram supplement which is particularly important for pregnant or nursing mothers.[25]

Vegetarians may also find B-12 in a few formulated or fermented non-animal foods. Table 4 lists several breakfast cereals which contain added or inherent cobalamin.[28] [29] Although we advise against regular consumption of the candy disguised as breakfast cereal (high in sugar) and some high-fat granola cereals, we can begin to see that the Kellogg, Post, Ralston Purina companies and others are becoming increasingly aware of the changing nutritional demands of their customers.

"Phony bologna" (meat analogs) also contains added B-12. But, like the real flesh counterparts, they also contain large amounts of fat. (There are a few exceptions.) The advice is to consume these products only sparingly, preferably in combination with robust amounts of grains, legumes, and other vegetable matter. Other non-animal foods containing B-12 include some frozen vegetables (small and unpredictable amounts), fermented soy products (nato, miso, etc.), exotic ocean vegetables (kombu and sakame), and some fortified yeasts. For those wishing to avoid all animal product, make certain to check the ingredient list on every food label. Occasionally dairy and/or egg products may find their way into a "vegetarian" meat analog or a breakfast food.

Again, reiterating, let's not be misled into thinking that vitamin B-12 is an inherent animal-produced nutrient, thereby confirming the apparent necessity of consuming flesh, milk, and embryos. When you consume B-12 laden meats, milk, and eggs, you're consuming the "warehouse," not the "factory." For those seeking better health, the B-12 issue is not an impasse. The use of supplements and consumption of select food products, as advised previously, will serve to sustain health using the only proven dietary approach to optimum wellness . . . pure vegetarianism.

TABLE 4

Vitamin B-12 Content of Non-Animal Foods[28] [29]

FOOD OR FOOD PRODUCT	SERVING SIZE	B-12 CONTENT
CEREALS:		
Alpha Bits	1 oz. (1 cup)	1.50 mcg
Bran, 100%	1 oz. (½ cup)	2.70 mcg
Bran Chex	1 oz. (⅔ cup)	1.50 mcg
Bran Flakes, 40%, Kelloggs	1 oz. (¾ cup)	1.50 mcg
Bran Flakes, 40%, Post	1 oz. (⅔ cup)	1.50 mcg
Bran Falkes, 40%, Ralston	1 oz. (¾ cup)	1.50 mcg
Cap'N Crunch	1 oz. (¾ cup)	1.79 mcg
Cap'N Crunch's Crunchberries	1 oz. (¾ cup)	2.03 mcg
Cap'N Crunch's Peanut Butter	1 oz. (¾ cup)	1.86 mcg
Cherrios	1 oz. (1¼ cup)	1.50 mcg
Cocoa Pebbles	1 oz. (7/8 cup)	1.50 mcg
Corn Bran	1 oz. (⅔ cup)	1.10 mcg
Corn Chex	1 oz. (1 cup)	1.50 mcg
Corn Flakes (Post Toasties)	1 oz. (1 cup)	1.50 mcg
Corn Flakes (Ralston)	1 oz. (1 cup)	0.10 mcg
Crispy Rice	1 oz. (1 cup)	0.08 mcg
Crispy Wheat and Raisins	1 oz. (¾ cup)	1.50 mcg
C.W. Post	1 oz. (¼ cup)	1.50 mcg
C.W. Post with Raisins	1 oz. (¼ cup)	1.50 mcg
Fortified Oat Flakes	1 oz. (⅔ cup)	1.50 mcg
Fruit & Fibre w/ Apples and Cinnamon	1 oz. (½ cup)	1.48 mcg
Fruit & Fibre w/ Dates, Raisins, Walnuts	1 oz. (½ cup)	1.48 mcg
Fruity Pebbles	1 oz. (7/8 cup)	1.50 mcg
Golden Grahams	1 oz. (¾ cup)	1.50 mcg
Grape-Nuts	1 oz. (¼ cup)	1.50 mcg
Grape-Nuts Flakes	1 oz. (7/8 cup)	1.50 mcg
Honey Bran	1 oz. (7/8 cup)	1.50 mcg
Honeycomb	1 oz. (1⅓ cup)	1.50 mcg
Honeynut Cherrios	1 oz. (¾ cup)	1.50 mcg
King Vitamin	1 oz. (1¼ cup)	5.57 mcg
Kix	1 oz. (1½ cup)	1.50 mcg
Lucky Charms	1 oz. (1 cup)	1.50 mcg
Maypo, Cooked	1 oz. (¾ cup)	2.10 mcg
Most	1 oz. (⅔ cup)	6.00 mcg
Nutri-Grain, Barley	1 oz. (¾ cup)	1.50 mcg

TABLE 4 *Continued*

Vitamin B-12 Content of Non-Animal Foods[28] [29]

FOOD OR FOOD PRODUCT	SERVING SIZE	B-12 CONTENT
Nutri-Grain, Corn	1 oz. (⅔ cup)	1.50 mcg
Nutri-Grain, Rye	1 oz. (¾ cup)	1.50 mcg
Nutri-Grain, Wheat	1 oz. (¾ cup)	1.50 mcg
Nutri-Grain, Wheat w/Raisins	1 oz. (½ cup)	1.07 mcg
Product 19	1 oz. (¾ cup)	6.00 mcg
Quaker 100% Natural w/Apples, Cinn.	1 oz. (½ cup)	0.08 mcg
Quisp	1 oz. (1 cup)	2.44 mcg
Raisin Bran, Kelloggs	1 oz. (¾ cup)	1.50 mcg
Raisin Bran, Post	1 oz. (½ cup)	1.50 mcg
Raisin Bran, Ralston	1 oz. (9/16 cup)	1.15 mcg
Raisins, Rice, and Rye	1 oz. (9/16 cup)	1.15 mcg
Ralston, Cooked	1 oz. (¾ cup)	0.08 mcg
Rice Chex	1 oz. (1-1/8 cup)	1.50 mcg
Sugar Frosted Flakes	1 oz. (¾ cup)	1.50 mcg
Sugar Frosted Rice	1 oz. (1 cup)	1.50 mcg
Sugar Puffs	1 oz. (7/8 cup)	1.50 mcg
Sugar Sparkled Flakes	1 oz.	1.50 mcg
Super Sugar Crisp	1 oz. (7/8 cup)	1.50 mcg
Tasteos	1 oz. (1¼ cup)	1.50 mcg
Team	1 oz. (1 cup)	1.50 mcg
Toasty-O's	1 oz. (1¼ cup)	1.50 mcg
Total	1 oz. (1 cup)	6.20 mcg
Trix	1 oz. (1 cup)	1.50 mcg
Waffelos	1 oz. (1 cup)	1.50 mcg
Wheat Chex	1 oz. (⅔ cup)	1.50 mcg
Wheat Chex w/Raisins	1 oz. (¾ cup)	1.50 mcg
Wheaties	1 oz. (1 cup)	1.50 mcg
MEAT ANALOGUES:		
Big Franks, Loma Linda	1 frank	1.20 mcg
Bologna, Loma Linda	2 slices	1.70 mcg
Breakfast links, Morningstar Farms	5 links	2.64 mcg
Breakfast patties, Morningstar Farms	2 patties	2.71 mcg
Breakfast strips, Morningstar Farms	3 strips	0.67 mcg
Chicken, fried, Loma Linda	1 piece	1.00 mcg
Chicken, fried w/gravy, Loma Linda	2 pieces	2.10 mcg

TABLE 4 *Continued*

Vitamin B-12 Content of Non-Animal Foods[28] [29]

FOOD OR FOOD PRODUCT	SERVING SIZE	B-12 CONTENT
Dinner cuts (Wheat Pro) w/sauce, Loma Linda	2 cuts	2.00 mcg
Griddle steaks, Loma Linda	1 steak	2.20 mcg
Grillers, Morningstar Farms	1 patty	2.16 mcg
Linketts, Loma Linda	2 links	2.20 mcg
Little Links, Loma Linda	2 links	2.00 mcg
Meatless meatballs, Loma Linda	4 pieces	1.40 mcg
Nuteena (peanuts & soy flour), Loma Linda	½" slice	1.30 mcg
Ocean fillet, Loma Linda	1 fillet	1.90 mcg
Proteena (lowfat nut loaf), Loma Linda	½" slice	1.60 mcg
Redi-burger, Loma Linda	½" slice	1.70 mcg
Sandwich spread, Loma Linda	3 Tbsp.	0.91 mcg
Savory dinner loaf, Loma Linda	1 slice	1.20 mcg
Sizzle burger, Loma Linda	1 burger	1.80 mcg
Sizzle franks, Loma Linda	2 franks	1.50 mcg
Stew pac w/sauce, Loma Linda	2 oz.	0.90 mcg
Swiss steak w/gravy, Loma Linda	1 steak	1.50 mcg
Tender bits, Loma Linda	4 pieces	0.63 mcg
Tender rounds w/gravy, Loma Linda	3 pieces	0.71 mcg
Vege-burger, Loma Linda	½ cup	1.80 mcg
Vegeloma, Loma Linda	½" slice	1.00 mcg
MOLASSES:		
Light	5 Tbsp.	0.20 mcg
Blackstrap	5 Tbsp.	2.10 mcg
RICE, LONG GRAIN & WILD	½ cup	0.01 mcg
SEA ALGAE	100 g	160.00 mcg
SEA VEGETABLES:		
Kombu	100 g	0-29 mcg
Wakame	100 g	0-29 mcg

TABLE 4 *Continued*

Vitamin B-12 Content of Non-Animal Foods[28] [29]

FOOD OR FOOD PRODUCT	SERVING SIZE	B-12 CONTENT
SOY PRODUCTS, FERMENTED:		
Miso...............................	100 g	0.17 mcg
Nato...............................	100 g	0.17 mcg
Soy sauce	1 Tbsp.	0.06 mcg
Soyu-Tamari sauce	100 g	0-10 mcg
Tempeh...........................	100 g	1.5-14.8 mcg
SQUASH, WINTER, FROZEN	2/5 cup	0.80 mcg
VEGETABLES, FROZEN:		
Chinese style	½ cup	0.01 mcg
Italian style	½ cup	0.01 mcg
Japanese style	½ cup	0.01 mcg
New England style.................	½ cup	0.01 mcg
San Francisco style	½ cup	0.01 mcg
YEAST, FORTIFIED W/B-12	100 g	50.00 mcg

REFERENCES

[1]Kofranyi, E. The minimum protein requirements in humans. In Akers, K. *A Vegetarian Sourcebook.* G.P. Putnam's Sons. New York. 1983.

[2]National Research Council. *Recommended Daily Allowances.* National Academy Press. Washington, D.C., 1980.

[3]Harris, W. The protein perplex. AHIMSA. 1991; 32(2):1, 3-9.

[4]Sherman, H. Protein requirement for maintenance in man. J Biol Chem 1920; 41:97.

[5]Hegsted, D. The protein requirements of adults. J Lab Clin Med 1946; 31:261.

[6]Bricker, M. The protein requirements of adult human subjects in terms of the protein contained in individual foods and food combinations. J Nutr 1945; 30:269.

[7]Hoffman, W. Nitrogen requirement of normal men on a diet of protein hydrolysate enriched with the limiting essential amino acids. J Nutr 1951; 44:123.

[8]Hegsted, D. Minimum protein requirements of adults. Am J Clin Nutr 1968; 21:352-357.

[9]Luyken, R. Nutrition studies in New Guinea. Am J Clin Nutr 1964; 14:13.

[10]Rose, W. The amino-acid requirements of adult man. Nutrition Abstracts and Reviews 1957; 27:631-637.

[11]Dahlberg, K. Medical care of Cambodian refugees. JAMA 1980; 243:1062.

[12]McLaren, D. A fresh look at protein-calorie malnutrition. Lancet 1966; 2:485.

[13]McLaren, D. The great protein fiasco. Lancet 1974; 2:93.

[14]Golden, M. Protein deficiency, energy deficiency, and the oedema of malnutrition. Lancet 1982; 1:1261.

[15]Rose, W. The role of amino acids in human nutrition. J Biol Chem 1943; 146:683 and 148:547.

[16]*Leverton, R. The qualitative amino acid requirements of young women. J Nutr 1956; 58:219.*

[17]Rose, W. The amino acid requirements of man XIV. The sparing effect of tyrosine on phenylalanine requirement. J Biol Chem 1955; 217:95.

[18]Rose, W. The amino acid requirements of man XIII. The sparing effect of cystine on methionine requirement. J Biol Chem 1955; 216:763-773.

[19]McDougall, J. *The McDougall Plan.* New Century, publishers, Piscataway, NJ, 1983, p. 99.

[20]Bell, G. *Textbook of Physiology and Biochemistry.* Williams and Wilkins. Baltimore, MD, 1959.

[21]Osborn, T. Amino acids in nutrition and growth. J Biol Chem 1914; 17:325.

[22]Netzer, C. *The Complete Book of Food Counts.* Dell Publishing, New York, NY, 1988. pp. 79, 120, 122-123, 198-199, 266-267, 304.

[23]Pennington, J. *Food Values of Portions Commonly Used.* Harper and Row, New York, NY, 1985, pp. 16-17, 33-34, 44, 62, 115-116.

[24]McDougall, J.A. *The McDougall Program: Twelve Days to Dynamic Health.* Penguin Books U.S.A., Inc., New York, NY, 1990, p. 369.

[25]Klaper, M. *Vegan Nutrition: Pure and Simple.* Gentle World, Inc., Umatilla, FL, 1987, p. 21.

[26]National Research Council. *Recommended Dietary Allowances,* 9th Rev. Ed. National Academy Press, Washington, D.C., 1980.

[27]McDougall, J.A. *The McDougall Program.* Penguin Books U.S.A., Inc., New York, NY, 1990, p. 46.

[28]Pennington, J.A.T. and Church, H.N. *Food Values of Portions Commonly Used.* Harper and Row, publishers, New York, NY, 1985, p. 112-114.

[29]McDougall, J.A. *The McDougall Plan.* New Century, publishers, Piscataway, NJ, 1983, p. 40.

9.

A Terrible Trio

9. *A Terrible Trio*

Little more could be said to implicate the high-fat, high-animal-product, low-fiber diet as a prime cause of debility and death. Likewise, the overwhelming evidence against tobacco products is so clear that only the most unconscionable representative of the tobacco industry would try to convince us that his merchandise has any redeeming value.

Considerable controversy exists, however, in regards to three particular products; namely, alcohol, artificial sweeteners and caffeine. Alcohol is now being touted as a help for heart disease, artificial sweeteners as an adjunct to weight control, and caffeine as an energy aid. This chapter will discuss the health-destroying influences of these substances in a way which will leave little doubt as to their true "worth."

DIET SWEETENERS: THE SLENDER TRAP

Diet sweeteners have been a huge success in terms of profit for the pharmaceutical companies that produce them. But, like other methods which supposedly help dieters to control weight by reducing calories, they have had rather sour results.

Cyclamates were the first to offer Americans the promise of slimmer waistlines, but due to the mounting evidence with regard to cancer risk, they were banned in all foods in 1969. Saccharin was the next to emerge, but as with cyclamates, overwhelming evidence of cancer-inducing effects could not be ignored. The FDA proposed a complete ban on saccharin in 1977 which resulted in such a public outcry that the issue quickly left the scientific arena and leaped into the realm of politics. The FDA settled for a warning label similar to that used on cigarette packages.

Then in 1981, food retailers acquired a new, widely acclaimed product which was destined to excel in the supermarket. The product was aspartame, and its promise was to provide virtually calorie-free sweetness with no aftertaste. From its grandiose introduction as a table-top sweetener through its approval for use in soft drinks, aspartame sales blossomed. Some sources have indicated, for instance, that between 100 and 150 million Americans (about 40-60% of the population) were consuming 800,000,000 pounds of this sweetener in 1985 which included 20 *billion* cans of diet sodas.[1] [2]

The commercial success of this product is based on the following beliefs by the consumer: (1) Diet sweeteners have little or no calories and therefore *must* be effective for weight control. (2) Since they are available on the supermarket shelves, they must be safe to eat.

Unfortunately, scientific data do not support either of these prevalent convictions.

Some "weighty" concerns

As established in the chapter on weight control, most of the methods purported to control weight actually promote weight gain. Aspartame and other sweeteners are no exception. Logically, one would question how the consumption of a substance void (or nearly void) of calories could cause an increase in stored fat. Yet, our previous discussions of obesity and diabetes presented incontrovertible evidence that calorie restriction activates physiological mechanisms which ultimately result in weight gain.

Artificial sweeteners are used to restrict calories by replacing the sugar which would normally be used to sweeten. We would expect, then, that these substances would contribute to overweight. We might also expect that, like sugar and fat, these sweeteners might raise the set point, resulting in an initial increase in food consumption until the "fat gap" had been filled. This would likewise culminate in a weight gain. (See the chapter on weight control.)

In studies using diet sweeteners, there have been absolutely no indications of successful long-term weight control. This idea that artificial sweeteners may be fattening is corroborated by several scientific studies. Animals fed saccharin or aspartame, for instance, become considerably fatter than abstinent littermates.[3] [4]

In a study of 78,694 women, the American Cancer Society determined that a significantly higher percentage of diet sweetener users gained weight than non-users (as shown in Table 1). Certainly if 32-44% of the diet sweetener consumers in the survey gained weight, the effectiveness of these products needs to be questioned.

TABLE 1
American Cancer Society Survey of 78,694 Women
Percent of Diet Sweetener Users and Non-Users
Gaining Weight in Five Weight Categories
Over A One Year Period.[43]

	Percent of Non-Diet Sweetener Users Gaining Weight	Percent of Diet Sweetener Users Gaining Weight
Very Low Weight	29.6%	32.3%
Low Weight.....................	33.5%	39.0%
Average Weight	35.0%	41.5%
High Weight	32.4%	41.5%
Very High Weight	26.3%	31.9%

One study did demonstrate a questionable benefit of aspartame. Six male subjects were given aspartame or sugar for a 24-day period. Those consuming aspartame gained weight *slower* than those consuming sugar. This is hardly a reason for endorsement of the sweeteners and small consolation to the multitudes who are continually at war with overweight.

The fattening effects of these chemicals may be due in part to the fact that they produce a proclivity for sugar and fat.[1] [5] Artificial sweeteners also produce an immediate insulin response as they are sensed on the tongue.[1] This is known as the cephalic phase of insulin release. Healthy people respond to sweet tastes (artificial sweeteners and simple carbohydrates) in exactly this way. The ultimate benefit derived from the cephalic phase is the inherent accompanying increased ability of the body to store more sugar as glycogen. For those who are obese, diet, or consume diet sweeteners on a regular basis, however, the cephalic phase of insulin release is gradually extinguished. The result? Let's look at the following sequence:

Regular use of artificial sweeteners ⟶ extinguished cephalic insulin response ⟶ less storage of simple sugars as glycogen ⟶ higher blood-sugar levels ⟶ higher *net* blood-insulin levels ⟶ higher LPL activity ⟶ weight gain

As we established in the chapter on obesity, insulin is essential to the fattening process—the more insulin produced, the fatter a person is likely to become.

Aspartame complaints

Aspartame was released to the supermarket shelves by the FDA under a gray cloud of questionable research with dubious results. Touted as "the most thoroughly tested additive in history," it has also accounted for more consumer complaints than any other food substance in recent times. According to Senator Howard Metzenbaum of Ohio, "We had better be sure that the questions which have been raised about the safety of this product are answered. I must say at the onset, this product was approved by the FDA in circumstances which can only be described as troubling" (U.S. Senate hearings, 1985).

In 1985, the FDA started its ARMS program (adverse reaction monitoring system) to focus on consumer complaints. During the first three years, it received a total of approximately 6,000 complaints, 80% of which involved aspartame! Unfortunately, the information gathered has been said to be "anecdotal"; in other words, based on personal experiences without scientifically substantiated conclusions. Hence, these complaints have been largely disregarded.

In 1986, Dr. H. J. Roberts[2] polled several sources for aspartame complaints, including the FDA, Centers for Disease Control, the manufacturer and a consumer group called Aspartame Victims and Their Friends (an organization founded by Shannon Roth of Ocala, Florida, who is steadfast in her belief that heavy aspartame consumption caused permanent blindness in one eye). Total complaints exceeded 10,000 and implied the existence of an imminent public health threat. There were 3,336 complaints received by the FDA. These are categorized and tabulated in Table 2.

Aspartame is composed of three substances: Phenylalnine, aspartic acid and methanol. Phenylalanine is an essential amino acid which composes about 4-5% of many food proteins. However, it may compose as much as 56% of aspartame. In high concentrations it is known to cause various toxic reactions (summarized in Table 3). Aspartic acid in high doses is known to destroy brain cells in experimental animals,[6] [7] [8] [9] and methanol (wood alcohol) is extremely toxic to humans, especially as regards the eyes.[10] [11] Although some scientists believe that the methanol produced in the breakdown of aspartame is far below the toxic level, investigations show that the recommended limit as defined by the Environmental Protection Agency has been exceeded in some cases by as much as 32-fold.[12]

Since these products do not help us to control weight, and in fact may contribute to weight gain, and since we have enough dietary toxins in the form of the high-fat diet, why use them?

TABLE 2
Complaints Reports To the
Food and Drug Administration
By 3,326 Aspartame Complainants[44]

Complaint	Total Received	Percent of Total (Rounded)
Headache.....................	951	19%
Dizziness/Balance Problems.......	419	9%
Mood Change—Quality or Level	349	7%
Vomiting and Nausea	329	7%
Abdominal Pain/Cramps	254	5%
Diarrhea	178	4%
Change in Vision	162	3%
Fatigue, Weakness..............	141	3%
Seizures and Convulsions	137	3%
Sleep Problems	127	3%
Memory Loss	125	3%
Rash.........................	111	2%
Numbness, Tingling.............	91	2%
Hives	80	2%
Other	1,464	30%

TABLE 3
Medical Conditions Associated with
High Phenylalanine Levels[1 2 45 46 47 48 49 50 51 52 53]

Chronic Kidney Failure (Uremia)
Mental Retardation in Infants and Children
Iron Deficiency
Cirrhosis of the Liver
Malnutrition
Obesity
Kidney Disease
Infection
Phenylketonuria (PKU)

COFFEE AND CAFFEINE:
A FAVORITE ADDICTION

Catherine the Great of Russia made a "great" cup of coffee. According to one historical account, she would treat palace dignitaries and guests to her own personal recipe consisting of one pound of ground coffee to four cups of water.[13] In these proportions, her thunderous concoction likely contained 2000-3000 milligrams of caffeine per five-ounce cup! Compared to a cup of java brewed today, which may contain up to 150 milligrams per five-ounce cup, we can begin to understand Catherine's reputation for anxious and compulsive behavior, which are familiar symptoms of excessive caffeine consumption. In modern vernacular, Catherine might have been described as "wired tight."

Caffeine is a stimulant to the central nervous system and can thus appropriately be termed a drug. Positive effects reports by those who use caffeine include increased alertness, improved sensory awareness, and enhanced work performance. These observations help to explain the popularity of coffee breaks in the work place as well as the devout consumption of coffee at breakfast. Unfortunately, caffeine also produces irritability, nervousness, restlessness, headaches, and insomnia.

Thirty to 60 minutes after consumption, caffeine attains its highest level in the blood. This level is usually accompanied by increases in heart rate and blood pressure, particularly during times of stress.[13] Light and moderate consumers can expect a rise of 5-15 millimeters of mercury on the upper (systolic) reading within 15 minutes of consuming 150 milligrams of caffeine.

The time of the drug's stimulating effects is gauged in terms of half-life, which is the amount of time required for the liver to remove one-half of the caffeine consumed. Caffeine half-lives average about four hours. Smoking can shorten the half-life of caffeine by as much as 50%, thus decreasing the stimulating effects of coffee. This may partially explain why smokers tend toward heavy coffee consumption.

Alcohol, and a few select drugs, however, decrease the rate of caffeine elimination. Oral contraceptives, for instance, more than triple the half-life of caffeine. Women using the "pill" will normally experience a strong reaction to a second serving of a caffeine-laden food because a high residual dose remains in the blood.[13]

Although many researchers regard caffeine as a minor health threat, the relationship of intake levels exceeding 650 milligrams per day correlates closely with several serious, troubling physical responses, including irregular heartbeat, high cholesterol levels (see the chapter on heart disease), bladder cancer in men, behavioral disorders and peptic ulcers.[13] [14]

Approximately 75% of all caffeine consumed in the U.S. is contained in coffee.[15] Other sources, however, do provide caffeine. They are listed in Table 4. The combined intake from coffee and other products is sufficient in our society to contribute to several important disease conditions; notably, heart disease (discussed in the chapter on that disease), fibrocystic breast disease, fetal defects and addiction.

TABLE 4
Food and Drug Sources of Caffeine[1] [13] [15] [36]

Source	Caffeine Mg.	Theobromine Mg.
Coffee, 5 ounces	110-146	
Coffee, decaffeinated, 5 ounces	2-5	
Tea, 5 ounces	9-36	
Tea, decaffeinated, 5 ounces	2-3	
Cola Drinks, 12 ounces	35-60	
Soft Drinks, 12 ounces	45-54	
Chocolate Bar, 1.8 ounces	3-63	68-314
Hot Cocoa, 5 ounces	1-8	40-80
Chocolate Milk, 8 ounces	2-7	37-104
Chocolate Chip Cookie, 1 ounce	3-5	21-30
Chocolate Ice Cream, 4 ounces	5-11	34-89
Over-The-Counter Drugs, 1 Pill		
Stimulants:		
No Doz	100	
Vivarin	200	
Pain Relievers:		
Anacin	32	
Excedrin	65	
Midol	32	
Vanquish	33	
Diuretics:		
Aqua-Ban	100	
Cold Remedies:		
Coryban-D	30	
Dristan	16	
Triaminicin	30	
Weight Control Aids:		
Dietac	200	
Prolamine	140	
Dexatrim	200	
Prescription Drugs, 1 Pill		
Migraine Remedies:		
Cafergot	100	
Migral	50	
Pain Relievers:		
Darvon	32	
Fiorinol	40	

Fibrocystic breast disease. Does coffee contribute?

Fibrocystic breast disease is a painful condition characterized by breast nodules that are particularly irritating just prior to the menstrual cycle. One of every two women in the U.S. will experience this discomfort during her reproductive years.[16] Suspicious lumps which turn out to be benign breast disease account for 75% of all breast biopsies performed in this country.[17] Women who acquire this condition, however, are at a three-fold risk for developing breast cancer.[18] Caffeine and related chemicals such as theobromine in chocolate stimulate breast tissue and may account for a significant number of cases of benign breast disease. Abstinence from caffeine-containing foods has also resulted in decreased lumps and less pain among sufferers.[19] [20]

Caffeine may cause birth defects.

Caffeine has been indicted in several studies as being a teratogen (a substance which causes birth defects or birthing problems). A study of 5,200 births found an indirect relationship between birth weight and coffee consumption of the mothers. Two studies also report a higher rate of spontaneous abortions among mothers who drink coffee.[21] [22] Japanese researchers studying 9,921 healthy women in their third trimester of pregnancy discovered a higher incidence of premature labor, smaller fetuses and birth defects among those who consumed more than five cups of coffee per day.

Other research appears to exonerate coffee drinking as a contributor to fetal defects.[23] [24] [25] Coffee consumption dropped by 36% from 1960-1982, yet sales of caffeinated beverages other than coffee increased by a startling 231% in the same period. The blatant discrepancies in the research may be due in part to the focus on coffee drinking rather than total caffeine consumption.

Caffeine *is* readily transferrable through the placental tissue and is an established animal teratogen.[26] For these reasons, the FDA advises pregnant women to eliminate or limit consumption of caffeine as a precautionary measure.

One organization, the Center for Science in the Public

Interest, has recommended that no more than a fraction of the caffeine found in a cup of coffee be consumed per day during the gestation period.[27] In fairness to the unborn, total abstinence from caffeine during pregnancy is the best advice.

Anxiety and addiction

Excessive caffeine intake has long been associated with anxious behavior and addiction. Typical characteristics of caffeinism are listed in Table 5. In one interesting study, 14 male psychiatric patients with a high susceptibility to anxiety attacks were given decaffeinated coffee for three weeks. All thought they were receiving their usual regular coffee. At the completion of the test period, all patients experienced significant drops in anxiety levels. When regular coffee servings were resumed, the original symptoms returned and to the same intensity previously observed.

Similarly, in a series of studies of the effects of caffeine in normal grade-school children, habitual dietary caffeine intake was found to be a significant indicator of anxious behavior.[28] [29] [30] [31] [32]

Those who exhibit anxious behavior are also likely to be addicted to the this popular stimulant. Individuals who consume coffee and other caffeine sources several times daily are likely to endure withdrawal symptoms such as headache, fatigue, shaking, and depression within two hours of cessation of the use of this drug.[33] Guests at National Institute of Fitness often experience severe headaches a day after giving up their caffeinated beverages. Suffice it to say that this stimulant cannot be good for the health.

ALCOHOL: TOOL OF THE GRIM REAPER

Perhaps you are inclined to enjoy a carafe of your favorite rose along with Saturday night's lasagna, an ice chest laden with "cold ones" for those weekends at the lake, or a double extra-dry martini before bedtime to "unwind." If so, you are engaging in

TABLE 5
Anxiety Manifestations of Caffeine[13]

Frequent Urination
Jitteriness
Tremulousness
Agitation
Irritability
Muscle Twitchings
Lightheadedness
Rapid Breathing
Rapid Heartbeat
Cardiac Palpitations
Upset Stomach
Loose Stools
Heartburn

the same insalubrious action in which two-thirds of the drinking age population regularly participates.

In view of the excessive social problems to which alcohol has been linked (see Table 6), it is inconceivable that any reputable or objective health authority would recommend ingestion of alcohol to promote wellness. Yet, the myths prevail. Tales of the "benefits" of moderate drinking abound. The perpetuation of these unsupported claims throughout the drinking community is, perhaps in part, rendered by the not-too-infrequent medical Rx's calling for 1-2 drinks per day to "help the heart," "build red blood cells," "help relax," or "thin the blood."

However, as one wise man said, "You can't fool all of the people all of the time." Alcohol use is declining. From 1977-1980, the per-capita consumption increased and then began a steady decline for seven years.[34] A concomitant drop occurred in deaths attributed to alcohol intake. For instance, deaths from cirrhosis had dropped by 20% whereas alcohol related automobile accidents decreased by nearly 8%.[35] Nevertheless, medical and social problems of alcohol use account for expenditures of $117 billion per year, and an estimated 18 million Americans are alcohol abusers.[35] One of every 16 users is addicted.

Alcohol and the disease process

Alcohol is readily absorbed from the digestive tract, causing blood levels to rise sharply shortly after ingestion. Only an estimated 5% of all alcohol consumed is eliminated through perspiration, urine, feces or breathing. The other 95% is processed by the liver, where it is broken down to carbon dioxide and water. Since the body cannot store alcohol, it must be broken down and eliminated, often at the expense of its responsibilities to process foods properly. As a result, lipids and proteins are often stored in the liver while they wait to be digested.

Stored proteins may raise havoc with health in two ways.[36] First, they absorb water, causing the liver to swell, eventually culminating in the liberation of active liver tissue into the fluids of the digestive cavity. The end result of this process is the development of dead, fibrous liver tissue—a condition known as cirrhosis. If a person consumes one pint of 80 proof liquor, or two six packs of beer, or one-half gallon of wine daily, his chance of acquiring cirrhosis is about 50%.[37] Up to 30% of those afflicted with cirrhosis will also acquire cancer of the liver.[37]

Secondly, stored liver proteins, under conditions of near-continuous alcohol oxidation, may only be partially broken down by a liver which is directing its attention to alcohol disposal. This partial breakdown of proteins produces ammonia and amines which can be destructive to brain tissue and also cause nerve damage.[37]

Fat metabolism is also rendered less efficient by alcohol consumption, causing a condition known as "fatty liver," which has been implicated in some deaths.[38]

Alcohol contributes to lung cancer.

When alcohol is combined with smoking, the chance of death

TABLE 6
Health and Social Problems with Increased Risk from Alcohol Consumption[26 34 35 36 37 38 39 40 41 42 43]

Accidents (Traffic and Other)	Impotency
Acne	Kwashiorkor
Alcoholic Hepatitis	Liquor Lung
Alcoholism	Marasmus
Birth Defects	Megacytosis
Cancer (All Types)	Memory Loss
Cardiomyopathy	Mineral Deficiencies
Cirrhosis of the Liver	Neurotoxicity
Constipation	Osteoporosis
Dehydration	Pancreatitis
Diarrhea	Premature Aging
"Feminization" of Men	Red Skin Breaks
Gout	Retarded Learning
Headaches	Seborrhea
Heart Disease	Sleep Apnea
Holiday Heart Syndrome	Sleep Disturbances
Homicides	Stroke
Hypertension	Ulcers
Hypoglycemia	Vitamin Deficiencies
Hypothermia	Wrinkles

due to lung cancer increases dramatically. As an example, consider the twins who each smoke ten cigarettes per day. The first twin consumes four to five drinks per day whereas the second twin is a teetotaler. The risk of lung cancer for the first twin is five times that of the second.

Other alcohol-related health problems

In addition to the obvious problems of accidents, addictions, cirrhosis and brain destruction, alcohol also contributes to gout[39] and birth defects.[40] Dr. James Schultz of the National Centers for Disease Control states that 2.7 million lives are lost each year due to alcohol consumption.[41] The chapter on heart disease discusses the one conceivable redeeming virtue of alcohol: a slight decrease in death from heart disease. Even with the slightly beneficial influence on heart disease, it is far outweighed by the increase in death and disability from other health problems.

REFERENCES

[1]Remington, D. *The Bitter Truth About Artificial Sweeteners.* Vitality House International, publishers, Provo, UT, 1987. p. 25.

[2]Roberts, H. *Aspartame (Nutrasweet): Is It Safe?* The Charles Press, publishers, Philadelphia, PA, 1990, pp. 1, 10-15.

[3]Merkel, A. Effects of glucose and saccharin solutions on subsequent food consumption. Physiol Behav 1979; 23:791-793.

[4]Rolls, B. Palatability and body fluid homeostasis. Physiol Behav 1978; 20:15-19.

[5]Hunter Warns: Beware of Aspartame. The Human Ecologist Nos. 23, 24, p. 13.

[6]Olney, J. Brain damage and oral intake of certain amino acids. Adv Exp Bio Med 1976; 69:597-506.

[7]Price, M. Uptake of exogenous glutamate and aspartate by circumventricular organs but not other regions of the brain. J Neurochem 1981; 36:1774-1780.

[8]Olney, J. Brain damage in infant mice following oral intake of glutamate, aspartate or cysteine. Nature 1970; 227:609-611.

[9]Finklestein, M. Correlation of aspartate dose, plasma decarboxylic acid concentration, and neuronal necrosis in infant mice. Toxicol 1983; 29:109-119.

[10]Gilger, A. Studies on the visual toxicity of methanol V. The role of acidosis in experimental methanol poisoning. Am J Opthamol 1955; 39:63-66.

[11]Roe, O. The ganglion cell of the retina in cases of methanol poisoning in human beings and experimental animals. Acta Opthamol 1948; 26:169-182.

[12]Monte, W. Aspartame: Methanol and the public health. J Appl Nutr 1984; 36:42-52.

[13]Gilbert, R. *The Encyclopedia of Psychoactive Drugs. Caffeine—The Most Popular Stimulant.* Chelsea House, publishers. New York, p. 33.

[14]McDougall, J. *The McDougall Plan.* New Century, publishers, Piscataway, NJ, 1983, pp. 175-176.

[15]Roberts, H. Biological effects of caffeine: History and use. Food Technology 1983; 37:32-39.

[16]Devitt, J. Clinical benign disorders of the breast and carcinoma of the breast. Surg Gynecol Obstet 1981; 152:437-440.

[17]Pilnik, S. Clinical diagnosis of benign breast disease. J Reprod Med 1979; 22:277.

[18]Coombs, L. A prospective study of the relationship between benign breast disease and breast carcinoma. Prev Med 1979; 8:40-52.

[19]Brooks, P. Measuring the effect of caffeine restriction on fibrocystic breast disease. The role of graphic stress telethermometry as an objective monitor of the disease. J Reprod Med 1981; 26:279-282.

[20]Minton, J. Caffeine, cyclic nucleotides, and breast disease. Surgery 1979; 86:105-109.

[21]Weatherbee, P. Caffeine and pregnancy: A retrospective survey. Postgrad Med 1977; 62:64-69.

[22]Srisuphan, W. Caffeine consumption during pregnancy and association with late spontaneous abortion. Am J Obstet Gynecol 1986; 154:14-20.

[23]Kurpa, K. Coffee consumption during pregnancy. New Engl J Med 1982; 306:1548.

[24]Linn, S. No association between coffee consumption an adverse outcomes of pregnancy. New Engl J Med 1982; 306:141-145.

[25]Rosenberg, L. Selected birth defects in relation to caffeine-containing beverages. JAMA 1982; 247:1429-1432.

[26]Surgeon General of the United States. The Surgeon General's Report on Nutrition and Health. U.S. Government Printing Office. Washington, D.C., 1988, pp. 560-561.

[27] Jacobsen, M. Caffeine poses risk of the fetus—FDA criticized for inaction. Brief submitted to the U.S. Food and Drug Administration. Center for Science in the Public Interest, Washington, D.C., 1978.

[28] Elkins, N. Acute effects of caffeine in normal prepubertal boys. Am J Psy 1981; 138(2):178-183.

[29] Rapoport, J. Behavioral and autonomic effects of caffeine in normal boys. Dev Pharmacol Therapeutics 1981; 3:74-82.

[30] Rapoport, J. Behavioral and cognitive effects of caffeine in boys and adult males. J Nerv Mental Dis. 1981; 169:726-732

[31] Rapoport, J. Effects of dietary substances in children. J Psychiatric Res 1983; 17:187-191.

[32] Rapoport, J. Behavioral aspects of caffeine in children. Arch Gen Psychiatry 1984; 41:1073-1079.

[33] Remington, D. *The Bitter Truth About Artificial Sweeteners.* Vitality House International, publishers, Provo, Utah, 1987, p. 125.

[34] National Institute on Alcohol Abuse and Alcoholism. In "Health United States 1989." National Center for Health Statistics. DHHS Publication # (PHS) 90-1232, 1990, pp. 70, 72.

[35] U.S. Department of Health and Human Services. Sixth special report to the U.S. Congress on alcohol and health from Secretary of Health and Human Services. DHHS publication # (ADM) 87-1519, 1987.

[36] Winick, M. *The Columbia Encyclopedia of Nutrition.* G.P. Putnam's Sons, publishers, New York, 1988, pp. 27-32, 76-79.

[37] Luks, A. *You Are What You Drink.* Villard Books, publishers. New York, 1989, p. 76-77.

[38] Lieber, C. To drink (moderately) or not to drink. New Engl J Med 1984; 310:846-848.

[39] McDougall, J. *McDougall's Medicine: A Challenging Second Opinion.* New Century, publishers, Piscataway, NJ, 1985, p. 234.

[40] Ernhart, C. Alcohol teratogenicity in the human: A detailed assessment of specificity, critical period, and threshold. Am J Obstet Gynecol 1987; 156:33-39.

[41] Schultz, J. National Centers for Disease Control. Quoted in the *Flagstaff Sun*, Sunday, March 25, 1990.

[42] American Cancer Society. Cancer Prevention Study 2. An epidemiological study of lifestyles and environment. CPS II Newsletter, Spring, 1986; 4:1,3.

[43] Tollefson, L. Monitoring of adverse reactions to aspartame reported to the U.S. Food and Drug Administration. In Wurtman, R. Proceedings of the First International Meeting on Dietary Phenylalanine and Brain Function, 1987, pp. 347-372.

[44] Furst, P. Effects of nutrition and catabolic stress on intracellular amino acid pools in uremia. Am J Clin Nutr 1980; 33:1387-1395.

[45]Lehman, W. Impaired phenylalanine-tyrosine conversion in patients with iron-deficiency anemia studied by a L-(2H5) phenylalanine-loading test. Am J Clin Nutr 1986; 44;468-474.

[46]Landau, R. The effect of progesterone on the concentration of plasma amino acids in man. Metabolism 1967; 16:1114-1122.

[47]Jagenburg, R. Kinetics of intravenously administered L-phenylalanine with cirrohosis of the liver. Clinica Chimica Acta 1977; 78;453-463.

[48]Antener, L. Biochemical study of malnutrition 5. Metabolism of phenylalanine and tyrosine. Inter J Vit Nutr Res 1981; 51:296-306.

[49]Brown, D. Effects of oral contraceptives and obesity on carrier tests for phenylketonuria. Clinica Chimica Acta 1973; 44:183-192.

[50]Pickford. Studies on the metabolism of phenylalnine and tyrosine in patients with renal disease. Clinica Chimica Acta 1973; 48:77-83.

[51]Wannecmacher, R. The significance and mechanism of an increased serum phenylalnine/tyrosine ratio during infection. Am J Clin Nutr 1976; 29:997-1006.

[52]Partridge, W. The safety of aspartame. JAMA 1987; 256:2678.

10.

Salt, Sodium and the Afflictions of Affluence

10. Salt, Sodium and the Afflictions of Affluence

> "Can that which is tasteless be eaten without salt?"
>
> —Job 6:6

The above quotation is thought to have originated over 3,500 years ago. Obviously, Job was well aware of the preference for salt as an addition to food. Throughout history, the popularity of this seasoning has been repeatedly acknowledged. Salt has been bartered, traded and used as currency up until the recent past. Ethiopia, for example, used salt disks for money well into the 20th century.

Salt occupies a unique place in human nutrition—as both an essential nutrient and health-destroying toxin (depending on the quantity consumed). As such, it deserves its own discussion, apart from such substances as alcohol, caffeine, tobacco and artificial sweeteners—which may have deleterious influences on health regardless of the quantity ingested.

Once considered a delicacy, salt is now an expected addition on the tables of homes and restaurants. People have acquired a preference for salinity. Moreover, salt not only adds its own taste to food but also increases aroma, enhances sweetness, tempers acidity, and performs several other culinary functions.[1] No wonder this inexpensive ingredient is used in vast quantities in formulated food products.

Salt is composed of two substances—sodium and chlorine—which separate from each other into charged electrolytes when dissolved in a water-laden system, such as the human body. When consumed, most sodium and chloride ions function in the blood, serving as regulators of acidity and water balance. However, when consumed in excess (as in the U.S. and other industrialized nations), disease is the predictable result. It has been estimated that 15% to 25% of the United States population have chronic high blood pressure,[2] [3] also known as hypertension—a predictable result of excessive sodium intake. As many as 58 million people may be affected.[3] Since those with this condition are at greater risk for stroke and cardiovascular disease,[4] salt cannot be relegated to a group of back-burner health issues. Children are not immune; an estimated 12% of the children (and 25% of the adults) from affluent nations are afflicted with chronic hypertension.[5] [6]

Most Americans will consume between 4000 and 6000 milligrams of sodium per day; most originating from salt.[4] The National Research Council has suggested that 1100-3300 milligrams per day is safe and adequate to sustain health.[7] However, the absolute minimum (threshold) level required by adults has been reported to be between 50 and 220 milligrams per day.[8] [9] The typical American, therefore, may be consuming somewhere between 20 to 300 times the minimum daily requirement!

It has been estimated that our healthy, primarily vegetarian ancestors consumed between 80 and 240 milligrams of sodium per day. Early meat-eating primitive people may have taken in up to 1600 milligrams.[8] From then to now, our consumption has increased anywhere from three-fold to 75-fold! With such an overabundance of salt entering our bodies, our kidneys, in many cases, cannot effectively remove the accumulated surplus.

One result is hypertension. Some experts cite government reports that suggest elimination of nearly all hypertension when sodium is reduced to less than 2000 milligrams per day.[8] In severe cases, less than 800 milligrams daily would be a wiser objective.[10] When sodium intake is reduced below 400 milligrams per day, high blood pressure virtually disappears.[10] Even moderate reductions in salt intake have been proven to be equally effective as medication for reducing blood pressure.[11] In addition, a salt-restricted diet may be helpful to many women in reducing the pre-menstrual weight gain caused by sodium retention.

Excess sodium in the blood draws water from the surrounding tissues, which increases the volume of blood (thereby increasing blood pressure). Since the heart is forced to work harder (diluted blood must be moved faster to the tissues), blood pressure is increased. When a diseased heart is unable to keep up with the augmented workload (or is inhibited by swelling of the surrounding tissues), water may back up into the lungs. This condition, known as congestive heart failure, is a serious threat to heavy salt consumers with cardiovascular disease. Water logging in other tissues, such as the legs, is known as edema and is a frequent malady among those whose kidneys are unable to remove excess sodium.

The risk of hypertension increases directly with the sodium consumed.[8] [10] For example, the highest incidence in the world (nearly 40% of the population) has been observed in Northern Japan where inhabitants consume about 10,000 milligrams of sodium per day. Not surprisingly, salt consumption in Japan has been conclusively linked to stroke, which is that country's number-one killer. As previously stated, 15% to 25% of the U.S. population have high blood pressure, while consuming 4000 to 6000 milligrams per day. And, despite all their other dietary-induced afflictions, Eskimos consume less than 2000 milligrams of sodium daily and are virtually free of hypertension. In primitive societies consuming low levels of sodium (such as the natives of the Kalahari Desert; Brazilian Indians; rural tribes of New Guinea, Malaysia, Polynesia, and the Solomon Islands), hypertension is non-existent—even in old age.

Those who consume large quantities of pickled and salt-cured foods are also at risk for certain cancers. Stomach cancer has been linked to a preference for pickled vegetables in Japan[12] and salted fish in Norway,[13] and several studies show a direct relationship between salt consumption and gastric cancer,[14] as well as cancer of the nasopharynx and esophagus.[15] [16] Conversely, there is a protective influence of fruit and vegetables in nearly all diet and stomach cancer studies.[17]

A HIGHLY ADDICTIVE SUBSTANCE

The taste for salt appears to be an acquired physiological addiction, since amounts ingested far surpass physiological needs. This has been borne out in laboratory studies where young rats develop a preference for salted food during infancy.

It is entirely possible that today's adult saltaholics may have acquired their addiction by consumption of highly salted baby foods. Because of the liberal use of sodium chloride in commercial infant formulations and the propensity of adults to prepare home baby foods with salt, infants in the U.S. had, until 1970, consumed the adult daily equivalent of 7200 milligrams of sodium, whereas toddlers ingested an amount equal to 10,000 milligrams![18] In 1970, the infant food industry responded responsibly to governmental commissions and consumer activists by voluntarily lowering the maximum salt content of commercial baby foods to 0.25%.

Further implicating the addictiveness of salt are studies with "primitive" low-sodium consumers. According to one account, when members of a rural Bolivian tribe were first introduced to salt, they found it offensive. Later, however, they found themselves using it in far greater amounts than their bodies required.

INDIRECTLY FATAL?

In spite of the direct, harmful effects of excessive salt consumption, it may well be an indirect effect of harm in our society. Salt causes us to eat more fat. Consider the potato. It contains about 1% of its total calories in fat. If the potato is sliced into thin wafers, baked in fat and then placed on a plate to cool, the end result will be a cold, greasy slice of potato. ANYBODY CAN EAT JUST ONE. Add salt to that process, however, and you create a potato chip—a product that contains about 53% of its calories in disease-causing fat. Now, as the people at Lay's Potato Chip Company will tell you, "NOBODY CAN EAT JUST ONE!"

Another problem is that fats are necessary to hold much of the salt we eat. The salt addict is very disappointed the first time he eats unsalted, air-popped popcorn. But, when he tries to salt it, the salt falls to the bottom of the bowl. His solution to this dilemma is to pour melted butter or some other grease on the popcorn in order to keep the salt from falling off. Many snack foods are laden with fat in order to pander to our proclivities for salt.

Of course, fat is also used to take advantage of our proclivities for sugar. Doughnuts made the "old fashioned" way used a pot of boiling lard into which circles of white flour dough were tossed to absorb the lard and cook. When they were pulled out of the boiling lard and cooled, they could have been described as little circular sponges, filled with pig grease. Bon appetit! Unless sugar is added to the outer coating of pig grease (the grease holds the sugar), the doughnut is inedible. With the sugar in place, however, we have a tasty little cancer-causing, diabetes-promoting, heart-disease enhancing, fattening pig-grease sponge!

By learning to consume only small amounts of sugar and salt, we will automatically decrease our consumption of fats dramatically, because most fats do not taste good without these products added. I have never seen anyone grasp a tablespoon and start eating lard by the spoonful. Nor have I seen anyone pour a cup of corn oil and drink it down. We don't like fat—what we like are the tastes of the substances which it holds in place—usually salt and sugar.

SHAKING THE SALT HABIT

If you are a saltaholic, beating your addiction may not be as difficult as you imagined. The following list of tips will assist you in reducing sodium intake to health-supporting levels:

1. Throw away your salt shaker. One-third of all sodium ingested in the U.S. has been added by the consumer. By removing salt and salt-laden spices from the table and pantry, we can immediately expect to reduce sodium intake by 1300 to 2000 milligrams per day.

2. 2. If your family refuses to give up the salt shaker, do not prepare foods with salt, and develop the habit of tasting food before salting. One nifty trick for adding more salty taste with less salt is to simply salt the

outside of foods. For example, a light dusting of salt over a mound of mashed potatoes will taste decidedly more salty than if the salt is mixed in. Most people find commercial rice cakes and popcorn cakes salty but are surprised to find only 40 to 60 milligrams of sodium per serving—about one-tenth the sodium found in potato chips. The reason: Salt is added to the surface and not mixed into the product.

3.   Become a good comparative shopper. Purchase low-sodium foods. One-third of the sodium we consume is in processed foods. Fortunately, many manufacturers are beginning to recognize the marketability of low-sodium products. Look for regulated terms on labels such as "low sodium" or "very low sodium" which signal beneficial reductions in salt. But don't trust the advertising label alone. Read the ingredients and beware *any* sodium.

4.   Acids increase the sensation of saltiness. Thus, using high-acid ingredients (lemon juice, lime juice, pineapple, vinegar, etc.) in garnishes and sauces increases the salty taste. In the spice section of many grocery stores is a product called "Sour Salt" which is nothing more than food grade citric acid (a harmless natural component of all food). By adding very small amounts of this product to entrees, salads, etc., the salt taste will increase. However, acid ingredients like "Sour Salt" have that characteristic zippiness inherent to low Ph food products. Therefore, very small amounts are recommended to prevent an overpowering astringent taste.

5.   If you are serious about lowering your sodium intake, it's important to know the sodium content of your drinking water. If it is greater than 45 parts per million, it would be wise to purchase or lease equipment designed to remove sodium. Purchasing distilled water for drinking and cooking is a viable alternative for many. This may be your best choice if your water is softened, since water softeners add sodium to the water supply while removing calcium and magnesium.

6. Exercise! Perspiration naturally removes salt from the body.

7. Avoid salt substitutes. Sea salt is sodium chloride. Formulations under labels such as "Lite Salt" replace much of the sodium chloride with potassium chloride. Consumption of high levels of potassium can cause irregular heartbeats and even death.[19] It is better to utilize salt-free spice blends such as those under the "Parsley Patch" and "Mrs. Dash" labels.

As you begin to eat foods that are not laden with salt, you will begin to experience the natural flavors of those foods. And the natural salt contained in what you eat will begin to manifest itself to your taste. You will have shaken the salt habit.

REFERENCES

[1] McFarland, P. Salt: Its use in the food industry. In Johnson, A. *Encyclopedia of Food Technology*. AVI Publishing Co., Inc., Westport, CT, 1974.

[2] U.S. Department of Health and Human Services. Health United States, 1989, DHHS Pub. No. (PHS) 90-1232. Superintendent of Documents, Washington, D.C., 1990.

[3] Subcommittee on Definition and Prevalence of the 1984 Joint National Committee on Detection, Evaluation, and Treatment of High Blood Pressure. Hypertension prevalence and the status of awareness, treatment, and control in the U.S. Hypertension 1985; 7:457

[4] U.S. Department of Health and Human Services. The Surgeon General's Report on Nutrition and Health 1988. DHHS (PHS) Pub. No. 88-50210. Superintendent of Documents, Washington, D.C., 1988.

[5] U.S. Department of Health, Education, and Welfare. Hypertension and heart disease in adults, U.S. 1960-1962. National Health Survey. National Center for Health Studies Services 11 No. 13. Superintendent of Documents, Washington, D.C., 1966.

[6] Loggie, J. Hypertension in the pediatric patient: A reappraisal. J Pediatr 1979; 94:685-687.

[7] National Research Council. Recommended dietary allowances. National Academy Press, Washington, D.C., 1980.

[8]Brody, J. *Jane Brody's Nutrition Book.* W.W. Norton & Co., New York, NY, 1981.

[9]Dahl, L. Salt intake and salt need. N Eng J Med 1958; 258:1152-1157.

[10]Fries, E. Salt, volume, and the prevention of hypertension. Circulation 1976; 53:589-595.

[11]Magnani, B., et al. Comparison of effects of pharmacological therapy and low sodium diet on milk hypertension. Clinical Science and Molecular Medicine 1976; 51:526S-530S.

[12]Haenszel, W. A case control study of large bowel cancer in Japan. J Natl Cancer Inst 1980; 64:17-21.

[13]Bjelke, E. Case-control study in Norway. Scandinavian Journal of Gastroenterology 1974; 9(Suppl. 31):42-45.

[14]Gebbers, J. Epidemiology of stomach cancer. In Joossens, J. *Diet and Human Carcinogenesis.* Elsevier Science. New York, NY 1985.

[15]Sasco, A. Diet and nasopharyngeal carcinoma: Epidemiological approach to comparative dietary assessment in different populations. In Joossens, J. *Diet and Human Carcinogenesis.* Elsevier Science. New York, NY 1985.

[16]Tuyns, A. Nutrition and cancer of the esophagus. In Joossens, J. *Diet and Human Carcinogenesis.* Elsevier Science. New York, NY 1985.

[17]Cordle, F. The use of epidemiology, scientific data, and regulatory authority to determine risk factors in cancers of some organs of the digestive system. Regulatory Toxicol Pharmacol 1986; 6:171-175.

[18]Mayer, J. White House Conference on Food, Nutrition and Health. J Am Diet Assn 1969; 55:553-560.

[19]McDougall, J. *The McDougall Plan.* New Century Publishers, Inc., Piscataway, New York 1983.

11.

Fitness Can Save Your Life!

11. *Fitness Can Save Your Life!*

> *"All parts of the body which have a function, if used in moderation and exercised in labours in which each is accustomed, become thereby healthy, well-developed and age more slowly, but if unused, they become liable to disease, defective in growth, and age quickly."*
>
> —Hippocrates

Tragic, unnecessary illnesses and deaths occur by the thousands each day—illnesses that could have been supplanted by years of vibrant health. These deaths can be described as death by deterioration. The coroner's report states it differently, but the myriad deaths from degenerative diseases are due in part to failure to use body systems in "labors for which each is intended." A more accurate coroner's report might state: *Death from disuse.* "Use it or lose it" is sage advice. Those who refuse to follow that advice discover that the bodies in which they reside are unfit servants, possessing decreased capacities for work and for defending against diseases which lie in wait.

Make no mistake: the primary cause of degenerative disease is improper nutrition; lack of movement is a close second. In fact, for those who flout the laws of good nutrition, an active lifestyle is the best insurance policy available. Not perfect, mind you, but better than anything else. Improper eating habits will ultimately kill a man or woman in spite of exercise, but death can be delayed and quality of life enhanced through proper physical activity. When the body is exercised and given the correct fuels, it becomes a bastion of strength against diseases that might otherwise prove fatal.

What was obvious to Hippocrates more than 2000 years ago has been lost on those who live in our modern world. Nothing is more natural for men and women than movement. Remove the skin from the human body and we find exposed a complex system of bones, muscles and tendons that enable that body to move in intricate and coordinated patterns. Disuse of this system causes deterioration and increases susceptibility to a host of maladies that afflict all other systems. Regular, vigorous movement, however, strengthens the body and furnishes protection against the ravages of diseases caused by poor choices of fuels (poor nutrition), stress, bad air, bad water and other environmental contaminants.

The relatively few men and women who do engage in regular, vigorous exercise do so for different reasons: to train for athletic contests, to improve appearance, to rehabilitate injured muscles and joints and to improve health. Whereas the benefits of exercise on appearance and athletic performance are obvious and incontrovertible, there is less agreement as to the beneficial effects of regular movement on longevity and disease.

Many who exercise believe that it will help them to live longer and in better health, but others believe that the benefits of exercise are imaginary, based on wishful thinking, and not scientifically sound. Some have labeled exercise a "myth" and have attempted to warp our thinking by trying to convince us that activities for fitness are a dangerous waste of time. Hence, the supposed salubrious effects of movement have been the subject of considerable controversy.

FITNESS AND FATALITY

Does regular exercise improve physical health and contribute to longevity? Indeed it does, and considering the voluminous research reported in the best scientific journals, it is surprising that there is any argument as to its benefits. Studies done many years ago, as well as important new research, confirm the positive influence which exercise has on the wellness of man.

As early as 1966, research reported in the British medical journal, *Lancet*, noted that the ticket takers on double-decker English buses, who were required to climb up and down stairs to perform their jobs, had a considerably lessened chance of fatal heart attacks than the drivers of the same busses who were required only to sit.[1] Figure 1 illustrates the difference in heart

FIGURE 1:
Heart Disease in London Busmen
(Rate Per 100 Men in 5 Years)

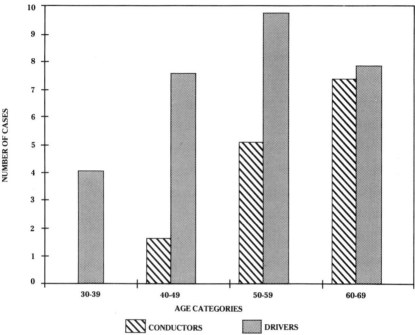

disease rates between drivers with low activity levels and conductors with higher activity levels.

Later, in 1975, it was determined from studies on longshoremen in the San Francisco Bay area that vigorous physical activity was associated with considerably reduced risk of death from heart disease, particularly from sudden death from heart attack.[2] Longshoremen who expended the most energy in their jobs had only about 55% of the number of heart disease deaths as their sedentary counterparts, and sudden deaths from heart attack were approximately three to three and one-half times higher in the most sedentary group. The researchers concluded that "repeated bursts of high-energy output established a plateau of protection against coronary mortality." "Bursts" is a poor term to describe effective exercise, however. "Periods" is a better choice.

Even moderate physical activity engaged in during leisure time protects against heart disease and death.[3] In a study conducted on middle-aged men who were at a high risk for heart disease, it was found that men with moderate or high levels of leisure-time physical activity had only 63% of the number of deaths from heart disease and 70% of the number of deaths from all causes as those with low levels of activity. The researchers concluded that there was a modest inverse relation between death rates and leisure-time physical activity. It is interesting that a reduction in death rate of 30 to 37% could be termed "modest." If a drug were found that could reduce death rates by a like percentage, the results would be emblazoned across the front pages of every paper in the country!

The aforementioned study noted that research conducted on healthy middle-aged railroad workers also showed that the least active men had about a 30% greater chance of dying of heart disease.

When the physical fitness of 2799 employees of the Los Angeles County fire and law enforcement departments was assessed by endurance tests on exercise bicycles and then followed up for a period of five years, it was found that men with below average fitness experienced more than twice the rate of myocardial infarctions (heart attacks) as those who had average or greater-than-average fitness.[4]

It should have been obvious by this time that exercise was protective against diseases, yet research on the subject was far from over. Those who were not inclined to exercise managed, by manipulating data, to pander to their indolence. Some of these people claimed that a person was much more apt to die of a heart attack while exercising than while resting. While such an assessment may be true, it is also true that during non-exercising time, the physically fit person has far less chance of death due to heart problems—a decrease which greatly surpasses the slightly increased risk during the exercise period itself. This will be discussed later in this chapter.

In terms of death rate from all causes, it has been determined that among people 60 years old and older, those who classified themselves as physically active had less than one-third the rate of death of those who were not active.[5]

Perhaps the most important research ever conducted regarding the influence of exercise on health and longevity was reported in the November 3, 1989 issue of the *Journal of the American Medical Association.*[6] This study, from the Institute for Aerobic Research in Dallas, Texas, showed conclusively that death rates are inversely associated with high levels of physical fitness: the higher the fitness level, the less the chance of dying from any cause. More than 13,000 men and women were assessed for fitness levels on an endurance-treadmill test and then followed up for an average of eight years to determine causes of death for those who died. The results were dramatic: The least fit men in the study had more than three times the death rate from all causes as the most fit men. Among women, all-cause deaths were five times as high in the least-fit women as in the most fit.

As to individual causes of death, the death rate due to cardiovascular diseases (heart disease and stroke) was eight times as high in the least fit men as compared to the most fit. Cancer deaths were nearly five times more common in the least-fit men. Among women the results were even more profound. Death from cardiovascular disease was seven times higher in the least-fit women, and death from cancer was an astounding 16 times as high in the least-fit women!

This study established poor fitness as a prime risk factor for both all-cause mortality and death due to heart disease—joining such infamous killers as cigarette smoking, high blood pressure and high blood sugar. According to the data, an unfit man could reduce his risk of death by almost 37% by becoming fit. A man with high blood pressure could reduce his risk by 27% if he lowered his blood pressure to ideal levels. A woman who quit smoking could reduce her risk of death by about 12%, but an unfit woman who became fit could lower her risk by about 48%!

FIGURE 2:
FITNESS SAVES LIVES
Deaths Per 10,000 Men Per Year

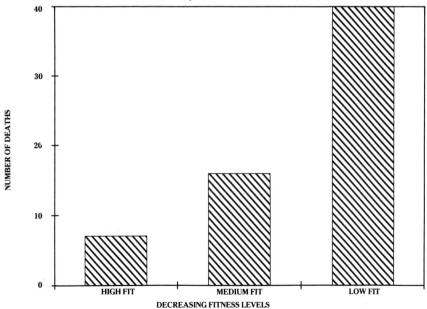

FIGURE 3:
FITNESS SAVES LIVES
Deaths Per 10,000 Women Per Year

FIGURE 4:
Deaths Per 10,000 Men Per Year
(Vascular Disease and Cancer)

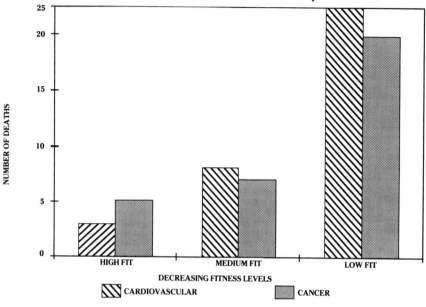

FIGURE 5:
Deaths Per 10,000 Women Per Year
(Vascular Disease and Cancer)

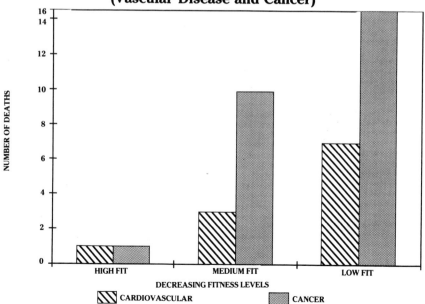

IS IT FITNESS OR ACTIVITY THAT ACCOUNTS FOR THE DECREASE IN DEATHS?

It has been postulated by some that it is physical activity, and not physical fitness per se, which is responsible for the increased health and decreased death rates. The reasoning is that any type of physical activity will improve health, even though the activity may not be intense enough to improve physical fitness levels. In the study just discussed, however, the measurement for fitness was the length of time which a subject could endure on a stress-treadmill test. This was definitely a measure of physical fitness and might indicate that fitness level, and not simply activity, is the factor which protects against disease and subsequent death.

Strong evidence from studies in Belgium indicates that it is indeed physical fitness which is the protective factor.[7] When more than 2000 men were assessed for fitness levels on an endurance-bicycle test and then followed after five years, it was found that those who were the most physically fit had only about one-eighth the number of cases of heart disease as the least fit.

It is obvious, however, that those who engage in some activity, regardless of the intensity, will become more fit than those who do nothing at all. We would, therefore, expect that increasing amounts of activity would build increasing amounts of fitness, even when the activity is not sufficiently intense to produce very-high levels of fitness. Therefore, any regular exercise is better than none at all and would be expected to produce dividends in terms of a healthier life.[8]

ACTIVITY EXTENDS LIFE SPAN

If physical activity lessens the chance of major killers such as cancer and heart disease, it should extend the life span. Such is exactly the case. Men who expend 3500 calories per week in physical activity can expect to live two years longer than those who do little or no physical activity.[9] Life span increases steadily as the number of calories expended in activity increases from 0 to 3500 calories per week. Beyond 3500 calories per week, there is no further increase. We might speculate that an even longer life span could be expected from those who exercised with sufficient intensity to make themselves highly fit—thus placing themselves into the highest and most disease-protected category as established in the research from the Institute for Aerobics Research.

It would take approximately 35 miles per week of walking for the average-weight individual to use 3500 calories. On hearing this fact, a person attending one of my lectures remarked, "One of the two extra years of life gained would be spent walking!"

A well taken point, *but* the time spent in hospitals, outpatient facilities and away from work are all substantially reduced in people who are physically active. Later on in this chapter, we will present figures to explain what can be expected in terms of time savings from an active lifestyle. We will also furnish a method by which the typical American can reap the benefits of fitness without any real investment in time whatsoever.

Fitness is also important to those who are in rehabilitation. For those who have had a non-fatal heart attack, a fitness program has proven to be effective therapy, increasing the average life span of the heart attack victim by an average of two years.[10]

HOW DOES FITNESS INFLUENCE HEART DISEASE?

To better understand the reasons behind increased longevity and better health among physically-fit people, it is well to look at the effects of physical fitness on some of the major risk factors for heart disease; namely, (1) high blood pressure, (2) cholesterol level and type, and (3) high blood sugar levels.

High blood pressure? Lower it with fitness.

An individual's current level of physical fitness greatly influences the chance of developing high blood pressure (hypertension).[11] A study of 4280 men and 1219 women ranging in age from 20 to 65 years found that persons with low fitness levels had a 50% greater risk of developing hypertension as those who were highly fit. Among people who had the highest "normal" levels of blood pressures at the beginning of the study, fitness had an even more profound protective influence. The unfit people whose blood pressures were in the normal range (120-129 systolic and 80-84 diastolic) had four times the chance of developing hypertension as the most highly fit subjects in the lowest blood pressure category.

Not only does this point out the protective influence of fitness against the development of high blood pressure, but it may also indicate that blood pressures considered "normal" may really be too high for good health.

Research confirms that sedentary railway workers have a much greater risk of death from heart disease and all other causes of death than their more physically fit counterparts.[12] The increased risk of death is attributed primarily to the higher blood pressure levels among the least-fit subjects.

Exercise heart rate, measured in beats per minute, is one indication of physical-fitness levels. One study reported that men with lower-than-average exercise heart rates had follow-up blood pressures 32 months later that were ten points lower on the systolic scale and five points lower on the diastolic scale than men who had higher than average heart rates.[13] It is obvious that a higher level of fitness helps to reduce the risk of hypertension in later life. And, since hypertension is one of the major risk factors for heart disease, regular physical activity will decrease the chance of death from that disease.

Exercise not only reduces the risk of developing hypertension but is also an effective treatment for those who already have it.[14] [14.1] As fitness increases, blood pressures become lower.

There is a strong, graded, inverse relationship between increased fitness and the lessening of a number of other heart disease risk factors. And, as already pointed out, there is an inverse relationship between high fitness and the risk of dying of heart disease. Even risk factors such as smoking tend to decrease dramatically as fitness increases.[15]

One researcher, in analyzing data on exercise and death from heart disease, stated the following: "By assessing physical fitness, we obtain a very strong predictor of the risk of dying from heart disease. The higher the level of fitness, the lower the risk, and vice versa."[15] Several studies besides those from the Aerobics Research Institute have corroborated this dose-response relationship.[16] [17]   It is quite conclusive that higher levels of fitness protect against death from all causes.[6] [15]

Since it is well known that eating habits also influence risk factors such as hypertension, we might conclude that better eating habits alone protect fit people against heart disease. This is not likely, since those who are fit eat the same types of food as their less fit counterparts.[18] It has also been shown that exercise protects against heart disease independent of other risk factors.[19]

Fitness helps cholesterol problems.

Physically-fit men, on the average, have significantly lower blood cholesterol than unfit men.[13] Since cholesterol levels are the best predictor of death from heart disease,[20] it is not surprising that high fitness levels are associated with a lessened risk. It has not been shown, however, that exercise will significantly lower cholesterol levels which are elevated; therefore, exercise probably exerts its influence as a protective factor against initially developing high levels.

Exercise, though, does change the type of cholesterol in the blood. "Good cholesterol," known as HDL (high-density lipoprotein) increases, while "bad cholesterol," known as LDL (low-density lipoprotein) decreases. HDL is associated with a decreased risk of death from heart disease, whereas LDL is associated with an increased death rate. A study reported in the *American Journal of Epidemiology* shows that as the ability to run on a treadmill increases, the ratio of total cholesterol to HDL decreases significantly.[21] Other risk factors also change positively, including decreases in body weight, blood-sugar levels, blood pressure and uric acid.

The weight loss that occurs with exercise is significantly linked to decreases in all other risk factors. This finding might lead some to believe that loss of weight in itself (via increased activity) is the primary ingredient in lessening the risk of heart disease. If so, then exercise would be relegated to the position of an indirect influence, rather than a direct cause of decreased cardiovascular disease. However, when data is adjusted to eliminate the confounding influence of weight loss, changes in fitness remain significantly associated with positive changes in cholesterol profiles.

Increasing levels of fitness, then, will improve blood profiles and lessen the chance of heart disease regardless of whether there is a need to lose weight. For those who need to lose weight, exercise would serve doubly well by decreasing risk factors (through its own direct effects) and by the indirect effect of lowering body weight. (For further information on the use of exercise as a therapy for weight-control problems, see the chapter on obesity.)

Many other studies indicate that exercise beneficially alters the type of cholesterol, thereby creating better blood profiles. The higher the fitness level, the better the profiles, indicating a lessened chance of death from heart disease.[22] [23] [24]

Can exercise protect against damage caused by high cholesterol levels?

In the study from the Aerobics Research Institute in Dallas[6] it was emphasized that highly-fit subjects lessened their risk of death from heart disease even when blood profiles were not good. Highly-fit subjects with very high levels of cholesterol or high blood pressure had a lower risk of death from heart disease than unfit subjects with low cholesterol levels or low blood pressure. *Fitness was so protective that the most-fit individuals with high levels of cholesterol had only about one-third the rate of death as those unfit subjects with low levels.*

This is not to say that exercise is a panacea which allows us to disregard high cholesterol levels. In fact, highly-fit subjects with high cholesterol levels had *twice* the risk of death from heart disease as their highly-fit counterparts with low cholesterol levels. We must never lose sight of the fact that high cholesterol levels are the primary predictors of heart disease and that it is high-fat nutrition (not sedentary living) which causes those high levels in nearly all cases. At best, fitness has a strong mitigating influence on heart disease for those who insist on harming themselves with dietary fat and cholesterol.

Unfortunately, most "experts" consider cholesterol levels below 200 to be "low," when in fact *levels above 150 may be dangerously high.* At a level below 150, death from heart disease is virtually non-existent. This level can be obtained by nearly anyone who is willing to free his diet of all animal products and saturated fats. (For a full discussion on cholesterol levels, please read the chapter on heart disease.)

Exercise would probably be of far less value in preventing heart disease in societies that consumed primarily fruits, grains and vegetables, since in such societies blood cholesterol levels average well under the threshold level of 150. We will probably never be quite sure, however, because these same societies in most cases tend toward a much higher level of physical activity than their meat-eating, fat-consuming counterparts.

High blood-sugar levels?
Help control them with fitness.

Physical activity also benefits the person who suffers from diabetes. Exercise lowers blood-sugar levels and increases the efficiency of insulin.[25] South Pacific urban populations that are sedentary have a much higher prevalence of diabetes when compared with rural populations that are more active. This is true even when obesity (an established risk factor for diabetes) is statistically eliminated from the comparison.[26]

Since diabetics have higher blood-sugar levels than non-diabetics and since high blood sugar has been established as an important risk factor for heart disease, it is evident that those who have higher levels of activity will not only suffer less from diabetes but heart disease as well. Perhaps part of the documented decrease in death from heart disease among highly fit persons could be due in part to the protective influences of exercise against high-blood-sugar levels and diabetes.

At National Institute of Fitness, we have seen well over 100 diabetics rid themselves of the need for insulin injections and hypoglycemic drugs, usually in a period of two weeks or less. Nearly all of the adult-onset diabetics who are injecting insulin at the beginning of their programs are needle-free within four weeks. The guests who remain dependent on some insulin injections usually dramatically reduce their dosages. We attribute part of this improvement in the diabetic condition to the fitness program, although there is no doubt that the low-fat nutrition program plays a major role. Those who cannot exercise still experience substantial improvements in short periods of time.

DOES EXERCISE REDUCE THE RISK OF OTHER DISEASES?

Some diseases not directly related to the vascular system respond favorably to exercise. Osteoporosis and cancer are two of the most important.

Osteoporosis: Use those bones!

Osteoporosis, or thinning of the bones, has become an epidemic among post-menopausal women. Although calcium supplementation of the diet through pills or dairy products seems to be the current therapy of choice, it has been virtually useless in preventing decalcification (calcium loss) of bones. At best, supplementation may slightly retard loss of bone, although even that is a moot point.

Exercise, however, has been shown not only to *retard bone loss* but to *increase bone mass*. Osteoporotic women who gradually conditioned themselves to an hour per day of vigorous weight-bearing activity were able to increase bone mass by 5% in nine months.[27] Other women gained 6.6% bone mass in a 12-month period with a program of aerobic activity and strength training.[28]

Dr. Nancy Lane reported in the *Journal of the American*

Medical Association that joggers between the ages of 50 and 70 have a 40% greater bone density of the spine than sedentary people of the same age.[29] Even senior citizens respond favorably to exercise. For instance, elderly women who squeezed a ball as hard as possible three times daily for a period of six weeks were able to increase their grip strengths by 14.5% and their forearm-bone mass by 3.4%![30]

Suffice it to say that exercise is a prime therapy for both the prevention and treatment of osteoporosis. More data on the benefits of exercise on osteoporosis can be found in the chapter on osteoporosis.

Fitness prevents some cancers.

In terms of cancer and the possible protective effect of physical activity and fitness against that disease, we need only look again at the study from the Aerobics Institute which was quoted earlier.[6] The study showed a highly significant correlation between low-fitness levels and all forms of cancer.

Since 1962 we've known that heavy physical activity has a protective effect against death from cancer.[31] Research in that year pointed out that sedentary employees of the railroad industries had one and one-half times the death rate from cancer as those who had heavy-labor jobs. Other research indicates a protective influence of exercise against specific carcinomas such as colon cancer,[32] [33] [34] [35] [35.1] breast cancer, and cancers of the reproductive system.[36] Studies done in 1984 and 1985[33] [34] reported a dose-response relationship between sedentary living and the rate of colon cancer. The less active a person was, the greater his risk of dying from the disease!

Recently, Dr. Alice Whittemore and her colleagues[35] reported that the incidences of colon and rectal cancer increased with the time spent sitting. And, as saturated-fat consumption increased, colon cancer among sedentary people skyrocketed compared to active people. Saturated fat is a known carcinogen (cancer causer). It appears that the influence of exercise is a protective one, helping the person at high risk of cancer to stave off the disease despite deplorable nutrition.

As with heart disease, the best preventive therapy for cancer is to eschew the foods which promote the disease in the first place. Exercise simply acts as extra insurance against a disease that lethally embraces those who consume foods that are anathema to human health.

FITNESS KEEPS THE MONEY
IN YOUR POCKET

There is another cost to a sedentary life style besides the cost in death and debility. That is the cost to the pocketbook, not only for the person who is unfit but for society as a whole.[37]

When shortened life, increased health-insurance costs, increased time away from work and increased hospitalizations for illness are considered, it has been calculated that the lifetime subsidy from society is $1900 per each sedentary individual. As part of this analysis, it was found that those who exercised vigorously had 20% fewer hospitalizations than those who were light exercisers or were inactive.[37]

Moderate exercisers had 18% fewer work-loss days than those who exercised little, and those who exercised vigorously missed 32% fewer days. In terms of outpatient care, the analysis showed that moderate exercisers had a 29% lower outpatient-use rate than sedentary people or light exercisers. *The authors of this research point out that the costs of a sedentary life style are almost double the costs of smoking!*

The cost of a sedentary life would be higher if it were not for the fact that sedentary people die sooner, thereby negating any added costs of hospitalization, insurance, etc., which would have accrued had they lived longer. Death, then, appears to be one method of stopping the physical and financial burden imposed by lack of exercise. A more sensible method is to shape up and enjoy the delights of an active life!

HOW MUCH EXERCISE IS NECESSARY?

Is it necessary to possess the same high levels of fitness as a competitive cyclist, long-distance runner, swimmer or triathlete to produce substantial benefits in health and longevity? It is not. By referring back to Figure 2, it can be seen that the greatest reduction in risk of death from all causes occurs when fitness improves from the lowest level to the next higher level. Thus, even a small improvement in fitness confers much better health.

An editorial in the *Journal of the American Medical Association* suggests that an exercise period of 20 minutes (such as a brisk walk) done three times weekly would be sufficient to produce many benefits.[38] Although some improvements may occur with such a minuscule effort, it would be much better to do more.

Dr. Steven Blair, who conducted the study from the Aerobics Institute, suggests a walk of 20 to 60 minutes daily. This would produce a greater level of fitness and place the individual in a much more protected category. Two miles per day walked in 30-40 minutes would move the sedentary person from the lowest level of fitness to the next highest level. To achieve the highest level of fitness it is necessary to move two miles in about 20 minutes or less for men and about 20-24 minutes for women.[39]

It is my opinion that this advice is correct. Thirty minutes of daily walking, cycling, cross-country skiing or the like would produce levels of fitness capable of furnishing most people with greatly improved health and length of life. Activity at this level of intensity is non-painful and non-threatening, therefore ensuring that the exercise is comfortable and more likely to be done on a consistent basis. This is very important, since the benefits of exercise cannot be banked. When the habit of regular exercise ceases, so do the benefits.

ARE WE EXERCISING ENOUGH AS A NATION?

Exercise is obviously good for the individual and the nation, but few people are doing the type of exercise that will produce benefits. The Centers for Disease Control[40] reported that the objectives for physical fitness and exercise for 1990 have not been met; and, in fact, the nation is not even close to meeting them. One of the objectives stated that by 1990, 90% of children ages 10 to 17 would be participating regularly in aerobic activity which could be carried into adulthood. Sixty-six percent participate occasionally in such activity, but only 36% of the children in this age group have daily physical education classes.

Of greater concern is the fact that the group who has the most to gain from regular exercise (those over 18 years of age) are falling woefully short of expectations. About 8% of those between the ages of 18 and 65 participate in regular exercise that produces the positive physiological changes and protection against disease which we have discussed. Only 5% of this group can identify the type, frequency and duration of activity necessary to make those changes.[40]

For the good of the nation, it is time to put the same kind of emphasis on physical fitness as we do on defense, environmental problems and education. Doctors could help by becoming knowledgeable in the area of fitness. Dr. Jeffrey Koplan and his associates have stated that "Physicians have taken a leading role in abandoning tobacco use as a health hazard and advising their patients to stop smoking. They should provide a similar model by adopting an active life style themselves and urging their patients and communities to do the same."[38]

What the government or the doctor may or may not do is important to the future health of the nation, but the individual can certainly benefit from an active lifestyle independent of those considerations. You, the reader, can begin today to avail yourself of the salutary effects of exercise and fitness, and expect a happier and healthier tomorrow for your efforts!

WHAT TYPE OF EXERCISE IS MOST CONDUCIVE TO GOOD HEALTH?

With the exception of the positive influence on bone strength, activities such as weight training and other strength exercises are not the types that protect against disease. These activities *are* necessary for overall fitness, however, and should not be neglected.

To produce the benefits discussed in this chapter, the activity must elevate the heart rate and sustain it for at least 20 minutes. Activities such as walking, cycling, dance, cross-country skiing and stair climbing are excellent. Jogging should be used only by those who are first properly conditioned by months of walking. Otherwise, injury to the joints is a distinct possibility. Swimming is a good conditioner but is not a good exercise for weight loss. As mentioned, 30 minutes to an hour of aerobic exercise daily will provide a superior workout.

A physician or other health professional who is familiar with the benefits of exercise should be consulted prior to beginning an exercise program. This person will be able to advise the neophyte as to proper intensities for activities which will help accrue the physiological improvements he or she expects. *Violent exercise can be life-threatening, especially to the person who suffers from heart disease.* Exercise which is too mild, however, is not likely to produce much in the way of improvement.

Much has been said about "aerobic target zones," meaning the range of heart rates, expressed in number of beats per minute, which are effective in conditioning the body. A person is usually considered to be "aerobic" when he or she has attained a heart rate which is 65%-80% of the maximal heart rate. Maximal heart rate can be calculated by subtracting a person's age from 220 and expressing the result in beats per minute (BPM). A person who is 40 years old, for example, would have a maximal heart rate of approximately 180 BPM. Sixty-five percent of that figure, or 117 BPM, would be the lower end of the "target zone," and 80% would be 144 BPM, which would represent the upper limit of the zone.

This formula represents ranges for heart rates which some scientists feel are necessary to cause improvements in fitness levels. In my opinion, the formula may serve as a useful tool for those who want to be scientific about their workouts. It is generally correct but not etched in stone. By measuring the pulse rate in terms of beats per minute or looking at the chart which follows, it can usually be determined whether or not a person is working at sufficient intensity to make the changes he seeks.

There are those people, however, who have a difficult time achieving a "target zone." If this is the case, they should exercise at an intensity that brings heart rates to a level lower than that suggested by the formula. To force oneself to achieve a heart rate that feels painful can be dangerous. If an individual feels that he is working hard, he is. If he cannot carry on a conversation without gasping for breath, he may be working dangerously hard, regardless of heart rate.

Usually, a person working within the target zone will feel comfortable enough to continue. But since individuals have different physiological makeups, some may find this rate of exercise to be too intense. If this is the case, they will probably scrap the exercise program within a few days anyway. No one voluntarily continues a program of misery.

If a person is to make exercise a viable and consistent part of life, then exercise must be enjoyable (or at least not miserable). When one cannot perform at the intensity that will cause his heart to reach the target zone, then he should simply do the exercise at an intensity which will let him exercise without pain for 30 to 60 minutes.

Some people who are beginning a program of exercise, of course, will find that it is not possible to exercise for more than a few minutes. Within a few weeks of gradually building up their exercise duration, however, most will be able to exercise for an hour.

The following chart will help you to estimate your approximate target zone for aerobic exercise, based on your age. If you prefer, you may find your exact heart rate by using the formula given.

MHR = MAXIMAL HEART RATE
LHR = LOWER HEART RATE
UHR = UPPER HEART RATE

AGE	MHR	LHR	UHR
20	200	130	160
25	195	127	156
30	190	124	152
35	185	120	148
40	180	117	144
45	175	114	140
50	170	111	136
55	165	107	132
60	160	104	128
65	155	101	124

Taking a pulse. To monitor your heart rate, you will need to learn to take a pulse count while exercising or for a brief period while ceasing to exercise. To do so, place two fingers flat against the inside of the wrist beneath the thumb (radial pulse) or against the groove under the jaw (carotid pulse). Count the number of beats in six seconds and multiply by 10 to determine beats per minute.

To be of any value whatsoever, exercise cannot be an on-again, off-again proposition. It should be as much a part of life as eating, breathing, sleeping and brushing the teeth. Sporadic bursts of exercise may do more harm than good, since the body never becomes conditioned to tolerate the increased effort. Regular, sustained, consistent exercise, which may be something as enjoyable as a brisk walk, is the *sine qua non* for a lean, vibrant and healthy body.

IS EXERCISE DANGEROUS?

There are a few nattering nudnicks of negativism who insist that exercise is dangerous and that it will shorten the life span. These are the people who would do anything to avoid the expedient of physical labor. They are also the people whose daily prayer is, "Please, Lord, don't make me work. Let me find a way to health and fitness that involves no effort on my part!"

Although we have set most of their nonsense to rest, it is well to debunk a few of the myths about the active life that are espoused by those who cannot bring themselves to sweat. A favorite method to rationalize their laziness is to twist figures of research studies to convince others that exercise is not only ineffective but harmful. After all, misery does love company.

Such prophets of doom, unfortunately, can usually find a large following of people who themselves have been praying for an excuse. Let's now dispel a couple of exercise myths that still persist in this age of enlightenment.

Does exercise increase risk of death by heart attack?

Indeed, it has been reported that during strenuous activity, the risk of dying suddenly from heart disease increases from four to seven times compared to non-exercise periods.[41] [42] [43] A study reported in the *New England Journal Of Medicine*[43] showed that habitually physically-active men had a six-times greater death rate during heavy exercise than during periods of inactivity. The same study also pointed out, however, that among a similar group of sedentary men, *the risk of sudden death was 50 times greater during strenuous activity than during inactivity!* This would indicate that a sedentary person who decided to shovel the snow on a winter morning would have about eight times the chance of dying as would the physically-fit person.

The study also pointed out that during periods of rest, the inactive men had several times the risk of sudden death as the physically-active men. Since a far greater part of the day is spent away from heavy exercise, even in physically-fit individuals, it is obvious that the benefits of fitness far outweigh the slightly increased risk during the period of exertion. In other words, the overall risk of having a heart attack during exercise *and* inactivity is much greater among those who are inactive.

As already discussed, the study from the Institute for Aerobics Research[6] points out the large decrease in deaths in those who are physically fit. We may put to rest the idea that exercise, when used in a safe and consistent manner, has much potential to shorten life. When there is heart disease present, exercise can bring on a heart attack, although the training effects of exercise will dramatically decrease that chance. Robert Pritikin once told me, "Exercise will lengthen life in the person with heart disease if he doesn't die during the exercise session."[44] Still, the odds of dying of heart attack are so greatly reduced through exercise that if one were playing the odds, he would certainly choose to keep himself fit.

Pritikin's point is nonetheless well taken. When we put the cart of exercise before the horse of low-cholesterol, low-fat nutrition, we are making a grave mistake. Heart disease is reversible, as pointed out in the chapter on that subject. This reversal is accomplished through proper nutrition. When the disease no longer exists, exercise is perfectly safe.

The "Lifetime Number of Heartbeats" myth

It has been said that a doctor once stated, "A person has only so many heart beats in a lifetime; exercising causes the heart to beat faster, thereby using up the beats at a faster rate and bringing on an early death. Therefore, whenever I have the urge to exercise, I lie down until the urge goes away!"

Whether such a thing was ever said is debatable, but as a fitness professional, I have heard similar arguments used to avoid exercise. If it were true that a person has only so many heartbeats in a lifetime, then fitness would be *more* effective than any method on earth in extending the life span, since *resting heart rate* is so dramatically *decreased* by a program of fitness.

Several physicians decided to determine just how many beats could be saved in a lifetime by lowering the pulse rate.[45] They compared the savings at rest against the number of extra beats which would be used during the exercise sessions. Thus they determined whether fitness would decrease or increase the life span.

To perform the calculations, they assumed that a person with a pulse rate of 72 (the average pulse rate for a man) would live to be 75 years old (the average age at death for a man). During that time, his heart would beat about 2.8 billion times. They then calculated that if the person ran 45 minutes, five days per week, at a pulse rate of 180 beats per minute, and thereby lowered his resting pulse from 72 to 45 beats per minute, that it would take him until he was 94 years old to use his 2.8 billion beats! To gain the extra 19 years of life would take less than one year of running!

I have lowered my own resting pulse rate by more than 30 beats per minute through a regular fitness program. My pulse rate was only about 66 beats per minute to begin with. Hmmm. I should live to be at least 114. With perfect nutrition maybe 130?

Such calculations, of course, are done in jest, and no one really expects to gain such length of life from physical fitness. At least such numerical manipulations serve to dispel the myth that exercise wears out the body.

DOES FITNESS TAKE TOO MUCH TIME?

A favorite excuse to avoid fitness is that it takes too much time. Nonsense! Exercise is not a waste of time but rather a wise investment in a healthier life. The time spent in exercise is returned many fold in life extension, fewer days away from work, and fewer days of hospitalization. Quality of life is greatly enhanced by fitness activities. There is less suffering from so many debilitating diseases, and a great deal of the financial burden is lifted through the decreased time spent in health-care facilities. Financial burdens to the company, the individual, and society as a whole are also lessened by decreasing the number of days away from the job.

The average American citizen spends several hours daily watching television. It seems that an investment of an hour per day away from the tube could hardly be considered too much time, especially in terms of the payoff. For anyone who watches television, it is entirely possible to watch while walking on a treadmill, riding an exercise bicycle, jogging on a mini-trampoline, using a cross-country-skiing machine, stair climber or other exercise apparati. In these cases, the investment in time is zero. One of the few remaining virtues of television may be to provide entertainment for the person who is exercising!

An intriguing analysis was performed regarding the investment in exercise time versus the return on that investment in increased life span.[46] The analysis used stair climbing as the method of exercise and determined that over a lifetime, it would require 101.6 days of stair climbing to gain 916.2 days of life. This would be a net gain of 814.6 days of life. Each flight of stairs climbed would increase waking life by about 1.47 minutes. Each step would increase life span by about four seconds!

The authors of these calculations admitted that their figures may not have been totally valid (due to variations in age, other activities, etc.) but felt that they were sufficiently accurate to recommend stair climbing as a time-effective way to increase health and life.

Analyses such as those discussed (which measure increases or decreases in heartbeats and stair steps versus life span) may be of some value to those who look at everything as investment and return and wish to "bank" some life for the future. This may give such people the impetus to relinquish a bit of their precious work time in order to increase fitness. Anyone who has experienced the joys of fitness, however, knows that exercise carries its own reward when it is performed in a safe and sane manner.

Nothing makes one feel better than a good workout after a day of stress at the office. There is little that can compete with the wonderful high achieved when one has overcome his baser inclination to stay in bed and instead has taken a brisk walk. Fitness may indeed add a few years to life and increase the number of disease-free days that a man or woman may experience on this earth. But we should not forget that fitness carries its own joy in a brightened outlook and a better self-image each day of our lives.

MAKING FITNESS WORK

Life often gets in the way of fitness programs, but it need not be that way. Excuses to skip exercise are myriad. But with a bit of thought, we can make exercise a delight rather than a dread. There are four basic keys that ensure that a person will succeed in following a program. If one is willing to implement these four suggestions, fitness will follow, and the quality of life will be greatly enhanced.

Key #1   Do it first!

Seventy-five percent of all people who schedule their exercise for any time other than morning eventually drop out. Seventy-five percent of those who do schedule it as the first activity of the day succeed in staying on a program.[47] If exercise is not placed in the number-one position, other concerns take precedence in the day. Exercise must be as much an integral part of one's existence as breathing and eating. *The only thing that should be done before exercise in the morning is going to the bathroom.* As the people at Nike say, "Just do it!" But do it first. If it isn't done first, there will be phone calls, unexpected visits, and a thousand other interruptions during the day. Toward the end of the day, it will be easy to say "I'm too tired" or "I'll wait until tomorrow." Too often, tomorrow never comes, and the fitness program becomes a memory.

Do it every day. Even when a full program cannot be done, at least do something. The slogan for exercise that we give to every guest at National Institute of Fitness is, "You need exercise only on the days that you breathe."

Key #2   Keep it pleasant

Remember, you are not training for the Olympics. Do not compete with anyone in your exercise program, not even yourself. It is not necessary to try to do your walk faster on Friday than you did on Wednesday. The main thing is that you do it. If you make it unpleasant by trying for faster times each day, you will dread getting up to do your exercise. You should, if walking, be able to enjoy the fresh air and the singing of the birds. If you do not notice these things, you are working too intensely and are apt to drop out. The aphorism, "The race is not to the swift, but to him who endureth to the end," is never truer than as it relates to a fitness program.

Unless you mentally stress yourself by brushing your teeth, you should not stress yourself with exercise. Both exercise and dental health should become habits that are part of healthful living. Fitness will come without misery. Walking times will improve as you walk briskly without pushing too hard. Don't remove the joy of physical activity by saying to yourself, "no pain, no gain." To paraphrase a popular slogan for an antacid pill, "Exercise doesn't need to taste bad to be good!"

Key #3   Exercise with a partner but rely on yourself.

Work with a partner for training. This will give that little extra incentive to keep an exercise appointment. However, you must be ready to carry on when your partner is unable to participate. Another thought: Never compete with your partner. He or she is there to provide an incentive to train, nothing more. If the two of you walk, bike or do other exercise at different speeds, so be it.

Key #4   Mix it up.

Should you tire of walking, change your route or bicycle for a day. When exercise becomes boring, change the form. You may want to walk one day per week, bike one day, hike one day, or take an aerobic dance class. Make it non-stressful, and if possible, fun. If you are the type of individual who cannot make exercise enjoyable, at least make it non-dreadful.

WHAT HAVE WE LEARNED?

1.   Fitness protects against such major killers as heart disease, cancer, diabetes and osteoporosis.

2.   Fitness also protects against obesity and is essential to weight control.

3.   It is not necessary to be a marathoner or a professional endurance athlete to derive great benefits from a fitness program. A half hour to an hour per day of brisk walking or other activity which raises and sustains the pulse rate is sufficient.

4.   Training for fitness should take precedence in a person's day. In other words, do it first! A program scheduled at a time other than the first part of the day is likely doomed to failure.

5.   Make it enjoyable. Or, if it can't be enjoyable, at least make it non-dreadful!

See your physician for his recommendations on target heart rates and then start on a safe and effective program. In a short time you will be addicted to this new habit and the magnificent benefits to your health that will accrue. However, if you should opt for a sedentary lifestyle, it is absolutely imperative that you consult a physician in order to determine whether your body can stand the strain of such an unnatural and unhealthful choice!

REFERENCES

[1] Morris, J. Incidence and prediction of ischaemic heart disease in London busmen. Lancet 1966; 2:553-559.

[2] Paffenbarger, R. Work activity and coronary heart mortality. N Engl J Med 1975; 292:545-550.

[3] Leon. Leisure-time physical activity levels and risk of coronary heart disease and death. JAMA 1987; 258:2388-2395.

[4] Peters, R. Physical fitness and subsequent myocardial infarction in healthy workers. JAMA 1983; 249:3052-3056.

[5] Grand, A. Disability, psychological factors and mortality among the elderly in a rural French population. J Clin Epidemiol 1990; 43:773-782.

[6] Blair, S. Physical fitness and all cause mortality. A prospective study of healthy men and women. JAMA 1989; 262:2395-2401.

[7]Sobloski, J. Protection against ischemic heart disease in the Belgian physical fitness study: Physical fitness rather than physical activity? Am J Epidemiol 1987; 125:601-610.

[8]Blair, S. Physical activity leads to fitness and pays off. Physician Sports Med 1985; 13:153-157.

[9]Paffenbarger, R. Physical activity, all cause mortality, and longevity of college alumni. N Engl J Med 1986; 314:605-613.

[10]Shepard, R. Exercise in the teritary prevention of ischemic heart disease: Experimental proof. Can J Sports Sci 1989; 14:74-84.

[11]Blair, S. Physical fitness and incidence of hypertension in normotensive men and women. JAMA 1984; 252:487-490.

[12]Slattery, M. Physical fitness and cardiovascular disease mortality. The U.S. railroad study. Am J Epidemiol 1988; 127:571-580.

[13]Gillum, R. Longitudinal study of exercise tolerance, breathing response, blood pressure, and blood lipids in young men. Arteriosclerosis 1981; 1:455-462.

[14]Duncan, J. The effects of an aerobic exercise program on sympathetic neural activity and blood pressure in mild hypertension. Circulation 1983; 68:285-288.

[14.1]Somers, V. Effects of endurance training on baroflex sensitivity and blood pressure in borderline hypertension. Lancet 1991; 337:1363-1368.

[15]Lie, H. Coronary risk factors and incidence of coronary death in relation to physical fitness. Seven year follow-up study of middle-aged and elderly men. European Heart J 1985; 6:147-157.

[16]Peters, R. Physical fitness and subsequent myocardial infarction in healthy workers. JAMA 1983; 249:3052-3056.

[17]Salonen, J. Physical activity and risk of myocardial infarction, cerebral stroke, and death. Am J Epidemiol 1982; 115:525-537.

[18]Blair, S. Comparison of nutrient intake in middle aged men and women runners and controls. Med Sci Sports Exerc 1981; 13:310-315.

[19]Ekelund, L. Physical fitness as a predictor of cardiovascular mortality in asymtomatic North American Men. N Engl J Med 1988; 319:1379-1384.

[20]Stamler, J. Is the risk between serum cholesterol and risk of premature death from coronary heart disease continuous and graded? JAMA 1986; 256:2823-2828.

[21]Blair, S. Changes in coronary heart-disease risk factors associated with increased treadmill time in 753 men. Am J Epidemiol 1983; 118:352-359.

[22]Huttenen, J. Effect of moderate physical exercise on serum lipoproteins. Circulation 1979; 60:1220-1229.

[23]Wood, P. Increased exercise level and plasma lipoprotein concentrations: A one year, randomized, controlled study in sedentary, middle-aged men. Metabolism 1983; 32:31-39.

[24]Hartung, G. Relation of diet to high-density-lipoprotein cholesterol in middle-aged marathon runners, joggers and inactive men. N Engl J Med 1980; 302:357-361.

[25]Richter, E. Diabetes and exercise. Am J Med 1984; 70:201-209.

[26]King, H. Non-insulin dependent diabetes in a newly independent nation: The island of Kirbati. Diabetes Care 1984; 7:409-415.

[27]Dalsky, G. Weight-bearing exercise training and lumbar bone-mineral content in postmenopausal women. Ann Intern Med 1988; 108:824-828.

[28]Chow, R. Effect of two randomized programmes on bone mass of healthy postmenopausal women. Br Med J 1987; 295:1441-1444.

[29]Lane, N. Long-distance running, bone density, and osteoarthritis. JAMA 1986; 255:1147-1151.

[30]Beverly, M. Local bone-mineral response to brief exercise that stresses the skeleton. Br Med J 1989; 299:233-235.

[31]Taylor, H. Death rates among physically active and sedentary employees of the railroad industries. Am J Pub Health 1962; 52:1697-1707.

[32]Kohl, H. Physical activity and cancer: An epidemiological perspective. Sports Medicine 1988; 6:222-237.

[33]Garabrant, D. Job activity and colon-cancer risk. Am J Epidemiol 1984; 119:1005-1014.

[34]Vena, J. Lifetime occupational exercise and colon cancer. Am J Epidemiol 1985; 12:357-365.

[35]Whittemore, A. Diet, physical activity and colorectal cancer among Chinese in North America and China. JNCI 1990 82:915-926.

[35.1]Lee, I. Physical activity and risk of developing colorectal cancer among college alumni. JNCI 1991; 83:1324-1329.

[36]Frisch, R. Lower prevalence of breast cancer and cancers of the reproductive system among former college athletes compared to non-athletes. Br J Cancer 1985; 52:885-891.

[37]Keeler, E. The external costs of a sedentary life-style. Am J Public Health 1989; 79:978-981.

[38]Koplan, J. Physical activity, physical fitness and health: Time to act. JAMA 1989; 262:2347.

[39]Interview with Dr. Steven Blair. Obesity Update. April 1990, p. 3.

[40]The Centers for Disease Control. Progress toward achieving the 1990 national objectives for physical fitness and exercise. MMWR 1989; 38:449-453.

[41]Thompson, P. Incidence of death during jogging in Rhode Island from 1975 through 1980. JAMA 1982; 247:2535-2536.

[42]Vuori, I. Studies on the feasibility of long-distance (20-90 kim) ski hikes as a mass sport. 20th World Congress of Sports Medicine. Melbourne, 1974.

[43]Siscovick, D. The incidence of primary cardiac arrest during vigorous exercise. N Engl J Med 1984; 311:874-877.

[44]Pritikin, R. Personal communication, Long Beach, California, November 1990.

[45]Stoller, J. Letter. N Engl J Med 1990; 318:708-709.

[46]Petty, B. Letter. N Engl J Med 1986; 315:399-400.

[47]A.M. Exercisers stay with it. Aviation Medical Bulletin, Dec. 1990, p. 1.

12.

Life Style and Longevity

12. Life Style and Longevity

An acquaintance once stated that he did not want to change his nutritional habits to live longer, because he was afraid of being miserable and debilitated by illnesses of old age. "I'd rather die young," he said, "while I still feel good."

Such a statement indicates a total misunderstanding of health and life span. As we have pointed out, healthful living habits reduce the rate of disease, and it is disease that causes both misery and shortened life. A person who spends his later years racked with pain might opt for a shorter life. But an elderly person who lives in good health will hardly wish to shorten his experience! If we must choose between quality and quantity of life, I'm sure that most would opt for quality. A better solution would be to live in such a manner that quality and quantity are both achieved. The achievement of that goal is entirely possible when we take responsibility for health and live in a manner which is consistent with life-long well-being.

From the information presented thus far, we would expect a higher average life span in populations that consume low-fat, high-fiber foods. This would be true, of course, only if other factors affecting longevity were equal. We would not expect societies with high death rates from communicable diseases to have long average life spans regardless of their dietary habits. Nor would we expect long average life spans from societies whose populations practice heavy smoking and alcoholism, even if their habits of nutrition bordered on perfection. Thirdly, we would not expect unusual longevity from populations with a high infant-mortality rate.

It is, therefore, difficult to compare one society with another in terms of the influence of life style factors on longevity. Within a society, however, it might be possible to assess the influence of life style factors on length of life by comparing different groups of people within that society. In other words, we could juxtapose smokers in the United States with non-smokers. Since life style factors other than smoking would be similar, any life span increase enjoyed by non-smokers would result primarily from their avoidance of that lethal habit. Similar comparisons could be made with vegetarians and non-vegetarians, drinkers and non-drinkers, etc.

There are groups in our society that choose to live one phase or another of their lives differently from "typical American living." Religious groups whose doctrines prohibit consumption of alcohol, tobacco or meat, furnish fertile fields for health assessment.

In studying such groups, of course, it is difficult to determine the influence that religion itself has on health and length of life. Nevertheless, religious people who are abstemious in their consumption of animal products, tobacco, and alcohol have lessened rates of the diseases of affluence. This decrease in degenerative diseases is consistent with whole populations of people such as the Tarahumaras and Chinese who also experience greatly decreased rates of the illnesses.

These people do not necessarily choose to be abstemious. The products that cause the sickness are simply in short supply. It is safe to assume, therefore, that at least a substantial part of the increased life span and decreased morbidity of certain religious groups is due to life style differences. At the same time, we should not discount the influence that a well-ordered existence, based on religious faith, may have on health and length of life. There are three groups we will discuss here, all of which have been studied as to their length of life and rate of various diseases.

THE MORMON ADVANTAGE

In the state of Utah, approximately 75% of the population belongs to the Church of Jesus Christ of Latter-day Saints, commonly referred to as the Mormon Church. If one were to look at death (mortality) statistics for the state of Utah, it would quickly become obvious that the rate of death through the years has been consistently less than 30-40% of the national average.[1] [2] In other words, in any given year, we would see only 30-40% of the number of deaths per capita that we would expect to see in the general population.

Science has provided several clues as to the potential for longer life among Mormons. They are guided by a doctrine known as "The Word of Wisdom," which advises against the use of coffee, tea, tobacco and alcohol. They are further encouraged to consume a diet high in vegetables, grains and fruits; to "eat sparingly of meat," and to "run and not be weary and walk and not faint."

Furthermore, the Mormon Church emphasizes strength in family life and service to others. Guided by these principles, an active 35-year-old Mormon man has about an 11% chance of dying before age 65, whereas a typical non-Mormon, 35-year-old U.S. Caucasian man has approximately a 30% chance of dying during the same time frame.[3]

This and other striking delays in mortality can be observed in Mormon High Priests (men in lay positions in the Church) who are much more likely to adhere strictly to Church doctrine.

Frequently, delays and quicker onsets of death for populations are expressed in terms of the standard mortality ratio (SMR). This statistic is simply the ratio of the actual death rate to the predicted death rate within a particular country. It is expressed as a percent:

SMR = (actual death rate / predicted death rate) x 100.

For example, Dr. James Enstrom of UCLA reports that the SMR for smoking-related cancer deaths for California High-Priest Mormons has, in the recent past, been 24.[4] This means that these Mormon men had only 24% of the smoking/cancer death rate of the general U.S population for Caucasian males, adjusted for age. Additional risk reduction of the major killer diseases by devout Mormons is shown in Table 1.

Clearly, the significant reduction in death rates by the Mormon High Priests (and their wives) is impressive. The devout males had an SMR for all cancers of 50, albeit prostate cancer deaths were about the same as the general population. Overall, the SMR for all causes for Mormon men was an astounding 53.

TABLE 1

Standard Mortality Ratios (SMR's) for
Mormon High Priests and Mormon High Priests' Wives[4]

Cause of Death	SMR: Mormon High Priests	SMR: Mormon High Priests' Wives
All Causes	53	66
Cardiovascular Disease	58	64
All Cancers	50	72
Colorectal Cancer	61	88
Lung Cancer	20	43
Breast Cancer	- - -	90
Prostate Cancer	100	- - -

Wives of High Priests also enjoyed longer lives as evinced by an all-cause SMR of 66. This overall advantage becomes even more luminous by the documented death rate for all cancers (SMR = 72) and cardiovascular diseases (SMR = 64). Because of the reduced risk of dying younger, expected life spans at birth for Mormon High Priests and their wives are about eight years and two years greater, respectively, than their typical non-Mormon counterparts.[5]

However, when researchers evaluated Mormon High Priests and their wives who never smoked, who engaged in regular physical activity and who had good sleep habits, the difference is even more impressive. A 25-year-old High Priest with those habits can expect to live 85 years compared to 74 for the typical white American male. His wife will live 86 years, which compares to 80 years for a typical non-Mormon woman.[6] This represents an 11- and six-year increase in life span, respectively. This may be the primary reason that Utah has been consistently rated as the "healthiest" state in the union.[7]

The fact that positive life style changes add more years to the male's life than the female's indicates that men are far more susceptible to early death due to bad habits. And, when habits are good, men gain far more years of life than do women. In view of this fact, we have the perfect explanation for the fact that there are far more widows than widowers in our country and that there are so many elderly women in comparison to the number of elderly men. A change in habits of nutrition, smoking, etc., would cause both sexes to live longer and better and would reduce by five years the time that a woman might be without her husband.

THE ADVENTIST ADVANTAGE

A gain in average life span has also been documented in studies of Seventh-day Adventists, a religious group which abstains from smoking, alcohol, coffee, tea, and (for about 50% of Adventists) meat.[8] This group has reduced mortality rates for nearly all causes as shown in Table 2.[8] As expected, the greatest risk reductions were with cancer deaths associated with smoking cigarettes and consuming alcoholic beverages; notably, cancers of the lung, mouth, pharynx, esophagus, and bladder (SMR's from 2 to 43).

The low mortality for other major cancers not associated with smoking and/or drinking, however, suggests that other components of the Adventist life style may also be very important. We have already established in our chapter on cancer that consumption of fat, meat and other animal products has been significantly linked to the risk of various cancers and heart disease. It is probable that decreased disease and the subsequent longer lives of Adventists are due, at least in part, to abstaining from meat.

Although Adventists have lower mortality than the general population and have significantly less cancer, malignancies do occur in accordance with dietary risk factors, particularly fat intake, which affect other populations.

One study assessed the SMR's for lifetime Adventists versus recent converts (church members for less than 12 years).[8] All of those studied were over 35 years old. As shown in Table 3, converts enjoyed nearly the same overall immunity from earlier

TABLE 2
Standard Mortality Ratios (SMR's) for Various Cancers Among California Seventh-day Adventists[8]

Type of Cancer	SMR: Men	SMR: Women	SMR: Men & Women
All Cancer	53	67	- - -
Strongly Related To Cigarettes/Alcohol			
Respiratory	10	43	- - -
Mouth/Pharynx	2	- - -	- - -
Esophagus	- - -	- - -	34
Bladder	- - -	- - -	28
Weakly Related To Cigarettes/Alcohol			
Gastrointestinal (All)	62	73	- - -
Colon	61	70	- - -
Stomach	69	71	- - -
Pancreas	50	76	- - -
Gall Bladder	- - -	- - -	83
Reproductive (All)	- - -	- - -	71
Breast	- - -	70-74	- - -
Ovary	- - -	53-88	- - -
Cervix	- - -	18-64	- - -
Other Uterus	- - -	60	- - -
Prostate	81	- - -	- - -
Kidney	- - -	- - -	98
Central Nervous System	- - -	- - -	113
Leukemia	70	66	- - -
Lymphoma	87	100	- - -
All Other Cancer	94	68	- - -

mortality from all causes of death, including all cancer, as their lifetime church member cohorts.

TABLE 3
Standard Mortality Ratios (SMR's) for All Causes and Various Cancers Among Lifetime and Converted Seventh-day Adventists[8]

Cause of Death	SMR-SDA Lifetime Members*	SMR-SDA Converts*
All Causes	50	51
All Cancer	53	52
Stomach Cancer	37	64
Colon/Rectal Cancer	60	44
Breast Cancer	71	57

Although the all-cancer SMR's were essentially the same for lifetime members and recent converts, distribution of the specific types of cancer deaths varied surprisingly. For reasons thus far beyond explanation, the converts had significantly less breast cancer and colon cancer but had nearly double the death rate for stomach cancer. Because overall death rates were nearly the same, it is suspected (but unsubstantiated) that new church members may be more zealous in pursuit of their religious mandates and may adhere more closely to dietary guidelines.

Whatever the reasons, one message comes through clearly: Those who change to a more favorable life style can expect to reduce the risk of disease and to live longer. In fact, the Mormons must take a back seat to the Adventists in terms of longevity. The Adventist man who adheres strictly to his church's nutritional doctrine can expect to live 12 years longer than the typical non-Adventist male. His adherent wife can expect to live six years longer than the typical non-Adventist female.[9] We can only surmise that the difference in longevity between these two long-lived groups is the difference in consumption of flesh. Adherent Adventists eat no meat of any kind; adherent Mormons eat it "sparingly."

LONG-LIVING PROTESTANT CLERGY

Like Mormon High Priests and Seventh-day Adventists, the Protestant clergy have for more than a century demonstrated their innate ability to keep the grim reaper at bay. Looking at Table 4, for example, one can see a continuously low SMR trend (44-81) for English and Welsh ministers from 1860 to 1972.[10] [11] Table 5 shows the SMRs for white Protestant clergy.

Even more remarkable are the lowered SMRs for younger clerics (age 20-65) who demonstrated an overall SMR for all causes of 56. Although not reported, it is strongly suspected that the Protestant cleric's inclination to avoid smoking, abstain from alcohol, pursue moderation in nutrition and in general assume a sense of responsibility for personal health and well-being, may be related to many of the lower SMRs.

SMOKING—THE "BIG KID'S" HABIT

Smoking has no role in the lives of those who aspire to avoid diseases and live to long and healthy lives. It is sometimes referred to as the "big kid's habit" (since many who started smoking in their youth did so because their older peers served as role models). Smoking is far from humorous from the standpoint of early death. It has been designated as the most important U.S. health risk by former Surgeon General, Dr. C. Everett Koop.

An individual with a two-pack-a-day habit can expect to shorten his/her life by 8-9 years due to a 70% increase in the risk of acquiring a fatal disease.[12] This estimate concurs with other predictions of the life hacking effects (pun intended) of smoking. For instance, the Veterans Administration has estimated a nine-

TABLE 4
Standard Mortality Ratios (SMR's) for
All Causes of Death Among
Clergymen in England and Wales From 1860-1972[10] [11]

Year(s)	SMR
1860, 1861, 1870	70
1880 - 1882	60
1890 - 1892	63
1900 - 1902	54
1910 - 1912	44
1921 - 1923	60
1930 - 1932	69
1949 - 1953	81
1959 - 1963	62
1970 - 1972	76

year life expectancy difference between smokers and non-smokers. The American Cancer Society estimates a seven-year difference. However, a recent study by the Social Security Administration showed smoking to shorten life by as much as 17.9 years!

The deleterious effects of passive exposure to tobacco smoke (inhaling the smoke of others) are quickly gaining the attention of our medical authorities. One recent study surveyed 191 lung cancer patients who had never smoked.[13] At least 17% of the cases were linked to excessive exposure to tobacco smoke during childhood. Risk doubled if the patient had been exposed to 25 or more "smoker years" (the number of years of home exposure to smoke multiplied by the number of smokers residing in the home).

It has sometimes been said that the shorter life span among smokers is due to the influence of other habits such as alcohol consumption and caffeine consumption which often accompany smoking. A study by Dr. C. E. Hammond has proven beyond any doubt that the smoking habit needs no help to dramatically reduce both health and longevity.

TABLE 5

**Standard Mortality Ratios (SMR's) for
Primary Causes of Death of
5,207 White Protestant Clergymen
Ages 20 Years and Older[19]**

Cause of Death	SMR
All Causes	72
Cardiovascular Disease	75
Renal Disease	49
Cancer	63
Tuberculosis	9
Syphilis	58
Diabetes	93
Influenza/Pneumonia	72
Hyperplasia of Prostate Gland	59
Accidents	52
Suicide	32
Other Causes	89

In Hammond's study, 36,975 men were computer matched with 36,975 other men who were alike in many ways such as race, height, birthplace, area of residence, religion, education, marital status, alcohol consumption, exercise, sleep habits, height, weight, use of tranquilizers, history of disease, etc. The only significant difference between the members of one group and their matched members of the other group was the fact that all the members of one group were smokers, and all of the other group were non-smokers. After nearly three years of observation, 1,385 smokers had died as opposed to only 662 non-smokers. A breakdown of the causes of death is submitted in Table 6.

As we can see, the smokers experienced nearly three times the deaths for all cancers (lung cancer was nine times greater); over twice the number of deaths due to heart attacks, stroke, aortic aneurysm, etc., and almost twice the deaths for other

TABLE 6

Matched Pair Analysis:
Number of Deaths from Various Causes Among
36,975 Men Who Never Smoked Regularly and
36,975 Men Who Were Currently Smoking
20 or More Cigarettes Per Day
Age Range: 40-79[20]

| | Number of Deaths | |
| | Never Smoked | Smoked 20 or More Cigarettes |
Cause of Death	Regularly	Per Day
Cancer..............	96	261
Heart & Circulatory Disorders..............	401	854
Other Diseases	73	127
Accidents/Violence/Suicide	58	66
Undetermined...........	34	77
GRAND TOTALS:	**662**	**1,385**

diseases. This data boldly dispels any lingering myths which insinuate that cigarette smoking is simply an interesting artifact, which by coincidence, happens to correlate to disease induced death. The indisputable quantitative relationship of smoking to death in addition to well-documented biological deterioration[14] should serve to convince even the most unconscionable member of the tobacco industry that there is a cause and effect relationship between smoking and death.

SOCIAL RELATIONSHIPS AND LONG LIFE

Other than the intake of toxic substances, there are important life style habits that influence the quality and quantity of life. One of these is social relationships. There is a virtual avalanche of research that reports significant direct correlations between mortality and a lack of supportive social contacts, both with human and animal studies. Among these, strong relationships have been reported between augmented death rates (as much as 50%) and individuals with sparse or non-existent human contact.[15]

The reason for the therapeutic benefits of gregarious behavior is unknown, although it is theorized that hermit-like lifestyles may be reflective of self-destructive dementia or perhaps socially incapacitating illness.

To assess the effect of various kinds of human interrelationships and health, let's look at a study that took place in Alameda County, California.[16] In 1965, 7,000 adult residents of that county were asked to complete a health questionnaire involving their health and behavior. Between 1965 and 1982, 1,219 of the residents died. After adjusting for risk factors such as smoking, obesity, age, etc., "relative hazards" were computed for four different classes of social relationships. A relative hazard of 1.0 indicates no increased risk of death. 2.0 would indicate double risk, and so on.

As seen in Table 7 on page 439, social relationships may have a small significant impact on mortality in all age groups. However, perhaps the most unexpected observation from these data is that marital status is of primary importance only for those under 60 year of age. It appears that with age, close association with relatives, friends, and church groups largely usurp the positive influences of marriage on abating death. Even when comparing only those who were not widows or widowers, this relationship still held fast. Regardless, when the influence of all social relationships are pooled and gauged against all-cause mortality, risk was significantly increased in low age groups. Simply stated: People live longer who enjoy a high quality and quantity of human interaction.

SLEEP—TOO MUCH OR TOO LITTLE?

Consistently long or short periods of sleep have long been suspected to be unhealthful in themselves or perhaps indicative of underlying illness. Confirmation of this suspicion is found in research.[17] Men who receive less than four hours of sleep per night are 2.8 times more likely to die in any given period than those who slept 7-7.9 hours per night.[17]

TABLE 7
Proportional Mortality Hazards for 4 Types of Social Relationships in Alameda County, California Adjusted for Age, Sex, Race, Baseline Health Status and Behavioral and Psychological Risk Factors[16]

| | Age Group | | | |
Type of Relationship	38-49	50-59	60-69	70 & Over
Not Married/Married	1.60	1.39	1.01	1.12
Socially Isolated/Not Socially Isolated	1.07	0.95	1.15	1.18
Church Group Membership: No/Yes	1.49	0.93	1.26	1.14
Membership in Other Groups: No/Yes	1.10	0.97	0.80	1.06

Women were about 1.5 times as likely to die if sleep periods were short. Both men and women also experienced increased mortality of about 80% when sleep patterns extended for ten hours or more. The maximum survival advantage is enjoyed by those who sleep about 7-8 hours per night. Figure 1 illustrates this data.

The use of sleeping pills also relates to a 50% greater death rate for men and women. Perhaps the sleeping pills used currently are safer, but, as with other drugs, one must question the wisdom of their chronic use. It is also quite possible that the real problem lies not in the pills as much as in the underlying problem for which they are used.

FIGURE 1:
Percent of Individuals Without A Past History of Heart Disease, Stroke, Diabetes, or High Blood Pressure; Ages 70 and Over; Within Specific Sleep Duration Groups; Who Died Within 6 Years After Completing An American Cancer Society Questionnaire in 1959-1960[17]

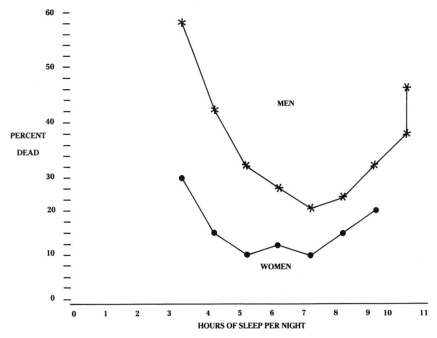

BE HAPPY, LIVE LONGER

In a study of 1200 centenarians, only 1½% had sour-looking dispositions[18] and showed an uncanny knack for avoiding stress associated with fear, suppressed and unsuppressed hate, exasperation, and frustration. Although habits associated with smoking, alcohol consumption and faulty nutrition are the prime causes of death and disability, there is no doubt that a sunny, happy disposition is an adjunct to living long and well. This is probably a good thing for many people. After all, who would want to live 100 years of life spent in anger, depression, and distrust? Unless old age is enjoyed, I can think of no reason to go through it.

WHAT HAVE WE LEARNED?

Life style factors are the primary determinants of longevity and health. A person throws the odds in his or her favor by abstaining from cigarettes, coffee, tobacco, alcohol and a diet loaded with animal products and fat. Proper habits of sleep and exercise, as well as a sunny disposition, can also add quality years to life.

REFERENCES

[1] National Center for Health statistics. Health United States, 1989. DHHS publication (PHS) 90-1232. U.S. Government Printing Office, Washington, D.C., 1990, p. 108.

[2] Bureau of the Census, USDC. Statistical Abstract of the U.S. Government Printing Office, Washington, D.C., 1986, p. 71.

[3] Enstrom, J. Health and dietary practices and cancer mortality among active California Mormons. Banbury Report #. In Cains, J. Cold Spring Harbor Laboratory, 1980, pp. 69-89.

[4] Enstrom, J. Health practices and cancer mortality among active California Mormons. J Nat Cancer Inst 1989; 81:1807-1813.

[5] Enstrom, J. Personal communication.

[6] American Cancer Society. Research updates. Cancer News, Spring 1990, p. 19.

[7] Northwestern National Life Insurance Company statistics, 1991.

[8] Phillips, R. Role of lifestyle and dietary habits in risk of cancer among Seventh-day Adventists. Cancer Res 1975; 35:3522.

[9] Nieman, C. Personal communication.

[10] Occupational mortality, England and Wales, 1951. Registrar General's Decennial Supplement, Part 2, Volumes 1 & 2. London: H.M. Stat Off, 1957.

[11] Occupational mortality, England and Wales, 1961. Registrar General's Decennial Supplement. Tables. London: H.M. Stat Off, 1971.

[12] Berger, S. Forever Young. William Morrow and Co., Inc., publishers, New York, 1989, p. 127.

[13] Janerich, D. N Engl J Med 1990.

[14] Wynder, E. (Ed) *The Biological Effects of Tobacco.* Little, Brown and Co., publishers, Boston, MA, 1955.

[15]House, J. Social relationships and health. Science 1988; 241:540-545.

[16]Seeman, T. Social network ties and mortality among the elderly in the Alameda County Study. Am J Epidemiol 1987; 126:714-723.

[17]Kripke, D. Short and long sleep and sleeping pills. Arch Gen Psychiat 1979; 36:103-116.

[18]Segerberg, J. *Living To Be 100*. Charles Scribner's Sons, publishers, New York, 1982, p. 340.

[19]King, H. American white protestant clergy as a low-risk population for mortality research. J Natl Cancer Inst 65; 5:1115-1124.

[20]Hammond, C. Smoking in relation to mortality and morbidity. Findings in first 34 months of follow-up in a perspective study started in 1955. J Natl Cancer Inst 1964; 32:1161-1188.

13.

Looking At the Bright Side

13. *Looking At the Bright Side*

Our options for good food are changing for the better, despite the advent of such nuisances as lactose-digesting pills and "lite" mayonnaise. Supermarkets have always offered grains, beans and vegetables and now carry relatively decent fat-free, cholesterol-free, low-fat products. And, by ordering a few days in advance, one can obtain a vegetarian, low-fat meal as he travels by air.

Dining at restaurants is also becoming simpler, especially if the patron makes very clear to the waitress that he doesn't want cheese on his steamed vegetables and that he will take his baked potato dry, thank you. Many restaurants boldly proclaim their desire to cook their foods to the specifications of the American Heart Association. While this is hardly a healthful way to eat, it can be considered a step in the right direction.

Many of the older generation will continue to cling to the "basic four" and will eventually pay the price in debility and degeneration. The reversal of their hardening of the arteries will be prevented by their "hardening of the attitudes." But not you, my friend. You value your health as a most prized possession. You will make the necessary changes. Rather than searching for excitement and pleasure in a greasy steak or a bowl of rich ice cream, you will, in vibrant health, experience your *joie de'vivre* as you hike the mountains with your children and grandchildren, live freer of degenerative diseases, and help to spread the truth to a modern world which has a dire need to return to its primitive basics of exercise and nutrition.

In a few short years, you will be part of a ground swell that will dramatically alter the way people live. The world you help to create will be a kinder world, a world which will choose to be more compassionate toward both humans and our animal friends. In 30 or 40 years, I hope to meet you as I mountain bike through the brush and pines of the Rockies. Perhaps later we can have lunch together. I think that I will order rice, beans, salad, whole-grain bread and fruit for dessert. I'll even pick up your tab. Until then, happy living and good health!

14.

You Can Make
It Work

14. *You Can Make It Work*

A large volume of information has been presented and documented that establishes the low-fat, animal-free nutrition program as the very best method to prevent and overcome the diseases that most commonly afflict our society. The question now arises, "How am I to put these principles into practice in my own life?' ' A good question indeed. With an overflow of advertisements screaming at you to consume double whoppers, pizza pizza, MacLean burgers, and cholesterol-free margarines, how are you to make this program practical? What can you eat? How do you order at restaurants?

This chapter will provide practical advice on comfortably thriving while making correct food choices in a world bent on poisoning itself. It will concentrate on how to shop, how to prepare foods, how to eat at restaurants, and how to enjoy social gatherings. You will then be ready to proceed with your lifetime program of healthful eating.

LET'S GO SHOPPING

Many supermarkets have special "health food" sections but beware. Some of the "healthy" foods include such "toxins" as cholesterol-free cooking oils, margarines, etc., and products that contain large amounts of vegetable oils in their ingredient lists. Remember that one cannot expect to enjoy megahealth while ingesting concentrated fat or oil sources of any kind. Obesity and certain forms of cancer are promoted by their consumption, and the processing of oils makes them doubly dangerous.

Nevertheless, the health food sections are a step in the right direction and do indeed contain foods free of fat, table sugar and cholesterol. These foods include breads, cookies, cereals and pastas that one can eat without the slightest compunction; and jams, jellies and other preserves which, when eaten sparingly, can add flavor to the breads and cereals. Also, fat-free salad dressings often are available in these sections.

Surprisingly, much of the rest of the supermarket contains foods that are perfectly "legal." One cannot go too far wrong in purchasing brown rice, potatoes, corn meal, vegetables and fruits. Even some canned goods advertise that they are fat-free, cholesterol-free or "canned in their own unsweetened juice."

If you can find these products organically grown in your area, so much the better, but well-washed vegetables and fruits from the local grocer can certainly be health-promoting. Animal products and fats cause nearly all of the degenerative disease, not insecticides and chemical fertilizers. Whereas these factors may be important, they form only the tip of the iceberg and should not be a great cause for alarm, especially in plant foods. At any rate, most food pollutants, including insecticides, are concentrated in products such as fish, milk, poultry, eggs and red meat; not in fruits, vegetables, legumes and grains.

To find good foods in the supermarket, it is also wise to understand how to read a food label. Many products that would otherwise be acceptable have powdered milk or casein (milk protein) lurking in the ingredients list and should be avoided. Of great concern is the quantity of fat contained in the product. We recommend that the total calories from fat not exceed 10% of the total calories in the product being purchased. Most food products now have nutritional breakdowns on the label which enable you to quickly assess the percentage of calories from fat.

Let's use an example. You look at the nutrition analysis list on a particular food package and find that one serving contains 100 calories. There are three grams of fat in that serving. Remember that each gram of fat contains 9 calories. The product in question, then, contains 27 calories in fat out of a total of 100 or 27% calories as fat. This product is far too high in fat, since our goal is 10% or less. Another food contains only one gram of fat per 100 calories. It has only 9% calories as fat and is therefore acceptable, provided it does not contain animal products. The mathematics are a bit more complicated when the portion contains more or less than 100 calories per serving, but fat content is certainly not difficult to assess. The basic formula is this:

(fat grams per portion x 9) x 100   = % calories from fat

———————————————————

Calories per portion

As an example, a food with 150 calories per portion, containing 4 grams of fat, would be assessed as follows:

$$\frac{(4\ fat\ grams\ per\ portion\ x\ 9\ x\ 100)}{150} = \frac{3600}{150} = 24\%$$

If you'd rather not be bothered with the mathematics, you may purchase a circular slide rule called a "Fat Finder." It is available for approximately $4.00 through National Institute of Fitness, Box 938, Ivins, Utah 84738. This device will immediately assess the fat content of any food product which has a nutritional breakdown.

When a food product does not have a nutritional breakdown, look at the ingredients list. If it lists oil, fat, or animal products as ingredients, don't buy it!

Some products containing too much fat can be combined with other products with very-low fat contents and still be acceptable. For instance, if you were to use 100 calories of a "light" soy milk (fat content, 18%) with 100 calories Grape Nuts cereal (fat content, 0%), the resultant fat content would be 9%. This would be an acceptable level.

The following chapter contains a partial list of products sold at either the supermarket or health food stores that are acceptable in terms of fat content and which contain no animal products. You will be able to find many other brands of "legal" foods as you begin your adventure in shopping.

An important point: If you cannot resist the temptation of shopping for good foods in a store replete with addictive "toxins," then you should not shop. There are many young men and women who would be glad to take your list and do your shopping for you for a small fee. Not only will you remove yourself from the temptation by using this method, but you will easily save enough to pay your helper by not buying unhealthful foods. And, if your helper decides to buy an ice cream bar to eat on the way home, it will not end up on your hips nor in your coronary arteries!

FOOD PREPARATION

Throw out the oil, margarine, butter, mayonnaise and all other fats. Cook your foods in non-stick cookware or, if you must, use a bit of non-stick spray such as PAM. For heaven sakes, use it *SPARINGLY*, since it is a vegetable oil. Used very sparingly, the amount of oil added will be negligible.

Other options include microwaving and broiling, and most cereals and pastas will be either baked or cooked in water. By using the sample recipes, you will learn how to prepare foods without using fat. A great bonus is that these methods are clean and will not cover your kitchen with a layer of grease and smoke.

A bit of creativity can help you to adapt many of your recipes to a Megahealth style of preparation. By leaving out fats and oils and by substituting more liquids or such ingredients as applesauce, you will produce some interesting and tasty dishes. Particularly easy to prepare in Megahealth style are Italian, Mexican and Chinese foods.

Don't expect the dishes to taste exactly like what you are used to. It will take time for you to adapt to the new style of eating and begin to taste the real flavors of foods that are not saturated in salt, fat and sugar. In a short time (and to your delight), these foods will taste as good as those which are filled with insalubrious ingredients; and they will be adequate and satisfying. And, after all, eating differently is a small price to pay for the benefits which accrue to those who are committed to a healthier life style. Cookbooks are crucial when you begin your new eating adventure. We recommend several good ones in the recipe section.

DINING WITH MEGAHEALTH

Those who eat no animal products and do eat low-fat meals can find gustatory pleasures at the most unlikely places; among them, Burger King, Golden Corral, Subway Sandwich Shop, Wendy's and Sizzler. (No, I haven't lost my mind.) In addition, there are many good restaurants which are more than happy to cater to the needs of those who wish to consume healthy fare.

Subway Sandwich is a favorite of mine. I order a vegetarian sandwich and tell them to hold the cheese, mayo, and oil and to add extra tomatoes and green pepper. I order the wheat bun. These sandwiches are much less expensive than the "killer" sandwiches which are served there, and consequently I usually have two in order to obtain sufficient calories for a good meal.

At Burger King, they will "do it your way." Tell them to hold the meat and load it up with veggies. Take a trip to the salad bar. Bring your own fat-free dressing and don't take anything from the bar but the vegetables and fruit. You will have eaten a surprisingly healthful meal and will not feel sluggish nor sleepy.

Sizzler and Golden Corral have excellent salad bars and baked potatoes. (Tell them to hold the butter and sour cream.) Salsas which contain no fat or animal products are available for the potatoes, though they may be a bit salty. You may wish to bring your own fat-free dressing. There is usually plenty of fresh fruit for dessert.

Restaurants will usually steam vegetables and prepare fruit plates for you. In addition, many of them will prepare dishes without fats or oils. Chinese restaurants will steam rice on request and will stir fry vegetables in water. Be sure that you inform them to leave out the MSG and let them know that you cannot tolerate fats.

Drink water at your meals, or at worst, a glass of juice or sparkling water with lemon.

Any good restaurant will generally have some fresh fruit on hand in order to prepare desserts such as strawberry shortcake. I have found no problem in ordering a bowl of fresh strawberries or other fruit. If you must have dessert, fruit is usually your best choice.

In a short time, you will become expert in ordering healthful meals in restaurants; and you will enjoy being alert and physically active afterward, rather than feeling lethargic and stuporous—common after a fat-laden meal.

SOCIAL GATHERINGS—LET'S
HAVE A HEALTHFUL PARTY!

The best way to survive a party is to either ask if the host or hostess will have some "edible" foods available or bring your own snacks and drinks. In the following shopping list you will note that there are many snack foods that are acceptable, including corn chips, dips, and drinks. Bring them with you to the party. For instance, Guiltless Gourmet tortilla chips and salsa can be carried along with you, and you can bring a bottle of Sundance Sparkler, which contains only fruit juice and sparkling water. (This is a special occasion drink, not to be consumed regularly.)

There are many other chips and snack foods, as well as cookies, muffins, etc., which can help you to socialize while avoiding the toxic substances being consumed by your less knowledgeable friends. You will find that these items make great topics of conversation also. It has been said that friends resent it when one is eating healthfully at a social gathering, but I certainly have not found this to be so. In fact, everyone is so interested in nutrition nowadays that a person who is doing something healthful quickly becomes the center of attention and is able to spread a few ideas about proper eating patterns.

For goodness sake, don't become preachy about your "pure" diet. Just answer questions and set a good example. Otherwise, you will quickly become an outcast. When the weight starts to come off and your eyes sparkle with energy and health, you will have ample opportunity to expound. Until then, please don't tell other people that they are consuming toxins, nor tell them that they are eating corpses. Just enjoy what you are accomplishing and let your actions and attitude speak for themselves.

15.

National Institute of Fitness Megahealth Nutrition Program

15. *N.I.F. Megahealth Nutrition Program*

The following dietary guidelines are those currently advocated at National Institute of Fitness for the maximum reduced risk of obesity and all major degenerative diseases:

DIETARY GUIDELINES

Guideline	Suggestions for Enactment
1. Avoid all foods derived from animals.	Simply do not eat meat, fish, eggs, or dairy products. Also, avoid eating foods containing ingredients of animal origin (casein, lactose, gelatin, egg whites, whey, milk solids, beef and chicken stocks, etc.).
2. Keep all meals and snacks at less than 10% of calories from fat.	Remove high-fat food sources (oils, lard, shortening, margarine, butter, sour cream, peanut butter, potato chips, etc., from the refrigerator and pantry.

Guideline	Suggestions for Enactment
3. Consume more than 70% of your calories from starch (complex carbohydrates).	Replace the fat removed from the diet with meals centered on whole grain foods (rice, pasta, cereals) and other starch-laden foods (potatoes, legumes, sweet potatoes, carrots, etc.).
4. Consume less than 2000 mg of sodium per day.	Throw away the salt shaker. Select foods that have the lowest amount of sodium (all other health factors considered). Use spices and small amounts of "Sour Salt" (citric acid) instead. Do not use sea salt or salt substitutes that contain potassium chloride.
5. If you are not down to your goal body size, consume no more than the equivalent of 3 fruit servings per day (approx. 60 grams of simple carbohydrate). For those who are at their goal body size and are continuing a program of daily aerobic exercise, we suggest you can enjoy fruit carte blanche.	Consume whole fruit, not the processed fruit product (example: You will go for longer periods of time between bouts of hunger if you consume 100 calories of a whole apple as opposed to 100 calories of apple juice). Remember, a serving of any sweetened food must constitute a part of your simple carb allotment. Do not consume diet sweeteners and eat sparingly of all sugars.

Guideline	Suggestions for Enactment
6. Do not consume foods containing caffeine or methyl xanthines.	Use carob for chocolate products. Incorporate more coffee substitutes and herbal teas into your nutrition program. Avoid soft drinks.
7. Avoid alcoholic beverages.	Unless used in cooking where the alcohol is evaporated, beverages containing ethanol are inappropriate in the homes of those seeking Megahealth. Even non-alcoholic beers may contain up to 0.5% ethyl alcohol.
8. Purchase "natural" food products, where possible.	Although not a hard and fast rule, it is best to purchase unprocessed food, void of additives (all other health factors considered). Several substances currently allowed in food have caused allergic reactions in select individuals.
9. Purchase organically-grown food where possible.	Some potentially carcinogenic agricultural pesticides may form a residue on fruits and vegetables. All other factors considered, plant foods produced without inorganic pesticides are best for the health.

PURCHASING AND PREPARATION TIPS

BAKING POWDER: Use the non-aluminum type. Example: Rumford.

BREADS & BAGELS: Make certain your selections contain less than 10% fat calories. If prepared from white flour, add wheat bran at meal time to replace the lost fiber, vitamins, and minerals. (Whole grains are always a better choice, however.) In this regard, nearly all wheat, rye, pumpernickel, sourdough, French, Italian, and white breads would be acceptable providing they do not contain ingredients of animal origin.

Most bagels are also prepared from white flour and would necessitate consumption of additional bran. Avoid egg and cheese bagels. Sprouted grain breads such as Essene and Ezekiel 4:9 products are great treats but tend to be a little high in fat (12% to 15% fat calories). Eat them sparingly. Some unique breads like Giusto's Vita Grain Sourdough Rye have inherent health value while offering unusual taste treats.

CEREALS, BREAKFAST: Avoid the candy-type of breakfast cereals (Count Chocula, Frankenberry, etc.) and the granola types (100% Natural). Corn Flakes, Shredded Wheat, Grapenuts, Wheaties, etc., all get the green light. Focus your breakfast cereal choices on the no- or low-sodium types (example: Shredded Wheat has no sodium as opposed to Corn Flakes which has 290 mg of sodium per serving).

CHEESES: Use (sparingly) 100% non-dairy cheese substitutes such as Soymage. Since these products contain considerable fat, use only as garnishes for enchiladas, pasta dishes, etc. Beware of the enticing fat-free mostly vegetable cheeses containing casein.

COFFEE/TEA SUBSTITUTES: Best advice: Use unsweetened caffeine-free products such as Mountain Roast, Caffix, Postum, and herbal teas (Select, Celestial Seasonings, Colonel Gordens, Lipton). Avoid herbal teas containing mate', a South American plant renowned for its high concentration of caffeine.

COOKIES: Best type: Non-fat whole-grain cookies sweetened with fruit juice and containing low sodium (example: Health Valley's Fat-Free line). Whole wheat Fig Newtons made with oil (not lard) should be eaten infrequently as they contain 15% to 23% fat calories. Avoid all others as they will invariably contain animal product and 30%-45% calories from fat.

CRACKERS: Suggestions:
1. Baked, fat-free crackers such as Westbrae Natural Brown Rice Wafers.
2. Nabisco's fat-free Saltines (a white flour product. Eat sparingly.)
3. Some melba toast products.
4. Hol-Grain Brown Rice Lite Snack Thins.
5. Some crispbreads (Siljans Knacke, Kavli Norwegian Crispbread, Finn Crisp)

DIPS: For bean dips, purchase only those which have no fat or lard (example: La Famous). You can also make a quick bean dip by blending the entire contents of a can of chili beans and chili sauce (no lard or oil, less than 300 mg sodium per 2 ounce serving) and spicing to taste.

EGG SUBSTITUTE: For baking, use an all vegetable product such as Egg Replacer.

FROZEN DESSERTS: Your most healthful selection is unsweetened fruit sorbet (example: Norvelle Sorbet). Second best advice would be to choose fat-free, dairy-free sherbets. Some all-vegetable desserts, such as Ice Bean and Rice Dream, have gotten rid of the cholesterol but not the fat. These should be avoided.

FRUIT, CANNED: Do not buy any canned fruit packed in syrup (even light or extra light syrup). Purchase only those packed in unsweetened fruit juice or water. Do not consume any product to which Nutrasweet or saccharin has been added.

GRANOLA BARS: Use those that are low in fat and sodium. Example: Nature's Warehouse High-Lite line (9% fat calories and 5 mg sodium per serving).

JAMS/JELLIES/PRESERVES: Use the concentrated fruit types that contain no added sugar or diet sweeteners. Examples include Smucker's Simply Fruit, Sorrel Ridge, Nature's Cuisine, R. W. Knudsen Family, and Halgrens.

KETCHUP/BBQ SAUCES: Most contain sugar, although many formulations use high-fructose corn syrup. The amounts contained are not excessively high and should not be a concern unless you're inclined to smother your 4-ounce hash brown patty with a quart of ketchup. Better ketchups: Westbrae Natural Fruit Sweetened Catsup (no salt added), Weight Watchers, Westbrae Natural Unsweetened Un-Ketchup.

MAPLE SYRUP SUBSTITUTE: Use formulated fructose products such as Featherweight's Lite Syrup. Since fructose is sugar, use it sparingly.

MEAT ANALOGS: Many meat analogs, like the product they're copying, contain copious fat. Use relatively lower fat products such as Worthington Cutlets (18% fat calories), Loma Linda Dinner Cuts With Sauce (8% fat calories), Worthington Granburger (8% fat calories), Loma Linda Vege-Burger (8% fat calories), etc.

MEXICAN FOODS: Most salsa and canned peppers have no fat added and tolerable amounts of sodium. For those who desire a better alternative to the Pace, Old El Paso, and Rosarita products, consider Enrico's, Hot Cha Cha, and Frontier Herbs line (and others) which offer more healthful salsas and sauces. Some enchilada and taco sauces (canned and mixes) contain added fat and should be avoided. Canned refried beans under the Little Pancho and generic labels are your best frijole choices as no lard (or oil) has been added. Most shelf stable taco shells and similar products have an oil residue from processing. A healthier alternative would be to bake your own shells from virtually fat-free tortillas (no lard) found in the frozen or refrigerated sections of your grocery store.

MILK SUBSTITUTES: Use diluted soy milk or products such as Edensoy, Soy Moo Lite, West Soy Lite, and some Rice Dream products. Even the "lite" substitutes tend to be slightly high in fat (12% to 18% fat calories) and should be used in combination with lower- or non-fat foods.

MUFFINS: Health Valley's Fat-Free Muffins (like their cookies) are your current best choice. These products are made from whole grains, free of animal products, sweetened with fruit juice, void of added oil, and contain only small amounts of sodium.

MUSTARDS: The mustard section of your supermarket has a wide array of choices, i.e., dijon style, Russian, Chinese, green peppercorn, tarragon, yellow, etc. The few that we should avoid are the oil-laden sweetened mustards such as Nance's. However, most should be used sparingly due to high sodium contents.

PANCAKE MIXES: Purchase lower-fat, fiber-laden mixes such as Kruteaz's Oat Bran Lite or some Fearn products (example: Fearn's Whole Wheat Pancake Mix).

PASTA: Use either whole wheat pasta or white pasta supplemented with wheat bran. Make certain that the pasta selected contains no egg. Most pastas made from corn (de Bole's wheat-Free Corn Pasta) and other whole-grain, no-egg pastas should prove to be acceptable.

PICKLES: Most pickles are high in salt which is a residue from the curing process. However, for those who enjoy one or two wedges on a sandwich or salad, there is virtually no sodium significance. For greater pickle consumption, consider purchasing products with reduced sodium such as those under the New Morning No-Salt brand. Some formulations (example: Featherweight) replace sodium chloride with potassium chloride. Avoid them.

RICE: Use brown rice or white rice supplemented with rice bran.

RICE CAKES, POPCORN CAKES, AND SIMILAR PRO-DUCTS: Select those that have less than 10% fat calories and 120 mg sodium per cake. Those that are fat and dairy-free and contain no added sugar and less than 60 mg of sodium per cake may be enjoyed anytime and in unlimited quantities. Applicable products: Quaker and Chico San lines (no butter or cheese), Crispy Cakes.

SALAD DRESSINGS: Suggestions:
1. Some Kraft "Free" dressing (example: Kraft's Free French Dressing)
2. Most Pritikin dressings. Watch out for Hains, Ci'Bella, and Westbrae dressings. Even though they're sold in health food stores, many are extremely high in fat. The sodium content is rather high, except for Pritikin brands, so use other brands sparingly.

SALT SUBSTITUTES: Use saltless products such as Mrs. Dash, Parsley Patch, small amounts of "Sour Salt" (food grade citric acid) and spices instead of sodium chloride (salt). Avoid using sea salt (same as regular salt except that it was harvested from the ocean) or potassium chloride substitutes (Lite Salt).

SNACK FOODS: Most snack food items are abounding with fat (35%-65% fat calories) and sodium (500-600 mg per one ounce serving). Forget the Fritos and Pringles and use the following instead:
1. Guiltless Gourmet Tortilla Chips, Arrowhead Mills Yellow Corn Chips, etc. (10%-12% fat calories, 0 to 200 mg of sodium per one ounce serving)
2. Make your own tortilla chips by broiling low-fat, non-lard tortillas until medium brown and breaking into chip size pieces.
3. Air-popped popcorn. Avoid mixes with fat or oil.
4. Low-fat, low-sodium pretzels
5. Non-fat, low sodium soft pretzels (example: Super Pretzels).

SOUPS: Best advice: Make your own. The Campbell Soup Company is the high-sodium champion, and many other popular brands are not far behind. Make certain that on those limited few soups that have drastic reductions in sodium (or no sodium) that they are equally beneficial from the fat standpoint (less than 10% fat calories). Recommendations: Health Valley Fat-Free Soups and some marketed under the Nile Spice and Fantastic labels. Avoid most Pritikin soups; they're inclined to use animal stock even in tomato soup.

SPAGHETTI SAUCES, PREPARED: Best choices: Ci'Bella Pasta Sauce and Robbies Spaghetti Sauce. Unfortunately, nearly all popular spaghetti sauces (Ragu, Prego, and Chef Boyardee) all contain added oil and may vary from 25% to 45% fat calories.

SUGAR SUBSTITUTE: Use fruit sugar (fructose) instead of table sugar (sucrose). For recipes calling for one cup of table sugar, use ⅔ cup of fructose instead. Remember that fructose is sugar. Use sparingly.

VEGETABLES, CANNED: Buy those with low or no sodium (no salt added). Avoid those packed in oil or syrup.

16.

Recipes

16. Recipes

The following recipes are furnished to help you to get started on low-fat, animal-free food preparation. We suggest that you purchase three cookbooks to add to the number of recipes in your repertoire:

1/2. *The McDougall Health Supporting Cookbooks, Numbers 1 & 2* by Mary McDougall. Available from The McDougall's, P.O. Box 14039, Santa Rosa, California 95402. Or call 707-576-1654.

3. *The Lighthearted Vegetarian Gourmet Cookbook* by Steve Victor. Pacific Press Publishing, Boise, Idaho. Or order through National Institute of Fitness, Box 938, Ivins, Utah 84738. Call 801-673-4905.

There are many other pure-vegetarian cookbooks on the market, but the three listed are the only books with which I am familiar that do not contain vegetable oils nor other high-fat vegetable foods.

We hope that you enjoy your new adventure in healthful meal preparation. As Steve Victor says in his cookbook, "Bon appetit, y'all!"

Familiarize yourself with the following products:

1. Fructose—A pure fruit sugar available in health-food stores. Use it sparingly in desserts.
2. Non-aluminum baking powder—Rumford is a brand that is available in supermarkets and health food stores.
3. Egg Replacer—This is a brand-name product which contains no animal products and is available in many supermarkets and health food stores.
4. Vegetable gelatin—A product available in most health food stores. It contains no animal products.

5. Arrowroot—This product is used like cornstarch to thicken liquids. It is available in most supermarkets.

6. Tofu—Tofu is a soy bean curd which should be used sparingly due to its high-fat content but which can add variety to vegetarian dishes. Prepared correctly, most dishes which use tofu can be kept to less than 15% fat calories. It is usually available in both supermarkets and health food stores.

7. TVP—TVP is textured vegetable protein which has a remarkably similar texture to meat. It is usually found in health food stores.

8. Jensen's Quick Sip—This product is a liquid seasoning (without added salt) that makes a delicious substitute for soy sauce and that can be used to spice up many foods.

9. Loma Linda Vege-Burger—This is a relatively low-fat all-vegetable canned burger substitute which is available in most health food stores and supermarkets.

10. Defatted soy flour—This product is available in most health food stores.

BREAKFAST DISHES

Fruit Delight

3 pears
4 oranges
2 grapefruit
1 pineapple *or* 3 lb. peaches
Juice from:
 ½ lemon
 ½ grapefruit
 3 oranges

Peel and slice pears and peaches and put into juice. Peel grapefruit and oranges and cut into small pieces. Dice pineapple after peeling and coring. Combine all fruit and add more fruit juice if needed. Serve with strawberries or blueberries.

Makes approximately 15 one-cup servings.

Approximate preparation time is 30 minutes.

PINEAPPLE OPTION = 4.1% Fat Calories

PEACH OPTION = 3.4% Fat Calories

Sunrise Fruit Extravaganza

4 apples
4 pears
2 bananas
1 c strawberries
8 chopped dates
⅓ c raisins
4 tbsp orange juice

Grate apples and stir in orange juice to prevent discoloration. Peel and slice pears and bananas. Add strawberries, chopped dates and raisins. Mix altogether gently and serve.

Makes approximately 11 one-cup servings.

Approximate preparation time is 15 minutes.

4.8% Fat Calories

Yummy Apple Cereal

3 c water
2 sliced apples
10 chopped dates
⅔ c cream of rye cereal
⅔ c rolled oats

Bring water to boil. Add apples and dates. Cook 2-3 minutes. Stir in cream of rye and rolled oats. Simmer about 5 minutes.

Makes 5 one-cup servings.

Approximate preparation time is 15-20 minutes.

4.1% Fat Calories

Niffer's Favorite Oatmeal

1 c old fashioned rolled oats
3¼ c boiling water
Dash cinnamon

Stir oats into boiling water in saucepan. Simmer 15-20 minutes, stirring occasionally until oats are cooked and mixture is thickened and not too watery.

Variations:

Before serving, add ¼ c raisins, sliced bananas, or other fresh fruits, or 1/8 tsp maple flavoring.

Makes 4 one-cup servings.

Approximate preparation time is 20 minutes.

15.0% Fat Calories

Pine Valley Flapjacks

4 c whole wheat flour
2 tbsp baking powder
½ c fructose (fruit sugar; available in most health food stores and supermarkets)
3 tbsp soy milk
3 pkgs vegetable gelatin (available in health food stores)
3 tbsp cornstarch
4 c water
½ tsp vinegar
Pam or other all-vegetable non-stick spray

Mix all ingredients. Spray griddle with Pam to prevent sticking. Pam is an oil. Use it sparingly! Prepare pancakes in the usual manner on a hot surface.

Makes approximately 12-16 pancakes.

Approximate preparation time is 25 minutes.

3.7% Fat Calories

Colleen's Whole Wheat Muffins

2 c whole wheat flour
2 tsp baking powder (non-aluminum; example, Rumford,
    which can be found in health-food stores and some super-
    markets)
¼ c fructose (available in health food stores)
1½ c water
2 tbsp unsweetened applesauce
1½ tsp Egg Replacer mixed with 2 tbsp water
    (This all-vegetable product can be purchased in the health
    food section of most grocery stores.)

Combine dry ingredients. Combine wet ingredients. Fold dry and
wet ingredients together until just moistened. Spoon onto non-
stick muffin pan or cupcake papers. Bake at 350° for 30 minutes.

Variations:
    Mix in ½ c raisins, currants or dates with dry ingredients.
    For unique, tantalizing flavor, try adding ½ tsp cinnamon,
    ½ tsp mace, ¼ tsp nutmeg, ¼ tsp allspice, ¼ tsp ginger or
    ¼ tsp cloves to the batter. (Mix first with dry ingredients.)

Makes one dozen muffins.

Approximate preparation time is 40-45 minutes.

3.3% Fat Calories

Rocky Mountain Hotcakes

1 c whole wheat flour
1½ tsp baking powder (non-aluminum)
1¼ c soy milk or apple juice
1¼ c unsweetened applesauce
½ tsp vanilla
1½ tsp Egg Replacer plus 2 tbsp water.
   (Egg Replacer is a powdered all-vegetable product available in health food stores and most grocery stores.)

Mix ingredients. Use slightest amount of Pam possible to prevent sticking on the hot skillet. Prepare hotcakes in the usual manner. Top with favorite unsweetened fruit syrups.

Makes 8-10 hotcakes.

Approximate preparation time is 15 minutes.

SOY MILK OPTION = 8.8% Fat Calories

APPLE JUICE OPTION = 2.6% Fat Calories

Apple 'n Spice French Toast

1 tsp Egg Replacer mixed with 2 tbsp water
2 tbsp apple juice
¼ tsp vanilla
1/8 tsp cinnamon
2 slices dry day old whole wheat bread

Combine egg mixture, juice, vanilla and cinnamon. Beat lightly. Heat non-stick griddle until hot (400°). Dip bread slices in egg mixture and cook until golden brown and crisp. Serve with applesauce or other fruit topping.

Makes 2 slices of French toast.

Approximate preparation time is 15 minutes.

8.1% Fat Calories

Saucey Cinnamon Toast

1 c unsweetened applesauce
Cinnamon to taste
4 slices whole wheat bread

Spread applesauce and a sprinkle of cinnamon on each slice of bread. Toast under broiler and serve.

Makes 4 slices of saucey cinnamon toast.

Approximate preparation time is 10 minutes.

7.3% Fat Calories

Granny's Homemade Apple Butter

1 jar applesauce — 32 oz.
1½ tsp cinnamon
½ tsp ground cloves
½ tsp allspice

Combine all ingredients in saucepan and cook uncovered over low heat 1 hour to thicken and blend flavors. Pour into covered container and refrigerate.

Use as a spread on toast, muffins, pancakes, waffles. Thin with a small amount of water to make syrupy. Serve hot or cold.

Makes one quart.

Approximate preparation time is 1 hour, ten minutes.

1.6% Fat Calories

"Dated" Blueberry Jam

2 c blueberries
24 pitted dates

Blend blueberries. Add dates a few at a time and blend until smooth. Put in jars.

Other jams can be made using strawberries, peaches, apples, etc. Jam keeps well up to 3 days in the refrigerator.

Makes 1¼ to 1½ cups.

Approximate preparation time is 5 minutes.

1.7% Fat Calories

This Is Grape! Sauce

1 c natural grape juice
2 tbsp arrowroot powder

Mix arrowroot powder with cold grape juice. Stir over heat until juice begins to thicken (about 5 minutes). It will thicken more when cool. Use as a hot or cold topping for vegetables, entrees, and desserts. Also good as a topping for pancakes and hot cereals.

Makes 1 cup.

Approximate preparation time is 10 minutes.

0.0% Fat Calories

ENTREES/MAIN DISHES

Sorensoni's Italian Style Spaghetti

4 oz. tofu
2 c tomato sauce
¼ lb. mushrooms thinly sliced
½ celery stalk thinly sliced
1 clove garlic
½ tsp basil
2 tbsp chopped parsley
1 tbsp chopped chives
6 oz. whole wheat spaghetti noodles

Cook spaghetti in boiling water until done. Drain.

Place tofu in medium saucepan. Mash tofu into small chunks. Add tomato sauce, mushrooms, celery, garlic and basil. Heat and stir until sauce is hot and mushrooms are cooked (5-10 minutes). Remove from heat and add parsley and chives. Serve over spaghetti.

Serves 4.

Approximate preparation time is 30 minutes.

9.0% Fat Calories

Bountiful Harvest Stew

4 tbsp canned, mixed vegetable juice such as V-8
1 large onion chopped
4 medium carrots chopped
4 medium potatoes cubed
2 stalks chopped celery
½ red pepper chopped
4½ oz TVP chunks
1 16 oz can tomatoes
2 cloves garlic
1 tbsp Jensen's Quik-sip
2 c vegetable stock or water
Seasonings or non-potassium, non-sodium salt substitute
Pepper

Lightly brown onions in vegetable juice. Add other vegetables and saute. Add TvP chunks and brown for 3 minutes over low heat. Add tomatoes and enough vegetable stock to cover. Season with Jensen's Quik-sip, seasoning and pepper. Cover stew and simmer 30-40 minutes or until thick and well cooked. Add extra vegetable stock or water if mixture seems dry.

Serves 4

Approximate preparation time is 1 hour.

2.1% Fat Calories

Rio Grande Rice Casserole

1 stalk celery chopped
1 large onion chopped
1 c brown rice
4½ oz TVP chunks
1 c vegetable juice (such as V-8) or water
2 16 oz can tomatoes chopped
1 tbsp Jensen's Quik-sip
Black pepper to taste
1 tsp chili powder
1 tsp mixed herbs (optional)

Preheat oven to 325°. Pam spray casserole dish. Saute celery and onion with ¼ c vegetable juice or water until tender. Add rice and TVP chunks, stir until chunks are slightly browned. Add remaining vegetable juices, tomatoes, Jensen's Quik-sip, pepper and optional seasonings, if desired. Stir well and bring to boil. Remove mixture from heat and pour into casserole dish. Bake, covered, 30 minutes.

Serves 4

Approximate preparation time is 1 hour.

1.1% Fat Calories

Vicki's Beefless Stroganoff Extrodinare

1 large onion, chopped
6 c mushrooms, sliced
1 tsp paprika
¼ c flour
4½ oz TVP chunks
1 c vegetable stock or water
1 tbsp Jensen's Quik-sip
4 oz soft tofu
½ tsp mustard
6 oz dry whole wheat noodles (no egg)

Saute onions, mushrooms and paprika for 10 minutes. Add flour and TVP chunks, stir well and brown. Pour in liquid and simmer on low heat for 10-15 minutes. Add more vegetable stock if mixture seems dry. Add tofu and mustard, then heat through but do not boil or simmer. Serve over brown rice or noodles that have been prepared according to package directions.

Serves 4

Approximate preparation time is 45 minutes.

9.3% Fat Calories

Dome Dwellers Favorite Veggie Chow Mein

3 c celery sliced diagonally
2 c onions thinly sliced
2 c bean sprouts
1 c sliced mushrooms
1 c cubed tofu
¼ c shopped parsley
2 tbsp Jensen's Quik-sip
4 c cooked brown rice
1¼ tbsp arrowroot starch
¼ tsp Mrs. Dash

Saute vegetables in ¼ c water and 2 tbsp Jensen's Quik-sip. Cook until tender (about 15 minutes). Add parsley last. Use 1¼ c water or liquid from vegetables and thicken with 1¼ tbsp arrowroot starch. Add ¼ tsp Mrs. Dash and stir until thick. Serve over hot brown rice.

Serves 4

Approximate preparation time is 30-45 minutes.

16.1% Fat Calories without Rice

4.8% Fat Calories

Bueno Chili Sin Carne

4 c cooked kidney beans
1 c chopped onion
1 chopped green pepper
1 c sliced celery
2½ tomatoes
1 tsp cumin
1 tsp celery seed
1 tsp tumeric
Onion powder
Garlic powder
¼ c vegetable juice (such as V-8) or water

In a skillet, brown onion and pepper in water or vegetable juice (5-10 minutes). Add celery and seasonings and cook until tender. Add tomatoes and cooked kidney beans. Add tofu. Serve hot garnished with chopped green onions, crushed low-fat corn chips (less than 10% fat calories such as "Skinny" brand corn chips), chopped green chilies and salsa.

Serves 4

Approximate preparation time is 30 minutes.

6.7% Fat Calories

Lasagna Supremo

½ c choppec celery
½ c tomato juice
1 6 oz can tomato paste
1 16 oz can tomatoes, chopped
1 medium onion, chopped
2 cloves garlic, crushed
12 to 15 strips wide lasagna, whole wheat
¼ tsp fructose
2 c tofu, finely chopped
Veg salt
Ground pepper to taste
Pam or other unflavored vegetable spray

Spray casserole dish lightly with Pam. Saute garlic and onion until soft and golden. Add celery, tomatoes, tomato paste, tomato juice, fructose, veg salt and pepper. Stir well, cover, and simmer on low heat for 45 minutes.

Cook lasagna in boiling water following recipe on box until it just begins to soften. Drain and cover with cold water until needed. Preheat oven to 350°. Arrange lasagna layers in casserole: pasta, sauce, tofu. Repeat until all ingredients are used.

Top lasagna with layer of tofu and bake at 350° until warmed through. Cut into portions and serve immediately.

Serves 6-8

Approximate preparation time is 1½-2 hours.

8.5% Fat Calories

Bake Spinach Mound

8 pkgs frozen chopped spinach, drained
2 large onions
1 c soft bread crumbs (ww) sauteed with 1 finely minced clove
    garlic
1 c chestnuts ground (optional)
½ c wheat germ
¼ c soy de-fatted flour or 4 tbsp arrowroot
Jensen's Quik-sip, veg salt and pepper to taste
½ c tomato sauce

Combine sauteed onion, nut meats and bread crums and other ingredients to spinach in large mixing baking dish coated with a small amount of Pam. Form spinach mixture into flattened mound. Surround with tomato sauce. Bake, uncovered, at 350° for 30 minutes.

Serves 8

Approximate preparation time is 1 hour.

No Chestnuts, Soy = 6.2% Fat Calories

No Chestnuts, Arrowroot = 6.7% Fat Calories

Chestnuts, Soy = 6.0% Fat Calories

Chestnuts, Arrowroot = 6.3% Fat Calories

Best Ever Casserole

1 c dry kidney beans
2 bay leaves
4 c water
1 c corn meal
1 c cold water
1¼ c boiling water

1 medium onion, diced
1 small eggplant (about 10 oz), diced
2 medium carrots sliced
2 stalks celery, dicked
1 green pepper, diced
½ c corn, fresh or frozen
3¼ crushed tomatoes
2 tbsp Jensen's Quik-sip
1 tsp garlic powder

Soak kidney beans overnight in water. Drain, rinse and cook the next day with bay leaves 1½ hours. Add diced vegetables and cook until tender.

Mix corn meal in cold water and stir into boiling water. Stir constantly until it begins to bubble. Partially cover pan and cook slowly for 5-7 minutes, stirring occasionally. Spray baking dish with Pam. Spread mush over bottom. Drain water from beans. Add tomatoes and seasonings to bean-vegetable mixture. Spoon into casserole. Bake at 350° for 45 minutes until bubbly.

Serves 8

Approximate preparation time is 12-14 hours.

5.1% Fat Calories

Baked Venetian-Style Eggplant Slices

2 lb eggplant cut into 8-10 slices
1 8-oz can tomato sauce
1 tbsp Jensen's Quik-sip
¼ c nutritional yeast flakes
2 tsp oregano
1 tsp garlic powder

Place eggplant slices on baking sheet sprayed with Pam. Sprinkle a little sauce on each slice; spread with back of spoon. Sprinkle a little garlic powder on each slice. Divide the tomato sauce among slices, spreading with back of spoon. Sprinkle on yeast flakes and oregano. Bake at 350° for 30 minutes or until they test done with a long fork.

Serves 6-8

Approximate preparation time is 40-45 minutes.

3.5% Fat Calories

Very Good Veggie Burgers with Mushrooms

½ lb fresh mushrooms diced
1 large onion diced
¼ c vegetable stock
½ tsp Mrs. Dash
5 c (old fashioned) rolled oats
4½ c water
⅓ c Jensen's Quik-sip
1 tsp garlic powder
¼ tsp oregano
½ tsp dried basil
½ tsp thyme
¼ c brewer's yeast (powder or flake)

Saute the first four ingredients in covered saucepan. Bring to boil all the other ingredients except oats. Lower heat, add the sauteed vegetables and oats, one cup at a time, allowing each cupful to sink a little before stirring gently. Cook up to 5 minutes until mixture starts to stick to bottom of pot. See aside to cool (about 10-15 minutes).

Form into patties and place on Pam cookie sheet. Bake at 350° for about 45 minutes. Turn once after about 20 minutes.

Variations: Add dill, parsley, celery, green or red peppers in place of mushrooms.

Serves 8-12

Approximate preparation time is 1½ hours.

13.6% Fat Calories

Italian Gardens Pasta Delight

1 tbsp vegetable stock
1 large onion
3 cloves garlic crushed
2 medium carrots, sliced
2 medium zucchini, sliced
2 tsp dried basil
2 tsp dried oregano
1 32-oz can unsalted whole tomatoes (reserve liquid)
2 c (16-oz) navy beans drained and rinsed
¾ lb whole wheat rigatoni or medium shells
Freshly ground pepper

Heat water to cook pasta in large skillet. Saute onion and garlic in vegetable stock. Add carrots, zucchini, basil, oregano, the tomatoes with their liquid and beans. Cook until vegetables are tender (about 10 minutes). Season with pepper to taste. While vegetables are cooking, boil pasta about 7 minutes. Divide pasta between 8 plates and spoon vegetables and sauce on top.

Serves 8

Approximate preparation time is 30 minutes.

6.1% Fat Calories

Extra Bueno Bean Dip

1 can Janet Lee "Mexican Style Chili Beans in Chili Sauce"
(or another similar product with less than 12% fat
calories, less than 300 mg of sodium per serving, and no
ingredients of animal origin)
Onion powder equal to ¼ onion
¼ tsp cumin
1 tsp diced jalapeno peppers (optional)
4 oz diced green chili peppers

Combine in a blender the entire contents of the can of beans,
onion powder, cumin, and jalapeno peppers (optional). Blend
until smooth. Mix in the diced green chili peppers. Store overnight in the refrigerator (covered) before serving.

Serves 8-10

Approximate preparation time is 10 minutes, plus overnight
storage.

8.0% Fat Calories

Healthy Bachelor's Skillet Dinner

3 onions, chopped coarsely
1 green bell pepper, chopped coarsely
1 19-oz can of Loma Linda's "Vege-Burger"
1 16-oz can of tomato wedges
1 7-oz can of diced green chilies
½ tsp garlic powder
¼ tsp basil
12-oz dry whole wheat macaroni

Saute Vege-Burger, chopped onions and bell pepper in a Pam-sprayed skilled until the onions become translucent. Add tomatoes, green chilies, garlic powder, and basil. Simmer slowly for 30 minutes. In a cooking pot, boil the macaroni until done. Mix the cooked macaroni with the Vege-Burger mixture and serve. Tastes even better re-heated the next day.

Serves 8

Approximate preparation time is 45-60 minutes.

7.8% Fat Calories

DESSERTS

Tropical Breeze Carrot Cake

¾ c unsweetened applesauce
½ c fructose
2 c ww pastry flour
¾ c soy de-fatted flour
1 tbsp aluminum free baking powder
2 tsp cinnamon
1 lb carrots, finely grated
¾ c raisins
1 tsp vanilla
½ c grapenuts
½ c shredded coconut
3½ c crushed pineapple with juice

Mix applesauce and fructose, add vanilla. Mix flours, baking powder and cinnamon. Add flours to applesauce. Stir in carrots, raisins and pineapple. Mix well. Spray Pam on baking pan and pour in ingredients. Top with Grapenuts and coconut and bake at 350° for 30 minutes.

Serves 8-16

Approximate preparation time is 45 minutes.

5.5% Fat Calories

Maple-Cinnamon Peach Crisp

2 c sliced peaches, packed without sugar or artificial
        sweeteners (drained) or 2 lbs fresh peaches
TOPPING:
    3 tbsp flour
    3 tbsp maple syrup
    1/8 tsp cinnamon
    Dash nutmeg
    2 tbsp quick oats, uncooked

Preheat oven to 400°. Pour peaches into shallow 1 quart
casserole. In bowl, combine dry ingredients for topping. Add
maple syrup. Mix well. Spread mixture over peaches. Bake 40
minutes or until lightly browned. Serve warm.

Serves 4

Approximate preparation time is 50-60 minutes.

3.9% Fat Calories

Date-Coconut Macaroons

1¼ c molasses
½ c unsweetened applesauce
1 c ww flour
1 c rolled oats
½ c apple juice
½ c chopped dates
½ c shredded coconut

Stir applesauce and molasses together. Add flour and rest of
ingredients. Mix. Spray Pam on cookie sheet and drop about 2
tbsp increments onto cookie sheet. Bake at 350° for 10-15
minutes.

Makes 20-24 cookies

Approximate preparation time is 30 minutes.

13.0% Fat Calories

Baked Cosmic Apples

3 apples sliced (4 cups)
⅔ c raisins
1⅓ c oats
1 tsp applesauce
⅔ c chopped dates

Put apples and raisins in layers in baking pan. Begin and end with apples. Mix oats, applesauce and chopped dates. Spread on top of apples. Bake at 400° for 15 minutes, then about 30 minutes at 325°.

Serves 8-12

Approximate preparation time is 1 hour.

6.3% Fat Calories

Proof of the Rice Pudding

¾ c brown rice
1½ c water
2 c water
½ c de-fatted soya powder
3/8 c molasses
⅔ c raisins
¾ c crushed pineapple

Wash rice. Cook in 1½ c water in covered pot for 45 minutes or until rice is cooked and water is absorbed. Mix in blender: 2 c water, soya powder, 1 tbsp molasses. Pour soya milk on rice. Stir. Add 3/8 c molasses, raisins and crushed pineapple. Stir well. Put in baking dish and bake at 350° for 50-60 minutes.

Serves 8-12

Approximate preparation time is 2 hours.

0.9% Fat Calories

17.

Recommendations for Further Reading

17. Recommendations for Further Reading

Three books by John McDougall, M.D.:

The McDougall Plan. New Century Publishers, 1983.

McDougall's Medicine: A Challenging Second Opinion. New Century Publishers, 1985.

The McDougall Program. NAL Books, 1990.

Dr. McDougall's books cut through all of the nutritional nonsense and confusion and leave no doubt as to the proper way to eat in order to live long and healthfully. His works are extensively documented from the best medical and nutritional journals and are must reading for anyone who seeks Megahealth.

Diet for a New America. John Robbins, Stillpoint Publishing, 1987.

A well-researched book which discusses the health implications of eating animals and makes a compassionate plea for better treatment of the animals themselves. This book was nominated for the Pulitzer Prize. It will make a lasting impression.

Vegan Nutrition. Gill Langley, Ph.D. Vegan Society, Oxford, England, 1988.

Dr. Langley analyzes all the research into the health and nutritional status of vegans. Recommended for those who might have any qualms about changing to a diet which contains no animal products.

The Power of Your Plate. Neal Barnard, M.D. Book
Publishing Co., 1990.

Dr. Barnard is the president of the Physician's Committee for
Responsible Medicine—a group of physicians who believe in
practicing preventive medicine through proper food choices.
Seventeen experts on health are interviewed, including Dr.
Denis Burkitt, Dr. John McDougall, and Dr. Jane Goodall. Very
interesting and easily read.

Dr. Dean Ornish's Program for Reversing Heart Disease.
Dean Ornish, M.D. Random House, 1990.

Dr. Ornish's work may be one of the most important of the 20th
Century. He has proved beyond any doubt that heart disease is
reversible with dietary means. His book explains what is
necessary for reversal and gives recipes, stress-reduction
techniques and other useful information.

Pregnancy, Children, and the Vegan Diet. Michael Klaper,
M.D. Gentle World, Inc., Umatilla, Florida 1987.

Dr. Klaper's book is excellent in calming any fears that
expectant mothers or parents may have about an animal-free
diet for themselves or their children. It is easily read and well-
documented.

18.

A Postscript

18. A Postscript

The secrets of happiness lie in following the golden rules of good health and good social relationships. Properly followed, these rules enable us to enjoy lives full of adventure, excitement and love.

Nevertheless, on numerous occasions, I am asked how I can possibly find pleasure in living without eating meat, drinking alcohol, or even (wonder of wonders) consuming ice cream and pizza. I usually answer that I find my joy in my family, my friends, and my senses, which—unencumbered by poor health—can observe the splendor of the sunrise and the sparkle of the morning dew on the grass. My pleasure comes from long rides on my mountain bike, serving my family and my fellowmen well, and from feeling far more fit at the age of 47 than I did at 20. My peace accrues from the knowledge that I am free from degenerative disease and that I will not take the life of another human being in an alcohol-related auto accident. There is also a freedom in being able to compete in sports without fear of dying during my exercise.

It is certainly an indictment of our society when life has grown so dull that we must seek our meaning in a bottle, a coffee cup, or a thick, bloody steak. The unfortunate who has established these elements as life's preeminent pleasures is one to be pitied indeed! The fully functioning individual needs no drugs to stupefy the senses, no rich foods to placate the palate. Vibrant health is a billion times more important than the taste of eggs or the stimulation of caffeine. Possessing a body and mind that serve one well should be of much greater significance. A person lives in his body and can accomplish nothing if it does not function properly. Where will I live if I wear out my body?

I am alive and appreciative of the gifts God has given me. It is my hope that you, the reader, will grasp the vision of *really living.* You will be happy only to the extent that you are in control of your health and your life. To the extent that you let your habits control you, you diminish that happiness. You can take control of all aspects of your life today and look forward to a healthier and happier tomorrow.

19.

Index

19. *Index*